Praise for
THE MAN FROM PAKISTAN

"Husband-and-wife team Douglas Frantz and Catherine Collins go beyond the James Bond cliches, to tell us the chilling, three-decades-long story of how the dangerous scientist spread nuclear research and development and changed the world forever . . . It's a tale of intrigue, international competition, terrorism, and rogue state leaders who operate far beyond the light of open media and the oversight of international intelligence organizations and regulatory agencies . . . Read and appreciate [THE MAN FROM PAKISTAN] for the detailed exposure of the A. Q. Khan network and a fuller awareness of the spread of nuclear weapons and the ultimate danger this poses for America and the free world."
—*New York Post*

"Details how well Dr. Khan in fact worked the Pakistani system, cutting some military officials into the deals, and using the air force to deliver nuclear goods."
—*New York Times*

"Thorough research and brisk prose propel a terrifying tale of greed, weaponry, and geopolitics."
—*Kirkus Reviews*

"Offers fresh, behind-the-scenes detail . . . In lively prose and well-chosen detail, it enumerates the dangers our world now faces thanks to Khan."
—*Christian Science Monitor*

"This is an exceptionally important book about the most dangerous criminal enterprise of our time . . . full of startling new details about A. Q. Khan's network and the investigations by the IAEA and the CIA that finally stopped him—it is a masterwork of investigative and historical reporting."
—Steve Coll, Pulitzer Prize–winning author of
*Ghost Wars: The Secret History of the CIA, Afghanistan, and Bin Laden,
from the Soviet Invasion to September 10, 2001*

more . . .

"The only book since *Helter Skelter* to keep me awake at night."
—Hugh Hewitt

"A revealing look at real-life intelligence operations . . . The authors wield old-school journalistic skills in weaving together facts with verve."
—*Denver Rocky Mountain News*

"Charting the hubristic ambition of one man and the 'strategic' indifference of many governments, this book describes in gripping and disturbing detail how our world became a very dangerous place."
—Pankaj Mishra, author of *Temptations of the West*

"A frightening book by two crack investigative reporters with no apparent ax to grind other than averting a holocaust."
—*Oregonian*

"Dissects the world's first nuclear black marketeer . . . From Iran to North Korea, A. Q. Khan supplied the most lethal weapons to the world's most menacing regimes."
—Graham Allison, author of *Nuclear Terrorism*, and Douglas Dillon, professor of government, John F. Kennedy School of Government, Harvard University

"A true triumph of investigative journalism."
—*Express*

"Revealing . . . Frantz and Collins know how to weave complicated material into a persuasive narrative."
—*The Economist*

"Has the potential to shake the foundations of the U.S. government and its intelligence operations."
—*San Francisco Chronicle*

THE
MAN FROM PAKISTAN

THE
MAN FROM PAKISTAN

The True Story of the World's Most

Dangerous Nuclear Smuggler

DOUGLAS FRANTZ

and

CATHERINE COLLINS

NEW YORK BOSTON

TWELVE

Twelve
Hachette Book Group
237 Park Avenue
New York, NY 10017

Visit our Web site at www.HachetteBookGroup.com.

Twelve is an imprint of Grand Central Publishing.
The Twelve name and logo are trademarks of Hachette Book Group, Inc.

Book design by Fearn Cutler de Vicq

Printed in the United States of America

Originally published in hardcover by Twelve as *The Nuclear Jihadist*.

First Trade Edition: November 2008
10 9 8 7 6 5 4 3 2 1

The Library of Congress has cataloged the hardcover edition as follows:
Frantz, Douglas.
    The nuclear jihadist : the true story of the man who sold the world's most dangerous
secrets—and how we could have stopped him / Douglas Frantz and Catherine Collins.
       p. cm.
    ISBN-13: 978-0-446-19957-5
    ISBN-10: 0-446-19957-5
    1. Nuclear nonproliferation. 2. Security, International. 3. Khan, A. Q. (Abdul
Qadeer), 1936- 4. Nuclear terrorism. I. Collins, Catherine. II. Title.
    JZ5675.F73 2007
    623.4'5119092—dc22
    [B]   2007023394

ISBN 978-0-446-19958-2 (pbk.)

CONTENTS

"The splitting of the atom has changed everything,
save our mode of thinking, and thus
we drift toward unparalleled catastrophe."

—ALBERT EINSTEIN

"The eyebrows of some were burned off and skin hung from their faces and hands. Others, because of pain, held their arms up as if carrying something in both hands. Some were vomiting as they walked. Many were naked or in shreds of clothing. On some undressed bodies, the burns had made patterns—of undershirt straps and suspenders and, on the skin of some women (since white repelled the heat from the bomb and dark clothes absorbed it and conducted it to the skin), the shapes of flowers they had had on their kimonos."

— JOHN HERSEY, *Hiroshima*

PROLOGUE

CROSSING THE RINGSTRASSE near Vienna's ornate State Opera House, a rumpled man with a shock of reddish hair tumbling across his forehead walked briskly past the cafés, where people lingered over their espressos and newspapers on the unseasonably warm day. He glanced anxiously at his watch as he tugged open the door on the Starbucks at the corner of Kärntner Strasse and Walfischgasse, two of the city's busiest streets. Olli Heinonen was a senior official with the International Atomic Energy Agency, the United Nations organization charged with stopping the spread of nuclear weapons around the world. Stout and in his early fifties, Heinonen had spent more than twenty years rising methodically through the agency's labyrinthine bureaucracy, his ascension built as much on his stubborn intelligence as on his ample scientific skills. On this particular day in May 2004, as he picked up his coffee and mounted the stairs to the second floor of the Starbucks, Heinonen's career was about to veer into the murky world of espionage and nuclear smuggling on an unprecedented and frightening scale. He would soon be playing a high-stakes game of hide-and-seek with an unseen man whose actions over the past thirty years had pushed the world closer to nuclear war than at any time in history.

Four months earlier, Mohamed ElBaradei, the Egyptian diplomat who was head of the IAEA, had put Heinonen in charge of the most significant and pressing investigation in the agency's fifty-year existence: the inquiry into the global black market in nuclear technology led by Abdul Qadeer Khan, a Pakistani scientist revered throughout the Muslim world as the father of the Islamic bomb. It was Khan who had exploded the myth that a developing country was too poor and too backward to join the nuclear powers. Heinonen soon found that Khan's nuclear trail led far beyond the borders of Pakistan. The scientist and a network of associates and middlemen had sold nuclear technology to a rogue's gallery of countries: Iran, North Korea, and Libya. If that were not bad enough, Khan had apparently provided nuclear secrets and possibly designs for an atomic weapon to customers still hidden behind the shroud of secrecy that had engulfed the scientist when, in late 2003, Pakistani authorities had arrested him but refused to turn him over to the IAEA for questioning. Pakistan was not alone in refusing to cooperate with the IAEA, as other foreign governments rebuffed queries, allowing members of Khan's ring to disappear underground throughout Europe, Africa, and the Middle East. Heinonen and his team were frustrated and fearful that the trails would disappear before they could unravel Khan's nuclear web.

Then a surprise telephone call offered Heinonen hope. A woman had contacted him at the IAEA headquarters, which rise high above the banks of the Danube in Vienna, requesting a meeting outside the agency's offices. She had refused to give her name, but she had promised that she could provide information that would be enormously helpful to his investigation of A. Q. Khan. Heinonen recognized the woman's accent as American and suspected that she was from the Central Intelligence Agency, which maintained a huge operation in the Austrian capital and had occasionally and grudgingly shared information with the IAEA. He agreed to meet with her on the second floor at the Starbucks. When he asked how he would know her, the woman assured Heinonen that she would recognize him.

Olli Heinonen and other senior officials at the IAEA were well aware of the dangers posed by nuclear proliferation, and they were deeply worried in the spring of 2004 that the genie was out of the bottle and that the weapons technology was spreading like a virus among some of the world's most unstable regimes. North Korea was on the brink of exploding its first nuclear device, to demonstrate its defiance of the United States and its allies. Iran was pushing ahead with a program that many experts at the agency were convinced was intended to lead to the capability of producing nuclear weapons, a threat that could destabilize the Middle East and lead to an all-out war. Libya had given up a clandestine nuclear-weapons program only after its exposure by British and American intelligence agencies. All three were customers of Khan and his network, but what Heinonen feared most was the possibility of other buyers.

WITHOUT any trumpets to herald the change, the world has entered a second nuclear age, and for the first time since the end of the Cold War the threat of nuclear annihilation is on the rise. Mohamed ElBaradei, whose Cassandra-like warnings won him the Nobel Peace Prize in 2005, fears that more nations are hedging their bets by developing nuclear technologies that could be diverted quickly from civilian energy plants into weapons programs. He estimated that as of the fall of 2006 thirty or more countries have both the technical know-how and motivation to opt for nuclear weapons. "Unfortunately the political environment is not a very secure one," ElBaradei cautioned. "So it's becoming very fashionable, if you like, for countries to look into the possibilities of protecting themselves through nuclear weapons."

Nuclear weapons are no longer the sole province of a handful of the most powerful nations. Since the dawn of the nuclear age more than sixty years ago, the technology for the most destructive weapon in history has spread far and wide. The basic design for a crude atomic weapon was widely available and well understood even before the Internet made it accessible to anyone with a computer. But rather than the traditional nuclear exchange between the United States and Russia or even between India and Pakistan, the gravest threat of catastrophic attack today may well come from a terrorist organization like Osama bin Laden's Al Qaeda. There is no doubt that bin Laden or his successor is seeking to buy or build a nuclear weapon for use in his holy war. As early as 1998, the Al Qaeda leader proclaimed possession of a nuclear weapon to be a "religious duty," later obtaining a dispensation from a Muslim cleric that justified its use against the West. A month before the September 11 attacks, bin Laden met with two Pakistani nuclear scientists to discuss acquiring nuclear-weapons technology. Later that year, following the American invasion of Afghanistan, U.S. troops found rudimentary designs for nuclear weapons inside an Al Qaeda safe house in Kabul. Intelligence agencies have tracked the group's efforts to obtain nuclear material across three continents.

The deaths of nearly three thousand people in New York City, Washington, D.C., and Pennsylvania on September 11, 2001, were a devastating demonstration of the willingness of a group like Al Qaeda to kill innocent civilians. Senior American officials were soon plunged into an even worse nightmare when the CIA was told that Al Qaeda terrorists had stolen a ten-kiloton nuclear bomb from the Russian arsenal and smuggled it into New York City. The information came from an informant code-named Dragonfire, and it seemed to gain credence when the National Security Agency picked up chatter in international communications that "an American Hiroshima" was imminent.

When President George W. Bush was told of the suspected plot on October 11, 2001, he ordered Vice President Dick Cheney to leave Washington for an undisclosed location—in the event that the target was not New York but Washington. Casualty estimates from such an explosion ranged as high as half a million people, while the psychological impact of a nuclear attack on American soil would be incalculable. Top-secret Nuclear Emergency Support Teams (NEST) were dispatched to New York City, where, under a cloak of secrecy that excluded even Mayor Rudolph Giuliani, searches were conducted. NEST was established in 1975 by the Department of Energy to respond to a terrorist incident involving a nuclear device or a bomb that contained radioactive material. Its members are drawn from more than three hundred scientists and technicians at the Energy Department and the national weapons laboratories; they are trained to detect the slightest evidence of radioactivity. Responding to Dragonfire's warning, more than a dozen teams of six members each were dispatched throughout Manhattan, working from unmarked vans and concealing detection instruments in backpacks and briefcases as they searched on foot. In the end, it turned out to be a false alarm. But the specter of terrorists unleashing a nuclear bomb in New York or London or Madrid remains a real possibility in the minds of many experts. The rules for what is thinkable have changed.

No science can calculate the precise chances of a rogue nation or terrorists detonating a nuclear device, but enough credible evidence exists to convince many experts that it is a matter of *when*, not *if.* Graham Allison, a Harvard professor and author of a book about nuclear terrorism, puts the odds of a nuclear attack by terrorists in the next ten years at better than 50 percent. One of his Harvard colleagues, proliferation expert Matthew Bunn, says he would not live in either New York or Washington because he fears a terrorist attack using atomic weapons is inevitable. Former defense secretary William Perry estimates the same odds of a nuclear attack, though he calculates it is likely to come before the end of the decade.

Smuggling a nuclear device into the United States is not regarded by experts as particularly difficult. A crude device the size of a large desk could be hidden inside one of the two hundred million freight containers moving in and out of the world's ports every year. A ten-kiloton nuclear weapon, which has the power of the Hiroshima bomb and weighs about one thousand pounds, could be hidden in the back of a delivery van. Detonating a device of that size at noon on a normal workday in Midtown Manhattan would destroy everything within a third of a mile: Half a million people would die instantly as a hurricane of fire vaporized buildings; hundreds of thousands more would perish in the raging infernos, collapsing structures, and radioactive fallout. Communications systems would be fried, hospitals and emergency teams overwhelmed.

Should such a horrific assault occur, there is a strong likelihood that the trail of devastation will lead back to Abdul Qadeer Khan. For three decades, Khan was the mastermind of a vast clandestine enterprise designed to obtain the technology and equipment to make atomic bombs—first for Pakistan and then later for the highest bidder. Khan started down the nuclear path as a patriot, stealing secret European nuclear designs out of determination to protect his country from its archrival, India. After playing a central role in developing Pakistan's nuclear arsenal, he shifted course and employed his global network to sell those same nuclear secrets to some of the most repressive regimes in the world, transforming himself into a nuclear jihadist devoted to payback for real and imagined griev-ances suffered by Muslims around the world. In the process, Khan grew arrogant, corrupt, and powerful, operating with impunity as he amassed a fortune from his black-market deals.

By the time he was stopped, Khan had done more to destabilize the world's delicate nuclear balance than anyone in history, emerging as the common thread woven through today's most dangerous nuclear threats, from the potential showdown between India and Pakistan to the inter-national standoffs with North Korea and Iran. The sheer scale of what Khan wrought is breathtaking, and so is the apparent ease with which he sold his wares. Khan's organization was a nuclear Wal-Mart, selling weapons blueprints, parts for thousands of centrifuges to manufacture fissile material for bombs, and the expertise to assemble the works into a bomb kit. The Pakistani scientist and his accomplices shattered the old proliferation model of state-to-state transfers, in which one government quietly shared nuclear secrets with an ally. For the first time, an individual demonstrated convincingly that the existing international safeguards and mind-set were no longer operative, leading to the grim conclusion that any ruthless or unstable regime—or individual, for that matter—with the will and money could acquire the bomb.

What is nearly as remarkable is that Khan spread this nuclear technol-ogy in partial view of successive administrations in Washington and in European capitals. What Pakistani government and military leaders knew about his activities is still in dispute. But it is certain that all of them, at various points in time, turned a blind eye when confronted with warnings from numerous intelligence agencies about what the Pakistani scientist was doing. There is no doubt that at key moments along the nuclear trail, Khan could have been stopped; but each time, more pressing strategic concerns trumped worries about proliferation to spare him and keep his global nuclear bazaar operating.

American intelligence first learned of Khan's activities in 1975, when the Dutch government informed the CIA that the scientist had stolen top-secret plans for the latest uranium-enrichment technology and taken them home to Pakistan. The CIA watched in the years that followed as Khan established a network of European and North American suppliers to obtain the sophisticated technology required to enrich uranium for atomic weapons. And they watched as Pakistan built its own nuclear arsenal. Yet for all of its detailed reporting on Pakistan and Khan, the CIA missed what occurred in the shadows. The agency failed to notice when Khan reversed the flow of the black market and began selling nuclear technology and expertise outside Pakistan, to the highest bidder.

This book explores the rise of A. Q. Khan and his role as one of the principal architects of the second nuclear age, examining how a scientist of mediocre skills and great ambition first helped Pakistan build the bomb and then had no qualms about spreading nuclear weapons to some of the most unstable regions of the world. It identifies the points at which American authorities and their allies could have halted his deadly operation, laying out what the Americans knew about Khan's operation and when they knew it. And finally the book follows Olli Heinonen and his small team of determined men and women from the International Atomic Energy Agency as they search for clues about Khan's activities from the clandestine nuclear plants in Iran to the hidden stockpiles of technology in Libya, from the dismantled atomic facilities in war-torn Iraq to a secret factory in South Africa. Evidence of the global reach of Khan's lethal bazaar has been unearthed in the capitals of Pakistan and European countries, from current and former intelligence officials, and among the written records of those who enabled Khan to turn the world into a more dangerous place. With little experience as detectives and facing a myriad of obstacles, the team plunged into a dark continent that had yet to be mapped, to search for the clues among the jungle of evasions and half-truths of Khan's accomplices, the false invoices, and the secret bank accounts. The goal was to reconstruct Khan's actions over the last three decades in a desperate fight to put the nuclear genie he had unleashed back in the bottle so they, and the rest of us, could stop waking, hearts pounding, in the middle of the night.

CHAPTER 1

THE SMILING MAN

IT WAS A WARM MORNING in late spring, with sunlight glinting off Amsterdam's famed canals. The man standing in the doorway of the laboratory's office seemed confident. He was Pakistani, thirty-six years old, just over six feet tall, with a broad forehead, fleshy face, and thick, close-cropped black hair. He wore a Western-style suit but tucked his tie behind his belt in a way that made the ensemble seem like an uncomfortable costume. He spoke adequate Dutch and very good German, but both were accented by the lilt of his native tongue. Arriving at the Physics Dynamic Research Laboratory on May 1, 1972, to begin his new job as a metallurgist, he had been escorted immediately to this office in the mechanical-science department, where he was to spend the next three years.

The man was smiling at no one in particular because, after a decade in Europe, he had learned that a simple smile was disarming. When his new colleague looked up from a large desk that dominated the room, he smiled even more broadly.

Frits Veerman, the laboratory's young photographer, was surprised. He had been told his new officemate would be an impressive person, a foreigner with a doctorate and a long list of academic publications. But Veerman had not expected the broad grin and the gleaming white teeth, not to mention the dark skin. The photographer stood, walked over, and stuck out his hand.

"Frits Veerman," he said in Dutch. "Welcome to FDO."

"I am Abdul Qadeer Khan," the man replied. "It is a pleasure to meet you."

Many of the people with whom Veerman worked had advanced degrees, and in the hierarchical structure of the laboratory—and of Dutch society in general—they tended to discount people like Veerman, who had only a technical degree and whose work as a photographer was deemed far less important than their own. He had braced himself for the usual cold shoulder, but Khan seemed different. Veerman thought him friendly and humble from the start, interested in all the workers and what they were doing inside the complex known by the initials FDO.

From that first day on, the men sat comfortably opposite each other at the large desk. Whenever Veerman ventured out to photograph minute design changes in some piece of sensitive technology, Khan tagged along, asking questions. Khan began praising Veerman's photographs—the prints were like works of art, he told him, with each detail clearly visible—and asked if he might have copies. The Dutchman thought this a bit odd, but he was flattered and complied happily. Khan eventually wanted to take his own photographs, and Veerman helped him buy a used high-quality camera. It all seemed to fit in with Khan's insatiable curiosity.

Khan had come to the research laboratory at the suggestion of a former classmate. The year before, he had completed his doctorate at the Catholic University of Leuven in Belgium and applied for a range of jobs in several countries, including Pakistan. He was interested in any company that required a specialist in the analysis and development of exotic metal alloys. He also seriously considered returning home to teach, as a way of honoring his late father, who had been a schoolteacher.

The place where he landed, however, was not just any company. FDO was the year-old in-house laboratory of Verenidge Machine Fabrieken, a major Dutch conglomerate, which worked closely with Urenco, a consortium formed by the governments of Britain, West Germany, and the Netherlands, in the design and manufacture of centrifuges. At the time, powerful companies such as Westinghouse and General Electric controlled the facilities that provided enriched uranium to civilian reactors throughout the Western world. In order to protect the fledgling commercial nuclear industry in the United States, President Richard M. Nixon had ordered in 1971 that the closely guarded enrichment technology not be shared with any other country, including allies. The decision forced other nations to begin developing their own enrichment technology to ensure an adequate fuel supply, eventually breaking the U.S. monopoly on uranium enrichment and unleashing the proliferation threat.

The key to the uranium-enrichment process is the ultracentrifuge, a sophisticated machine that spins uranium gas into enriched uranium. The centrifuges under development by Urenco were intended to manufacture fuel for a nuclear program that was to generate electricity for the three sponsor countries. The work was highly classified because the same process could be used to produce fissile material for nuclear weapons.

A friendship quickly developed between the lonely Dutch photographer and the newly arrived foreigner. During that first summer, they spent their lunch hours wandering along the canals, eyeing the scantily clad young women who thronged the city's sidewalks and perched on the bridges. Amsterdam was probably the most dramatic contrast one could find to the modest Islamic society in which Khan had grown up. He was not prepared for the culture of legalized marijuana and prostitution that marked Amsterdam in those years as the hottest, hippest corner of Europe. The contrast seemed to enthrall him, and though Khan was recently married, he was intrigued by the festive and confident young women. Sometimes during their lunchtime strolls, Veerman watched with concern as Khan followed a young woman for blocks on end. Even though Khan always kept a distance, Veerman worried that the Pakistani's fascination would one day land him in serious trouble.

Their weekend jaunts were less eventful: the two men rode bicycles through the lush Dutch countryside, threading their way through the lacework of canals, stopping for cheese and drinks at small cafés along the way. Veerman understood Khan's polite refusal to drink alcohol or smoke but was surprised that he never brought his Dutch wife, Henny, along. The truth was that while Khan had lived in Europe for a decade and been drawn to the life of Amsterdam's streets, he had not escaped the religious and cultural constraints of his homeland and his upbringing.

———

KHAN was born to a Muslim family on April 27, 1936, in Bhopal, British India. Half a century later, the city became known for the eighteen thousand deaths caused by an accident at a Union Carbide insecticide plant. When Khan was born, however, Bhopal was known only as a peaceful place shared by Hindus and Muslims, who had lived side by side for centuries. Khan was one of seven children. His father, Abdul Ghafoor Khan, had been a teacher in the central provinces of India. He retired the year before Khan's birth, devoting his energy to working with the All-India Muslim League, which began as a political party in British India to protect the rights of Muslims and later became the driving force in the creation of Pakistan as a separate Muslim state. Throughout his life, Khan modeled himself on his father's humility and politeness. Like his father, he rarely raised his voice and often referred to himself as a man of peace, recalling that his father had stopped him from shooting birds when he was a young boy and instilled in him a reverence for life. But the son also inherited the father's fervor for an Islamic state and his hatred of India.

Shortly after Khan's birth, his mother, Zulekha, visited a fortune-teller and received a prediction about her newborn's fate: "The birth of this child will bring good fortune to his family. The child is very lucky; he is going to do a lot of good deeds in his life ahead. He is going to do very important and useful work for his nation and will earn immense respect."

Prediction aside, Khan's early years were typical of a young boy in British India. When time came to enroll him in school, his striving parents backdated his birth to allow him to start attending early. He was considered a good, though not exceptional, student, and he often seemed more interested in fishing and playing field hockey with his friends than in studying. He was more disciplined when it came to religion, attending prayers regularly at the neighborhood mosque with his father and four brothers. His favorite books were histories of the Muslim heroes who had created the Mughal Empire, gaining control over South Asia by vanquishing infidels in the sixteenth century. Eventually the Mughals were defeated by the British in the nineteenth century, instantly transforming India's Muslim rulers into a powerless minority.

The indignity stained Muslim life in India, fostering a widespread belief that the British who governed the vast subcontinent of India favored the majority Hindus and fueling the Muslim desire for a separate state, which finally came to fruition a century later. On August 14, 1947, Pakistan was created as an Islamic nation and refuge for Muslims. As so often in the building or breaking up of nations, logic was not part of the plan, and so the newly created Pakistan did not comprise a single territory but two—East and West, with India between them. The next day, India gained its independence and control over the remainder of its territory. The division of British India deteriorated rapidly into massive communal warfare, with tens of thousands of Muslims slaughtered in riots as they tried to leave for their newly created state. Khan was eleven years old at the time, and the violence was seared into his memory. His family watched in horror as Muslims flooded their neighborhood in Bhopal, still considered a sanctuary in those bitter days, bringing spine-chilling tales of atrocities committed by Hindus. Khan later described having seen trains packed with the corpses of Muslims killed in the sectarian fighting.

Two of Khan's brothers fled immediately to Karachi, the bustling port on the Arabian Sea in the newly established West Pakistan. Another brother and his elder sister joined them in 1950. Khan's father was determined not to be driven from his home, which he viewed as surrender to the Hindus, and he refused to permit his youngest son to join his siblings. Finally, after Khan finished high school in 1952, Abdul Ghafoor decided that there was no future for his youngest son in India, which he believed discriminated against the Muslims who had remained behind rather than immigrate to Pakistan. At sixteen, Khan bid his parents goodbye and set off for West Pakistan by train.

But Khan never really left India behind. The scars of his last years there remained, creating an instinctive fear of India that came to define his personal and professional worlds. Often in later years he recounted the violence and discrimination he had endured as a Muslim, invariably beginning with his own journey out of harm's way by train.

"I was alone," Khan would recall. "Luckily there were a number of Muslim families traveling with us. The attitude of the Indian police and the railway authorities toward these shattered families was extremely hostile, degrading and insulting. The mischievous behavior will always remain fresh in my memory. They snatched every valuable thing from these poor people." As the teenager huddled in the jammed train car, he clutched his meager belongings to his thin chest. All around him, women tried to hush the cries of babies and children, as men suffered the indignities of departure in silent anger. Khan carried little of value—his beloved Mughal history books and a gold pen given to him by his brother upon graduation—but he was not safe from the predations of the Indian authorities. He had watched the police rifle through the luggage of his fellow passengers, taking whatever they wanted, and just before the train arrived at its last stop near the border, his turn came. A police officer spotted something shiny and reached a fat hand into the boy's shirt pocket, plucking out his treasured pen. Khan was helpless to resist, humiliated by his loss and his weakness. The incident, seemingly minor compared with the tens of thousands of deaths, was a transforming event. The theft framed his view of Indians for a lifetime, and he recounted it whenever he talked about his distrust of Pakistan's neighbor. "It was something I'll never forget," he said over and over.

The train was forbidden to cross the border into Pakistan, so the final leg of Khan's pilgrimage required navigating a sandy, five-mile stretch of no-man's-land on foot. Khan stepped off the train and peered at the expanse in front of him as other passengers disembarked and began to trudge slowly toward the promised land, fathers and sons first, mothers and daughters bringing up the rear. After a few tentative steps in the shifting sand, Khan removed his shoes and walked barefoot. The hike took nearly two hours, leaving him exhausted and parched when he reached the other side. There, he saw for the first time the flag of Pakistan, with its white Islamic crescent emblazoned on a field of green. He sat on the bare ground and ate a meal of bread and meat from a stranger's tandoori oven, thinking that no food had ever tasted so good.

Khan had just enough money to buy a train ticket to Karachi, where his older brothers were living. A few months later, his mother arrived, carrying tales of continued violence against Muslims and describing her husband's stubborn refusal to surrender to the Hindus and leave Bhopal. Khan's father died there in 1956, four years after his last son's departure. By then, Khan had enrolled at the D. J. Science College of Karachi.

Less than a decade after its birth, Pakistan remained mired in poverty, with few of the industries, schools, and financial institutions necessary for economic progress. Pakistanis invariably blamed the Indians for keeping the riches of the British Empire for themselves, a resentment fueled by India's faster economic growth. Pakistan had lost a war with the Indians over the disputed territory of Kashmir in 1948 and watched in fear as India's army grew larger and more powerful, creating a widespread belief that the Indians harbored ambitions of taking over their Muslim neighbor. "Hindus are crooks and mischievous," Khan told a friend in those days. "They are dreaming of destroying Pakistan to create a united India."

Khan graduated from college in 1957, landing his first job as a government inspector of weights and measures in Karachi. He soon discovered the job was a dead end, leaving the ambitious young man restless and unsure about where his future lay. Pakistan's literacy rate was a paltry 16 percent, and there were no great universities. To compensate, the government adopted the common practice in the developing world of encouraging its brightest young graduates to seek higher education abroad. In 1961, Khan received a government grant, resigned from his job, and booked a flight to Düsseldorf, West Germany, where he planned to learn German and enroll in a technical university.

A few days before leaving, a friend took Khan again to visit a fortune-teller. Though Khan considered himself a man of science, like many Pakistanis he was intrigued by the ancient ritual. The old man took Khan's right hand, traced the lines on his upturned palm, and murmured for a minute. Then he said: "I'm surprised you are still here. You should be abroad." The palmist predicted that Khan would leave Pakistan soon and that his initial studies would be difficult, but he reassured the young man that he would fall in love, achieve great success, and then return to Pakistan. "Here in Pakistan, you will do outstanding work in your field, which will bring you a big name," the fortune-teller said.

Khan found an eerie significance in the prediction. His departure had in fact been delayed by a snafu with his German visa. Whether his friend had tipped off the fortune-teller or not, Khan seized on the shaman's vision of his bright future. Even a man of science could find solace in the predictions of a fortune-teller, particularly if they matched his own determination to accomplish great things.

CHAPTER 2

AN ACCIDENTAL OPPORTUNITY

NEARLY TWENTY YEARS BEFORE A. Q. Khan began work at the Amsterdam research laboratory, President Dwight D. Eisenhower reversed the American policy of zealously guarding its atomic secrets, opening the door to the spread of nuclear technology and ultimately permitting people like Khan to bridge the illusory divide between peaceful atomic energy and its darker applications.

The Cold War was well under way and events in the 1950s led to Eisenhower's determination to increase the country's nuclear arsenal in preparation for a possible encounter with the Soviet Union. The first Soviet atomic test had been detected in 1949, ending the American nuclear monopoly. The British conducted their first test in 1952. The next year, the Americans detected yet another Soviet test of a thermonuclear device, and U.S. analysts were shocked to discover that it was more advanced than anything in the American or British atomic arsenals, leading to Eisenhower's decision to expand the American capability. The prospect of developing more lethal weapons at a time when the public's fear of nuclear Armageddon was on the rise meant the escalation would have to be cast in terms that allowed the administration to conceal its true military plans— thus the façade of creating a civilian nuclear sector to harness the atom for peaceful purposes. The speech was still being drafted as Eisenhower flew to New York on December 8, 1953, to unveil the proposal to the UN General Assembly.

Eisenhower began his address by emphasizing the destructive power of the arsenals of the United States and Soviet Union, reminding his audience that the U.S. stockpile alone already exceeded the power of all of the munitions used in World War II combined. The only way to avoid mutual destruction, he said, was to harness the peaceful power of the atom. Eisenhower proposed that the existing nuclear powers contribute uranium and other fissile material to a new International Atomic Energy Agency under the sponsorship of the United Nations. The agency would promote the safe and peaceful uses of atomic energy in something akin to a nuclear Marshall Plan, which he called Atoms for Peace. The concept was greeted with surprising enthusiasm, drawing thunderous applause from the UN delegates and almost immediate acceptance around the world.

What few knew was that the proposal for what was to become the IAEA was serendipitous. During a late draft of Ike's speech, a physicist on the U.S. Atomic Energy Commission had sent the White House a memo drafted by Ronald I. Spiers, one of the commission's young foreign-affairs specialists. Spiers laid out plans for such an international agency, affiliated with the United Nations, to control and promote civilian uses of nuclear energy much as the Atomic Energy Commission did in the United States. The idea was incorporated directly into the Eisenhower speech without much thought about how such an agency would be set up or the full extent of its mandate. The enthusiastic international response left the Eisenhower administration scrambling to figure out the details. Civilian and military nuclear programs run on parallel courses and are nearly inseparable, which meant Eisenhower was going to unleash the nuclear genie before any real guidelines were in place to prevent a peaceful effort from turning into a weapons program.

A few days after the speech, Spiers was at his desk in Washington when Secretary of State John Foster Dulles's office telephoned, asking Spiers to make his proposal a reality. Over the next three years, Spiers worked on the evolving treaty to create the IAEA. Early plans were for the agency to have its own intelligence operation to ensure that peaceful nuclear activities were not diverted to military programs, but powerful forces in the Eisenhower administration and Congress were leery of ceding real power to any international organization. "There was a lot of distaste for the UN, and they felt it was an intrusion on U.S. sovereignty," said Spiers. There was no chance that Congress would ratify the treaty to join unless the new agency's authority was watered down. Among the elements jettisoned was its independent intelligence arm, a step seen as giving the new organization too much power. The IAEA came into being in 1957, when it opened its headquarters in Vienna, but questions were raised from the outset about whether the agency had the powers necessary to cope with the spread of nuclear technology.

By the time of the IAEA's creation, the United States was already using taxpayer money to subsidize the sale of small nuclear reactors to a host of countries, including Iran, Israel, India, Pakistan, and South Africa. Attempting to counter American influence, the Soviets were also handing out nuclear goodies to countries aligned with them. The dangers were recognized almost immediately. Top-secret intelligence reports prepared by the CIA and other American intelligence agencies in the late 1950s and early 1960s warned that the spread of nuclear know-how was creating the capability for small-scale nuclear-weapons programs in many countries. The classified reports warned that some countries would try to convert peaceful nuclear research into weapons programs. France, China, West Germany, Japan, Sweden, and Israel were identified initially as the countries most likely to develop nuclear weapons, with India and Pakistan joining the list a few years later. The barrier between peaceful nuclear energy and its military uses was turning out to be an illusion. No better example existed than centrifuges, the narrow cylinders about six feet tall that were being developed at FDO in Amsterdam when A. Q. Khan arrived on the scene in 1972. The same machines could be used to produce nuclear fuel for civilian reactors—or, with some minor modifications—for atomic weapons.

CENTRIFUGES have many uses. Washing machines are simple versions, using centrifugal motion to remove water from wet clothes during the spin cycle by creating enough artificial gravity to separate the heavy water from the lighter clothes. A good washing machine spins at twelve to twenty revolutions per second. The sophisticated ultracentrifuges used to enrich uranium need to spin about one hundred times faster, near the speed of sound. But the concept remains the same: In the uranium-enrichment process, the centrifuge must spin fast enough to separate the highly prized U-235 isotope from the other isotopes found in natural uranium. The U-235 is desirable because it easily splits in two, producing bursts of atomic energy.

Enriching uranium cannot be done with just one centrifuge, however, but thousands of the slender cylinders linked by a series of pipes and specialized valves in arrays called cascades. A basic cascade contains 164 centrifuges, and as few as five cascades concealed in a school classroom could eventually produce enough highly enriched uranium for a small bomb. But a working enrichment plant requires thousands of cascades stretching the length of a football field. Each centrifuge increases the concentration of rarer U-235 ever so slightly as it spins and feeds the material into the next centrifuge, where it is enriched further and further. Centrifuges can run for months, and in some commercial plants they never stop. So they must be balanced perfectly atop precision bearings and magnets.

When uranium is enriched to 3 percent U-235, it is suitable to fuel reactors for generating power. As is common with many forms of technology, the difference between commercial and military applications of the technology is only minor. Slight adjustments to the enrichment process can increase the concentration of the explosive U-235 to 90 percent, the level deemed most efficient for atom bombs. This end product is called highly enriched uranium, or HEU, and it was the fissionable material used by the Americans in the bomb that devastated Hiroshima on August 6, 1945.

Despite the goal of sharing uranium to be used for fuel set forth in Atoms for Peace, the United States maintained a near monopoly on producing enriched uranium for civilian plants. In 1970, Britain, West Germany, and the Netherlands sought to escape their dependence on the Americans. The result was a joint program called Urenco, which became the largest nuclear project in Europe. Its mission was to guarantee a consistent and independent supply of enriched uranium fuel for their civilian power plants.

Together, the governments built a sprawling uranium-enrichment plant in the quiet rolling hills near the Dutch town of Almelo, about fifteen miles west of the German border. The plant was intended to use the most advanced centrifuge technology available, and the three countries engaged in a competition to come up with the best design. Though Almelo's purpose was strictly civilian, it was built behind rings of barbed wire, and security clearances were required for entry because of fears that the advanced technology could be stolen.

Competing against their German and British partners, Urenco's Dutch arm and its subcontractors were working at full speed to perfect their version of the advanced centrifuge, increasing the demand for qualified engineers and scientists. The need for new blood was particularly great at FDO, where Khan worked, because it was a new company set up to work on the big Urenco contract. The result was that security measures often took a backseat to filling key spots on the scientific roster.

KHAN'S journey from Karachi to his new office at FDO had been difficult, just as the fortune-teller had predicted. Mastering German had proven tougher than he expected when he arrived in Düsseldorf in 1961. His frustrations were magnified by homesickness. In January 1962, he had been studying without a break for several months when he took a vacation in the Netherlands. Visiting The Hague, Khan was watching the crowds pass by when he worked up the courage to approach a young woman who appeared to be by herself, asking in his halting German if she knew the cost of postage to Pakistan. Transparent as the pickup line was, the woman knew not only the answer but a little about Pakistan. Khan struggled to keep the conversation going, but the plain young woman was in no hurry to escape the dashing older man. She told him that her name was Hendrina, but she said she preferred to be called Henny. She explained that she was on a day trip from Amsterdam, where she lived with her parents.

Henny Reterink had been born in South Africa to expatriate Dutch parents, had been raised mostly in Northern Rhodesia, and carried a British passport. She had returned to Holland with her parents a few years earlier and learned to speak Dutch and German, though she was not a Dutch citizen. Khan and Henny chatted for several minutes before moving to an outdoor café. They found that they shared a sense of being outsiders and, before parting, exchanged addresses and promises to write. Henny did not expect to hear again from the handsome man. "To tell you the truth I never thought that this would lead to anything," she said. "To me he was a lonely young man who was very homesick."

But he did write, and she replied. After exchanging several letters, she took an uncharacteristically bold step and agreed to visit him in Düsseldorf, where he was completing his German lessons before transferring to the Technical University of Berlin to begin his scientific studies. Several months later, the relationship became serious enough that Henny took a secretarial job in Berlin to be close to Khan. They were engaged in early 1963, and both families seemed to accept the couple's decision. "Neither my parents nor my husband's mother were against this relationship," Henny said. "After having lived in many countries with different people, my parents were quite broad-minded. This does not mean there were no misunderstandings. There were, but luckily we resolved them amicably."

In September of that year, Khan transferred from Berlin to the Delft University of Technology in the Netherlands to continue his graduate work. The university's science and engineering departments were well regarded, and the medieval city had a charming combination of canals and cobblestones. Henny wanted to get married at Delft's historic city hall, but that was prohibited because both of them were foreigners. Instead, a modest Muslim ceremony was performed at the Pakistani embassy at The Hague, where the ambassador served as Khan's witness because his family had been unable to travel to Holland. The embassy staff arranged a tea party for the newlyweds, which was followed by a reception hosted by Henny's parents. Khan was twenty-seven, and his wife was twenty-one.

The newlyweds formed a world unto themselves. Henny had lived in Rhodesia until she was sixteen and never felt at home in the Netherlands. By the time of his wedding, Khan had spent two years in Europe and did not feel at home. People who knew Khan at Delft remembered him as quiet and serious about his studies. They said he seemed to enjoy strolling through the city arm in arm with his wife and appeared oblivious to the occasional ethnic slights sent his way. The assumption was that he intended to finish his degree and remain in Europe. One of his few friends at Delft was a Dutch student named Henk Slebos, who was also studying metallurgy. "He was a serious student," Slebos recalled. "He was not what one would call a bon vivant."

Khan had been too busy to involve himself in politics. In 1965, however, events reached a stage that he felt he could not ignore. In 1948, Pakistan had lost a war with India over the disputed territory of Kashmir, and in 1965 the Pakistani army made a second attempt to liberate the predominantly Muslim region from Indian rule, resulting in a full-scale war and second defeat. The international community was critical of Pakistan's continued designs on Kashmir, and a professor at Delft screened a documentary condemning the country. Khan heard about the film and sent off a series of angry letters to the professor and local newspapers in which he tried to correct what he saw as a biased view of his country.

Pakistan's defeat had struck a chord deep within Khan, dredging up his old hatred of India and foreshadowing events in his own life. The next year, he decided that the time had come for Henny to visit Pakistan for the first time. He wanted to introduce her to his family, and he wanted to test the waters for a possible return home. Initially, Khan's mother and sisters-in-law insisted that the couple reenact their wedding with an imam presiding in a traditional Muslim ceremony, and Henny was relieved when her husband rejected the proposal. Much to Henny's chagrin, her relatives asked continually when the couple planned to have children. She smiled and said time would tell, declining to share with them the fact that she was undergoing medical treatment because of fears of infertility.

As for Khan, he was overjoyed to find himself back in the folds of his large family. His mother filled the family home in Karachi with the aromas of foods from his childhood, strengthening his resolve to return permanently. Pakistan remained poor and technologically backward, and Khan confided in Henny that he was determined to return home permanently and contribute to the country's progress in a significant way. But when he applied for a job at the national steel mill in Karachi, he was turned down and told that he lacked the proper credentials. Dumbfounded, Khan and

Henny returned to Delft, where he completed his master's degree in 1967 and earned a research scholarship in metallurgy at the Catholic University in Leuven, Belgium.

His time at Leuven was to prove a turning point for Khan. Angered by his rejection in Karachi, he made a determined effort to become a European. Though not deemed a brilliant student, he worked fanatically on his doctorate, impressing his adviser with his ability to persuade his rival students and top-ranked academics to work toward a common goal. In one case, the adviser, Professor Martin Brabers, and Khan were editing a textbook on the esoteric topic of physical metallurgy, and the student persuaded senior scientists from around the world to contribute chapters. In the meantime, his family life thrived. Henny, who worked as a secretary, gave birth to their first child in 1968, a daughter named Dina. Two years later, when Henny was pregnant again, she asked her husband if he hoped for a son, something every Pakistani family seemed to want. He told her it did not matter whether the next one was a boy or a girl, but they agreed that they should stop at two, even when the second child turned out to be another girl. Khan still spent long hours at the university, but he always made it home in time to cook dinner for the family, a practice that had started after they were married because Khan considered himself the better cook.

When the topic of Pakistan arose, Khan displayed little more than passing affection for his homeland. To Brabers, he appeared to be proud of his country and occasionally irritated that it was not treated well by its neighbors and the West, but Brabers saw nothing of the burning nationalist who was soon to emerge. "He had an international mind," Brabers said years later. "He could live in any country, I think, and that's what he tried to do."

Try as he might to blend in, however, Khan could not shake his past. For him, Pakistan was not an obscure chapter in a history book but something that he had seen written in blood. As he was finishing his dissertation on metallurgy in late 1971, he found himself distracted by violent new events unfolding on television. Pakistan's capital, Islamabad, was in the western portion of the divided country, leaving those in the eastern half feeling constantly slighted. With India separating the two, it was a

difficult situation. Toward the end of 1971, the Pakistani military determined to put down the separatist-minded Muslims in the eastern portion,
sparking a series of brutal clashes that left hundreds of East Pakistanis
dead and sent tens of thousands more fleeing across the border into India.
From bases there, the refugees launched retaliatory attacks on the Pakistani military. When the army replied with strikes that reached into Indian territory, Pakistan found itself once again facing all-out war with its
much larger neighbor. The Indians both outnumbered and outmaneu-
vered the Pakistanis, leading to a humiliating surrender in December of
that year. One of the most stinging conditions of the cease-fire was the
permanent division of Pakistan, with the eastern portion splitting off to
form the new nation of Bangladesh.

Khan wept as he watched the Pakistani surrender, sobbing over the
images of thousands of Pakistani soldiers being kicked and caned by the
Indian army. Memories of his childhood flooded back, and he prayed to
Allah to help his country. For Khan, the division of Pakistan was the first
step in India's campaign to dismember and annihilate the Muslim nation, and he vowed to himself that his country would never suffer another
humiliating defeat if he could help it. "All he thought about," his biographer later wrote melodramatically, "was to make Pakistan so strong that it
would never have to face such a trauma again."

The 1971 war marked Khan's transformation from expatriate to patriot, the point at which he gave up the notion of becoming a European
and made up his mind that he would return to Pakistan. After completing
his dissertation, he enthusiastically began his job search by mailing out
applications for a series of jobs in Pakistan, ranging from the steel industry to government and academic posts. But again, he was turned down
without explanation, leaving him befuddled and disheartened. With two
young children and a wife, he couldn't wait until something came through
in Pakistan, so he grudgingly sent out inquiries to universities and industries in Europe; again, he got no job offers.

In the spring of 1971, Khan told Henk Slebos he was worried about
how to make ends meet. Slebos mentioned that he had heard about an
opening for a metallurgist at FDO, which was developing new centrifuge
designs for the Dutch government. Khan's dissertation on the ability of

exotic metals to withstand the strains of the high speeds seemed to make him a natural candidate, so he sent in an application, accompanied by a strong recommendation from Brabers. Within days, he heard back—he had the job and could start as soon as he could get to Amsterdam. This was not Pakistan, and Khan wouldn't be saving his country, but he would be able to provide for his family.

Khan probably should not have been given the job at FDO, at least not that particular job. Security regulations adopted by the three Urenco governments stipulated that anyone who worked in the centrifuge program needed a top security clearance, a process that was designed to be particularly difficult for anyone who was not British, Dutch, or German. For employees from other countries, even a routine clearance required a complete background check and special clearance from a review committee representing all three countries. But the rush to hire new workers and bureaucratic missteps meant that Khan underwent little scrutiny, and his name was never submitted to the review group. He started work without the clearance, and receiving it turned out to be only a formality. When FDO submitted Khan's name to the Dutch Ministry of Economic Affairs as the first step in the security process, the company specified that he would not work on centrifuges, which meant that his security clearance did not need to be higher than "restricted." In addition, FDO specified that Khan's wife was Dutch and that he was applying for Dutch citizenship. Whether the citizenship issues were the result of lies by Khan or bureaucratic blunders, they meant that he was given only a cursory check by Dutch authorities, and by the time his "restricted" clearance came through, he was already at work.

CHAPTER 3

THE MUSLIM ALLIANCE

O N JANUARY 24, 1972, only five weeks after being installed by the military as Pakistan's leader, Zulfikar Ali Bhutto stood beneath a gaily colored canopy on the lawn of a colonial-era mansion. Seated in front of him were fifty of the country's top scientists and military officials, flown aboard military planes in the greatest secrecy to the remote town of Multan, about 250 miles southwest of Islamabad and close to the border with India. The setting reflected Bhutto's flair for drama. His words were calculated to stir the nationalism of his audience.

Pakistan's new leader had been dreaming for years of an Islamic nuclear bomb, which would put his country on a par with its much larger rival. The humiliating partition of Pakistan had disgraced the military and ushered Bhutto into power. He was determined that no similar disgrace would lead to his ouster. He had first talked publicly of a nuclear weapon in the early 1960s when he was the government's energy minister. Then, in his 1967 autobiography, he had laid out his argument for going nuclear, writing: "All wars of our age have become total wars; all European strategy is based on the concept of total war; and it will have to be assumed that a war waged against Pakistan is capable of becoming total war. It would be dangerous to plan for less and our plans should, therefore, include the nuclear deterrent." The generals in power at the time had rejected Bhutto's plans, arguing that the costs would cut too deeply into spending on conventional forces. Once he took charge, however, Bhutto was eager to carry out his plan.

Beneath the canopy, he began his remarks sedately and then gradually increased the intensity by recounting the recent crushing defeat by India and promising to restore the country's honor. He reminded his audience that he had long wanted Pakistan to counter India's greater military numbers by developing a nuclear deterrent, though until that time no one had embraced his vision. Because the latest battlefield loss had had the effect of entrusting him with the country's destiny, he said, he had decided to take the single most important step to protect Pakistan's security: building an atomic bomb. His voice rising and trembling, he told his rapt audience, "You men here will make it for me and for Pakistan."

There were men inside the tent who knew well the enormous scale and the dangers of what Bhutto was asking. Abdus Salam had founded a respected theoretical-physics center in Italy and recognized the difficulty of building an atomic weapon. Munir Ahmed Khan had just returned to Pakistan from a senior job at the International Atomic Energy Agency, so he was aware of the obstacles to obtaining the technology. I. J. Usmani, who had spent the previous decade building up the Pakistan Atomic Energy Commission, knew that the country lacked the technology and skill to build a nuclear weapon, and he had spent the previous days trying to persuade Bhutto to abandon the idea.

But enthusiasm born of frustration and bitterness coursed through the crowd of generals and lesser scientists. Khaled Hasan, Bhutto's press secretary, saw emotions sweep over the group as the realization dawned that they might be present at a historic turning point for their young country. To the scientific and military elite of a nation suffering from yet another defeat at the hands of its worst enemy, Bhutto offered salvation and even retribution. Many were ready to embrace the challenge, no matter how outlandish or risky the goal seemed. "He had great charisma, and he really moved those people," Hasan said years later, remembering the day as if it had just happened. "They cheered him. They said they could do it. Everyone believed in Bhutto."

"Can you give it to me?" Bhutto exhorted the audience, like an

evangelical preacher warming up a tent sanctuary packed with true
believers.

"Oh, yes, yes, yes. You can have it. You can have it," they chanted.

"How long will it take?" he demanded.

The harsh reality of the question silenced the group. It was one thing
to hoist the banner of building a nuclear weapon, another entirely to carry
out one of the most complicated tasks of modern science. The murmuring
began, and slowly the skeptics emerged. As the group pondered the challenge, some questioned whether Pakistan had the scientific and technical
expertise to build a bomb, and others wondered whether it could afford to
drain scarce resources to finance such a massive project. The country possessed only the barest beginnings of a nuclear industry—a small research
reactor provided by the United States under the Atoms for Peace program
sat in Rawalpindi, the garrison town next to Islamabad. A larger reactor
was under construction by Canadians near Karachi, but it was designed to
generate electricity, and the Canadians had insisted as part of the contract
that its operation be monitored by the IAEA. Building a nuclear weapon
required thousands of trained technicians and access to the most sophisticated technology in the world. Starting from scratch would cost hundreds
of millions of dollars and could take many years.

Some of the senior people at Multan were brave enough to stand up to
Bhutto and tell him that it was impossible to predict how long it would
take to complete such an enormous project. A few suggested Pakistan
lacked the scientific foundation and resources to accomplish the task. But
before long, emotion overpowered reason, and one man jumped to his feet
and embraced Bhutto's challenge.

"It can be done in five years," he said.

"Three years," Bhutto fired back. "I want it in three years."

Another scientist, a young physicist named Siddique A. Butt, shouted,
"It can be done in three years."

Bhutto smiled broadly, promising his audience that he would scour the
globe for the financial resources and scientific talent to make the dream a
reality. Usmani was fired as head of the PAEC, replaced by Munir Khan;
Salam opposed the whole idea of building a bomb and left the country
in 1974, going on to share in the Nobel Prize for physics in 1979 for

work done at Imperial College in London and the International Center for Theoretical Physics in Trieste.

BHUTTO needed millions of dollars for his bomb, but his country was poor, so within weeks of the Multan meeting he embarked on a whirlwind tour of twenty countries, mostly in the Middle East, with stops in Iran, Saudi Arabia, and Egypt. Hasan, who traveled with Bhutto, called the trip the president's Islamic offensive. In Libya, he met with Colonel Moammar Gadhafi, the revolutionary who had seized power in a military coup in 1969 at the age of twenty-seven and established one of the world's most repressive regimes. Gadhafi was a wild-eyed man of the desert who had enormous ambitions for himself and his country, which included using oil revenue to finance international terrorism and turn his country into a regional superpower. Gadhafi had already tried without success to buy a bomb from China. He was intrigued by Bhutto's proposal.

Gadhafi was not the only one interested; the prospect of an atomic bomb manufactured in Pakistan had broad appeal across the Muslim world. Arab rulers in the Middle East were realistic enough to understand that the world, and particularly Israel, would not tolerate a nuclear-weapons program in the volatile, oil-rich region, but they believed that Pakistan stood a better chance of avoiding international interference because its bomb might be seen as a counter to India's superior forces and its rumored nuclear program. Certainly there would be loud opposition, but the conventional wisdom was that no one was likely to launch an attack against a Pakistani nuclear effort, except perhaps India.

Bhutto did not have to wait long for help. The international oil crisis of 1973 sent prices through the roof. In February 1974, he planned to cash in on his allies' bonanza under the guise of an Islamic summit. He chose the perfect backdrop to rally Muslims: the historic and beautiful city of Lahore. A former capital of the Mughal Empire, Lahore's brick-and-limestone fort and luxurious gardens were reminders of the Muslims' lost glory on the subcontinent. The leaders of thirty-seven Muslim nations arrived in Lahore at a time when some saw the possibility of a new era for their people. Arab armies had exhibited newfound strength in fighting Israel a few months earlier, and many governments were fat from oil revenue. Pakistan had no oil, but Bhutto saw another role for his country. He used the forum to lay out a broad vision of a new Muslim alliance that would join poor Islamic countries with their wealthy brothers to fight the Zionists and their Western backers. He envisioned Pakistan at the forefront of Islamic nations, if it could develop the weapons necessary to challenge the world's superpowers.

"Israel has gorged and fattened on the West's sympathies, nurtured itself on violence and expanded through aggression," he told the conference. Now was the moment, he said, that oil money and military strength could shift the balance in favor of the Muslim world. "This may well be a watershed in history," he said.

Bhutto singled out Gadhafi for special attention, determined to secure his support for Pakistan's bomb. Though both had a flair for the dramatic, the men were a study in contradictions. Bhutto was a son of privilege who had a degree from the University of California at Berkeley and had studied law at Oxford University. Gadhafi was the last child and only son of a poor Bedouin family. He had risen to power through the Libyan military, engineering the overthrow of King Idris and promoting himself to colonel. Bhutto honored his new friend by naming the largest cricket stadium in Pakistan after the Libyan strongman. Bhutto gave him a rare personal tour of the country's military installations and the Canadian-built nuclear reactor nearing completion outside Karachi. The courtship worked, and Gadhafi agreed to help finance the nuclear effort. "Mr. Bhutto told me that during the Islamic summit in Lahore, he had several discussions with Colonel Gadhafi about the manufacture of an atomic bomb by Pakistan," said Mohammed Beg, a former Pakistani diplomat and journalist. "[Gadhafi] promised Mr. Bhutto that he would provide however much money was needed. And, in return, he asked Mr. Bhutto if Libya could have the first bomb." In the months that followed, two couriers arrived in Pakistan from Libya, each carrying $100 million in cash. There were also reliable reports that Saudi Arabia's King Faisal agreed to provide money for the program in return for a promise that Pakistan's nuclear program would provide a security umbrella for the kingdom. Bhutto later demonstrated his appreciation by renaming the former colonial city of Lyallpur as Faisalabad.

Arab support for Pakistan's bomb reflected the lessons of the first nuclear age. The world had been divided into two camps: those who had the bomb and those who did not. No Muslim country had the bomb, and some Arab leaders were convinced that acquiring it was the only deterrent against attack from the West and Israel. For others, an Islamic bomb was a potent symbol of their importance on the world stage. Certainly both rationales were part of Bhutto's mind-set, but fear of India weighed heaviest on his mind. Pakistan had little chance of defeating the larger forces of India through conventional warfare, so Bhutto turned to nuclear deterrence. Not everyone in Pakistan agreed, and some of the generals openly opposed the nuclear path, arguing that they could hold their own against the Indians with conventional forces. This argument defied recent military history, and it was rendered moot three months after the Lahore summit.

ON MAY 18, 1974, about one hundred miles from the Pakistani border, India detonated a nuclear device roughly equivalent in power to the bomb that destroyed Hiroshima. Prime Minister Indira Gandhi watched as the floor of the Rajasthan desert heaved from the blast set off 350 feet underground. A message was sent to New Delhi, the capital, which read simply, "The Buddha is smiling." Gandhi later insisted it was a "peaceful nuclear explosive," but that benign nomenclature did not stop world condemnation or the anxiety spike in Islamabad.

India's detonation demonstrated the utter folly of believing that nuclear technology could be divided neatly between civilian and military programs. Up to this time, only five countries openly possessed nuclear weapons: Britain, China, France, the Soviet Union, and the United States. President John F. Kennedy's prediction in 1963 that fifteen to twenty countries would have nuclear arms by 1975 had not come true, thanks largely to the technical and political barriers to proliferation. The chief regulatory mechanism was the Nuclear Non-Proliferation Treaty, which had taken effect in 1970 as part of a so-called grand bargain to stop the spread of nuclear weapons. The treaty allowed the five weapons states to keep their arsenals but required them to begin reductions through future negotiations. In exchange for pledging to forgo nuclear weapons, other countries were offered access to technology and expertise to develop civilian nuclear programs to generate power and conduct scientific and medical research. More than seventy countries had ratified the treaty by the time of the Indian test, and among them were Iran and most Arab states, in addition to Britain, the Soviet Union, and the United States. China and France had refused to sign, and so had a handful of countries with nuclear-weapons ambitions of their own, including India, Pakistan, and Israel, which was widely suspected of already possessing the bomb. The Indian test threatened to undermine the treaty, and a contingent of policymakers in Washington wanted to issue a sharp rebuke to Delhi and impose economic sanctions. They were convinced tough action was necessary as a lesson to India and other countries that defying the international prohibition against developing nuclear weapons would not go unpunished. But President Nixon and his powerful secretary of state, Henry Kissinger, refused to go along with new sanctions or even permit a harsh condemnation. Dennis Kux, who drafted the initial response, later wrote that Kissinger determined that "public scolding would not undo the event, but only add to US-Indian bilateral problems and reduce the influence Washington might have on India's future nuclear policy."

Kissinger's decision was the first in a series of failures by American policymakers to take the significant steps required to halt the spread of nuclear weapons. In the case of India and other countries that would follow, bilateral considerations trumped concerns about nuclear weapons, setting the stage for what would become regular complaints from have-nots over a basic inequity and inconsistency concerning possession of nuclear weapons. Israel's rumored arsenal was ignored for political expediency, and India's test did not provoke new sanctions or tough talk from the United States. The lack of American retaliation was not lost on the Pakistanis, and in the years to come Bhutto and his successors came to understand just how far they could go without provoking the United States.

Canada did take action, freezing all assistance to a second reactor being built in India and blocking new parts for an existing one. Ottawa felt betrayed because India had used spent fuel from a Canadian-supplied reactor to produce the plutonium for its nuclear device. The reactor was supposed to be used solely for peaceful purposes, but the diversion of fissile material to a secret weapons program underscored the difficulty in enforcing the separation of civilian and military nuclear uses, particularly in a country like India, which had refused to sign the treaty. The blame was shared by the Atoms for Peace program, which had provided vital knowledge to Indian scientists. Homi Sethna, chairman of the Indian Atomic Energy Commission later in the 1970s, described the impact of Eisenhower's program by saying, "I can say with confidence that the initial cooperation agreement itself has been the bedrock on which our nuclear program has been built."

Though India's bomb was intended primarily as deterrence against China, the Pakistanis saw it as a direct threat, prompting Bhutto to declare that his country would not be intimidated or submit to "nuclear blackmail." The test hardened Bhutto's resolve to move forward, erased any doubts among the generals, and ultimately opened the door for A. Q. Khan's return. But even as the Multan project took on more importance, it became more difficult because the Indian test stiffened some of the international community's resolve to get tougher on proliferation. Like India, Pakistan's weapons program centered on fissile material from reprocessed plutonium extracted from spent fuel from its own Canadian-built power reactor, which had just come on line near Karachi. The next step was to build a reprocessing plant to extract the plutonium from the reactor's spent fuel, but the British had already refused to sell Pakistan the necessary technology because of fears it could be used for weapons. Negotiations with the French for the construction of such a plant suddenly came under more international scrutiny.

The Canadians demanded that Pakistan open its Karachi reactor to full inspections by the International Atomic Energy Agency, even though Pakistan had not signed the nonproliferation treaty. The Pakistanis called the demands unreasonable and refused to comply, prompting Canada to cut off spare parts for the reactor and stop shipping uranium fuel rods that would have brought the core to full strength. Still, the means for imposing tighter restrictions on the Pakistanis and other potential proliferators were limited. The IAEA lacked authority over countries that had not signed the nonproliferation treaty, and it had no authority to regulate or even monitor the export of nuclear-related technology to such countries.

The Indian test marked the official start of what Austrian writer Robert Jungk described as the Age of Proliferation, an era in which the threat of nuclear weapons no longer rested with the five original nuclear states but with India and Israel and likely Pakistan. No one could be sure when it would stop or how to stop it. Before the Indian explosion, a handful of countries had been working on a list of specific technologies and equipment that should be subject to tighter export controls because of their nuclear applications. The controls would prohibit sales to any country that had not signed the nonproliferation treaty and had not accepted IAEA safeguards, but the regulations were informal and difficult to enforce, particularly because many countries regarded the sales of such advanced technology as commercial transactions, with little regard for proliferation dangers. Nonetheless, a month after the Indian test, fifteen countries gathered in Vienna for an emergency session to hammer out the final list of restricted technology. Two months later, a remarkably short time for a broad international agreement, the group published two separate memos establishing a category of equipment and technology that would come under tighter controls; it was known as a "trigger list" because any attempt to buy the goods would trigger the restrictions. But the regulations were only as effective as the ability and willingness of the individual countries to enforce them.

This was, in fact, one of the moments when the world might have stopped Pakistan from following the nuclear path. Some experts argue it was already too late—once India went nuclear, there was no chance to stop Pakistan from matching its neighbor, bomb for bomb. The more convincing argument is that strong international condemnation of India coupled with genuine enforcement of tougher restrictions on sales of nuclear-related technology could have at the least tacked many years onto the time it would take Pakistan to match India's bomb. But that didn't happen because more powerful forces took over in Pakistan and the United States.

THERE is no doubt that the American government knew that Pakistan had embarked on a nuclear-weapons program by the time of the Indian test. The CIA had reported on Bhutto's speech at Multan and monitored the beginnings of the scientific effort inside Pakistan, much of which rested with physicists and other scientists who had been educated in the United States and were open to discreet conversations with quiet Americans. At the State Department, efforts were under way to start a diplomatic campaign to block the sale of the French reprocessing plant to Pakistan.

Bob Gallucci understood the Pakistani program better than almost anyone in the American government, and he recognized the urgency of stopping it, though he was among those who suspected that it was already too late. Gallucci had joined the U.S. Arms Control and Disarmament Agency, an independent government body set up in 1961 to monitor nuclear-weapons developments worldwide, in early 1974 after receiving a doctorate in politics from Brandeis University. He was completing a manuscript about the politics of American involvement in Vietnam, but the new focus on proliferation after the Indian explosion meant his superiors assigned Gallucci the task of analyzing how long it might take Pakistan to develop a nuclear counterstrike capability. Gallucci appreciated Bhutto's rationale that a nuclear weapon would serve Pakistan's political and military purposes by providing a rallying point for a disheartened and anxious people, while also solidifying Bhutto's power. He also recognized that the chances that the international community would take truly punitive action against Pakistan were slim because of the country's strategic value as a buffer against China and India.

On January 22, 1975, Gallucci turned his analysis into a classified memo that predicted Pakistan would proceed with its nuclear plans and that the objections of the international community would be both muted and ineffective. His examination of CIA intelligence reports and State Department documents convinced him that a concerted crackdown might delay Pakistan's program substantially. The available evidence indicated that Pakistan would concentrate on developing a device with plutonium as the fissile material, not on using centrifuges to enrich uranium, so Gallucci advocated focusing international diplomacy on preventing the sale of plutonium-related technology to Islamabad.

There are two paths to a nuclear device. The bomb that the United States dropped on Hiroshima used enriched uranium as its core fissile material; the one that devastated Nagasaki three days later was a plutonium device. Each method offered advantages and disadvantages. Plutonium is generally regarded as less complicated, but the reactor and reprocessing facilities required inevitably leave visible clues, such as shape, size, and connections to sources of water and electricity. In addition, gases released through reprocessing can be detected. Enriching uranium through centrifuges, on the other hand, can be concealed easily. A small factory, even a school gymnasium, could hide the thousand or so centrifuges necessary to produce sufficient enriched uranium for a single nuclear weapon, though not an arsenal. A clandestine enrichment facility does not emit environmental signatures or consume large amounts of electricity. The drawback, however, is that enrichment technology can take years to master, even for countries with strong technological skills.

In Pakistan's case, plutonium seemed the surer route. The Canadian reactor near Karachi was operational, and negotiations were under way with France and others to obtain additional technology that could be used to extract plutonium from the spent reactor fuel. With the right outside help, Gallucci concluded, Pakistan could produce a plutonium-based atomic device in the not-too-distant future.

"Pakistan's nuclear industry is not particularly worrisome now, but its potential for expansion and the intentions of the Pakistani government once it achieves a significant capacity are cause for concern," Gallucci wrote in the memo. He warned that French and Belgian companies could provide Pakistan with the additional technology to convert fuel from the Karachi reactor into plutonium for a nuclear device. He said Pakistan had "clearly decided to have the capability" to build a nuclear weapon, which might be completed as soon as 1980. The only way to stop it would be blocking transfers of technology from Western countries.

"Because of the Indian explosion, the Pakistanis have a solid incentive to produce a bomb and they can also do so with less world condemnation than might otherwise be expected," he wrote. "If an explosion is perceived as a source of political cohesion, current disintegrative tendencies within Pakistan may be seen as more reason to acquire the status of a nuclear weapon state. In sum, the Pakistanis appear quite prepared to proceed to a weapons capability, but they may encounter difficulties if political barriers are sustained."

Gallucci was right about everything save one detail: He had no way of knowing about the future impact of an anonymous scientist who was then toiling away inside a Dutch laboratory, working on the latest designs in centrifuges and yearning to help his country fight back against India.

CHAPTER 4

GOING HOME

A T THE AGE OF THIRTY-EIGHT, Dr. Abdul Qadeer Khan was a
middle-ranking scientist working for FDO, applying the theoretical concepts from his academic work to the real-life development of
ultracentrifuges. Security restrictions never impinged on his movement,
and he traveled easily and frequently between the FDO lab in Amsterdam and the enrichment plant being built at the village of Almelo in the
countryside. Khan was maturing as a rational scientist, but he remained
a man shaped by the violent reality of his early years, who still believed in
the fortune-teller's prediction that a great fate awaited him, and who had
never forsaken his desire to return to Pakistan. Word of the Indian nuclear
detonation stirred Khan's patriotism and renewed conversations he had
had with Henny before they married about his desire to go home one day.
Providence seemed to offer him an opportunity in June 1974, when two
Pakistani nuclear scientists arrived at FDO.

Despite the rising concerns in both the United States and Europe about
Pakistan's nuclear activities, the two scientists were touring a number of
European nuclear facilities as representatives of the PAEC. Khan sought
them out as they were having tea in the cafeteria. The two visitors were
surprised when he approached them and started speaking Urdu—they
had no idea that a fellow countryman was working in one of Europe's

most advanced centrifuge-development programs. Khan was eager to impress the scientists, hopeful that they might open the way for him to go home. Boasting about his academic background and the work he was engaged in at FDO, he told them that he was convinced India's nuclear test foretold the death of his country unless it developed its own atomic bomb. He said that he wanted nothing more than to return to Pakistan and work to build a nuclear weapon to save the country.

To Khan's surprise, his appeal fell on deaf ears. Whether it was his middle-class background or his adopted European manners, he encountered a stone wall. The two Pakistanis told him in hushed tones that they had grave doubts about their country's ability to build a nuclear weapon, urging Khan to remain in Europe, where he had a secure job and a bright future. "Nobody would appreciate your talents, and you would be disappointed not to find any employment," one of them, Sibtain Bhokari, explained to the disheartened Khan. The rebuff, however mild, angered Khan, and he stalked out of the cafeteria. He had not been taken seriously as a scientist or a patriot.

Khan was not going to go away easily. He later said that he knew nothing at the time about Bhutto's secret quest for an atomic bomb, though he was certainly aware of the small civilian nuclear program that employed Bhokari and his colleague. Refusing to give up on his plan, Khan took another route. In August, he wrote a personal letter to Bhutto in which he described his accomplishments and offered his services. He wrote that he was an expert in uranium enrichment, working on advanced designs for the European consortium, and that he had published many research papers and edited a well-received book on metallurgy. Again, Khan was ignored, but he repeated his offer in a second letter, on September 17.

Somehow, the second letter caught Bhutto's eye. Perhaps the prime minister was growing desperate because of the slow progress of the plutonium project. Facing the new international concerns over proliferation, France was dithering over its commitment to provide the reprocessing plant that was vital to the plutonium plan. Regardless of the reason, Pakistan's nuclear history was about to be rewritten. One of Bhutto's aides said Khan's letter prompted the Pakistani leader to ask that inquiries be made about the writer and the legitimacy of his claims. "He seemed to be talking sense," Bhutto scrawled in the margin of Khan's letter. The task of evaluating the scientist and his motives was assigned to the embassy in The Hague. "Bhutto asked the embassy to see who this character was," recalled the aide, Khaled Hasan. "All kinds of nutcases write."

By late that month, a Pakistani diplomat confirmed that Khan was the genuine article and that the research center where he worked was involved in nuclear projects. On instructions from Bhutto, the Pakistani ambassador in Holland, J. G. Kharas, contacted Khan, explaining that the prime minister was intrigued by his offer and would like Khan to come to Islamabad to meet with Major General Imtiaz Ali, Bhutto's chief military adviser.

Khan finally faced the choice that was to determine his future. He suffered no inner conflict over abandoning the place where he had lived and worked for more than a decade, no remorse about packing up his wife and children and taking them to a country they barely knew. Khan was convinced that his destiny was within his grasp, but he was calculating enough to recognize that he had to be prepared as fully as possible, because there would be no possibility of return. That meant taking a step beyond simply offering his scientific experience to Pakistan: Khan realized that he needed to be equipped with the actual technical plans that would ensure his success. So, though he was willing to leave at that minute, he explained to the ambassador that he needed to delay the trip because he was on the verge of starting an important new assignment with FDO, one that he suggested could provide crucial benefits for Pakistan. While he and his family had made three previous trips to Pakistan for holidays without raising suspicions at FDO, a visit home at this point without his family might attract undue attention, particularly given the new concerns about proliferation in South Asia. Khan asked to postpone the meeting until late December, when he and his family made their annual visit to his home and after he had completed his new assignment at FDO. Kharas sent a cable to Islamabad explaining the obstacle and received approval for the delay.

But the promise of Khan's return to Pakistan and the validation of his credentials prompted Bhutto to authorize the construction of two small pilot plants, where the first steps could be taken to learn to enrich uranium for a nuclear weapon. The pilot program was placed under the control of a Pakistani scientist named Sultan Bashiruddin Mahmood, who would one day play a far different role in the world of nuclear proliferation.

In Europe, the three countries that formed the Urenco consortium were competing with one another at the same time that they were cooperating. Each wanted to boost its domestic nuclear industry by winning the right to develop the new centrifuges for the huge enrichment facility being built at Almelo. For the Dutch scientists and engineers working for Urenco, the race translated into long hours of work and an atmosphere that encouraged the open exchange of information. Security concerns took a backseat. Khan was drawn into the process despite his low-level security clearance, which should have kept him away from the most sensitive aspects of the work. He found himself with access to almost every part of Almelo and working with every phase of the enrichment process. As part of his job, he helped devise detailed specifications for some of the specialty metals used in the manufacture of the new centrifuges. This work in turn brought him into contact with the outside contractors who were selling components and material to Urenco.

In the fall of 1974, Urenco decided that the Dutch centrifuges were to be augmented with an improved version developed by German scientists, called the G-2. The Dutch engineers at Almelo needed to learn the intricacies of the new machines, but the designs and production specifications were in German. Khan was one of the few scientists in the organization who spoke both German and Dutch, so he was enlisted to translate the documents, which represented the most advanced centrifuge technology in Europe. This was the opportunity that kept him from going to see Bhutto.

Since arriving in Europe, Khan had been accumulating knowledge that he hoped would translate into an important job for him in Pakistan. It wasn't exactly espionage, but his learning always carried an ulterior motive. At FDO, he had picked up extensive information about centrifuges and a general understanding of what was required to build a uranium-enrichment plant. His hobby of photographing centrifuge components had resulted in a collection that would be invaluable in manufacturing the machines. Now he faced the opportunity to expand his knowledge, to acquire the cutting edge of centrifuge technology just as he finally prepared for the journey home.

The German documents were contained in twelve fat volumes. Because of their sensitivity, they were stored inside a small metal structure called the "brain box," which was separate from the main centrifuge plant at Almelo. In addition, the brain box contained the most sensitive records for the overall project. Khan had never been granted a high enough security clearance to walk inside the brain box, let alone work there, but that was where he was sent in October 1974 to translate the critical material. Security regulations required that the Dutch Ministry of Economic Affairs be notified of an employee's transfer to an area this sensitive. Khan should have been required to obtain a higher security clearance. Again, security was a myth, as Khan discovered when he arrived.

Regulations dictated that all doors and desk drawers in the brain box remain locked at all times. Access to the sensitive documents was supposed to be restricted. The reality was that the same collegial atmosphere and free exchange of information that permeated the main plant was operating in its nerve center, too. There was none of the culture of suspicion that the governments would have preferred. Even the segregation of the brain box from the rest of the plant was a fiction—there was a constant flow of people between the two locations, partly because the temporary structure had no canteen or bathroom, so workers there had to use the facilities in the larger building.

On the morning that he started his new assignment, Khan checked in through security as usual, but he needed a special escort to the brain box. Once inside, he met several engineers with whom he had had dealings in the past, and one of them showed him around. After the quick tour, he was handed two of the twelve volumes. Khan was asked to translate them into Dutch as quickly as possible.

Khan worked diligently for sixteen straight days, rewriting the material in Dutch and surreptitiously taking his own notes in Urdu. To anyone casually watching, Khan seemed only to be hard at work. For the first time, he was operating consciously as a spy, gathering material that he planned to take back to Pakistan. Whether sitting at his desk or walking through the larger sections of the plant, Khan seemed always to be jotting in a small notebook. If anyone bothered to ask what he was writing, he said they were letters to family back home. His transparent friendliness and the relaxed atmosphere blunted further questions.

The Dutch made it easy for Khan to steal everything he needed. People working in the brain box had to make do with a single typist, so Khan was permitted to take his handwritten translations back to FDO, where a secretary typed them. The extraordinary arrangement meant that Khan regularly left Almelo with the translations in his briefcase; sometimes, he also carried the originals, saying that he needed help from his wife, who spoke better Dutch. The arrangement violated all of the security rules and provided Khan the chance to make his own set of production designs.

At the time, there were no outward indications that the Pakistani scientist was anything more than a middle-class technocrat commuting by train to Amsterdam from the suburb of Zwanenburg, where he and Henny were raising their young daughters, Dina and Ayesha. Their two-story brick house at 71 Amestelle Street was tidy and identical to the others that lined the narrow streets. Most of Khan's neighbors also worked for FDO and, like him, rented their houses from the company. Ria Hollabrands lived a few doors away from the Khans and found them to be a quiet couple who neither stood out nor blended in. Mrs. Khan participated in occasional functions at the neighborhood school, but she was not Dutch, and she was never welcomed fully into the tight social circles. "My only memory of the mister was visiting the house once and finding him cooking something in the kitchen," said Hollabrands. "It was a surprise, finding a man cooking, but he didn't say anything and I didn't either."

One of Khan's specialties was fried chicken, a favorite of Frits Veerman's. The Dutch bachelor and Khan had remained friends. They still took occasional weekend jaunts on their bicycles, and Veerman was a frequent dinner guest at Khan's home. One night in October, as Veerman sat at the compact table with the Khans, he noticed a stack of blue documents on a nearby table. He thought the color looked familiar, and after dinner he slipped over for a closer look while Henny and Khan cleared the dishes. What he saw surprised him. "I could see these were very secure drawings for the ultracentrifuge, marked with a UC in the corners," he said. "They should never have left the office. They belonged in the fire-resistant safe at FDO or somewhere else. I did not want to ask Abdul why he had them."

Veerman stayed on for another hour, sipping coffee and chatting nervously, unhinged by the sight of the documents. He knew Khan was working on something top secret at Almelo and was certain the drawings were highly classified and did not belong at his friend's house. Veerman could not relax until Khan dropped him at the train station around ten o'clock that night. As he rode back to his apartment in Amsterdam, Veerman was unsure what he should do with this explosive information. Thinking back over the past two years, he examined previous incidents in a new light. Perhaps Khan's interest in Veerman's photographs had not been so innocent. Maybe Khan bought the specialized camera for something other than a hobby, and his endless questions about shutter speeds and lighting might have had a sinister implication. But in the hierarchy of the laboratory, Veerman was a lowly technician, and he could not imagine speaking out against a scientist of Khan's stature. Plus, Veerman, a perpetual outsider, didn't want to lose one of his few friends. He rationalized his silence, concluding that all the details probably added up to nothing.

KHAN finished the translation work at the end of October and returned to work in Amsterdam. Veerman remained concerned, and he kept a close eye on his friend, though he spoke to no one about his suspicions. As the weeks passed, he put the secret papers on the table out of his mind. By then, Khan's copies of the plans were tucked away in a closet at his home. He tried to concentrate on his work, but he could think of little but the upcoming trip back to Pakistan and his meeting with the prime minister's military adviser.

In the middle of December, Khan flew home for his regular holiday. He settled Henny and the girls with his family in Karachi and took the two-hour flight to Islamabad for his meeting. Any pretense that the meeting was normal was contradicted by the fact that Khan had been instructed to use the code name "Karim" when he arrived at the prime minister's office building. After passing through security, he was escorted into a large, formal office, where he expected to meet General Ali. When the military officer entered through a side door, Khan was surprised to see that he was followed by an even more imposing figure. Khan jumped to his feet, bowed slightly, and shook hands with Prime Minister Bhutto. Khan had brought his trove of plans and photographs with him, and he was fully prepared to say yes if Bhutto asked him to stay and join the nuclear program.

Khan wasted no time in presenting his plan to Bhutto. He argued that Pakistan's reliance on plutonium as a fissile material left the country open to interference from its antagonists in the West. Using a centrifuge plant to enrich uranium, on the other hand, Pakistan could achieve nuclear capability in a relatively short time, for less money, and in absolute secrecy. Material and equipment could be purchased quietly abroad, attracting less outside attention than the reprocessing plant Pakistan was trying to buy from France. Khan promised that Pakistan would be enriching uranium to the levels needed for a weapon in five years, a timetable that must have appealed to Bhutto, since the deadline he had imposed at Multan had been missed.

Bhutto was skeptical. He had studied nuclear-weapons development enough to know that only a few countries had mastered the complicated processes of enriching uranium, and even those developed countries had taken years and spent millions of dollars. Still, facing delays with the plutonium project and the threat of American objections to the French deal, Bhutto was inclined to give Khan's proposal serious consideration. Two paths to the bomb could prove better than one, and the prospect of working secretly to enrich uranium while the West watched the plutonium program was intriguing. Bhutto sent Khan on a Cook's tour of Pakistan's nuclear installations. After a few days, Khan returned to Islamabad and met again with the prime minister to report his observations. Khan said he had not been impressed by the progress, claiming that the plutonium route seemed impossible. To his surprise, Bhutto did not ask him to remain in Pakistan and start an enrichment program. Instead, the prime minister instructed him to go back to his job and supervise the beginnings of a secret procurement network to obtain the necessary equipment and technology. Once that was accomplished, the prime minister promised Khan that he would return and lead the enrichment program. No timetable was set, but Khan was elated with his new role.

In meetings over the next few days, Khan learned the rudimentary tradecraft of espionage. He was given the name and telephone number of a contact at the embassy in Brussels named Siddique A. Butt and instructed to keep their conversations to a minimum. He was to come up with a shopping list and the names of suppliers from whom the material could be purchased, but the actual contacts with the outside companies would be handled by embassy personnel, who were protected by diplomatic immunity if something went wrong. In those days, Khan crossed the line from scientist to full-fledged spy and helped to lay the foundations for what was to become a global black market in nuclear technology.

In early January, Khan returned to Amsterdam, bringing sweets for the secretaries and tiny carpets for the desktops of his colleagues, as was his habit. But he was a different man, with a different purpose. Veerman saw a subtle change in his office mate, noticing that he spent more time on the telephone, speaking what Veerman assumed was Urdu, and ducked out for meetings at odd hours of the day. Once he saw Khan stuff rolls of film into an envelope and seal it. Another time, Khan asked him to take photographs of some specific centrifuge components at FDO. On a visit to Khan's house that spring, Veerman noticed some actual centrifuge components. Unlike when he saw the papers, this time the Dutchman spoke up, asking what Khan was doing with the parts. Khan explained that he had scavenged them as souvenirs from the discard bin at FDO and assured Veerman there was no cause for concern.

Veerman could not rid himself of his suspicions this time, and they deepened a few weeks later when he was invited to a small afternoon party at Khan's house. As he arrived, he noticed a car with diplomatic plates parked in front. Inside, he found his friend deep in conversation with two other men. Khan rose immediately and introduced Veerman to the pair, identifying them as Pakistani diplomats.

Later that spring, as Khan was casually extolling the beauties of Pakistan, Veerman said he might like to go there on a holiday. Two weeks later, Khan told Veerman that he had arranged for the Pakistani government to pay for Veerman's trip. He said they would provide airline tickets and a guesthouse in Lahore.

"No, no," Veerman insisted, somewhat surprised. "I will go there as a private person. I have no connection with your government."

Khan assured his friend there was no obligation, but the suggestion of a government-sponsored trip alarmed Veerman, and he anguished over whether this was yet another indication that his friend should be reported to the authorities. Again, he chose to wait, fearing that he was wrong. But if Veerman's suspicions turned out to be well founded, he worried that the innocent help he had provided to Khan for so long might wind up implicating him. Faced with the possibility of being seen as an accomplice, he chose to stay silent, and the opportunity to stop Khan before he really got started was lost.

CHAPTER 5

THE PAKISTANI PIPELINE

O NE OF THE DIPLOMATS who had been at Khan's house during Veerman's visit was Siddique Butt, who was listed as a science and technology officer at the Pakistani embassy in Brussels. When Bhutto had unveiled his plan at Multan in 1972, it was Butt who had stood up and enthusiastically embraced the audacious goal. His contribution had come not in the laboratory, however, but in the covert world of procurement. In 1974, Butt had been assigned to begin buying equipment in Europe for the plutonium project run by the Pakistan Atomic Energy Commission. When Khan offered his services to Bhutto in September 1974, Butt's assignment was expanded to encompass the new world of centrifuge enrichment.

Khan had been given Butt's name and contact details while he was in Pakistan in late 1974, and he wasted no time setting up a meeting with the young physicist when he returned to Amsterdam. With their shared background as scientists and belief in the need for a Pakistani bomb, the two men hit it off from the start. The relationship formed then was to extend for years, proving so effective that insiders gave it the nickname "the Pakistani pipeline." Khan used a secure telephone number to set up meetings with Butt or convey simple information, and some of those conversations in Urdu were what Veerman had overheard at FDO. When it came to more complicated written information, like precision specifications for centrifuge components and reports on enrichment techniques, Khan copied the material and handed it over at his home or in crowded public places, where a casual encounter was unlikely to attract attention. In one case that had implications later, Khan worked on a Urenco team that developed specifications for a new type of ultrathin metal foil for the centrifuge process and copied the specs for Butt. Just six months after meeting with Bhutto, Khan had provided a nearly complete shopping list for the equipment and raw material for a centrifuge plant, as well as the names of suppliers in the Netherlands, Germany, and other countries working with Urenco.

Butt's job was to buy the equipment and get it shipped to Pakistan, employing a network of other diplomats, covert agents, and front companies. As the flow of information from Khan increased, the procurement effort grew more elaborate, and Butt enlisted the help of Pakistanis whose diplomatic or scientific credentials allowed them to visit sensitive nuclear installations across Europe and in Canada and in the United States. Many of these people were part of the wave of bright young men sent overseas for training as nuclear scientists in the 1960s. Together, they managed to turn a handful of the country's embassies into miniprocurement offices for the two secret nuclear programs and inaugurate a practice that came to be known as the gray market. The modus operandi was to develop a list of the required technology and equipment and assign to each item a potential civilian use, which would be used to describe the item to prospective sellers and government export officials. For example, frequency inverters required for centrifuges would be designated for use in textile factories, which also require spinning machines.

As the procurement orders grew more specific, the risk that the scheme would be discovered increased, too. In the summer of 1975, Butt set up two separate front companies to mask his plans for obtaining restricted metal that would be used to form the cylindrical rotors central to centrifuge assemblies. Both companies placed orders for tubes manufactured from high-strength aluminum at a handful of manufacturing plants in the Netherlands that were already supplying the same material to Urenco. The coincidence was not lost on officials at the Dutch companies. When they recognized that the technical specifications exactly matched those for centrifuges under development by the consortium, the orders were politely rebuffed. Similarly, when Butt wrote to one of the Dutch firms on Khan's list about buying a large number of high-frequency transformers to regulate the flow of electricity that keep centrifuges spinning at a consistent speed, the specifications raised another red flag, and the order was refused.

Those incidents were reported to the Dutch authorities, who passed on the information to the CIA and European intelligence agencies. The Americans knew the Pakistanis were buying nuclear equipment, but they misinterpreted the purchase patterns and believed that the acquisitions were related only to the plutonium program. In response, diplomatic and export-control efforts were concentrated on blocking the French deal on the reprocessing plant. What the Americans and the rest of the world did not yet understand was that Bhutto had set his country on a second, more secret path, which relied on the cleverness of his new volunteer, A. Q. Khan. It simply did not occur to Western experts and intelligence agents that Pakistan could acquire the technological expertise to enrich uranium. The failure to recognize the significance of the threat was part of a pattern of underestimating the Pakistanis that contributed to their ultimate success.

Stopping the trade in nuclear technology rested officially with the International Atomic Energy Agency, but few American officials thought the IAEA was up to the task. The agency was regarded primarily as a promoter of civilian nuclear energy and its applications, rather than a proliferation watch dog. The Americans also understood that the agency's investigative capabilities had been restricted from the outset. As a result, Washington made diplomatic approaches to European governments to tighten controls over the exports of nuclear technology, an effort that ran into opposition in several countries. Washington wanted to stop the export of equipment that fell into the category of "dual-use technology," which could be used in either a civilian nuclear program or a military one. The argument worked best with the Dutch and British, both of whom already cooperated closely with the United States on many issues. Germany and Switzerland were among the countries that were less receptive, suspicious of the American motives and willing to put their commercial interests ahead of proliferation concerns.

The German economy had boomed after the Marshall Plan following World War II, with a civilian nuclear sector thriving under a massive government program to achieve energy independence. The Germans had signed the Nuclear Non-Proliferation Treaty, but their officials and industrial leaders had viewed the agreement primarily as a means to jump-start their own nuclear industry. When Germany tried to sell eight reactors, a uranium-enrichment plant, and plutonium-reprocessing facilities to Brazil, which had refused to sign the nonproliferation treaty, the Americans objected. The Germans eventually put the deal on hold, but killing the multibillion-dollar project left them with an unpleasant sense that the Americans were not as interested in counterproliferation as they were in aiding their own nuclear giants, such as Westinghouse and General Electric.

Germany's lax attitude toward proliferation and its general irritation with the United States provided fertile ground for Butt. He bought enough of a steel alloy known as maraging steel to produce 532 centrifuges. The steel was not on the restricted export list, and the German supplier, Rochling, filled the order and shipped it to Pakistan. In another case, a British technician working at the Almelo plant visited a company in Germany's Rhine Valley to inspect specialized, free-flowing lathes being assembled for shipment to Urenco, where they would be used to manufacture centrifuge components. As he walked across the assembly floor, the technician noticed an extra lathe that appeared identical to the ones ordered by Urenco. When he asked where that lathe was headed, he was told it had been ordered by a company in Pakistan. The technician reported his discovery to British Nuclear Fuels Limited, the British partner in Urenco. When the British relayed their concerns to the German government, they were told that the sale did not violate any export controls. All the British could do was put on a watch list the Pakistani front company buying the lathe.

For all its success in Germany, the Pakistani pipeline kept running into obstacles in the Netherlands, where authorities kept a closer eye on sales of nuclear-related technology and material. Despite several failures, however, Butt and his crew had to keep trying Dutch companies because they were the only sources for some of the components specified by Khan. These repeated attempts eventually became impossible to ignore.

The discovery of Khan's duplicity occurred because of the need for the special metal foil that Khan had helped to develop for Urenco. In September 1975, Butt placed an order for a large quantity of the foil with its Dutch manufacturers. As had happened with orders at other companies, officials at the firm recognized immediately that the order's specifications were identical to those used by Urenco. The company alerted Urenco's Dutch arm.

Pakistan's earlier attempts to acquire sensitive technology had been passed off as isolated incidents, but this attempt convinced FDO officials that the order could only be based on inside knowledge. In an attempt to discover if there was a mole, FDO security officials tracked the development path of the foil, tracing the specifications to a nonclassified research report prepared by a team of FDO scientists. Going down the list of scientists involved in the research, the security personnel stopped at a suspicious name: A. Q. Khan. The connection between the order placed by a Pakistani diplomat and a Pakistani scientist at FDO was circumstantial, but it raised the possibility that the laboratory had been infiltrated. FDO security investigators were worried enough that they went to the Binnenlandse Veiligheidsdienst (BVD), the Dutch national security service.

Khan, granted a measure of immunity on account of his courtesy and friendliness, had been passing information to Butt for months without attracting suspicion. When the BVD launched its investigation, the agency discovered that Khan had worked on far more than the foil design—he had spent more than three years at the company, much of the time dealing with sensitive information, including the top-secret German designs. The potential for damage was enormous, and Khan was immediately placed under surveillance.

In October, Khan was scheduled to travel to a nuclear-industry exhibition in Basel, Switzerland. The BVD and Urenco debated whether to permit him to leave the Netherlands and Dutch jurisdiction, fearing that he would bolt for Pakistan if he suspected anything was amiss. But canceling his trip, even on a pretext, risked alerting Khan that he was under suspicion before it could be determined how much damage he might have done to the centrifuge program. In the end, the decision was made to let him go to the meeting, with a pair of BVD agents on his trail.

Khan was in his element at the exhibition. He circulated from booth to booth, chatting with engineers and gathering promotional brochures. When the BVD agents approached the engineers with whom Khan had been speaking, they learned that he was asking about classified aspects of nuclear-weapons work, something far outside his responsibilities at FDO—a discovery that seemed to confirm suspicions that Khan was more than an innocent metallurgist.

Something else caught the attention of the BVD agents. They spotted Khan deep in conversation several times with Henk Slebos, the former classmate who had suggested the job at FDO to Khan four years earlier. Since then, Slebos had gone to work for a company that supplied welding material to FDO, and the two men had quietly renewed their ties. The BVD knew nothing of the earlier connection between Khan and Slebos, but the Dutchman was already on the radar of the security service because Urenco authorities had voiced suspicions about his unusual curiosity regarding secret aspects of the centrifuge program. The possibility that Khan was connected to Slebos heightened the concerns of the BVD agents, though they lacked hard evidence the two men were engaged in wrongdoing.

Khan returned to Amsterdam unaware of the drama that was unfolding around him, threatening to expose him and fatally derail Pakistan's enrichment plans. The BVD delivered a full report on Khan's role in the foil research and his activities at the exhibition to the Ministry of Economic Affairs, which oversaw the Dutch part of the Urenco consortium. The findings fell short of proof of espionage, but they sparked a fateful debate. One faction within the security service and the ministry felt that the minimum action required was to fire Khan and ban him from the industry, while hard-liners wanted him arrested and charged with espionage. Led by a contingent from Urenco, another group counseled against taking any harsh action, arguing that the evidence was inconclusive and amounted to nothing more than a string of coincidences. They wanted to move Khan into a job where he would no longer be in contact with sensitive information and sweep the episode under the rug to avoid a scandal. This line of thinking was particularly appealing to some because the Dutch government was struggling to develop a high-tech industry, and exposure of a spy inside a top-secret area could jeopardize the effort and its economic rewards.

The contingent that argued against a splashy espionage arrest was led by Ruud Lubbers, the economics minister, who would later become prime minister. "It was about economic interests," Lubbers said later in recounting the debate. "My title was economics minister, and economics was my job. The Foreign Ministry insisted on arresting him for proliferation, but we did not."

The BVD was determined to arrest Khan, and it went so far as to plan an operation to nab him. Two teams of agents would be used for simultaneous actions, with one group waiting at FDO to arrest Khan as he arrived at work in the morning and another team poised to launch a raid on his home in Zwanenburg to search for stolen documents. Before executing the operation, a senior BVD agent contacted the CIA station chief in the Netherlands and briefed him on the discovery of an apparent Pakistani agent with access to top-secret nuclear designs. The Dutch and American intelligence agencies cooperated extensively in those days, and sharing the information was not unusual. After all, the Americans were making the most noise about proliferation, and they might want to interrogate Khan after the arrest. The BVD expected American support for arresting Khan, but they got a surprise. The station chief said he needed to run the matter past his superiors in Langley, Virginia, and he asked the BVD to wait.

In November 1975, the CIA was an agency in turmoil. Its director, William Colby, had been fired by President Gerald Ford following both a string of revelations about assassination attempts on foreign leaders, some of which were successful, and the failures to anticipate the Soviet invasion of Czechoslovakia in 1968 and the Arab-Israeli war in 1973. Colby's replacement was to be George H. W. Bush, the future president, and he would immediately find himself fending off attacks in Congress from the Church Committee. The request for advice on whether to back the arrest of a Pakistani scientist reached the upper levels of the agency, where the decision was made to watch Khan in hopes of learning more about Pakistan's procurement pipeline in Europe. Better to watch and wait, said the CIA man to the BVD a few days later, particularly given the criticism the agency was under for its recent intelligence failures.

When the Dutch authorities reconvened for a final decision, Lubbers said, the American position tipped the balance. If the CIA had agreed, the BVD would have gone ahead and arrested Khan. Instead, the Pakistani would remain at FDO. Still, the suspicions could not be ignored, and the Dutch devised another plan for dealing with what most people agreed was a rogue scientist, deciding to remove him quietly from sensitive work while the investigation continued into the extent of his espionage. In November, Khan was given a small promotion and told that he would be transferred to another part of FDO. He also was informed that his new job meant he would no longer need to visit Almelo.

Lubbers and a former CIA division chief who monitored the Pakistani nuclear program at the time said the solution met the Dutch goal of maintaining the economic status quo and satisfied the Americans. In fact, the CIA was exultant because the Khan episode opened a new window onto Pakistan's procurement operation at a critical moment. A few weeks earlier, a Pakistani nuclear scientist who had been providing the CIA with intelligence from inside the PAEC had been exposed and arrested. The CIA feared that its spotlight on Pakistani nuclear work would go dark at a critical moment. Said the former CIA official, "We were nervous about rebuilding our espionage network, so it makes sense that the agency would not have asked the Dutch to arrest Khan. We were rebuilding, and we would have wanted to see a lot more."

The decision to recommend against arresting Khan marked the first time that American intelligence agencies could have stopped Khan. The decision was understandable in light of the agency's culture and worldview—the CIA is not a law-enforcement agency, and its responsibility is to gather intelligence and pass it on to American policymakers. Looking back, however, current and former government proliferation experts and intelligence officers questioned the decision. What if Khan had been stopped before he really got started? He had kept the centrifuge designs to himself to ensure a triumphal return, and his arrest would almost certainly have stopped the transfer of key information to Pakistan and delayed its nuclear program for years, perhaps decades.

"That was the first monumental error," said Robert Einhorn, who was assistant secretary of state in charge of counterproliferation and arms control under presidents Bill Clinton and George W. Bush.

There is no conclusive evidence that Khan knew how narrowly he escaped, but his later actions suggest he realized that the abrupt change in his responsibilities hinted that he was in some jeopardy. Though there were still gaps in his purloined library of plans, he had stolen most of what he needed to build the most advanced centrifuges in the world and, almost as important, he had collected a list of Urenco subcontractors to supply the equipment.

Khan might not have sought out the role of a spy, but he had jumped enthusiastically into espionage when the opportunity arose. He was a scholar and a scientist, but he was also an ambitious man placed by fate in the right place at the right time. Motivated by his animosity toward India, driven by a growing nationalism and his own outsized ego, he took advantage of his situation to lay the groundwork for building the nuclear bomb that Bhutto had called for at Multan. The time had come to return home for the starring role he had long envisioned for himself.

On December 15, 1975, he and his family left for their annual pilgrimage to Pakistan, telling friends they would be visiting relatives for a couple of weeks. While he was unaware of how close he came to being arrested, Khan suspected he would not return to his job at FDO.

CHAPTER 6

DOUBLE STANDARDS

LEONARD WEISS stood in Senator John Glenn's outer office in Washington, D.C., chatting with a staff member while he waited to meet the man whose heroics in space had helped him win political office. Weiss, forty-one years old, was a tenured professor of applied mathematics and electrical engineering at the University of Maryland. Yet here he was applying for a year-long job on Glenn's staff as part of a fellowship sponsored by an engineering association. His goal was to find a staff job in which his background in science and engineering could translate into useful insights and a role in crafting policy. It was about noon on a cold day in December 1975, about the same time A. Q. Khan was flying home to Pakistan, and Weiss was about to embark on a new career. And unlike Khan, Weiss would devote himself to stopping the spread of nuclear weapons.

Weiss was tall and slender, a distance runner in a time before the sport had become popular. He had grown up in a liberal Jewish household in Brooklyn. His father, a self-educated Russian immigrant with socialist tendencies, had worked a series of factory jobs to make ends meet for his wife and three children. Len was the youngest, and as a child he absorbed the lessons of his parents' struggle for economic survival, as well as the lessons of World War II. Dinner conversations at the Weiss table often turned to the need to combat fascism and to the plight of Europe's Jews at the hands of the Nazis. Max Weiss had left several relatives behind in Russia, and concerns about their fate rose as word of the Holocaust filtered out. But his son's outlook also was shaped by events on the other side of the world.

For many Americans, the horror of the Holocaust was compounded by the impact of the atomic weapons dropped on Hiroshima and Nagasaki in the waning days of the war. For Weiss, the destructive reality of the atomic bomb made the victory bleak. CBS Radio commentator Edward R. Murrow seemed to be speaking directly to young Weiss on August 12, 1945, when he said, "Seldom if ever has a war ended leaving the victors with such a sense of uncertainty and fear, with such a realization that the future is obscure and that survival is not assured." Within two weeks of Hiroshima, *The New Yorker* magazine published a cartoon that envisioned a nuclear-arms race that would make the first atomic bombs obsolete and lead to an even larger disaster. Nuclear proliferation entered the lexicon of the intellectual and popular press. John W. Campbell illustrated his 1947 book, *The Atomic Story*, with a drawing of two mad scientists assembling a crude weapon. The caption read, "In a cave or forgotten cellar, an atomic bomb can soon be set up." For a generation of Americans growing up in the new atomic age, fear became a constant companion. Two thirds of Americans, pollsters found, felt a real danger that atomic bombs would be used against the United States someday. Bomb shelters became household features; duck-and-cover drills were staples of school classrooms. Some sought humor in the blackness—Bob Hope joked about the fear, saying on Valentine's Day 1946: "Have you noticed the modern trend in verses? No more roses are red, violets are blue. I picked up one that read, 'Will you be my little geranium until we are both blown up by uranium?'"

A darker image was burned into the mind of young Len Weiss, who as a freshman in high school read John Hersey's iconic *Hiroshima* and Erich Maria Remarque's *All Quiet on the Western Front*, two seminal works about the horrors of war. The books had such a powerful effect on Weiss that he never thought of war without empathy and sorrow for its military and civilian victims and visceral anger at its perpetrators. Weiss devoted hours to reading political tracts, which increased his fear that America's blustery postwar policies could lead to a nuclear confrontation with the Soviets. As a fourteen-year-old, he worked as a volunteer in the 1948 presidential campaign of dovish Henry Wallace.

When it came time for college, Weiss could not afford a private school, so he enrolled in New York's free university system. He graduated from City College with an engineering degree and went on to get a doctorate from Johns Hopkins University. He taught at Brown University and then moved to the University of Maryland when his wife, Sandy, got a job in Washington, D.C. While he concentrated on research and teaching, he remained active politically, joining protests against the Vietnam War and arguing for a reduction in nuclear arms in the United States and the Soviet Union.

In late 1975, Weiss was awarded a fellowship that offered scientists the opportunity to bring the rigors of their discipline to the political process on Capitol Hill. Weiss had the choice of working for any senator or congressman who would have him; his first candidates were liberal Democrats, whose policies meshed with his own views. Weiss was not some young intern, looking for a foot in any door. He wanted to work for someone who would take serious advantage of his scientific skills, so he interviewed with old-time and novice politicians alike, insisting on a personal meeting with the congressman or senator as a condition for taking a job. He initially tried legendary liberals like Senator Walter Mondale and Senator Hubert Humphrey, but they were too busy to see him personally. He met with Representative Bella Abzug, the fiery liberal from New York, but was put off by her high-handed treatment of her staff. "Though I liked her politics, I decided to strike a blow for the workingman," he said with a laugh. Eventually someone suggested that Weiss go see John Glenn, the freshman senator from Ohio and a true American hero.

Like most Americans of a certain age, Weiss had strong memories of Glenn's role as a pioneer in the country's space program. He remembered watching televised reports in February 1962 as Glenn waited through weather delays for his chance to pilot the first American-manned orbital spaceflight. He recalled being slightly put off when Glenn brushed aside questions about the stress of the delays by saying that his religion had sustained him. In 1974, Glenn had traded on his hero's reputation for a run for the Senate as a Democrat from Ohio, his home state. It was the height of Watergate, and the images from that summer were fresh in the minds of Americans: the helicopter on the South Lawn of the White House, the final salute from Richard M. Nixon, the only president in American history to resign from office. Glenn had ridden the wave of public indignation to the Senate, along with other Democrats who became known as the Watergate babies.

"John Glenn didn't quite fit my political profile," Weiss said later. "I knew him as a conservative Democrat. I am a liberal Democrat. So I didn't come to that first meeting prepared for the idea that this was a guy I would particularly like or want to work for. But he was famous, and I was curious."

When Weiss was ushered into Glenn's office, he found the man across the desk from him funny and charming and smart. Most important, Glenn was interested in Weiss's scientific research and said he believed science had a role in the political process. When Glenn asked what he wanted to do in Washington, Weiss listed a range of interests, from energy and arms control to environment and health.

"If you come here, you can work in all these areas," Glenn promised.

Weiss had arrived in Washington without personal ambition, driven only by the belief that he had a duty to make a difference. He found Glenn's open-ended offer irresistible. As a freshman senator, Glenn had a small staff, which translated into plenty of opportunities for the newcomer. Before agreeing to take the job, however, Weiss went home and discussed the prospect with Sandy and some close friends. One of the friends was well to the left on the political spectrum and active in a variety of causes. She urged Weiss to sign up with Glenn, explaining: "If you go with a liberal, they will vote the way they vote regardless of what you do. But with Glenn, you might have some influence in swinging him to some position he might not have chosen otherwise."

Accepting the logic of her argument, Weiss signed on to Glenn's staff, starting his yearlong fellowship in January 1976. It turned out to be a banner year for arms control and a turning point for the senator and the intern.

Within weeks, Weiss was deeply involved in nuclear issues. The Indian explosion two years earlier had raised the profile of proliferation concerns in Congress, and some members believed the new administration of Gerald Ford was not exercising enough influence to avert a nuclear-arms race in South Asia. Glenn in particular worried that the United States needed to get tougher on proliferation, and he assigned Weiss to examine the issue and draft legislation if it seemed necessary.

The first thing Weiss did was upgrade his security clearances. As a university professor, he had consulted occasionally for the navy and other parts of the government, so he had clearances that granted him access to some classified information. But if he was to take a lead role in developing counterproliferation legislation, he needed to understand the issue in all its manifestations, and that meant digging deeper into the secrets being gathered by the CIA, the electronic sleuths at the National Security Agency, and other government intelligence operations. His existing clearance allowed him to upgrade quickly to level Q, which granted him access to the mostly highly classified information on nuclear issues. Later, he added another level, called "compartmentalized," which permitted him to see information related to specific countries and regions. The clearances also authorized Weiss to receive the highest-level briefings from U.S. intelligence agencies.

Within weeks, Weiss found himself walking from Glenn's office to the Capitol, where he took a special elevator to the fourth floor. There, the Senate Intelligence Committee maintained a secure hearing room and a library open only to staff members with top security clearances. Emerging from the elevator, Weiss walked down a short corridor to the receptionist's desk, leaving his briefcase there as he was ushered into a windowless anteroom, where he was seated at a small table. The clerk brought some classified material to the table, where Weiss signed a sheet acknowledging its receipt. The rules were so strict that when he left the room, the notes he had written were automatically classified and had to be left in the folder with the documents.

In his growing knowledge of America's nuclear secrets, Weiss began to discover that the information often appeared contradictory and confusing, and the briefings provided by CIA officers seemed designed to obfuscate rather than enlighten. "They would give you a briefing in which they would speak very quickly," he said. "They would give you the facts, but they would throw them at you at a speed at which you found it hard to take notes. I would try to slow them down. It was a game they would play. It was annoying, but it didn't stop me from asking pointed questions. The main problem was that I would ask these questions, and I wouldn't get answers, or I would get answers that were inconsistent with information I already had from other sources. I was treated with condescension until they discovered my background as a scientist. They assumed that meeting with someone representing Congress meant they would be briefing an ignoramus, so they exhibited a smart-alecky attitude until they realized I had done my homework."

After attending a dozen or more briefings and reading countless classified intelligence reports, Weiss concluded that the threat of nuclear proliferation was far more serious than Congress, let alone the average American, knew. U.S. export controls were not strong enough to block the transfers of critical technology, and neither were the laws of its allies. If the threat was to be contained, new legislation would be required, and the United States would have to enforce the resulting restrictions.

One country that kept coming up in the raw intelligence and the briefings about likely candidates to pursue an atomic bomb was Pakistan. In fact, the consensus among U.S. intelligence agencies was that the Pakistanis had already launched a campaign to go nuclear. It didn't really require much intelligence work. Zulfikar Ali Bhutto had proclaimed long ago that his country needed a nuclear weapon, and India's test had underscored the threat next door. Even before the military installed him as president, Bhutto had warned that Pakistan would make any sacrifice to match its rival. "If India builds the bomb, we will eat grass or leaves, even go hungry, but we will get one of our own," he had written. "We have no alternative."

Threats existed elsewhere, too. The French were not only trying to sell a reprocessing plant to Pakistan but negotiating to provide the same technology to South Korea. The Germans were trying to sell an entire nuclear fuel cycle to Brazil. South Africa and Iraq were also suspected of having designs on nuclear weapons. American intelligence had already concluded that Israel had used technology supplied by France in the mid-1950s to develop a nuclear arsenal. President Kennedy's earlier prediction of fifteen to twenty nuclear nations seemed to be coming true.

IN 1957, four years after he was restored to the throne in an American-backed coup that ousted a democratically elected government, the shah of Iran, Mohammed Reza Pahlavi, signed a nuclear-cooperation agreement with the Eisenhower administration. In the years that followed, thousands of Iranian students and scientists were trained in nuclear physics at top universities in the United States and Europe. In 1960, as part of Atoms for Peace, the Americans agreed to provide Iran with a five-megawatt research reactor. The reactor went on line in 1967, and three years later Iran ratified the new Nuclear Non-Proliferation Treaty, opening the door to a full-fledged civilian nuclear industry. The Iranians opened negotiations with the Americans, French, and Germans to spend billions of dollars on civilian reactors to generate electricity. Concerns were raised in mid-1974 by newspaper articles in the United States and Europe suggesting that the shah's real goal was a nuclear arsenal. The Iranian embassy in Paris issued a statement denying any weapons aspirations, and the shah said that "not only Iran, but also other nations in the region should refrain from planning to gain atomic arsenals," but the suspicions remained.

Since the 1950s, the United States had depended on Iran and the shah to watch over its interests in the Persian Gulf. The relationship had been cemented in May 1972 when President Richard Nixon and National Security Advisor Henry Kissinger stopped off to visit the shah in Tehran after a trip to Moscow. Nixon agreed to increase the number of American military advisers in Iran and to sell the shah billions of dollars' worth of advanced weaponry, ranging from F-14 fighter jets and fourteen thousand missiles to four destroyers and three submarines. With his foreign policy under pressure from the debacle in Vietnam, Nixon ended his meeting with the shah by pleading, "Protect me."

But no one could protect the president. On August 9, 1974, Nixon resigned as a result of the Watergate affair, succeeded by Gerald Ford, a former congressman from Michigan who had been appointed vice president less than a year earlier, following the resignation of Spiro Agnew in a bribery scandal. Ford was inexperienced when it came to foreign policy, so he retained Kissinger as both secretary of state and the White House national-security adviser, the two positions he had held under Nixon. Much of the rest of the hierarchy from the Nixon administration was tainted by Watergate, so Ford had to reach out to form his own leadership team. As chief of staff, he picked Donald Rumsfeld, who had served in Congress with Ford and was currently ambassador to NATO in Brussels, far enough removed from Washington to be clear of the controversy. Rumsfeld chose as his deputy a thirty-three-year-old former aide named Dick Cheney.

Cheney had grown up in Wyoming and received a scholarship to Yale University after his girlfriend, Lynne Vincent, intervened on his behalf with a powerful Yale donor. He spent three semesters in New Haven, mostly playing cards and hanging out with the football team, before he was asked to leave. Returning home, he married Vincent in 1964 and graduated from the University of Wyoming a year later. After starting work on a doctorate in political science at the University of Wisconsin in 1968, he had gone to Washington on a fellowship and met Rumsfeld, at the time a powerful congressman from Illinois. As White House deputy chief of staff, Cheney became known for his attention to detail. In one famous incident, he questioned the use in the White House residence of "little dishes of salt with funny little spoons" instead of "regular salt shakers."

Cheney's chief attribute appeared to be his loyalty to Rumsfeld, a trait that earned him the Secret Service code name "Backseat." With Cheney at his side, Rumsfeld quickly established control over the White House staff and domestic policy, pushing aside staff members who had been brought in from Ford's congressional office or were leftovers from his days as vice president. By early 1975, Rumsfeld and Cheney were working to undermine Vice President Nelson Rockefeller, the former New York governor whom they considered too liberal, and Kissinger, whose policy on détente and arms control with the Soviet Union was anathema to the two conservatives.

At the time, Kissinger held unusual sway over American foreign policy, controlling both the State Department and the National Security Council at the White House. He was trying to strengthen ties with the shah by selling billions of dollars' worth of the most advanced American nuclear technology to Iran. In April 1975, Kissinger circulated a memo outlining the administration's plan to sell Iran six to eight reactors and grant the shah the unprecedented opportunity to purchase an American-built reprocessing plant to extract plutonium from the spent fuel.

Iran's oil-based economy was booming, rolling up an amazing 42 percent growth rate after the Organization of Petroleum Exporting Countries quadrupled the price of oil. Iran was pumping six million barrels of oil per day, but the shah preferred to sell it abroad rather than consume it at home, arguing that Iran needed twenty or more reactors to generate electricity for domestic needs and thus maintain its reserves. A strategy paper prepared by the Ford administration in 1976 supported Iran's determination to build nuclear plants, saying that Tehran needed to "prepare against the time—about 15 years in the future—when Iranian oil production is expected to decline sharply." Among the companies eager to get a share of the billions the shah planned to spend were the giants of the American civilian nuclear industry, Westinghouse and General Electric. The United States dominated sales of nuclear technology to the world, accounting for 70 percent of the international market, but in Iran they were competing against West German and French companies.

Competition with the Europeans was fierce, so the Ford administration sweetened the deal by reversing U.S. policy on the export of reprocessing technology. In previous transactions, Washington had refused to approve exports of the technology to reprocess spent fuel into plutonium. A nuclear power plant capable of generating electricity to serve a city of one million people generates enough spent fuel per year to produce five hundred pounds of plutonium, which could be used to destroy several cities of the same size. But the spent fuel cannot be turned into plutonium for weapons without a reprocessing plant. Yet as it pushed the sale of this technology to Iran, Washington was citing proliferation fears in objecting to plans by France to sell reprocessing technology to Pakistan, an apparent double standard that angered the French.

Kissinger said later that the administration was not concerned that Iran might build nuclear weapons because it was a friend. "I don't think the issue of proliferation came up," he recalled. "They were an allied country and this was a commercial transaction. We didn't address the question of them one day moving toward nuclear weapons." Other members of the administration, however, had different recollections. Charles Naas, the deputy U.S. ambassador in Iran at the time, later said that nuclear experts expressed concerns about the proliferation impact of the deal, but he said it was "attractive in terms of commerce, and the relationship as a whole was very important."

Tony Benn, Britain's energy secretary, visited the shah in January 1976 and spent a long time discussing Iran's nuclear ambitions, which envisioned an industry far larger than that of Britain itself. In addition to buying the plutonium-reprocessing technology from the United States, the shah told Benn that he wanted centrifuges for uranium enrichment and that he knew he could get them from the Germans and the French if the British and Americans would not sell them. If the shah succeeded, he would have the ability to build nuclear weapons from plutonium and enriched uranium. Despite those concerns, the Americans were clearly willing to do business and, reflecting on the conversation thirty years later, Benn said: "Most astonishing of all, in the light of the present discussions, is that the problem of Iran developing such a huge nuclear capacity caused no problems for the Americans because, at that time, the shah was seen as a strong ally, and had indeed been put on the throne with American help. There could hardly be a clearer example of double standards than this."

While Kissinger was the architect of the nuclear agreement with Iran, Rumsfeld and Cheney eventually usurped much of Kissinger's authority. In the fall of 1975, the two men persuaded Ford to take away Kissinger's title as national-security adviser, reducing his influence. Ford also ousted James Schlesinger as defense secretary, replacing him with Rumsfeld. Cheney moved into Rumsfeld's job as White House chief of staff. George H. W. Bush, who had been head of the U.S. liaison office in Beijing, was brought back to serve as director of the CIA.

Rumsfeld, a strong believer in American military power, was skeptical about arms-control treaties and other agreements that he feared might weaken U.S. supremacy. As a result, Rumsfeld advocated the sale of nuclear technology to Iran as a way to bolster American influence in the region, a view that aligned him with Kissinger and other administration officials, including Cheney and Paul Wolfowitz, a young former congressional aide who was responsible for nonproliferation issues at the U.S. Arms Control and Disarmament Agency, the government's top counterproliferation office. With the support of Rumsfeld, Cheney, and Wolfowitz, Ford signed a directive authorizing the sale to Iran in January 1976, which marked a dramatic divergence in U.S. nonproliferation policy.

As an accidental president, Ford went into the 1976 election with little mandate from voters. He had appeased some elements of the Republican party with his pardon of Nixon for Watergate, but the same action had angered Democrats. After beating back a challenge from California governor Ronald Reagan to win the Republican nomination, Ford faced Democratic nominee Jimmy Carter, the populist governor from Georgia. Carter, who had served as a nuclear officer aboard a submarine in the navy, made proliferation an issue in the campaign, which forced Ford onto the defensive over the pending sales to Iran. In October, a month before the election, the president said that he had reviewed U.S. nuclear policy and concluded that avoiding proliferation had to take precedence over economic considerations. He said that he would prohibit the export of reprocessing technology and equipment. More than politics were behind Ford's change of heart—earlier in 1976, the CIA had obtained new evidence that Iran was buying technology to develop a nuclear weapon.

It remains an open question whether Ford would have scuttled the deal with Iran, but he never got the chance because he lost to Carter. Although Carter promised to prohibit the sale of reprocessing technology, when he met with the shah at the end of 1977 he surprised his aides by assuring him that he could buy any nuclear technology he wanted from the United States, including reprocessing equipment. So the deal remained alive despite a worsening political situation in Iran, where the shah embarked on a brutal crackdown against militants and religious supporters of a fiery Islamic cleric named Ayatollah Ruhollah Khomeini.

On Capitol Hill, Len Weiss was concerned about the prospective sales to Iran and pushed Senator Glenn to persuade the new Democratic administration to abandon the idea. From a national-security viewpoint, Weiss argued, allowing large numbers of nuclear reactors and reprocessing technology into the Middle East was incendiary. "While we couldn't stop the French or Germans from selling this technology, I didn't see any reason why the United States should participate," he explained later.

Westinghouse, which hoped to sell six billion dollars' worth of nuclear technology to Iran, had more than one hundred employees in Tehran preparing for what would be a major commercial venture. Both Westinghouse and General Electric used their influence in Washington to push for the sale. In Westinghouse's case, its chief lobbyist, former U.S. ambassador Dwight Porter, was a close friend of the shah's, and he worked tirelessly to persuade Congress that selling nuclear equipment to Iran would cement an important geopolitical alliance. Porter knew Glenn's office was the leading opponent of proliferation on the Hill, so he tried more than once to convince Weiss that the deal was justified. But Weiss refused to relent, maintaining that even an ally should be denied access to such technology.

ALMOST every country that has pursued nuclear weapons has relied to one degree or another on technology and equipment obtained from other countries. As the original nuclear power, the United States has long maintained a double standard about sharing nuclear technology. After World War II, the Americans helped Britain develop its nuclear arsenal but refused assistance to France, which was regarded as a less reliable ally. But the most dramatic illustration is the evolution of America's attitude toward a nuclear Israel.

In 1956, the Israelis struck a secret agreement with France to build a plutonium reactor in a remote corner of the Negev desert, near the village of Dimona. The project was massive, with as many as 1,500 Israeli and French workers building an extensive underground complex that covered fourteen square miles. Not long after work started, American U-2 spy planes spotted the construction, and the Eisenhower administration demanded to know what was happening. Israel initially claimed the site was for a textile factory, yet later described it as a metallurgical-research facility. By 1960, the CIA had identified the Dimona complex as a nuclear reactor and suspected that it was part of a weapons program. The Israelis acknowledged the existence of the reactor but claimed it was solely for civilian purposes.

Soon after taking office in 1961, President John F. Kennedy, who opposed nuclear weapons in the Middle East, pressured the Israelis to allow an American team to inspect Dimona. A postvisit memo written by the team said that the scientists were "satisfied that nothing was concealed from them and that the reactor is of the scope and peaceful character previously described to the United States." In fact, critical portions of the complex were hidden from them and six other inspection teams that followed during the 1960s. The weapons work was conducted deep underground in laboratories accessible only through elevator banks that had been disguised.

By the end of the decade, the CIA had nevertheless concluded that Israel was developing nuclear weapons at Dimona, a determination that led to growing concern that the discovery could prompt an Arab attack on the complex and destabilize the region. In the first months of the Nixon administration in 1969, senior officials argued that Washington had to persuade Israel to halt its weapons work for the sake of stability. Later that year, however, President Nixon struck a deal with Israeli prime minister Golda Meir: As long as Israel did not test a nuclear weapon or otherwise publicize its existence, the United States would not pressure its ally to shelve the program. Since then, Israel's possession of a nuclear arsenal has remained an open secret, dubbed "nuclear ambiguity" by the Israeli press.

Israel and Iran both demonstrate the conveniently permissive attitude adopted by the United States toward proliferation. Different rules have applied to different countries. In the case of allies, the United States was willing to turn a blind eye or even to sell billions of dollars' worth of technology. India and Pakistan, on the other hand, were regarded as unreliable allies, and government policy was to block such sales to them.

Weiss played a central role in crafting legislation aimed at restricting sales to India and Pakistan. He worked closely with the staffs of Senator Stuart Symington, a Democrat from Missouri, and Senator Jacob Javits, a New York Republican. There was talk about establishing an entirely new export-control regime for nuclear technology that would impose tight restrictions on sales to any country, but the plan was abandoned as too ambitious. Instead, the staffs drew up more specific legislation that focused on plutonium and reprocessing technology because enrichment know-how remained classified. The legislation, known as the Symington amendment, required countries that wanted to buy nuclear technology or receive American military assistance to allow regular inspections by the International Atomic Energy Agency, and it passed Congress in May 1976 as part of the Foreign Assistance Act, which governed American foreign aid. The legislation assigned the White House the job of determining who was violating the amendment and taking action against them. It was not a popular requirement at the White House because the executive branch instinctively dislikes laws that it feels ties its hands, especially on foreign-policy matters.

The legislation marked a U-turn in congressional thinking about nuclear proliferation. Since Atoms for Peace in the 1950s, U.S. policy had encouraged free trade in nuclear technology to promote its civilian use. But attitudes had begun to change in response to the Indian nuclear test and worries over Pakistan's intentions. The Symington amendment was the first effort by Congress to force the White House to take action against proliferators.

While the amendment grew out of worries about both India and Pakistan, it hit Pakistan harder. The Indians already had much of their nuclear-weapons infrastructure in place and had tested a device two years earlier. Pakistan, on the other hand, was in the early stages of its nuclear program, and its diplomats and politicians complained bitterly that the legislation discriminated against what they claimed was a legitimate civilian program.

On May 12, 1976, the day after the amendment's passage, Secretary of State Henry Kissinger convened a meeting of his senior staff to discuss nuclear proliferation and develop a strategy for dealing with Pakistan. One suggestion was to push Pakistan to sign the Nuclear Non-Proliferation Treaty and accept IAEA inspections of its nuclear installations. That way, the Pakistanis could buy the French plant without triggering the Symington sanctions. Pakistan was an ally, albeit not a fully trusted one, and Kissinger worried that applying pressure to sign the treaty would make Bhutto feel that Pakistan was once again being singled out.

"It is a little rough on the Pakistanis to require them to do what the Indians don't have to do," said Kissinger.

"The important distinction here is that there is no economic basis for the project," said Reginald Bartholomew, a State Department counterproliferation official. "Pakistan has no need for reprocessed fuel at the present time, and its future needs, when they develop, could be better met in other ways."

"Why do they want a reprocessing plant?" asked Kissinger.

"They want to be in a position to produce a weapon, and a reprocessing facility clearly puts them in that position," Bartholomew replied.

Kissinger was told that there was no doubt that Pakistan had started its own nuclear program. Alfred Atherton, a deputy assistant secretary of state, said the shah had recently warned the United States that Bhutto intended to develop nuclear weapons. Adding to the worries, he said, a recent CIA report said that Libya had agreed to finance a significant portion of Pakistan's effort to go nuclear "in return for some unspecified future nuclear cooperation."

Three months later, on August 8, Kissinger flew to Islamabad for a showdown with Bhutto. Kissinger remained grateful to Pakistan for its help in arranging his secret trip to Beijing in 1971, which had paved the way for President Nixon's opening of relations with China. But he recognized that Pakistan's atomic ambitions threatened to bring nuclear warfare to the region, so he was determined to stop Bhutto. In an off-the-record briefing to reporters traveling with him, Kissinger said that Washington would invoke the Symington amendment to cut off all aid to Pakistan if Bhutto insisted on going ahead with the reprocessing plant. As an incentive, he planned to offer Pakistan a fleet of 110 Corsair A-7 jet fighters, complete with missiles, rockets, and cannons. Some administration factions, led by the CIA, believed that buttressing Pakistan's conventional forces against India might persuade it to take its eye off the ultimate weapon.

"He told me that I should not insult the intelligence of the United States by saying that Pakistan needed the reprocessing plant for her energy needs," Bhutto later wrote in his diaries, describing the encounter with Kissinger. "In reply, I told him that I will not insult the intelligence of the U.S. by discussing the energy needs of Pakistan, but by the same token, he should not discuss the plant at all."

As the Americans anticipated, the Pakistani leader felt like he was coming under discriminatory pressure. Later, Bhutto summed up his anger by saying that if the Christians, Jews, Hindus, and communists had atomic weapons, why exclude Muslims? America's inconsistent policy on the spread of nuclear weapons was already a major grievance among many Muslim countries, which were angered by the American failure to stop the Israelis from developing its suspected nuclear arsenal. Bhutto had tapped into that resentment earlier when he had persuaded the Libyans and Saudis to help finance Pakistan's nuclear-weapons project.

Kissinger's failure to secure a voluntary halt to Pakistan's program increased the pressure on the United States and its allies to find another means of thwarting Bhutto's nuclear aspirations. The challenge was part and parcel of the growing complexity and seriousness of proliferation as a whole, which led Len Weiss to reconsider his plan to leave Senator Glenn's staff and return to the University of Maryland. Near the end of 1976, Glenn took over as chairman of a subcommittee of the Senate Governmental Affairs Committee and asked Weiss to stay on as chief of the staff for it, as it had jurisdiction over nuclear proliferation. Weiss agreed. He was determined to expose the people, the companies, and the governments that were spreading nuclear technology, at least for another year.

CHAPTER 7

THE ROAD TO KAHUTA

A **.Q. KHAN RETURNED** to Pakistan at a time when the nuclear-weapons program was in peril. Canada had crippled the reactor in Karachi by cutting off spare parts and fuel rods, and, in the face of international pressure, France was considering backing out of its agreement to sell Pakistan the reprocessing plant. The stage was set for the return of the prodigal scientist.

By the end of 1975, some of the equipment for the uranium-enrichment plant had arrived through front companies, and more was on the way. After settling his wife and daughters temporarily with his family in Karachi once again, Khan arranged to take a tour of a warehouse in the village of Sihala, a few miles from Islamabad, where the enrichment equipment was being stored. He hoped to find that they had started laying out the bare bones of a pilot centrifuge plant according to his instructions, but he was disappointed to encounter only unopened crates of machinery.

Bhutto had been on a trip with the shah of Iran. In Khan's telling of events, when the prime minister returned he immediately summoned Khan to his office. Khan told him that the lack of progress was such that he was contemplating going back to the Netherlands. Appealing to Khan's patriotism, the prime minister asked him to stay, but the scientist hesitated, saying he wanted to talk to his wife first. Khan was never shy about embellishing his role in history, and he later said that when he returned the next day to inform Bhutto of his decision to remain, the prime minister banged his fist on his desk and said, "I will see the Hindu bastards now."

His years in Europe had left Khan ill prepared to deal with the convolutions of Pakistan's bureaucracy. His awakening began when he learned that the pilot plant in Sihala was to be established and operated under the umbrella of the Pakistan Atomic Energy Commission, meaning Khan would report to the agency's head, Munir Khan (no relation). Khan knew his new boss had only a master's degree, and he had no intention of sharing his anticipated glory with someone he considered his scientific and intellectual inferior. His concerns became more personal when he discovered that his salary would be three thousand rupees per month, about three hundred dollars, a tenth of what he had earned at FDO. Khan and his family had not lived lavishly in the Netherlands, but feeling like a pauper in his own country was intolerable. Pakistan was highly class-conscious, steeped in the traditions of the British Raj. To some people, Khan, no matter what his education or accomplishments, would never rise above his roots as the son of a schoolteacher. But Khan was determined to find a way to stay and rise.

Even after telling Bhutto he would remain, his worries increased in the days that followed as he toured the rest of the installations overseen by the PAEC. The procurement effort in Europe had yielded less than Khan had expected. Worse, there was no coordinated program to start the first stage of the pilot plant. Several factors had delayed its start. Munir Khan remained focused on using plutonium in the core of Pakistan's first atomic device, and he still harbored hopes of reaching an agreement with France over the reprocessing plant. But Munir Khan was also worried about the way the technology was being obtained for the centrifuge program and how the world would respond to Pakistan's treachery. Munir Khan had joined the IAEA in Vienna in 1958, the year after the agency had been founded, and he had developed a high regard for the organization and its agenda. He had not returned to Pakistan until 1972, when he attended the Multan conference. Bhutto had prevailed on Munir Khan to take over the PAEC from I. H. Usmani. From his experience in Vienna, Khan knew some countries and companies would willingly sell sensitive goods to Pakistan or anyone else. But he also recognized that obtaining much of the most critical equipment would involve false invoices, front companies, and other forms of subterfuge, which made him uncomfortable. Already his reluctance to engage in the necessary lies was so strong that the control over Siddique A. Butt and his procurement ring had been transferred by Bhutto from the atomic-energy agency to the military.

When A. Q. Khan confronted Munir Khan about the lack of progress on the pilot plant that Bhutto had ordered started in late 1974, Munir Khan explained that the PAEC had many priorities, and uranium enrichment would wait its turn. As far as Munir Khan was concerned, it could wait forever. For Khan, that was unacceptable. He had no intention of playing second fiddle to a man he considered his inferior, and he had no intention of being denied his role at the forefront of Pakistan's nuclear efforts. So A. Q. Khan decided to take the second big risk of his career, embarking on a scheme to push aside his new rival and gain personal control over the enrichment project. By this time, he had resigned from FDO, fueling suspicions in Amsterdam. If the gamble backfired, he knew he could end up trapped and marginalized in Pakistan. There was no way to predict the outcome of his plot with a scientist's certainty, leaving him to count on his own cunning and Bhutto's desperation.

His first move was to plant the seed of dissension, complaining to Bhutto's military adviser that the lack of progress on enrichment was imperiling the nuclear effort. He said the PAEC and its head refused to provide the resources to carry out the work assigned to him by the prime minister, and he said he was worried about disappointing Bhutto. The adviser dutifully passed on the concerns to Bhutto, who summoned A. Q. Khan for what was to be a defining moment for the ambitious scientist.

As he sat face-to-face with Bhutto in the prime minister's office, Khan launched a withering attack on Munir Khan and the PAEC, saying they had misled Bhutto about the nuclear program's progress. Not only had they refused to start an enrichment program, but the plutonium project was stalled by the French and most likely doomed. He called his rival a liar and a cheat, claiming that he was incapable of ever delivering a bomb. "If you really want this atomic bomb," Khan argued, "you must free me from this stifling bureaucracy. I cannot work with the PAEC, and I cannot work beneath someone as incompetent as Munir Khan. He has never participated in any scientific research. He doesn't even have a single research paper to his credit. He is an enemy of Pakistan. I must have complete independence from this man, and I must report to no one but you, sahib."

Khan bemoaned the lack of technology and infrastructure to develop the sophisticated equipment necessary to enrich uranium, saying the only way to build the bomb was to buy the equipment and the technology on the open market. In the most audacious element of his plan, the scientist told Bhutto that he needed complete freedom to use the Pakistani network already operating in Europe, without oversight or budget constraints.

"This will take large sums of money," he told Bhutto. "I must be able to spend it without anyone looking over my shoulder. Many of the deals will be in cash because that's the way these people do business. I know them because I've dealt with them and their kind for years."

Bhutto promised to weigh the proposal. The prime minister had known Munir Khan for many years, and he liked and respected him. He didn't trust the brash and egotistical new arrival, but he was desperate to have his bomb and willing to take a risk of his own. A few days later, Bhutto's military adviser telephoned Khan and said the prime minister had granted his request, giving him complete control of the enrichment program and granting him the authority to operate outside the reach of the atomic-energy agency, with all the money he needed and without the troubling hassles of financial oversight. Bhutto, who was not averse to his own scheming, planned to pit the two Khans against each other, with one chasing the dream of enriching uranium in secret and the other leading a team trying to produce plutonium. Bhutto figured that just as American scientists in the Manhattan Project had manufactured bombs from plutonium and enriched uranium simultaneously, the two Khans, walking their two roads, offered twice the chance of success.

On July 31, 1976, Bhutto signed a secret order establishing the enrichment program, code-named Project 706. A. Q. Khan was in charge, reporting directly to the prime minister. The finance minister, Ghulam Ishaq Khan, who was not related to A. Q. or Munir, was told to give Khan a blank check for whatever he needed to get the project running. Bhutto's army chief of staff, General Mohammed Zia ul-Haq, was instructed to assign the military's Special Works Organization, Pakistan's equivalent of the U.S. Army Corps of Engineers, to build a pilot enrichment plant as quickly as possible. Khan's dream was under way. His gamble had paid off, but now he had to deliver on his promise, which meant that he would be taking another kind of gamble.

To DELIVER, Khan needed equipment and people from the outside, and he needed them in a hurry. Obviously, the nuclear-armed Western countries and their allies were not going to share the technology willingly, particularly with a Muslim country. Khan would have to be crafty and careful, but he was confident that he could outwit the world.

Normally, years or even decades would be necessary to build a uranium-enrichment plant, with each step coming in sequence; a pilot plant would be built and a small number of centrifuges tested there; then a plant would be constructed to supply the gaseous uranium to spin the machines and produce the enriched uranium. Each step would involve lengthy studies and research and extensive tests. Khan did not have that kind of time or patience, so he had a far more radical approach in mind. He would not wait for completion of the pilot plant, nor would he delay construction of the centrifuges until prototypes were perfected. Everything would take place simultaneously. Within weeks of getting the green light, work had started on the pilot plant in Sihala, and the search was on for a site for the full-scale enrichment plant, which would be capable of running ten thousand centrifuges at a time, to turn out enough highly enriched uranium for several bombs per year. It was a daring move because it left no room for error, but Khan had great faith in the European technology he had stolen and the ability of the Pakistani pipeline to find the companies and people who would be willing to sell him what he needed. Along with the technology and equipment, he would use the government's funds to hire the best minds away from the PAEC and recruit Pakistani scientists working abroad.

Seven months after his homecoming and just past his fortieth birthday, Khan had carved out his own fiefdom and begun enlisting a small army of people loyal only to him. In bypassing the bureaucracy, Khan dealt directly not only with Bhutto but with his two most powerful aides, Ghulam Khan and General Zia. The alliance with Zia offered a particular kind of insurance for Khan's longevity—civilians leaders might come and go, but the military remained in power forever in Pakistan.

In a short space of time, Khan had positioned himself to reap the maximum benefits from his education as a scientist and the knowledge that he had gained and stolen in the Netherlands. He was poised to launch not just an enrichment project but himself. In both cases, he was driven by his fierce desire to be perceived as both a brilliant scientist and the savior of his nation.

THE ENRICHMENT program and the self-imposed deadline entailed enormous logistical and technological obstacles. Even an advanced industrial country would be hard-pressed to meet the timetable set by Khan, and Pakistan did not have the basic manufacturing ability to produce far less sophisticated products than a nuclear bomb. Its literacy rate was barely into double digits, and there were still no great universities to turn out legions of scientists and engineers. "The task was gigantic, and there were no visible means to accomplish it," Khan said in describing the beginnings of the project. "Not a slightest sign of any advanced scientific infrastructure was available from where one could kick off, and we had to start afresh. But as they say, 'Where there is a will, there's a way.' This is a long chain of steps and usually takes a very long time, especially if you are dealing with one of the most difficult and sophisticated technologies of the world. We took a very bold step and started with all the steps simultaneously."

Finding a location for the main enrichment plant was critical. Khan wanted it close enough to Islamabad to give him access to the centers of power, yet far enough from the city to discourage unnecessary intrusions by outsiders or bureaucrats. Eventually, a hundred-acre site was selected about twenty miles southeast of Islamabad, outside an obscure village called Kahuta. Khan thought the heavily forested location was perfect. To deter the curious, the plant would be given the innocuous name Engineering Research Laboratories.

"With no charm for the outer world, the place would not draw crowds, and security would be maintained, but with it so near to the capital, it was always for our benefit to take quick decisions and implement them without any delay," Khan explained later.

Kahuta was not a unanimous choice. The village and Islamabad are in the eastern portion of Pakistan, closer to the Indian border—and within the reach of Indian missiles and aircraft—than some of the generals would like. But taking the facility to a far-flung location, like the Baluchistan desert in the southwest, would have made it harder for Khan to recruit top engineers and scientists and would have removed him from Islamabad. Khan prevailed. Ground was broken in late 1976.

In those frantic early days, Khan spent little time with his wife and two daughters, who were five and seven years old. They had settled into a small bungalow on Shalimar Road in a middle-class neighborhood of Islamabad. The city had been laid out a decade earlier in accordance with the rules of modern planning, with broad avenues, impressive white-washed government buildings, and modern villas. A running joke among foreign diplomats was that Islamabad was "ten miles from Pakistan." It was also far from the suburbs of Amsterdam, and Henny and the girls had been unprepared for the strangeness of the place.

Henny had visited Pakistan several times, and she had long recognized her husband's determination to live there, but the brief holidays had not prepared her for the gigantic pushing and shoving throng that was her new home. The crowded streets of Karachi had been an urban jungle of beggars, street vendors, staring passersby, careening rickshaws, and traffickers in unidentifiable goods. Islamabad had offered a relative respite, with calmer and less crowded streets, many of them lined with neat white houses, mature trees, and flowering bushes. She knew her husband's work was vital and secret, and she understood that security considerations dictated that she not develop the sorts of casual friendships that might have eased her isolation. Her only solace was her family and the late-night conversations in which her husband confided in her about the challenges he encountered in trying to make Pakistan safe from India and other enemies. In the years that followed, she developed her own code of silence, even to the point of denying to outsiders that she was married to the famous scientist, saying, "Khan is a common name in Pakistan."

While Kahuta was being built, Khan ran Project 706 from a temporary office near Army House, the military headquarters in Rawalpindi. The trappings of power were already present. Late each night, he would leave the office and get into a chauffeur-driven car for the short ride home, accompanied by an armed guard and an escort car carrying soldiers assigned to his security. As the enrichment project grew, no detail was too small for Khan. He established a pattern that he was to follow until the end of his career: Every piece of paper had to cross his desk; every purchase was approved by him; every new hire understood he was Khan's man.

"Khan centralized everything, and nothing went out without his review," said a Pakistani engineer who worked alongside Khan for two decades and both admired and detested him. "At least subliminally, he wanted to rule everyone. Khan was no Einstein. He wasn't very creative, but he knew how to get things done."

CHAPTER 8

OPERATION BUTTER FACTORY

BEFORE LEAVING AMSTERDAM, Khan had realized that he might
need more information from the experts at FDO and Urenco, so he
had taken steps to leave a back door open by arranging for two Pakistani
agents to obtain low-level jobs in the purchasing department. Perhaps because they were outside the sensitive areas of the lab or because of the same
sloppy security that had allowed Khan to start work at FDO, the two men
had avoided losing their jobs or even coming under scrutiny after Khan's
departure. From their positions, they were able to pass on some of the information that Khan needed. But their access was limited, so to fill bigger
gaps he turned to his old friends at FDO, Urenco's outside suppliers, and
at least one unusual source.

In the spring of 1976, Khan found that he needed some things he
had left behind in his desk at FDO. Henny was planning a trip back to
Amsterdam to pack up the belongings in their house, and he asked her to
collect a cache of documents and other material from his office. He wrote
a letter for her to give to Frits Veerman, asking the Dutchman to escort
her to the office. But Veerman's earlier anxiety over Khan's activities had
deepened in his friend's absence, and he was unwilling to take any step
that might expose him to charges later. When Henny telephoned him
shortly after her arrival in Amsterdam, he said that he was too busy to

help. He rebuffed her second attempt and later said that, as far as he knew, she did not get into the office.

When Henny returned empty-handed, Khan had to try a different tack, so he mailed a more brazen letter to Veerman. "Very confidentially I request you to help us," he wrote to his old friend. "I urgently need the following information for our research programme." What followed was a list of sensitive components for ultracentrifuges and design information. "Frits, these are very urgently required, without which the research would come to a standstill," he said. "I am sure you can provide me with these. These things are very small, and I hope you will not disappoint me." In addition, Khan asked Veerman to get in touch with another former colleague at FDO and arrange for both men to come to Pakistan. "I have a little technical work for him and much photographic work for you," Khan wrote. "Both of you could take a holiday and at the same time earn something as well." Because of the candid nature of his request, Khan tried to cover his tracks by asking his friend to address his reply to Henny or one of the children and not use his own name or address on the envelope.

By this time, Veerman had concluded that his former colleague was engaged in industrial espionage, and he worried that he could be dragged into the mess if he remained silent. So he took Khan's letter to one of his superiors at FDO, who recognized the dangers immediately and alerted the BVD. A few days later, Veerman was sitting in front of the television at home when two agents from the security police knocked on his door. Veerman spent the rest of the night describing how he had taken photographs for his friend, recounting the visits from Pakistani diplomats to Khan's home, and mentioning the secret drawings that he had seen there. The intelligence agents showed Veerman an array of photographs of diplomats attached to the Pakistani embassy, and he was able to pick out two of them as men he had met at Khan's home. Veerman was warned to keep quiet about the investigation or he would put himself in danger.

After the men left, Veerman was frightened because he could not figure out exactly what the security policeman meant. There was an implied threat from Khan's associates, but it also seemed that his worst fear might be coming true: The BVD could suspect that he had knowingly helped Khan.

The BVD agents prepared a lengthy written report on the interview with Veerman, including the accusation that Khan had stolen classified centrifuge designs. As the report moved through the chain of command and into other parts of the Dutch government, no one rang the alarm bell. Instead of fully investigating Khan's activities, the government decided again not to follow up on the suspicions or take precautions against Khan's continuing efforts to obtain technology and assistance. Exposing Khan's deception risked embarrassing the Dutch government at a critical time in the partnership with the British and Germans on Urenco. As a result, senior ministers decided to turn a blind eye once again to evidence that Khan had plundered their nuclear trove.

The government's inaction allowed others associated with Urenco to respond positively to Khan's entreaties. A handful of Urenco contractors agreed to sell equipment to the Pakistani pipeline, and some of them traveled to Pakistan to inspect the plant under construction there. Khan's former mentor at the university in Leuven, Martin Brabers, was among those who accepted an invitation. He came away impressed, saying later: "He had a good setup, a good organization. He could choose the people he really wanted. He knew who the good people were. He gave them good salaries so they would not want to leave the job. Also, in buying equipment, he knew all the companies. He knew so many people abroad in many countries. Why, he knew so many languages, and he was so charming [that] he managed to buy many things that other Pakistanis could not manage to buy."

SIDDIQUE BUTT also was proving to be a gifted man in the field, emerging as Khan's top purchasing agent in Europe as the buying campaign moved into high gear. Butt and his ring of fellow diplomats exploited a combination of weak export regulations and greedy businessmen to buy sensitive equipment for the centrifuge program. In some cases, the ring hid the true destination for the parts behind front companies and fake invoices; other times, they were able to make their purchases openly by claiming the equipment was for nonnuclear civilian use. Butt also developed a technique aimed at overwhelming officials who oversaw exports:

Critical equipment was concealed in large shipments of material that had no nuclear application, compelling customs and law enforcement to send whole lots along without proper inspection.

But some items on Khan's shopping list were clearly designed solely for a nuclear plant. Among them was a huge and complex system of pipes and vacuum valves to feed uranium-hexafluoride gas into the centrifuges, which would be a main component of the Kahuta plant. This elaborate, specially designed system had no civilian application, and its central role in an enrichment plant could not be disguised. Butt and two associates approached a Swiss company, CORA Engineering, and outlined what they wanted. The Swiss engineers were willing to design and build the system, but the procurement team didn't understand the technical details well enough to explain exactly what was required. As a result, Khan and another Pakistani scientist flew to Switzerland to meet with the company. After the visit, CORA consulted the Swiss government and was reassured that the system did not require an export license because its individual components were not on the government's list of restricted technology. Several months later, it took three huge C-130 cargo planes to transport hundreds of tons of the sophisticated machinery to Pakistan. Rudolph Walti, an executive at CORA, defended the sale, saying that it did not violate any regulations. "We are not producing revolvers or cannons, and we are not producing bombs," Walti told the BBC years later. "We are not involved in nuclear weapons in any respect because we wouldn't even know how to make a nuclear weapon."

It was not unusual for Khan to travel to Europe to explain the technical aspects of an order or offer a final nudge to reluctant suppliers. He arrived again in November 1976 to conclude negotiations with a German engineering firm run by Heinz Mebus. The company, CES Kalthof, agreed to build a fluorine plant in Pakistan, an important step in the production of uranium hexafluoride. The transaction was the ring's first contact with Mebus, an important figure in the years to come. Other contacts were old friends of Khan's. From its earliest days, the pipeline got a major assist from Henk Slebos. After graduating, Slebos had gone to work for the Dutch Navy as a troubleshooter assigned to find parts for the submarine fleet, which enabled him to develop an encyclopedic knowledge of high-tech companies in the Netherlands. In 1974, two years after Khan started at FDO, Slebos had become commercial director of a specialized welding firm that had a contract with Urenco, and the two men reestablished their friendship.

By the time Khan returned to Pakistan, Slebos had formed his own business, and he flew to Pakistan just as the clandestine purchasing operation was gathering steam. Khan had requested his help obtaining 6,500 tubes manufactured of hardened steel for centrifuge rotors, and Slebos agreed to find them. Returning home, Slebos placed a small order with a Dutch firm, Van Doorne Transmissie (VDT), but the request caught the attention of the Dutch Ministry of Economic Affairs, and an export officer visited the company. VDT officials acknowledged that the tubes were for a Pakistani centrifuge project, and the Dutch government refused to provide an export license. The order proved too big for the company to ignore, however, so it challenged the government's prohibition. When the ministry was unable to find a specific export regulation that prohibited the sale of the tubes, the first batch of three hundred was sent to Pakistan on November 2, 1976. Khan was so pleased with the quality that he risked returning to the Netherlands to persuade the company to send the remainder of the 6,500. When Khan showed up there in early 1977, VDT readily agreed to sell him all the tubes he needed, though it would take three years to fill the order.

The transaction marked the beginning of a long and lucrative relationship between Slebos and Khan, which brought wealth to the Dutchman and delivered critical equipment to the Pakistani. A short, slender man with a stern military bearing, Slebos later boasted about his relationship with Khan. "I delivered him . . . the whole lot, the whole range from electronics to the construction materials, all kinds of things that were not forbidden to deal in," he said, later explaining that he was well aware that the products he sold were destined for Pakistan's nuclear program. Slebos even exhibited a degree of pride, justifying his actions by contending that Pakistan was within its rights to build a nuclear weapon to maintain the balance of power against India. Still, when he was shipping equipment to Pakistan, Slebos sought to evade detection and gave the deals a code name: Operation Butter Factory.

HAAG is one of those chocolate-box Swiss villages, with tidy houses and neat gardens, dwarfed by the towering peaks of the Alvier range, near the border with Liechtenstein. The valley had been part of the marshlands that spread out from the Rhine until the 1960s, when a vast reclamation project created a series of small hamlets along the great river's tributaries. Swiss authorities persuaded a number of high-tech companies to relocate to the area; many of them specialized in vacuum technology, giving the region its new nickname, "Vacuum Valley."

After World War II, the Swiss had flirted with the idea of developing their own nuclear arsenal. In the late 1960s they abandoned the plan for financial and political reasons, choosing instead to sign the nonproliferation treaty in 1969. Instead of becoming a nuclear power, Switzerland decided to focus its ample technical capabilities on becoming a major exporter of nuclear technology. Many of the industry's hot new companies had set up shop in Vacuum Valley. That was where Butt had found CORA Engineering and where Khan later came across one of CORA's competitors, Vakuum Apparat Technik. VAT manufactured a particular type of vacuum valve critical in controlling the gas that flowed into centrifuges. The inventor was a Swiss engineer named Friedrich Tinner, who was also in charge of export sales for VAT.

When Khan needed tens of thousands of dollars' worth of valves for Kahuta, the natural choice was Tinner, an old acquaintance from his Urenco days. Tinner had supplied valves for FDO, and he was more than pleased to renew his ties with Khan when the Pakistani arrived at his office. Khan was frank, explaining to Tinner that he was building a centrifuge plant for his own country and needed VAT's assistance. Regardless of the purpose or destination, Tinner and VAT were eager for the sale, but the firm checked with the authorities in Berne, the Swiss capital. The bureaucrats there replied by sending a list of export regulations, which included the trigger list published by the IAEA and the ad-hoc group of nuclear-export nations known as the Zangger Committee, named for its first chairman, a Swiss professor. Complete centrifuge units were on the list, but individual components like vacuum valves were not, despite their specific use in centrifuges. As in the CORA sale, the Swiss reasoning was that since the valves were not involved directly in the separation of isotopes at the heart of enrichment, they were not "nuclear sensitive," an obscure rationalization concocted by countries and companies that wanted to keep commercial avenues open.

The negotiations ran over several months, and Khan and some of his colleagues visited Haag so often that Tinner grew tired of making sure local restaurants did not cook meals that violated Muslim prohibitions on serving pork or alcohol. Eventually, he found it simpler to invite Khan to his home, where his wife would cook. "This was a business friendship, not a personal one," Tinner's daughter, Sonja Haas, said years later.

Other reasons might have been in play. Tinner was an important man in the village. He was active in civic organizations, including the board of the local school attended by his three young children. The valley was fairly isolated in those days, and strangers attracted attention. Like most of his countrymen, Tinner wanted to avoid anything that called attention to him or his business. This would have been particularly true when it came to selling nuclear-related items to foreigners.

As Khan and the network progressed, his patron's fortunes declined. In the spring and early summer of 1977, protests swept Pakistan. The March elections that had returned Bhutto to office appeared to have been rigged. The religious parties, never happy with Bhutto's leadership, sent their disciplined cadres into the streets in protest, leading to the most violent clashes between civilians and the police in Pakistan's history. On July 4, a weakened Bhutto met with his senior advisers to tell them that he would resume negotiations with the Pakistan National Alliance, a right-wing coalition dominated by the ultrareligious Jamaat-i-Islami party, in an attempt to defuse the situation. Yet there was to be no chance for an accord because the next day the country's military commander, Mohammed Zia ul-Haq, ordered Bhutto and his ministers arrested, imposed martial law, and suspended the constitution. Zia said the military was forced to intervene because the country was on the verge of a complete breakdown. Zia said he had no political ambitions and promised new elections in October.

Bhutto saw the coup as Kissinger's revenge. In memoirs written eighteen months later from his jail cell, where he faced a death sentence, Bhutto inferred that his fall was orchestrated by the Americans because of his refusal to back down from his pursuit of nuclear weapons after Kissinger visited him in August 1976. To be sure, the Americans were unhappy with Bhutto's stubbornness on a number of issues, but there was no evidence that they were involved in his overthrow. Still, the speculation refused to die, particularly among some Bhutto supporters and factions within Pakistan's primary intelligence service, the Inter-Services Intelligence Directorate. Known universally by the initials ISI, the agency was regarded as a state within the state that operated as something like an invisible government.

If the Americans were counting on a new policy from Zia's military government, they misjudged him. Two weeks after the coup, U.S. envoy Joseph Nye met with Zia and was told that the change of government had not changed Pakistan's stance on the development of nuclear capabilities.

Zia had dealt extensively with American military officers and intelligence agents in his years as a rising star in the military and later as commander of the armed forces. He was a hardened nationalist and an Islamist. The son of a devout Muslim civil servant in British India, Zia had been a young captain in the colonial army at the time of partition in 1947. He later recalled the nightmarish assignment to escort the final trainload of Muslim refugees from northern India to Pakistan. The weeklong journey took them past a landscape littered with mutilated corpses. "We were under constant fire," he said later. "The country was burning until we reached Lahore. Life had become so cheap between Hindu and Muslim." In his new country, Zia resumed his military career and eventually rose to the rank of general, growing more pious along the way. For him, Islam was not just a religion but the political framework that should govern the country. He liked to compare Pakistan to Israel, saying that he believed Pakistan would fail without Islam just as Israel would collapse without Judaism. And he was not going to back away from the country's nuclear ambitions. Zia had developed a close relationship with Khan as they worked to build the plant at Kahuta. Not long after taking control, the general took the scientist aside and assured him that his pursuit of atomic weapons should go forward at full speed.

Going full speed meant not only acquiring the equipment and technology but also developing a cadre of trained scientists and technicians almost from scratch. "A country which could not make sewing needles, good and durable bicycles or even ordinary durable roads was embarking on one of the latest and most difficult technologies," Khan observed later. But a pool of candidates existed, provided he could persuade them to come home. Like Khan, hundreds of bright young Pakistanis had enrolled in advanced science programs at universities in Europe and North America, with the government's encouragement. The United States alone had trained more than one hundred Pakistani scientists in nuclear specialties as part of Atoms for Peace. As Khan had discovered himself, there were few job opportunities in Pakistan for well-educated young Pakistanis, so most of them had remained abroad. The enormous challenge of the nuclear program opened the possibility of a technical career at home and, coupled with a bottomless pocketbook and patriotic appeal, Khan began to lure back many of the scientists, engineers, and technicians he needed.

Much of the recruitment was done through advertisements in small newspapers aimed at the Pakistani community living abroad. The effort was organized by the Pakistani diplomatic missions, and the fruits of the recruiting were to be shared by Khan's program and the PAEC. A typical ad, placed in a Canadian newspaper called the *Crescent*, invited scientists and engineers of Pakistani origin to come home to share their knowledge as the country embarked on new ventures in challenging scientific fields. There was no suggestion that the projects had anything to do with weapons. Applicants were instructed to apply at the embassy in Ottawa. Candidates were divided according to specialty, and those with backgrounds in physics or nuclear science were asked about their knowledge of uranium-235 and plutonium-239, the two versions of fissile material used in weapons. Anyone who was interviewed at that point would have had a pretty good idea of what was going on.

Competing with the atomic-energy commission for the most promising recruits, Khan didn't hesitate to get involved personally and use his experience as an example of how returnees could make a difference. In a letter in 1977 to Abdul Aziz Khan, a soft-spoken Pakistani electrical engineer living in Canada, Khan appealed to his sense of patriotism and promised him a role in a project of national importance. Reluctant to leave Canada, where he had citizenship, and sensing something was amiss, the engineer declined the offer. He later agreed to collect technical literature and use his vacations to travel to Pakistan to help train engineers for the centrifuge program, but he rejected the offer of first-class tickets to Pakistan and large sums of money, saying he wanted to avoid attracting the attention of Canadian authorities.

Aziz Khan went to Pakistan in the spring of 1978, visiting Kahuta and other facilities and meeting a handful of scientists and technicians who had returned permanently. A. Q. Khan described his band of workers as "crazy people" who were "working day and night," buoyed by the heady progress being made on the centrifuges and other technical aspects. Not every returnee could handle the workload or living conditions. One scientist who had been living in London had come primarily for the money, but his wife was unable to adjust to life in Pakistan, and the couple fought so bitterly that Khan dismissed him. "It is . . . the bad luck of this country that people do not want to stay here," Khan wrote to his Canadian pen pal in early 1979. "When one leaves he does not want to come back." In an apparent reference to his continuing feud with Munir Khan, he said that some people were trying to force him out of his job, but he vowed to remain until the task was finished.

No influx of expatriates could provide the full range of expertise required to start an enrichment program from scratch, so Khan called on the fraternity of European engineers, salesmen, and middlemen from his Urenco days to come to Pakistan to train what Khan called "local boys" on the sophisticated machinery being assembled at Kahuta. The visitors came from the most advanced countries in the world—places such as Germany, Switzerland, the Netherlands, Russia, and Japan, as well as China and the Middle East. The extent of the outside help did not escape the notice of Western intelligence agencies, but no one was willing to take the action that could have shut down or at least delayed Pakistan's rush to the bomb because they underestimated its nuclear capabilities.

CHAPTER 9

ACTIONABLE INTELLIGENCE

T HE U.S. EMBASSY in Islamabad—set amid a thirty-two-acre compound graced by a swimming pool and private club and surrounded by a high wall—employed about 150 diplomats, administrators, aid workers, and assorted spies. The CIA station was tucked away on the third floor, the walls of its warren of offices lined with locked file cabinets, a vault, and shredders. A small, gas-fired incinerator stood ready for burning the most sensitive classified material in the event an attack shut down the electricity. The station was usually home to three or four full-time case agents, who ran a network of operatives within the country. Throughout the 1960s and 1970s, Pakistan had served primarily as a listening post on Soviet activities in Central Asia and on the Chinese. American U-2s flew secretly out of a base in the northwestern city of Peshawar, and CIA agents moved about Islamabad with relative freedom, maintaining cordial relations with their counterparts at ISI.

When American policymakers began to worry that Pakistan was developing nuclear weapons after the Indian detonation, the CIA was in a good position to put its ear to the ground. The agents used their contacts and ability to get around the country to achieve some notable successes in the early going, managing to recruit at least one worker inside the Pakistan Atomic Energy Commission and a string of informants elsewhere. The

CIA knew when Chinese nuclear engineers started visiting several nuclear- and conventional-weapons facilities, and they were informed when Libyan couriers arrived by commercial aircraft, carrying suitcases filled with what was rumored to be cash. The CIA reported back to Washington that Colonel Gadhafi appeared to be fulfilling his pledge to help pay for the Islamic bomb. There was a slight hiccup in the summer of 1975 when the PAEC worker was detained by the ISI, but the Pakistani authorities never connected the scientist to the CIA, so the game went on.

A. Q. Khan first appeared on the radar of the CIA agents in Islamabad in early 1976. After Khan failed to return to his job at FDO, the Dutch security service assumed that he had bolted and notified the local CIA chief in the Netherlands. The information quickly circled back through CIA headquarters in Langley, Virginia, and arrived on the third floor of the embassy in Islamabad. The CIA and others in Washington failed to recognize Khan's significance, regarding him as a minor player even after his formal resignation from FDO.

Near the end of 1977, a CIA officer in Islamabad was told by a source that construction had started on a huge installation near Kahuta. The informant said the plant was to be a production center for enriched uranium as part of the country's weapons program, prompting an urgent cable to CIA headquarters. Spy satellites were redirected to photograph the location, providing CIA analysts with surprising images of a vast complex going up in the middle of nowhere. The warning, coupled with the huge amount of centrifuge-related technology arriving in Pakistan, indicated that something was clearly brewing. But the CIA technical analysts at Langley were convinced Pakistan did not have the technological or scientific base to get far in the complicated field of uranium enrichment, so the Islamabad station was instructed only to keep an eye on the construction at Kahuta.

The threat of nuclear proliferation was being taken more seriously in Washington. In the spring of 1977, Len Weiss flew to Paris to meet with senior French nuclear officials to relay John Glenn's opposition to the pending sale of the reprocessing plant to Pakistan. His most important meeting was with Bertrand Goldschmidt, one of the directors of the French nuclear agency and a physicist with a worldwide reputation. Even before Weiss finished laying out Glenn's concerns, Goldschmidt said the French had decided to stop the transaction. Weiss was surprised and pleased, but his mood soured a bit when Goldschmidt told him that unfortunately the French company involved in the deal had already sold Pakistan the blueprints for the plant. Getting them back, he said, would be impossible.

Weiss paused to consider the implications, unsure of how much damage had been done. "What stops them from going ahead with the reprocessing plant and eventually building a bomb?" he asked.

"We didn't give them critical pieces of equipment," Goldschmidt said. The French had not yet provided Pakistan with a device known as a "chopper," which sliced the highly radioactive spent fuel rods into pieces as part of producing plutonium. The Pakistanis would have to find another source for the chopper, which could add years to the effort. Weiss found some solace in Goldschmidt's revelation, but it also planted a seed in his mind: What if the reprocessing plant was not the true focus of the Pakistani nuclear plans? What if the plutonium route was a ruse? What if, while the United States spent precious diplomatic capital and intelligence resources trying to stop the French deal, Pakistan had another option for developing a weapon? As a scientist, Weiss was trained to look at issues from unorthodox angles. His method of evaluating a problem emphasized starting with a set of facts and following them wherever they led, without trying to fit them into a predetermined pattern. He therefore saw the situation differently from politicians or intelligence agents. Based on CIA reports and classified briefings over the previous year, Weiss knew that Pakistan was pursuing uranium enrichment at some level. Perhaps, he began to think, enrichment was the real way the Pakistanis planned to produce fissile material.

Weiss headed back to Washington to put the finishing touches on an amendment to the Foreign Assistance Act. The legislation threatened to bring sanctions against countries that acquired or sold nuclear-reprocessing technology with or without IAEA safeguards, which meant Pakistan and France both could face U.S. sanctions if their transaction went forward. Passed in August 1977 and signed into law by President Carter, the measure became known as the Glenn amendment.

But Weiss continued to worry, particularly as more information came to him about the expanding Pakistani procurement network. Sifting through reams of intelligence reports and ordering briefings from the CIA and the National Security Agency, Weiss began to assemble a clear picture of an enrichment operation that was far larger and potentially more dangerous than anyone had imagined previously. Weiss felt alarm bells should have been ringing, and he wasn't sure why they were not.

In the midst of his research, Weiss encountered the name of A. Q. Khan. Either a CIA briefer or an analyst's report mentioned the Pakistani scientist, explaining that he had stolen material from an advanced European centrifuge project and appeared to be playing a role in Pakistan's procurement effort. The NSA had even monitored telephone conversations in which Khan discussed specifications of certain equipment. His trips to Swiss and German high-tech companies had been documented, too. Khan was one of many people identified in the intelligence reports, but the name stuck with Weiss because of his concerns about enrichment. "Actionable intelligence was there, right from the beginning," said Weiss. "Inverters from England, maraging steel, Swiss valves—we knew about this at the time it was going on."

"Actionable intelligence" describes information regarded as solid enough to demand a response. Based on what he had seen, Weiss believed the Ford administration could have cut off assistance to Pakistan under the terms of the Symington amendment a year earlier. So he used his influence with Glenn to try to push the Carter administration to act, playing a key role in persuading President Carter to shut off most economic assistance and all military sales to Pakistan in the fall of 1977. Carter was worried about Pakistan's nuclear program, and he also had been angered that summer about Zia's coup. As a result, relations between the United States and Pakistan went into a tailspin, albeit a temporary one.

Earlier that year, Weiss had drafted an important piece of legislation, known as the Nuclear Non-Proliferation Act, which imposed new restrictions on U.S. nuclear exports and aimed to reverse the drive by a number of countries to build enrichment and reprocessing facilities. He was not naïve enough to believe that sanctions alone could stop a country determined to build the bomb, but he was confident that restrictions could delay the process, perhaps allowing the international community additional time to step in. He knew that the real solution was to address the underlying political and security motivations that led countries to acquire nuclear weapons.

Despite his reservations about the impact of the legislation, Weiss felt his trust in Glenn had been affirmed. He went ahead and resigned his tenured post at the University of Maryland and signed on full-time with the senator from Ohio. In the years that followed, he was to become one of the Senate's most influential staff members on nuclear proliferation, staying on the trail of A. Q. Khan.

IN WASHINGTON'S Foggy Bottom neighborhood, someone else was absorbing the same intelligence dispatches about Pakistan's purchases of enrichment-related equipment in Europe. Bob Gallucci had left the Arms Control and Disarmament Agency for the State Department, where he was a division chief in the Bureau of Intelligence and Research. Known as INR, the bureau was a fraction of the size of the CIA or NSA, and the people who worked there were not spies. Instead, INR drew on classified information generated by the U.S. intelligence community to develop policies and guidance for American diplomats in Washington and worldwide. Gallucci's specialty was proliferation, and he and his analysts were focused on India and Pakistan.

Pakistan was overtaking India as a source of worry. On January 1, 1978, President Carter traveled to New Delhi for a two-day visit. Normally, the president would have stopped next door in Pakistan, if only out of courtesy, but Carter snubbed Zia by deciding to skip his country. The American president rubbed salt in the Pakistani's wound by praising India's human-rights record and its democracy, capping the trip by signing a declaration with Indian prime minister Morarji Desai that affirmed the commitment of both countries to reduce and eventually eliminate nuclear weapons. Carter's visit and Desai's long-standing opposition to nuclear weapons put India's weapons program into what Gallucci called a "cryogenic freeze."

The American-Indian agreement signaled genuine progress, but it depended on stopping Pakistan's nuclear efforts, too. If Pakistan tested a nuclear weapon, India would resurrect its program. On his way home from India, Carter stopped in Paris to meet with French president Valéry Giscard d'Estaing and discuss U.S. concerns about Pakistan. The French had already promised privately not to proceed with the sale of the reprocessing plant, but Carter was eager to get a formal agreement. D'Estaing agreed to make the decision official, but he insisted on waiting long enough to make it seem as if France was not submitting to American pressure. Six months later, the French Council on Nuclear Policy declared the contract with Pakistan null and void.

By then, the French decision was not a surprise, but it still constituted a setback for Islamabad. In preparation for the French action, Pakistan had been devoting more of its resources to Khan and his enrichment program, a shift that was monitored by CIA stations across Europe. Gallucci was reading the new intelligence with increasing alarm, particularly reports about the new profile of A. Q. Khan. "He was all over the place," Gallucci said. "Did the CIA know exactly what he was doing? Probably not. But it was clear he was up to something. I think we had a pretty good handle on his stuff."

The Carter administration was at a critical juncture, if it had the will to stop the Pakistani march toward nuclear weapons. The intelligence agencies, led by the CIA and NSA, had provided undeniable evidence of what the Pakistanis were doing. Congress was aware of the threat, and the president had already been concerned enough to impose sanctions. The outcome hinged on taking significant action to stop Pakistan by stepping up enforcement of export regulations and enlisting American allies in the effort. If those steps failed, some in the American government were prepared to consider more drastic action.

In mid-1978, a working group was convened within the State Department to try to find a way to thwart Pakistan. But the question was how. Relations with Zia were terrible, so there was little hope of gaining political leverage. In the midst of the discussion of various options, Secretary of State Cyrus Vance took the highly unusual step of asking his diplomats to develop an outline of the pros and cons of launching air strikes to level the construction under way at Kahuta. Vance recognized the risk he was taking in even asking for the information, so he put the request in the form of a private memo, to avoid embarrassment if word leaked. After reviewing the outline developed by his staff, Vance abandoned the idea as too fraught with political danger, including the possibility of touching off a major conflict in South Asia. Despite the precautions, word did leak to the Pakistanis, and they responded by installing French-made antiaircraft-missile batteries around the perimeter of the complex.

Another option that was debated in the most hushed terms was a plan to assassinate Khan. "Many of us wondered why somebody doesn't just stop this guy," said Gallucci. "It wouldn't be us, but somebody." That option, too, was never acted on, but years later another senior government official at the time rued the decision not to kill the Pakistani scientist. "The best thing would have been to take Khan into an alley somewhere and put a bullet in his head," he said.

A more prosaic task for the working group was to understand the full scope of Pakistan's enrichment program in order to assess how far along it was and what its vulnerabilities might be. For this, Gallucci turned to nuclear-weapons analysts at the CIA and experts at Lawrence Livermore National Laboratories in Berkeley, California. As proliferation concerns grew during the Cold War, the CIA had sought help from the weapons designers and other experts who worked for the giant lab, leading to the creation of a special-projects group known as Z Division. Its top-secret job was to provide the intelligence community and the State Department with the kinds of highly detailed technical assessments of foreign nuclear programs and weapons capabilities that could be made only by nuclear scientists. As time went on, Z Division grew within the laboratory, with teams assigned to specific regions and countries. The partnership allowed the CIA and other agencies to tap the reservoir of technical knowledge at Livermore, but the experts weren't always right. Often there were disagreements between the analysts at the CIA and the scientists at Livermore and other laboratories.

That summer, Gallucci's working group brought the top Z Division scientists and the senior CIA analysts together in a secure briefing room on the seventh floor of the State Department. Instead of disagreeing, both groups were unanimous in their assessment of Pakistan's enrichment program: There was no threat, and it would take decades for Pakistan to master the arcane principles of developing centrifuges to enrich uranium. They were certain that the Pakistanis would never be up to the task because the country was too backward, no matter how much technology it smuggled in from Europe. There was arrogance in the assumption, best exemplified when one of the CIA analysts told Gallucci, "You should be happy that they are pursuing centrifuges, because they will never get those centrifuges to work."

Doubt began to arise about that assessment by early 1979, when an American spy satellite above the Indian subcontinent beamed back images showing surprising progress—the roof was going on a massive installation situated on more than fifty acres and surrounded by high fences and antiaircraft batteries. The sheer size of the construction project caused Gallucci to go back to his experts for a second opinion. Pakistan appeared to have marshaled a huge effort to build the structure, and the question was, Would they have done so without some assurance that the centrifuges they planned to install would work? None of the experts was willing to abandon the idea that Pakistan wasn't up to the technological challenge, but Gallucci felt that he could no longer count on Pakistan's failure. He feared time was not on his side.

CHAPTER 10

A NUCLEAR COWSHED

DESPITE THE PROGRESS of the construction at Kahuta, Khan's team was having trouble with the prototypes for the centrifuges that were to form the heart of the enrichment plant—they kept spinning out of balance and breaking loose from their moorings, sending technicians ducking for cover as the cylinders ricocheted through the test hall at Sihala. Some engineers thought they had identified the problem and come up with a solution. Because centrifuges spin at up to twice the speed of sound, the electricity that propels them has to flow at a consistent voltage. The slightest variation throws the machine out of balance and leads to potentially disastrous accidents. The cause of the voltage fluctuation was traced to the type of high-frequency inverter purchased the previous year from a German company. The engineers felt the device was inferior and told the boss that the only way to cure the problem was to find a better one. Khan relayed the assignment to Siddique Butt, who was rebuffed when he tried to buy more advanced inverters from a Dutch company on Khan's list from Urenco.

In running the Pakistani pipeline, Butt had maintained security by using only fellow Pakistanis to place orders for technology. Under pressure to get the inverters, however, he took a chance and turned to an outsider. The man he chose was Abdus Salam, a Muslim of Indian origin who was a British citizen and ran a small electronics business in North London. At Butt's request, Salam and a partner, a British engineer named Peter Griffin, set up a new company to place orders for top-quality inverters with the British subsidiary of Emerson Electric, the American firm that provided the devices to U.S. and British nuclear plants. Salam and Griffin started small, placing an initial order for thirty inverters after telling Emerson that the devices were for a textile plant in Pakistan. Emerson approved the first order. Before the initial shipment was made, Salam requested sixty more.

British export law did not prohibit the export of the inverters, and both shipments likely would have gone without notice except for an article published in the summer of 1978 in *Nucleonics Week*, a specialty publication for nuclear experts in and out of government. The article disclosed that the Emerson inverters were intended for use by Pakistan in a secret uranium-enrichment program for military purposes. The article's sources were unclear, though Khan later blamed the German businessman whose company had filled the earlier order but lost the business because his inverters didn't work.

Regardless of its origins, the scoop caught the attention of Frann Allaun, a Labor Party member of the British Parliament and an advocate of nuclear disarmament. His staff inquired with British export authorities and learned that Emerson was selling inverters to a Pakistani textile company. Allaun took to the floor of the House of Commons to denounce the transaction and the ineffectiveness of British export regulations. "Was the British Government aware that the firm Emerson Electric had supplied Pakistan with a quantity of special inverters for driving ultracentrifuges in a uranium-enrichment plant?" Allaun demanded. Later, the MP explained that he raised concerns because the inverters were identical to those used by the British Atomic Energy Authority, so he doubted they were destined for a textile plant. Despite the flap, Emerson officials shipped the first batch of thirty inverters.

The outcry forced the British government to conduct a quick investigation, leading export authorities to conclude that no law was violated. Still, the government had no desire to be seen as abetting Pakistan's nuclear efforts, so high-frequency inverters were added quickly to the prohibited export list, and the second shipment was blocked. Tony Benn, the British energy minister, said the inverters were clearly intended for Pakistan's bomb program, and the British action appeared to be too little and too late.

Still, Khan would need far more than thirty inverters. In letters to Abdul Aziz Khan, the Pakistani nuclear engineer living in Canada, late in 1978 and early in 1979, Khan complained that his engineers were running short of inverters, and he worried that the furious pace of work would be interrupted if a new supplier were not found soon. "Work is progressing satisfactorily, but the frustration is increasing," Khan wrote. "It is just like a man who waited for thirty years but cannot wait for a few hours after the marriage ceremony. As now the work has started to progress and you can see the light through the tunnel, it is hard to wait till that time. We all want that instead of finishing the work tomorrow, we should finish it today."

The letters to Aziz Khan provide an intriguing glimpse inside the program at a critical time. The United States and its allies were working to strengthen export laws, so in response A. Q. Khan was expanding his procurement operation outside the reach of the West, to the Soviet Union and China, an effort that he recounted in the letters, often resorting to an awkward code to conceal the topic. In describing apparent efforts to get centrifuge components from the Soviet Union, he wrote: "The dam is ready and a week ago we put the flow of water in it and now it is filled. It has become quite scenic. Presently we are trying to obtain some information about where we can get the fish and put them in it so that our angler friends could have a good time. Hopefully in winter there will be ducks from Russia." In February 1979, he said construction was almost finished on the laboratories and administration building and that he expected the first technicians and engineers to be transferred to Kahuta by April.

The correspondence sometimes veered into personal matters, with Khan describing his heavy workload in the same paragraph in which he recounted the slow progress on the new house he and Henny were building on Margalla Road in Islamabad's most affluent neighborhood. The house was a symbol of Khan's rising status and improved financial situation, but it was a headache, too. "Construction of the house is continuing," he said. "Contractors keep on saying it is only a question of one or two months. These days it is nearly on the finishing stages, it is being polished, bathroom fixtures are being installed, doors are being installed." He looked forward to moving into the house by spring, explaining that he had promised his daughters that they would be able to swim in the pool by April 1.

The controversy over the British inverters had done more than just threaten Khan's centrifuge program. The *Nucleonics Week* article and Allaun's outburst had attracted the attention of a number of European publications and television networks, which responded by assigning teams of investigative reporters to dig further into Pakistan's procurement operation and its nuclear program. Khan had operated in relative secrecy since arriving home, but that came crashing down on March 28, 1979, when the German television network Zweites Deutsches Fernsehen broadcast a program disclosing that Khan had obtained access to centrifuge technology while working under contract to the Urenco consortium and taken it back to Pakistan. "Today, Dr. Khan is the director of the top-secret project for the construction of a similar plant in Pakistan," said the program. More detailed broadcasts and investigative articles followed quickly, portraying Khan as a spy and a thief who had stolen the designs that had given Pakistan the keys to a nuclear arsenal. Exactly as Ruud Lubbers had feared years before, exposure of Khan's misdeeds embarrassed the Dutch government and Urenco, prompting demands from their German and British partners to know what exactly had happened at FDO: How had a Pakistani scientist gained access to the sensitive centrifuge technology? How much he had learned? The Dutch tried to shift the blame from one agency to another in hopes outside interest would soon fade, but there was no quelling the storm, and its consequences turned personal for Khan.

Slightly more than three years after his return to Pakistan, Khan felt that he was on the verge of success at Kahuta, and he expected to be regarded as a national hero, not a thief. Khan thought of himself as a great scientist and a leader, someone who exercised almost total control over his environment, colleagues, and family. His self-image as well as his centrifuge program was threatened by these exposures, so Khan railed against the articles and broadcasts, insisting to anyone who would listen that he was the victim of a vicious smear campaign that sought to undermine not just him but the very idea that Muslims could build the bomb. His rage boiled over and provoked his first public response after an article in *Der Spiegel,* the German newsmagazine. "I want to question the bloody holier-than-thou attitudes of the Americans and the British," Khan wrote to the magazine, lashing out at his enemies in hyperbolic terms. "Are these bastards God-appointed guardians of the world to stockpile hundreds of thousands of nuclear warheads and have they the God-given authority to carry out explosions every month? If we start a modest program, we are the Satans, the devils, and all the Western journalists consider it a crusade to publish fabricated and malicious stories about us."

Khan's wildest accusations were reserved for private correspondence with trusted friends. Writing to them, he added Jews to his list of tormentors and lamented the impact on his efforts. "American and Jewish [officials] have advertised my name and another and showing it on T.V. has created the problem of security, but we are working, depending on God," he wrote in one tirade. "All our material has been stopped; everywhere they are making it delayed. The materials which we were buying from British and Americans have been stopped. Now we will have to do some work ourselves." His troubles extended to relations with Munir Khan and the PAEC, too. "On one side the whole world is after us and on the other side the internal enemies are going to finish us," he said. "But at least we have one satisfaction, that from one end to another end we have made other people sleepless."

Despite the external pressure, Khan promised that he would provide the enriched uranium he had promised on time. He even found an upside in the bad publicity, telling his future biographer Zahid Malik that the press onslaught had served as a gigantic advertisement for Pakistan's nuclear-procurement program. "Many suppliers approached us with details of the machinery and with figures and numbers of instruments and material they had sold to Almelo," he said. "In the true sense of the word, they begged us to purchase their goods. And for the first time, the truth of the saying, 'They will sell their mothers for money,' dawned on me."

The press accounts played a role in increasing the resolve of officials in Washington to stop Pakistan, and so did General Zia's decision to execute former Prime Minister Bhutto on April 4. International legal observers had described Bhutto's conviction for plotting to murder political opponents as a political act in itself. President Carter was outraged at the hanging. On April 6, a week after the German television program about Khan and two days after the execution, Carter announced that Washington was expanding the sanctions against Pakistan to withhold additional types of economic assistance. The amounts were relatively small—$40 million for the remainder of fiscal 1979 and $45 million for the following year—but the symbolism was strong. "U.S. laws require countries importing armaments components for atomic installations not subject to international security controls to be deprived of development funds," Tom Reston, a State Department spokesman, said. "Our information is that Pakistan is developing a centrifuge for the enrichment of uranium. In the long term this might give Pakistan a nuclear weapon capability. According to our laws, we have decided to cut back significantly on development aid to Pakistan."

Even the modest sanctions were major news in Pakistan, where they were regarded as not only a blow to the country's economy but an insult to Zia. The Pakistan Foreign Ministry claimed that the Americans had singled out Pakistan because they wrongly believed that it was building nuclear devices for the Muslim world to use against the Israelis. As they would over and over, Pakistani officials maintained that their country's nuclear program was a peaceful one, intended only to generate electricity. A Pakistani diplomat assigned to the embassy in Washington during this tumultuous period said later that he and his colleagues were instructed to lie about the country's nuclear intentions. "Those of us who knew what was going on, we were given clear orders not to tell the truth to anyone, not other diplomats or U.S. officials or anyone," said the diplomat, who had a long career in government service before retiring in the late 1990s.

Washington used its influence to stop the World Bank from making any further loans to Pakistan. Other countries agreed to modest restrictions, but few officials expected the sanctions to sway Pakistan, and simultaneous efforts were under way to find a carrot to accompany the stick. In an echo of the offer made in 1976 by Kissinger to Bhutto, the Pentagon proposed selling advanced F-16 fighter jets if Pakistan agreed to give up its weapons program and submit to outside verification. As with Kissinger's proposed quid pro quo with Bhutto, the bargain seemed unlikely to deter the Pakistanis.

EFFORTS were under way on the diplomatic front, too. That summer, Carter appointed Gerard Smith, a retired diplomat, as his special envoy on nonproliferation. Smith had helped negotiate the first strategic arms limitation treaty, or SALT I, with the Soviets, and he had headed the Arms Control and Disarmament Agency. On his first mission, he was sent to Europe to deliver the president's warning about the threat posed by Pakistan's nuclear efforts; accompanying him was Bob Gallucci. After stops for meetings in London and Paris, the two men headed to Vienna on June 25. Their arrival was timed to coincide with a regular meeting of the IAEA's board of governors, a gathering of hundreds of diplomats that would provide some cover for the Americans. They wanted to present their case quietly to Sigvard Eklund, the director general of the IAEA, and convince him to back tough steps to isolate Pakistan and stop the flow of nuclear technology from IAEA member countries. Eklund was a thoughtful Swedish nuclear scientist; although his worries about the spread of atomic weapons had deepened during the eighteen years he had been in charge of the IAEA, he remained a cautious international bureaucrat.

Smith and Gallucci slipped into the huge complex overlooking the Danube the next morning and went straight to Eklund's office on the twenty-seventh floor. Smith cautioned the Swede that the information he was about to hear had to remain secret and turned the presentation over to Gallucci, who had a better grasp of the details and significance of the intelligence. He had to strike a balance between giving Eklund enough information to alarm him into taking the threat seriously without disclosing anything that would jeopardize the methods used by U.S. intelligence agencies. This was always a tricky balance and often a point of friction between intelligence agencies and policymakers. Gallucci's version of what the United States knew about Pakistan was broad and heavily censored, but he promised there was clear evidence that Pakistan had not abandoned its attempts to reprocess spent fuel into plutonium for a nuclear weapon. But the more pressing concern, he told the silent Swede, was the ongoing project to enrich uranium, which had been in the news in recent weeks. He gave Eklund a sketchy but frightening outline of Pakistan's progress, describing the construction at Kahuta. Lest the IAEA director had any remaining doubts, Gallucci said American intelligence had solid information that the Pakistanis were working on a nuclear-weapon design that would incorporate the enriched uranium from Kahuta.

Eklund knew that the French had not provided Pakistan with all of the technology necessary to reprocess plutonium into usable fissile material, so he was less worried about that part of the briefing. The progress on uranium enrichment concerned him more. "Does Pakistan have the technical capability to manufacture centrifuge machines?" he asked the two Americans.

Gallucci said that the complexity and extent of Pakistan's shopping list indicated that they were making good progress on centrifuges and that it was likely that Islamabad could soon be producing large quantities of weapons-grade uranium. This assessment was a dramatic turnaround from the recent days when the CIA and Livermore were downplaying Pakistan's ability to master enrichment, and it underscored the peril of underestimating the skill and tenacity of Pakistan's nuclear establishment.

Eklund was in a quandary. The IAEA was restricted in its ability to inspect nuclear facilities in Pakistan because the country had not signed the Nuclear Non-Proliferation Treaty. Though the Canadian-built reactor in Karachi and the small U.S.-supplied research reactor were under IAEA safeguards, Kahuta and the rest of the country were off-limits to agency inspectors. Twenty-four years after its creation, the world's nuclear watchdog relied almost entirely on the voluntary declarations of its member countries and occasional intelligence passed on by the United States and others. Eklund said he had already written to Pakistan to inquire about the news reports, and the government had assured him that no nuclear installation was being operated outside the safeguards agreement and that it had no secret program.

Faced with the American intelligence, however, Eklund began to doubt that the Pakistanis were telling the truth. He agreed that the situation was extremely serious, but he recognized that the IAEA had no real way to stop the Pakistanis. "The only chance of stopping the Pakistanis would be to give wide publicity to the information, which might lead the responsible countries of the world to put enough pressure on them to stop the program," he told Smith and Gallucci.

Smith said it might be effective in the future, but for the time being the American government did not want its secret information getting out.

"May I discuss this information with members of my staff?" Eklund asked.

"Unfortunately, no, not at this time," said Smith.

A troubled Eklund spent the next day pondering the warning. The contradiction between what Pakistan was telling the IAEA and what the Americans were claiming exposed a dangerous gap that was a continuing, nagging problem for the IAEA. Designed primarily to promote the peaceful use of nuclear energy, the agency lacked investigative facilities or enforcement authority. Increasing the agency's authority was problematic because it was controlled by a board of governors whose thirty-five members were chosen from the agency's overall membership. Few of those countries were willing to sacrifice their sovereign rights to make the IAEA more effective, and some of them were downright hostile; Pakistan, India, and Israel were all IAEA members.

Two days later, Eklund requested a second session with Smith and Gallucci. The IAEA chief was struggling for a strategy. In the conference room outside his office, he told Smith that economic and military sanctions were unlikely to be effective because of Pakistan's access to oil revenue from some of its fellow Islamic countries. "Muslim solidarity might mean that countries such as Libya would be willing to finance the project and might want to use nuclear weapons in the Middle East," he said. The United Nations Security Council was the forum of last resort for bringing pressure on rogue countries, but Eklund said the chances of success there were not good. He repeated his belief that publicizing key portions of the evidence offered the best chance of stopping them.

Smith again rejected the suggestion. "I feel we still have some time," he said. "I doubt if the Pakistanis will be able to explode a device for two or three years."

"That is not so much time," Eklund replied, adding, "The more work the Pakistanis do, the harder it will be to stop them."

The clock was ticking. Planners at the Pentagon were already developing a strategy for an air assault on Kahuta and other nuclear sites in Pakistan if the diplomatic route failed. On August 12, 1979, *The New York Times* reported that Smith was directing an interagency task force developing a military strike as a last resort. The article hit like a bombshell in Pakistan, forcing the United States to issue a categorical denial that it had any intentions of an armed attack. But the Americans were not the only ones who regarded Pakistan's nuclear program as a threat that might merit military action. Israel was secretly considering air strikes against the same targets, fearing that Pakistan was building an "Islamic bomb" that could erase Israel from the map.

On September 13, senior U.S. officials met for two days of closed-door sessions about the growing threat from Pakistan in the secure conference room on the seventh floor at the State Department. Among those who attended were Lieutenant General Brent Scowcroft, former President Ford's national-security adviser and a member of President Carter's non-proliferation advisory council; General George Seignious, director of the Arms Control and Disarmament Agency; several analysts from INR; and a number of other intelligence analysts. The talk was blunt, and the results were classified. Over two days, the discussion made clear that U.S. officials were aware of the broad strokes of Pakistan's enrichment program. They reviewed Khan's theft of Urenco plans and his high-tech shopping spree in Europe. Tougher export controls might slow down Pakistan but probably would not stop it. The consensus was that Pakistan was several years away from manufacturing a nuclear weapon, though some participants were concerned that Pakistan might set off some type of improvised nuclear explosion in the coming weeks for political purposes. Zia was running for election to the office he had grabbed, and a show of strength could assure him of victory that November.

Conventional wisdom was that Israel possessed nuclear weapons, but the Israelis maintained an official policy of nuclear ambiguity—the mere threat was enough to keep its enemies from launching an attack anything short of completely destroying the Jewish state. Pakistan's position was different: The Indian nuclear explosion in 1974 was a direct challenge that demanded a response for purposes of national honor as much as actual deterrence of the Indians, whose conventional forces far outnumbered those of Pakistan.

"This is a railroad train that is going down the track very fast, and I am not sure anything will turn it off," said Charles N. Van Doren, assistant director of the arms-control agency.

No one was able to offer a solution. Some agreed with Van Doren that it was probably too late and the best the United States could do was delay the day Pakistan got the bomb. Others argued that a strong security guarantee from Washington might convince Pakistan that it did not need nuclear weapons to counter the threat from India.

The same challenge hung over talks that occurred a month later in the same conference room. In mid-October, Secretary of State Cyrus Vance and Pakistani foreign minister Agha Shahi met to discuss the deteriorating relations between the two countries. The American-imposed sanctions were damaging Pakistan's economy, and Shahi was desperate to win some sort of concession in advance of the elections at home. He complained that the restrictions threatened the country's stability, and he said General Zia and Pakistan's military leaders were very concerned by the reports that the United States was considering an attack on the country's nuclear installations. Vance assured Shahi that no military action was planned, but he refused to back down on the issue of economic and military sanctions until Pakistan abandoned its nuclear efforts. Without acknowledging that Pakistan was pursuing nuclear weapons, Shahi asked Vance whether the United States would provide Pakistan with a security guarantee similar to the agreement that committed the Americans to defending any NATO member attacked from the outside. This, he suggested, would go a long way toward easing Pakistan's fears of India and, implicitly, remove the need for a nuclear arsenal. Vance replied that Washington valued its alliance with Pakistan and he hoped that ties could return to normal soon, but the United States could not provide such an assurance.

Gallucci was in the room during the talks with Shahi, and later he discussed the dilemma with colleagues, reaching a consensus that the outlook for stopping Pakistan was grim. The two options appeared to be equally unpalatable: A military attack, even if successful, would enrage the Muslim world; the NATO-like security guarantee could involve the United States in war in a place where its national interests were not strong enough to justify it. Even without war, such a pledge would outrage India at a time when the administration was rebuilding its ties to the world's largest democracy.

By this time, Gallucci knew more about the Pakistani nuclear program than did anyone at the State Department. During one of his many trips to Islamabad, he had taken along satellite photos of Kahuta to show Zia. The Pakistani leader scoffed at the images, saying they depicted nothing more than a cowshed. Curious to see for himself, Gallucci had persuaded the American ambassador to allow the embassy's political officer, Marc Grossman, to accompany him on a drive to Kahuta. Accompanied by an intelligence officer, the pair drove an embassy jeep to the barbed-wire fence surrounding the complex, where Grossman talked his way past the guard shack by claiming that they were going for a picnic on one of the hilltops. Once inside the perimeter, they glimpsed some of the construction work under way and snapped some quick photographs before caution prevailed and they left. The Pakistanis later learned of the so-called picnic but took no action against the Americans. A week after the Gallucci-Grossman incursion, however, the French ambassador tried to repeat the visit. This time, the Pakistanis were on alert, and the ambassador and his driver were beaten badly by the guards.

When Zia learned of this, he told a British reporter, "I wish it had been the American bastard."

CHAPTER 11

SEE NO EVIL

O N NOVEMBER 21, 1979, residents and shopkeepers in the garri-son town of Rawalpindi awoke to a startling sight: the country's military strongman, President Zia ul-Haq, riding a bicycle through streets jammed with buses, cars, and motorized rickshaws. As Zia, surrounded by a small army of bodyguards, pedaled to promote an alternative form of transportation, the radio reported accusations that infidels had taken control of the sacred Grand Mosque in the Saudi Arabian city of Mecca, the holiest site in Islam. Saudi national guardsmen had surrounded the mosque, and the occupiers had opened fire with automatic weapons, re-sulting in a bloodbath. Zia was mobbed by angry people shouting ques-tions about the still-unfolding drama when he paused outside a local market. He inflamed the crowd by telling them that the United States was behind the attack at a site so revered that non-Muslims are not even allowed to enter it.

Anti-American sentiment was already red-hot in the Muslim world, ig-nited by events in Iran fewer than three weeks earlier. On November 4, mil-itant Iranian students had stormed the U.S. embassy in Tehran and taken sixty-six diplomats, military personnel, and others hostage. The students, incited by fiery rhetoric from religious leaders, were angered by decades of American interference in Iran's internal affairs, dating to the 1953 coup that overthrew the elected government of Prime Minister Mohammed Mossadegh and reinstalled the Shah, Mohammed Reza Pahlevi, a man widely reviled in the country. The CIA and British intelligence had organized the coup after Mossadegh nationalized Iranian oil, and secret documents later declassified showed that the Americans and British were determined to maintain Western control over Iranian oil. The student takeover of the American embassy twenty-six years later, perhaps the first instance of what would become known as "blowback," quickly escalated into an international crisis. The streets of Arab capitals filled with outraged protestors chanting "Death to America," provoked by the glowering, black-turbaned Ayatollah Ruhollah Khomeini, whose sermons pushed the debate beyond the political realm and provided a theological basis for using violence and terrorism against perceived enemies of Islam. "Islam says: Whatever good there is exists thanks to the sword and in the shadow of the sword," Khomeini said in sermons broadcast throughout the Middle East. "People cannot be made obedient except with the sword. The sword is the key to paradise, which can be opened only for holy warriors."

The mood on the streets of Pakistan was ripe for Zia's accusation, and within minutes a huge throng began marching toward the American embassy, several miles away. With each block along the route, the crowd grew more unruly and threatening. As they neared the embassy compound, the protestors were joined by students from Quaid-i-Azam University, where militant students had recently taken control of the student union and begun persecuting secular-minded professors and vilifying women who refused to wear the veil.

When the mob reached the embassy, its fury boiled over into a full-blown siege. Young men tore down part of the outer wall, flooded into the compound, and set fire to the main building. The six Marine guards were easily overwhelmed and retreated into the embassy. As the mayhem raged, the 139 American and Pakistani employees trapped inside fled to the third floor and huddled inside a secure vault.

Stephen Crowley, a young Marine, rushed to the roof of the embassy to report on the melee below. Blond and six-foot-six, he was an easy target—a rioter shot him in the head. Other Marines hauled him down to the third floor and into the vault, where Fran Fields, a registered nurse and the wife of an embassy officer, fitted an oxygen mask to his face as blood pooled around his head. Inside the vault, people arranged themselves in groups by blood type, so Crowley could get an immediate transfusion in case they were rescued.

The ambassador, Arthur Hummel Jr., and the CIA station chief, John Reagan, pleaded by telephone with the Pakistani government to send troops to protect them. At one point, a Pakistani military helicopter circled the compound, its pilot nearly blinded by the smoke rising from fires. Still, no help arrived, even though Pakistani troops were stationed in a barracks less than half an hour away. The first contingent did not show up for more than five hours, as the embassy smoldered and the rioters were dispersing. In the interim, Crowley died, and another American, Army warrant officer Brian Ellis, and two Pakistani employees were killed. All six buildings inside the compound had been destroyed.

Instead of outrage, official reaction from Washington was muted. Everyone from President Carter on down remained obsessed with the ongoing hostage crisis in Iran, so instead of condemning what happened in Islamabad, Carter telephoned Zia to thank him for his assistance. No one challenged the Pakistani president's false assertion that Americans were behind the Mecca attack, which was actually carried out by a disgruntled Islamic theology student and his fundamentalist followers. No one contradicted the Pakistani ambassador in Washington when he crowed that his country's troops had responded promptly to the assault on the embassy in Islamabad. The State Department, however, ordered all nonessential personnel evacuated from Pakistan. The diplomats and CIA agents who stayed behind were bitter because they knew a much greater death toll had been only narrowly averted.

Carter and his administration feared that challenging Zia would drive him deeper into the camp of the Islamic fundamentalists gaining power in Pakistan and across the Muslim world. After assuming the presidency, Zia had courted political support from religious militants by promising a "genuine Islamic order." He had approved amputations for thieves and floggings for adulterers, both traditional punishments under Sharia law. He had also authorized the establishment of hundreds of religious schools across the country, where the curriculum included virulent doses of anti-American and anti-Israeli teachings. The proliferation of these schools was to play a major role in the spread of religious extremism across Pakistan.

Following Zia's election, the State Department's INR produced an analysis examining how far toward religious extremism he might take the country, and whether such a movement would raise the risk for the region dramatically by bringing nuclear weapons into the equation. The report found that the Koran could be interpreted to justify the use of terror in a holy war and that Zia and other members of Pakistan's military elite regarded an atomic bomb as the ultimate weapon of terror. "This concept leads strategists to maintain the importance of a nuclear deterrent, the weapon most capable of weakening the enemy's self-confidence and leading in turn to his utter defeat," said the study. "Thus, as one officer put it: 'Nuclear weapons are modern terror weapons, and Islam enjoins us to strike terror into the heart of the enemy.' The weapon that at first glance seems to be the most undisciplined one thus is placed within rigid theological-ideological boundaries."

As Carter and his aides grappled with the hostage crisis, another momentous event took place on Christmas Eve when the first planeloads of Soviet troops landed at Kabul International Airport in Afghanistan. By early Christmas morning, Soviet tanks were rolling across pontoon bridges in the north, and army troops were fanning out across the country. The CIA had been watching Soviet troop deployments and had already warned that an invasion was imminent. Rather than a threat, Zbigniew Brzezinski, the president's national-security adviser, saw the invasion as an opportunity. He regarded it as a desperate act by the Soviets to prop up the puppet regime they had established in Kabul and saw a chance for the United States to confront the Soviets through proxies. The rebellious forces with whom the Americans were about to throw in their lot were dominated by devout Muslims who were angered by efforts by the Soviet-backed government to undertake numerous reforms, including educating women, abolishing arranged marriages, and banning dowries.

Carter had authorized a secret assistance program to the disorganized

Afghan rebels the previous summer, in advance of the Soviet invasion. Now that the Soviets had made their move, Brzezinski wondered how far he could go without provoking a confrontation with Moscow. The day after Christmas, he wrote a memo to Carter outlining a plan to increase the covert backing to make sure the Afghan resistance survived the invasion. Some resources would come from U.S. coffers, but Brzezinski proposed seeking additional help from Islamic countries such as Saudi Arabia and Pakistan. Because of Pakistan's proximity to Afghanistan, enlisting it was critical to the plan, even if it meant sacrificing one of Carter's signature policies by reversing American opposition to Pakistan's nuclear ambitions. "To make the above possible, we must both reassure Pakistan and encourage it to help the rebels," he wrote. "This will require a review of our policy toward Pakistan, more guarantees to it, more arms aid, and, alas, a decision that our security policy toward Pakistan cannot be dictated by our nonproliferation policy."

Carter faced a historic decision, one that would shape American nuclear policy and determine the fate of Pakistan's nuclear ambitions. The president was dogged by the ongoing Iranian hostage crisis, which was damaging his political standing at home and America's image in the world. So Carter accepted Brzezinski's argument that the prospect of defeating the Soviets outweighed the goal of stopping Pakistan's nuclear program, agreeing to lift the sanctions imposed two years earlier. Then, he went so far as to offer four hundred million dollars in economic and military aid to Pakistan.

President Carter justified his decision by telling Congress in his State of the Union address on January 23, 1980, that the United States needed to support Pakistan's territorial integrity by easing sanctions. The only mention of the nuclear arms race in the speech was in the context of controlling the threat from the Soviets; Carter said nothing about Pakistan's nuclear ambitions, though a statement sent out a few days later by the State Department pledged that the renewed assistance to Islamabad was not intended to diminish the American commitment to preventing the spread of nuclear weapons in Pakistan or elsewhere.

For a second time the American government had decided that short-term strategic considerations outweighed the future danger from Pakistan's nuclear ambitions, again opening the door to Khan and his associates.

Four years earlier, the CIA had decided to let the Pakistani scientist escape Dutch arrest and continue gathering the know-how and equipment for the enrichment plant, so that the Americans could keep track of what the Pakistanis were doing on the nuclear front. Now, Carter and Brzezinski were giving the Pakistani government carte blanche to carry on its nuclear-weapons development in exchange for its help against the Soviets. The goal of stopping Pakistan's nuclear effort was sacrificed, and American moral authority to advocate for the cause of nonproliferation was severely damaged.

Anyone who doubted the lasting damage of that decision on American proliferation policy needed only to listen to Ronald Reagan, the former California governor who was seeking the Republican presidential nomination to run against Carter. Reagan was determined to go much further: During a campaign stop in Jacksonville, Florida, on January 31, 1980, he was asked his concerns about Pakistan's nuclear-weapons ambitions. "I just don't think it's any of our business," he replied.

Reagan won the Republican nomination and defeated Carter, who had been damaged by both his inability to extricate the hostages from Tehran and a sagging domestic economy. The hostages were released in January 1981 as Reagan moved into the White House, but the fight against the Soviets in Afghanistan was just beginning, and the new president wasted no time embracing the new leniency on Pakistan's nuclear program. It was decided that Washington could live with Pakistan's pursuit of an atomic bomb as long as it got the help it needed against the Soviets. Reagan's first secretary of state, General Alexander Haig, told Pakistani officials that their nuclear program "need not become the centerpiece of the U.S.-Pakistan relationship." For the next eight years, the Reagan administration concentrated on keeping Pakistan on its side in the war against the Soviets, while Pakistan concentrated on perfecting its bomb.

BY COINCIDENCE, Reagan's selection as ambassador to Pakistan was Ronald Spiers, a strong supporter of nuclear containment whose memo nearly three decades earlier had planted the seeds for the creation of the International Atomic Energy Agency as part of the Atoms for Peace program.

Before his appointment, Spiers had been in charge of the Bureau of Intelligence and Research at the State Department, where he had overseen the report warning that elements of Pakistan's military leadership considered nuclear weapons part of the arsenal of terror. But Spiers was a career foreign-service officer who knew that his job was to execute the policies established by the president, and it was clear that proliferation was a much lower priority than prosecuting the Afghan war. "We would not have done anything to jeopardize Pakistani cooperation by taking too hard a position on the nuclear issue," he said, years later. "The administration had made a very pragmatic, though probably unarticulated, decision to keep an eye on nuclear matters, but not to do anything to jeopardize the Afghan business. Washington put it to the Pakistanis in a way that signaled, 'Don't do anything to embarrass us.' The Pakistanis probably understood this as a go-ahead."

The message was reinforced in the spring of 1981 when Reagan submitted a request to Congress for $3.2 billion in aid to Pakistan over the next six years, a dramatic escalation. The assistance was to be divided equally between economic and military assistance, including the option to buy forty F-16s, which the Pakistani Air Force had been trying to buy since the Soviet invasion of Afghanistan. Senator Alan Cranston, a liberal Democrat from California, was one of the few members of Congress who spoke out against the plan, warning that Congress was being kept in the dark about Pakistan's nuclear ambitions.

Len Weiss agreed with Cranston, but he was unable to persuade his boss to oppose the package. Like most of his colleagues, Senator Glenn proved too much the Cold Warrior and voted to open the flow of military and economic aid to Pakistan. Weiss did succeed, however, in convincing Glenn to insist that the aid package include a provision that required it be cut off if Pakistan tested a nuclear weapon. In the end, however, Congress approved what became the largest American assistance package in the world, including the F-16s and other advanced weapons. The legislation also gave the president the authority to waive the Symington and Glenn amendments for six years if he deemed doing so to be in the national interest. The action effectively removed the remaining impediment to Pakistan's nuclear efforts.

Weiss had invested enormous intellectual and emotional energy advocating a tough policy on proliferation, and he was convinced waiving the sanctions and ignoring hard evidence of Pakistan's pursuit of nuclear weapons spelled the end of Washington's attempt to be an honest broker concerning proliferation. "As a result of supporting the Afghan rebels and refusing to act against Pakistan, our credibility on nonproliferation policy was destroyed," he said.

If Zia had any lingering doubts about American tolerance of his nuclear agenda, they were resolved in December 1982 when he visited Reagan at the White House. A briefing paper prepared for Reagan pointed out that concerns remained about Pakistan's human-rights record, its opium production, and its nuclear program, but the emphasis was on maintaining close ties with Islamabad. "The fundamental aim of U.S. policy toward Pakistan today is to help this front-line nation provide for its own security and independence in the face of the threat from 100,000 Soviet troops across the border in Afghanistan and general instability in the region," said the paper.

Reagan stayed on message, telling Zia that his administration would pretend Pakistan's nuclear program did not exist, so long as the Pakistanis adhered to three main points. First, it would not actually manufacture a nuclear weapon. Second, it would not transfer nuclear technology to another country. Finally, it would not embarrass the United States by going public with its progress toward a weapon. The deal erected a convenient fiction that was to exist as long as Pakistan remained useful to the United States. In the years to come, maintaining the illusion would require hairsplitting by administration lawyers over what constituted possession of a nuclear weapon and, eventually, outright lying to Congress.

Along with the turning of a blind eye to Pakistan's nuclear ambitions, Reagan's determination to defeat the Soviets in Afghanistan led to other consequences that would one day boomerang on America. The Afghan war attracted a new breed of Islamic fighter, eager to embrace the holy war and oust the Soviets. Among them was Osama bin Laden, the son of a wealthy construction-company owner in Saudi Arabia. Bin Laden later claimed that he went to Afghanistan within two weeks of the invasion, though others said that he did not arrive until 1982. In either case, bin

Laden's operations in the first years of the war were based in the Pakistani city of Peshawar, not far from the Afghan border. From there, he recruited fighters from Saudi Arabia and other Muslim countries, providing them with cash and equipment and dispatching them to expel the Soviets and install a fundamentalist regime in Kabul. Bin Laden did not conceal his disdain for the United States because of its alliances with Israel and moderate Muslim countries, and before the end of the Afghan war the Saudi firebrand started building a new global organization dedicated to carrying the fight beyond Afghanistan to the United States.

WITH AMERICAN attention diverted, Pakistan's nuclear work went ahead at a remarkable pace. By 1981, construction was completed on the outer shell of the enrichment plant at Kahuta, and technicians were preparing the huge halls for thousands of centrifuges. In honor of the milestone, Zia attended a public dedication ceremony, and he renamed the plant the Dr. A. Q. Khan Research Laboratories. Khan basked in the glory. In the five years since his return, his achievements had gone beyond the realm of science. Since the execution of Bhutto, Khan had cultivated a close relationship with Zia that allowed him to maintain his freedom from government oversight. Like a chameleon, Khan had adopted a style of dress that amounted to protective coloration. He initially abandoned his Western suits and ties in favor of the traditional flowing pants and baggy shirts known as *shalwar kameez* worn by Bhutto and most Pakistani men. But with Zia's ascension, Khan switched to well-tailored beige safari suits. Not quite military, not quite civilian, they provided a distinctive uniform for the man who straddled both worlds. Rarely was he seen in public wearing anything else. Khan's religious coloration changed, too, under Zia. Although Khan had observed the religious prohibitions against alcohol and pork throughout his life, friends saw a new pious streak emerge as the scientist began referring to Allah in conversations and public remarks and denouncing the United States and Israel.

Though still operating in a cocoon of secrecy, Khan started courting a small group of high-level Pakistani journalists. Occasionally, he reached out to them to make a comment in the Urdu press about the progress of his work or to react to criticism of his country from the Western press. Always, he was careful to couch any reference to Pakistan's nuclear program in civilian terms.

Khan's long hours and frequent trips abroad meant he was often absent from home. His daughters were growing up without him, but the family's circumstances had improved sharply. They had moved into the grand house on Margalla Road, where the neighbors were foreign ambassadors and wealthy Pakistani businessmen. Khan's home was a gracious white building surrounded by a large yard enclosed behind a high wall, with a guard shack at the gated entrance manned twenty-four hours per day by military police. Behind the wall were fruit and flowering trees, inhabited by monkeys that Khan fed regularly, and a swimming pool where he exercised and the children played. Inside, dominating one wall of Khan's study, was a constant reminder of his past: a large painting showing red flames spewing from the last train leaving strife-torn India for the new country of Pakistan.

Khan was growing imperious at work. While he could still turn on the charms of the friendly, humble man who had seduced his colleagues in the Netherlands, workers who crossed him quickly discovered his nasty temper. More than one technician was fired for angering the boss, but those who did well and remained in his favor could count on top salaries and regular cash bonuses.

By this time, Khan had surpassed his rival, Munir Khan. The plutonium effort was still stumbling, and enrichment looked more than ever like Pakistan's quickest path to a nuclear weapon, with the huge halls of the main plant at Kahuta almost finished. A test cascade of fifty-four centrifuges set up at the pilot plant in Sihala had run smoothly, and engineers were resolving last-minute problems so Khan could give the green light to begin mass production of the machines for Kahuta. Work at related installations was progressing quickly, too. Using equipment purchased in Germany, a plant to convert uranium ore into uranium hexafluoride was being completed in Dera Ghazi Khan, adjacent to the country's only uranium mine and a mill capable of producing thirty metric tons of uranium ore per year. When the conversion plant was up and running, it could supply enough uranium gas to operate thousands of centrifuges.

While Khan concentrated on enriching uranium, scientists at the PAEC used a front company to purchase two powerful computers to conduct research on a nuclear warhead. The progress on the design worried Khan, who wanted to maintain complete control over the entire nuclear program, so he assigned a team of his own engineers to begin a secret effort to design a competing warhead, which was based on plans that he had obtained from the Chinese.

Sometime in the early 1980s British intelligence had discovered that Khan had the Chinese plans. Though the Americans were no longer pushing strict controls on sales of nuclear technology to Pakistan, the CIA and Britain's MI6 were continuing to monitor Kahuta and Khan's travels. On several occasions, agents tried to strike up conversations with him at technical conferences outside Pakistan, but they had no luck, and Khan joked to colleagues about the ineptitude of Western intelligence agencies. During one trip, however, MI6 agents broke into his hotel room and photographed the documents in his suitcase. They shipped the film to London, where nuclear experts determined that they were designs for a nuclear device tested by the Chinese in 1966. The British shared their find with the CIA.

Vernon Walters, a former CIA deputy director serving as President Reagan's roving envoy, was dispatched by Washington to confront Zia about the obvious violation of his agreement not to embarrass Reagan. Sitting opposite the Pakistani president and Munir Khan in the president's office, Walters spread copies of the drawings across a table and watched their reaction. "What is this thing that looks like anyone could have drawn?" asked Zia. Munir Khan seemed surprised, too. Walters explained what he was certain Zia already knew—that the designs were for a nuclear warhead. He warned Zia not to build the warhead or do anything else that would provoke Reagan.

PAKISTAN was not the only country trying to cloak a nuclear-weapons program in civilian clothes. About the same time that Zulfikar Ali Bhutto had launched his campaign for the bomb at Multan in 1972, Saddam Hussein had started a clandestine weapons program in Iraq. At the time,

Saddam was the country's vice president and second in command of the ruling Revolutionary Council. He recognized that building an atomic bomb would require orchestrating a grand deception to persuade the international community that his only goal was generating electricity. Iraq had been among the first signatories of the Nuclear Non-Proliferation Treaty, which entitled the country to buy advanced nuclear technology as long as it was used for civilian purposes only.

The French nuclear industry had taken the lead in helping Iraq build its first nuclear reactor at Tuwaitha, a dusty outpost ten miles southeast of Baghdad. The French called the reactor Osirak, a combination of the name of the Egyptian god of the dead, Osiris, and Iraq. Like the Indians and the Pakistanis, the Iraqis planned to reprocess the spent reactor-fuel plutonium for weapons, but the reactor also contained highly enriched uranium at its core, which could be used to manufacture a crude nuclear device. While the French may have thought the Iraqi program was civilian, the Israelis recognized it as a military effort from the start and conveyed their concerns to the French on several occasions. In the late 1970s, the Israelis persuaded the French to propose fueling the Osirak reactor with a form of low-enriched uranium, which could not be used for a weapon, but the Iraqis refused to change to their agreement. When diplomacy failed, the Israelis turned to other means.

Israeli intelligence set up a fictitious group, the Committee to Safeguard the Islamic Revolution, to send threatening letters to scientists and technicians working at Tuwaitha, but they did not stop there. Early on the morning of April 6, 1979, several Israeli demolition experts broke into a hangar operated by a French nuclear company at La Seyne-sur-Mer, near the port of Toulon, and destroyed reactor cores scheduled to be shipped to Iraq. The sabotage was attributed to a previously unknown organization, the French Ecological Group, but French intelligence suspected the sophistication of the operation meant it was carried out by Mossad, the Israeli intelligence service.

Slightly more than a year later, French intelligence again suspected Mossad of taking matters into its own hands. Yahya el-Meshad, an Egyptian-born nuclear scientist trained in the Soviet Union, had been recruited by Iraq to work in its nuclear program. On June 14, 1980, Meshad was on a trip to France to inspect work being done for Osirak. That afternoon, a chambermaid at the Paris hotel where he was staying let herself into his room, despite the "Do Not Disturb" sign that had been hanging on the door since the previous night. Inside, she found the Egyptian scientist, lying across his bed, fully clothed and bludgeoned to death. When police arrived, they determined that the only item missing was the scientist's personal diary. The sole lead appeared to be makeup smeared on a bathroom towel, and police quickly discovered that Meshad had been accompanied to his room the night before by a prostitute. The police eventually identified the prostitute as Marie Claude Magal, but when she was tracked down and questioned, she claimed that Meshad had turned her away and gone into his room alone. Magal acknowledged hearing noises inside the room as she walked away, but she insisted that they did not appear to indicate violence. A few days after her initial interrogation, the police sought Magal for additional questioning and found that she had been hit by a car and killed.

The police dismissed her death as an accident, but her mother said that her daughter had been receiving threatening telephone calls in the days before her death. The French press speculated that Israel was behind both killings, but the Israelis denied any involvement. "It's getting so that whatever happens in the Middle East, we're blamed for what we don't do as well as what we do," an official with the Israeli Foreign Office later complained.

Despite the ruined reactor cores and the dead scientist, work continued at Osirak. By the summer of 1981, the reactor was nearing completion, and two hundred pounds of enriched-uranium fuel rods were being prepared for shipment to the site as the final step before activation. Frantic diplomatic efforts by Israel to stop the shipment failed, and Mossad estimated that Iraq could possess a nuclear weapon within a year of starting the reactor. The members of the Israeli cabinet met and concluded that they had to take action.

On June 7, six of Israel's American-built F-15 and eight of its F-16 jet fighters left the runway at Etzion Air Force Base in the Negev desert, bound for Tuwaitha. The F-16s had been stripped of some of their fuel tanks so each could carry two one-ton bombs, capable of destroying the huge concrete-and-steel reactor container. The F-15s were along to provide protection for a flight that would take them through Jordanian, Saudi, and Iraqi airspace. The formation roared low over the rooftops on the southeastern edge of Baghdad, and only moments later residents heard a series of thunderous explosions from the direction of Tuwaitha. The surprise attack wiped out the Osirak reactor and destroyed several nearby buildings that were part of the complex.

It was a dramatic sabotage operation, one that risked world condemnation and possible retaliation. But the Israeli government wanted the world to see how it would treat efforts by any of its adversaries to develop a nuclear weapon. "For a long time we have been watching with growing concern the construction of the atomic reactor," said a government statement. "From sources whose reliability is beyond any doubt, we learned that this reactor, despite its camouflage, is designed to produce atomic bombs." The statement said the reactor would have been completed the following month and that the Israelis had acted before the uranium cores were installed to avoid radioactive fallout over Baghdad and other parts of the Middle East.

Reviewing satellite photos and other information on July 1, American intelligence agencies concluded that the strike had caused long-term damage to Iraq's nuclear program. "It will take Iraq several years to rebuild its nuclear facilities, even if Baghdad finds cooperative suppliers of nuclear technology," the authors wrote. Still, the Americans recognized that Saddam would not abandon his goal of becoming a nuclear-weapons power. A top-secret report by the CIA in 1983 warned that the attack had not changed Iraq's long-range nuclear ambitions. CIA analysts had not yet discovered a renewed nuclear program, but they pointed out that Baghdad had taken steps to obtain nuclear technology and material from abroad. The CIA speculated that there had been contacts between Iraq and Pakistan on nuclear matters, including the possible acquisition of equipment, but the analysts had no hard evidence of collaboration.

The destruction of Osirak heightened Khan's fears that Kahuta might be next, and he insisted that more antiaircraft batteries be installed around the perimeter of the plant. Publicly, in response to international concerns about what was happening at Kahuta, Khan replied, "The Islamic bomb is a figment of the Zionist mind."

CHAPTER 12

CRIMES AND COVER-UPS

P AKISTAN'S NUCLEAR SHOPPING SPREE reached well beyond Europe. In July 1980, two government officials were sent to Canada on diplomatic visas, which said they were there to deal with internal matters at the consulate in Montreal. When Canadian authorities reviewed the visas, they became suspicious because the men worked for the PAEC. The Canadians had been worried about Pakistan's nuclear ambitions since 1974, when the Indians diverted plutonium from their Canadian-supplied reactor for their first nuclear test. As a result, by the time the Pakistanis checked into the Queen Elizabeth Hotel in Montreal, they were under surveillance.

It took only a few days before the Canadians' suspicions were confirmed. The Royal Canadian Mounted Police watched the men enter two small electronics stores owned by fellow Pakistanis. At each location, they bought a variety of electrical components manufactured by General Electric, Westinghouse, RCA, and Motorola, including high-frequency inverters that could be used in centrifuge operations. Most of the goods required an export license, but the shops packaged them for immediate shipment to Pakistan. The police intercepted the packages. When the Pakistani consulate learned the equipment had been seized, the two men used their diplomatic immunity to get on the next plane out of Canada.

Suspecting Pakistan had not given up, police continued to keep the shops under surveillance. A month later, their patience paid off. Nineteen boxes of sophisticated electronics being prepared for shipment to Pakistan were seized, leading to the arrest of a Pakistani engineer and the owner one of the shops. When the Mounties examined records at the electronics stores, they found that ten shipments of inverters had already been shipped to Pakistan. Those records led to the arrest of a third man, Abdul Aziz Khan. Searching the engineer's home, police discovered the letters that he had received from A. Q. Khan over the years. After the letters were translated from Urdu, the authorities found the men's crude code for discussing progress at Kahuta and other nuclear installations, and they learned that Abdul Aziz Khan had sent technical literature on nuclear-related subjects to Pakistan.

Abdul Aziz Khan was released after twenty-four hours because he could not be linked directly to the shipments. From the moment he walked out the door, however, the police were on his trail, watching as he went to the city's cavernous central train station and wound his way among the shops and ticket offices before stopping at a row of lockers. He opened one of them, removed a medium-sized suitcase, and withdrew some papers. He tore the papers into pieces, threw them into a trash can, and left the station. One officer stayed behind to collect the discarded papers, and another followed the quarry to the bus terminal, where Khan boarded the airport bus. When he arrived there, police were waiting to arrest him. In his pocket they found an airline ticket to Pakistan.

Reassembling the torn pages, police found a scientific paper describing advances in uranium enrichment, written by an American government scientist. The paper was available at research libraries. Abdul Aziz Khan claimed that he knew nothing about its contents or Pakistan's nuclear industry. Still, Khan was charged with violating export laws, although when his case came to trial a few months later he continued to claim that he had no involvement with the nuclear industry and that a friend had asked him to get the inverters for a textile plant and a butter factory. The jury found that the correspondence with A. Q. Khan uncovered at Abdul Aziz Khan's home did not amount to conclusive evidence and acquitted the engineer.

The case illustrated the difficulty in prosecuting even someone caught red-handed, because of the dual civilian and military uses of the technology and the vagueness of export laws. "It does seem a bit of a laugher when you're dealing with atomic-energy materials," said Jack Waissman, one of the prosecutors. The sergeant who developed the case for the RCMP, René Garceau, said, "The whole thing was a farce."

The police had come across only a small portion of the Pakistani pipeline. Intelligence agencies, however, knew the operation was far larger. A secret analysis by MI6 conducted about the same time as Abdul Aziz Khan's arrest described how the network was set up. "It is known that Pakistan is actively engaged in the construction of gas centrifuge plants required for the production of nuclear weapons grade highly enriched uranium and in the development and construction of nuclear explosive devices," said the classified report. "To facilitate this, Pakistanis have at their disposal an effective and widespread network for the procurement overseas of equipment, components, materials and services required for these programmes. Not surprisingly, the end users, and destinations, of goods acquired through this Procurement Network are usually disguised." Fifty-one companies, organizations, and fronts were being used as false destinations for the nuclear-related goods. Among them were well-known institutions like Quaid-i-Azam University and fronts with innocuous names like Northern Traders and Punjab Fertilizer Company.

Despite the subterfuge, there were other opportunities to stop the supply chain. In one case, an American was charged with trying to ship a specialized metal used in nuclear installations to Pakistan. In another, a retired Pakistani army colonel described by authorities as a friend of President Zia's was accused of shipping restricted high-tech goods. In neither case did the American government lodge a protest with Pakistan. The "don't ask, don't tell" policy adopted at the start of the Afghan war was holding firm, though one episode threatened to blow the lid off the charade.

That case involved krytrons, which are inch-long cathode tubes developed as specialized high-speed switches for radar transmitters during World War II. The gas-filled devices turn extremely high voltages of electric current into a precise burst as short as one millionth of a second. The precision is essential to detonate a nuclear device, which relies on the simultaneous triggering of conventional explosives to unleash the critical mass of fissile material that leads to an atomic explosion. The tubes have limited civilian uses, and their essential role in nuclear weapons means that all exports require a government license, and each prospective sale is reviewed by the State Department.

In the early 1980s, the Pakistanis had reached the critical point at which tests of their warhead design required a supply of krytrons, but the only company that manufactured them was the EG&G Corporation in Salem, Massachusetts. The attempt to get the krytrons was scarcely the stuff of James Bond. A Pakistani living in Houston named Nazir Ahmed Vaid had recently purchased a number of unregulated chemicals for the PAEC when he was asked to buy fifty krytrons by Siddique Butt, who had abandoned his diplomatic cover in Europe and returned home to continue his work. On October 18, 1983, Vaid walked into the EG&G offices dressed in traditional Pakistani garb. He said he was in the import-export business in Houston and Pakistan, and he wanted to place an order for fifty krytrons for Quaid-i-Azam University. Company officials were surprised and suspicious. No one had ever tried to buy these sophisticated devices over the counter, and the size of the order was unusual—the few businesses that use krytrons for civilian purposes need only a handful over the course of a year. When told that he needed an export license for the four thousand dollar order, Vaid asked the company to prepare the proper paperwork and said he would return when the krytrons were ready.

EG&G officials contacted the Federal Bureau of Investigation. The FBI lacked jurisdiction, so the matter was turned over to the U.S. Customs Service. Agents from the Customs Service criminal-investigations division recognized the potential danger and set up a sting, telling EG&G officials to wait for Vaid to make contact again. When he called ten days later to check on the export license, Vaid was told that there would be a slight delay. Impatient and suddenly wary, he canceled the order.

Customs thought they'd lost their prey, until October 31, when Vaid showed up at a small electrical-supply shop in Houston and placed a new order for krytrons. Presumably in hopes of avoiding scrutiny, he described the item only by its catalog number, KN 22, and specified that he intended to use them within the United States. Store owner Jerry Simon telephoned EG&G to place the large order and was told that it would take about six months to manufacture the krytrons. When Simon relayed the news, Vaid said he had to go to Pakistan on business in the interim and would pick up the devices when he got back.

A second order for fifty krytrons in such a short period raised a red flag at EG&G, and company officials alerted the team from Customs. Customs agents approached Simon, who agreed to cooperate with a sting. When the krytrons arrived in April 1984, Vaid was still in Pakistan, but he got Simon's message and relayed instructions to deliver them to a photocopying shop operated by a relative of Vaid's. The deliveryman was an undercover customs agent, and the shop was placed under surveillance while the authorities waited for Vaid to return for the devices. Because possession of the devices domestically was not illegal, they would have to catch Vaid in the act of shipping the krytrons overseas. On June 22, three days after returning to Houston, Vaid appeared at the store and arranged to ship the tubes to Pakistan. The bill of lading identified the contents as office products, including "50 bulbs/switches." An agent posing as a deliveryman picked up the sealed package at the photocopy shop and took it to the customs office. Opening the box, agents found the krytrons. A customs team went to Vaid's Houston office and arrested him. In a briefcase confiscated at the office, agents found telexes indicating that Vaid intended to ship the krytrons to two people in Pakistan associated with the country's nuclear program, Siddique Butt and an army colonel. Other documents showed that Vaid had made other purchases on behalf of the nuclear project.

At a federal court hearing six days later, prosecutor Samuel Longoria told the magistrate that the krytrons had a direct use in nuclear munitions and that Vaid appeared to be a Pakistani agent. "We strongly suspect that Mr. Vaid is operating at the instance of the Pakistani government and that the purpose of the export of these krytrons was specifically for the Pakistani government's use in obtaining a nuclear weapon," he said. "The allegations in this complaint are not simply technical violations of United States export laws. The Department of State has serious concern regarding the nature and direction of Pakistan's nuclear program." The next month, a federal grand jury charged Vaid and two accomplices from the photocopy shop with conspiring to ship krytrons overseas without a license, specifying that they were "part of a firing set for a nuclear explosive device."

The case appeared to be a clear example of Pakistan's nuclear intentions and its willingness to flout U.S. law. In the months that followed, however, the case took a strange turn. Federal prosecutors mysteriously agreed to rewrite the indictment, removing references to nuclear weapons and Vaid's role as a Pakistani agent. In addition, the judge handling the case issued a gag order on everyone involved. Both developments were so unusual that Vaid's own lawyer, William Burge, was surprised. He said he did not understand the government's actions but assumed that the changes were orchestrated because Pakistan was an American ally. "The case apparently was embarrassing to the Government of Pakistan and they didn't want any more publicity than was necessary," said Burge.

Vaid agreed to plead guilty to a single count. He still faced up to twelve years in prison, but the judge gave Vaid a two-year suspended sentence and ordered him deported to Pakistan. The judge took the trouble to underscore the innocent nature of the attempt to export the krytrons, saying at sentencing that he was "left with the impression that this man was not acting in any capacity as an enemy agent. He apparently had no malicious intent beyond trying to expedite what he thought was a business deal and trying to accommodate a customer and in doing so made a false report."

The Pakistani government had been busted, but the damning elements of the case were erased from the record. The concealment allowed the Reagan administration to maintain the fiction that Pakistan was not pursuing a nuclear weapon and kept American financial and military assistance flowing through Pakistani intelligence to the Muslim fighters in Afghanistan. After whitewashing the public record, Reagan sent Zia a top-secret letter warning him not to enrich uranium beyond 5 percent, the level that could be used in civilian power-generating plants. Exceeding 5 percent, Reagan said, would constitute crossing a "red line" and jeopardize the relationship between the two countries. Zia responded by promising not to go beyond the limit and repeating his assurance that Pakistan's nuclear program was purely civilian.

By this time the CIA had a nearly complete picture of what was going on and dutifully reported it to policymakers in Washington. Deane Hinton, who had replaced Spiers as the American ambassador in Islamabad, spelled out the scope of the intelligence findings in late 1984 in a classified evaluation of Howard Hart, who was leaving Islamabad after serving as CIA station chief since 1981. As a young man, Hart had chosen the CIA over the Marines, but he retained a fascination with weaponry that made him the perfect person to oversee the supplying of guns and training for the Afghan *mujahideen*. Hart also paid attention to Pakistan's nuclear efforts. Hinton wrote: "His collection efforts on the Pakistani effort to develop nuclear weapons is amazingly successful and disturbing. I would sleep better if he and his people did not find out so much about what is really going on in secret and contrary to President Zia's assurances to us." Yet the evidence provoked no action. In November, Richard Kennedy, the American ambassador at large for nonproliferation, gave an interview to the Pakistani press in which he publicly reassured the Pakistanis that Washington had no intention of confronting them. "We accept President Zia ul-Haq's statement that Pakistan's nuclear program is devoted entirely to power generation," he said.

Short of actually detonating a nuclear weapon, there seemed to be nothing that Pakistan could do to provoke sanctions from the Reagan administration. In fact, Munir Khan later said the warnings from American diplomats over the years had no effect on the country's plans, save that they disclosed how much the Americans knew about what Pakistan was doing. The gap between what Washington knew and its public statements was growing larger, yet the Reagan administration accepted this act of geopolitical expedience.

THE AMERICANS may have backed off, but A. Q. Khan was facing legal troubles of his own. The press reports about his thefts from Urenco had finally forced the Dutch government to dig into its own dirty laundry. A team of investigators questioned officials and workers at FDO and Almelo about Khan's activities and examined evidence of the network's purchases of nuclear-related technology from Dutch and German firms. The inquiry was by no means exhaustive, but the results painted a sorry picture of security at FDO and Almelo and pointed an accusatory finger at Khan. "Although there is no conclusive proof . . . it seems reasonable to assume that through Dr. Khan, Pakistan has been able to obtain possession of essential gas centrifuge know-how, which could mean a considerable time saving," said a declassified version of the Dutch report. "According to information from reliable sources, Pakistan now possesses a pilot installation with a very small enrichment capacity."

In 1982, prosecutors charged Khan with stealing classified information. From the start, the case was weak. Not even Frits Veerman could say conclusively that he had seen Khan take classified material from FDO or Almelo because he had not looked closely at the documents he had seen at Khan's home. Instead, the charges relied on two letters that Khan had written after his return to Pakistan, seeking classified information about centrifuge components. The Dutch government tried to serve court papers on Khan by delivering the summons to the Pakistani Foreign Office in Islamabad. A month later, the Foreign Office returned the undelivered summons to the Dutch embassy, saying that Khan could not travel because of national-security concerns related to his work. And yet Khan continued to travel extensively to other countries and even made a couple of clandestine visits to his relatives in the Netherlands.

The Dutch put Khan on trial in absentia, beginning on November 14, 1983. Khan said later that he did not learn of the charges against him until three days before the trial started, when Henk Slebos arrived in Islamabad with a copy of an Amsterdam newspaper that contained a story about the proceedings. Khan said that he sent a telegram to the Dutch authorities, explaining that he had not been notified of the charges or the trial and asking for a delay. Despite his protest, the trial went forward, and Khan was convicted and sentenced to four years in prison.

Khan later railed to his biographer that the proceedings were rigged against him. "This court was comprised of three judges, and was presided over by a woman who was a Jew," Khan said. "Another of the judges was also a Jew. It looked as if the court was presided over by the Israeli prime minister and its verdict written in Tel Aviv."

The conviction was a blow. The notion that he had stolen the plans contradicted his self-created image as a scientist whose brilliance and innovation were leading Pakistan into the nuclear elite. He hired lawyers in the Netherlands to appeal his conviction and was so determined to clear his name that he started his own search for information that he believed would exonerate him. Eventually, he located a reference to an academic article that he thought would buttress his case that the information he sought from Veerman was available to the general public, but when he tried to get a copy of the article from the library of the PAEC, he found his access blocked: His old rival Munir Khan had ordered his agency to withhold any support from A. Q. Khan because his actions had embarrassed the government and endangered the weapons program.

Khan returned home that night in a rage, berating Munir Khan and others in the Pakistani nuclear establishment for jealously attempting to thwart him. Henny had never seen her husband so angry. "I would never have imagined that this sort of thing could happen to you," she told him. "Perhaps we should pack up and go back to Holland." The suggestion was naïve at best and an indication that Henny was not fully aware of what her husband had done in Amsterdam or what he was doing at Kahuta. Khan knew going back meant the possibility of prison, so he decided to find another way to clear his reputation.

IN JULY 1982, Bob Gallucci was at the State Department's Bureau of Intelligence and Research when he wrote a top-secret memo outlining the ways in which Pakistan had violated the three-pronged agreement it had reached with the Reagan administration to stop work on a nuclear weapon. "It was the best memo of my life," Gallucci recalled with some pride. "It was the only top-secret memo I ever originated. I never saw it again after I sent it off." More than two decades later, however, he still remembered the main points. Zia and his government, he had written, had crossed all three red lines drawn by the administration when it approved the $3.2 billion aid package in 1981. "We said that you will not manufacture nuclear weapons, you will not transfer nuclear technology, and you will not embarrass the president over this issue," said Gallucci. Pakistan was violating all three provisions, regularly and routinely.

The following year, Gallucci and his staff prepared a twelve-page report that was both blunt and thorough in assessing Pakistan's nuclear program and Khan's critical role. "There is unambiguous evidence that Pakistan is actively pursuing a nuclear weapons development program," said the opening paragraph. "Pakistan's near-term goal is evidently to have a nuclear test capability, enabling it to explode a nuclear device if Zia decides it's appropriate for diplomatic and domestic political gains. Pakistan's long-term goal is to establish a nuclear deterrent to aggression by India, which remains Pakistan's greatest security concern." The report said the plutonium and uranium-enrichment projects were having technical difficulties but predicted that both operations would ultimately succeed. Khan's clandestine activities were described in varying amounts of detail, from his theft of plans from Urenco to his reliance on the pipeline. The report said Kahuta was too large for only research and development and pointed out that the IAEA was forbidden to enter the complex. "We believe the ultimate application of the enriched uranium produced at Kahuta, which is unsafeguarded, is clearly nuclear weapons," it said. Kahuta would produce enough highly enriched uranium for Pakistan's first atomic bomb within two to three years, according to the report's calculations, and it would eventually turn out enough highly enriched uranium for several devices per year.

A secret CIA report dated May 20, 1983, also confirmed that Pakistan was on course to develop a nuclear weapon. "In our view, Zia and his advisers continue to believe that they must acquire nuclear weapons," said the CIA analysis. "We have detected continuation of longstanding efforts to acquire components for nuclear devices."

The CIA and the State Department delivered the truth about Pakistan to President Reagan and his advisers, who chose to ignore it in favor of routing the Soviets in Afghanistan.

Pakistan's desire for a nuclear arsenal was intended to deter India, but deterrence does not work if no one knows you have the bomb. For several years, some elements within the ISI had argued for orchestrated leaks to let the Indians know that Pakistan had gone nuclear, too. In early 1984, Zia and his military advisers decided that a little boasting was in order, and Khan was chosen as the messenger. In February, Khan gave an interview to an Urdu-language newspaper in which he bragged about his work.

"By the grace of God, Pakistan is now among the few countries in the world that can efficiently enrich uranium," he said. Asked specifically if Pakistan could manufacture an atomic bomb, the scientist said: "In brief, Pakistan has a proficient and patriotic team capable of performing the most difficult tasks. Forty years ago no one was familiar with the secrets of the atom bomb and education was not so widespread, but American scientists did the job. Today, 40 years later, we have ended their monopoly in this most difficult field of the enrichment of uranium in only 10 years. This job is undoubtedly not beyond our reach." In an article published in the same newspaper the following day, Khan went further, suggesting that Pakistan could achieve nuclear capability without an actual test by conducting experiments and nonnuclear explosions.

Pakistan's small English-language press operated with a certain amount of freedom because its readership was restricted to the educated elite and foreigners, but the government maintained tight control over the Urdu press because it reached the masses. The intelligence agency had helped set up Khan's interview on the assumption that its distribution would be restricted to the Urdu press, which was monitored by Indian intelligence. What the Pakistanis had not counted on was that the news would spill over into the English-language press not only in Pakistan but worldwide. When Khan's assertion reached foreign capitals, it created a furor that forced Zia to call a press conference to try to avoid antagonizing or embarrassing the Reagan administration further. "Pakistan has acquired very modest research and development capability of uranium enrichment . . . for peaceful purposes," he said, contradicting his own senior nuclear scientist.

The denial did not stop some U.S. congressmen from calling attention to the wealth of information attesting to Pakistan's push toward the bomb. On June 20, 1984, Senator Cranston took to the Senate floor and delivered a blistering and prescient attack on Pakistan and the Reagan administration. He said government officials had told him that Pakistan could turn out at least a dozen atomic weapons within the next three to five years, setting the stage for nuclear war with India. The program, he said, had been subsidized with American finances and misrepresented by the Reagan administration. Cranston warned that Khan and other

Pakistani scientists could turn the country into a distribution point for nuclear technology, sharing it with other Muslim countries, such as Saudi Arabia, Iran, and Libya. Cranston put his finger on the central dilemma. "As with India and Israel, we may never be able to say exactly when it was that Pakistan crossed the threshold to achieve a nuclear-weapons capability, or exactly how many bombs they might have in hand at a given time," he said. "The point is that they now have what they need to produce their own nuclear weapons."

LEN WEISS worked closely with Cranston's staff on proliferation legislation and listened to the senator's speech with the knowledge that the charges were true. A recent classified briefing from the CIA had escalated his worries about Pakistan and the potential for nuclear war on the subcontinent. U.S. intelligence had learned that Pakistan was planning to retrofit its F-16s to carry nuclear weapons, and Pakistani pilots were learning the "dive-and-drop" maneuvers necessary to release nuclear payloads and escape the ensuing fireball. At the same time, senior Pentagon officials were telling Congress exactly the opposite in public sessions and closed briefings. The military officers said that F-16s could not be equipped to deliver nuclear weapons. The discrepancy was critical because India and its chief ally, the Soviet Union, would erupt if they discovered that Pakistan was outfitting American-supplied aircraft thus.

Weiss had limited means of determining who was telling the truth, though he was certain Congress was not getting the whole story. After eight years on Capitol Hill, Weiss recognized that little could be done to change the administration's policy as long as the Soviets remained in Afghanistan. Still, the mounting lies ate at him. "This is part of a pattern of clear-cut examples of where the government of Pakistan was in violation of the law and the United States didn't do anything about it," he said. "It is not an intelligence failure. It is a policy failure. They knew but refused to act on it because they had a more important agenda when it came to the Pakistanis."

Someone else in Washington had noticed the pattern, too. Richard Barlow was a newly minted CIA analyst whose job was to monitor and assess sensitive diplomatic information and top-secret intelligence reports, to determine which countries were trying to develop nuclear weapons. One of the blips looming on his radar was Pakistan and, though he was new in his job, he was not a neophyte when it came to the Pakistanis. In his senior honors thesis at Western Washington University in 1980, Barlow had used press and academic articles and testimony from congressional hearings to conclude that Pakistan was acquiring the knowledge and technology for a nuclear-weapons program with little interference from the U.S. government. "The failure of the government to prevent such clandestine activities, indeed to even provide the equipment for them, would seem to indicate an intelligence failure of major proportions or a failure of capability," the young student wrote. "In fact, Pakistan's success was neither. It was a clear cut failure of policy perpetuated by the consumers of intelligence, not intelligence staff."

But Barlow was in the real world now, and he was about to plunge into the treacherous gap between those who collect intelligence and those who twist it to suit their own purposes.

CHAPTER 13

NUCLEAR AMBIGUITY

THE SON AND GRANDSON of New York City surgeons, Rich Barlow exhibited an independent streak in his teenage years. When he graduated from the elite Ethical Culture School in New York in the early 1970s, Barlow was the only member of his class who refused to go to college immediately, preferring to work for a collection agency and later as assistant manager of a bicycle store. His goal was to get out of New York City, and in 1976 he enrolled in Western Washington University in Bellingham. His father tried to insist that Barlow carry on the family's medical tradition, and in a compromise the young rebel agreed to major in science. Barlow struggled with the courses and soon switched to political science and international relations, where he turned out to be a stellar student.

Nuclear power caught his eye in 1977 when the State of Washington was embroiled in a controversy over plans to develop several nuclear plants to generate electricity. Barlow got a summer internship in the local congressman's office and, in a brazen move, used the position to get in touch with a senior military-intelligence official in Washington, D.C., for help on his senior thesis about the relationship between intelligence gathering and proliferation policy. "The general was amused to be questioned by a kid," Barlow said later. "But he still gave me valuable tidbits about Pakistan."

The experience shaped Barlow's future both in terms of his professional interests and his determination to use unconventional means to get to the bottom of an issue. His thesis earned an A and appeared to reflect a deeper knowledge of the dangers of proliferation than that of the average member of Congress. After graduating in 1980, Barlow used contacts in Washington to get an internship with the Arms Control and Disarmament Agency. The agency had been established in 1961 primarily to negotiate treaties with the Soviets on banning nuclear tests and chemical and biological weapons, but over the years its mission had expanded to cover broader aspects of proliferation policy. Barlow worked days at the agency as an intelligence officer specializing in Pakistan and attended graduate school at Georgetown University at night. When the internship ended, Barlow had developed enough expertise on proliferation and Pakistan that he was offered a full-time job. Before Barlow got through the probationary period, however, President Reagan put the agency on his hit list, and Barlow's position was eliminated.

Not sure of his next step, Barlow moved to a small town in Connecticut with his college sweetheart, Cindy, and took a series of odd jobs, such as mucking out horse barns and working as a butcher in a supermarket. He got married in 1983 and returned to Bellingham a short time later, where he took another job that did not reflect his real interests: advertising copywriter. That's where he was in 1984 when he got an unexpected telephone call from a man who identified himself as a recruiter for the CIA. Barlow jumped at the chance, and a few days later he received a plain envelope containing a formal inquiry from the CIA about his willingness to sign up. The weeks and months that followed were a crash course in how the nation's intelligence service vets a potential agent. Barlow had a series of clandestine meetings with anonymous case officers at hotels in and around Bellingham and answered earnestly as they probed his background and his motivation for joining the agency. He was, he told them, a patriot who was worried deeply about the threat of nuclear proliferation. Eventually, he flew to Washington for a series of psychological examinations and polygraph tests. Finally, he was offered a job with the CIA in 1985.

Barlow seemed a perfect fit for the role of undercover agent. Slender and handsome, with light-brown hair and an easy banter, he has the ability to put people at ease in any situation. His new employers considered training him as a case officer within its directorate of operations. The D.O., as it is called, was the covert arm of the CIA, and its members were the agency's core, men and women responsible for collecting foreign intelligence through classic spying operations. They operated in the field, often developing disdain for the analysts, many of whom sit safely behind desks in the CIA's sprawling campuslike headquarters in Langley, Virginia. But Barlow's knowledge of proliferation led him to the analytical side of the shop, where he was assigned to the agency's directorate of intelligence, the analytical arm. Its mission is to provide timely, accurate, and objective analysis of national-security threats and foreign-policy issues facing the United States. Barlow went to work initially in the office of global issues, which monitored proliferation and a host of other security matters. His job was to cover an area with which he was already familiar: the nuclear-proliferation threat from Pakistan. As it turned out, the time he had spent studying chemistry and physics in college served him well, as he underwent training in nuclear technology at the national weapons laboratories and developed an expertise in the scientific aspects of atomic weapons. He received security clearances that entitled him to see some of the most secret information the country possessed. His job was to digest the sensitive diplomatic and intelligence reports from the field and develop the most accurate assessment possible of Pakistan's nuclear capabilities.

Barlow stood out early as an analyst because of his ability to absorb vast amounts of complex data and produce a cogent analysis of what they meant for operational use. He was an activist in a field where many were passive readers. "He brought the agency a unique skill," said Richard Kerr, who was the CIA associate deputy director for intelligence when Barlow arrived at the agency. "He was an investigative analyst. It was a different kind of skill from the kind we had historically used." He was soon moved to the elite office of scientific and weapons research, which housed the CIA's technical experts.

Like others who had seen the intelligence coming out of Pakistan, Barlow recognized that there was no doubt about the country's nuclear intentions. At the same time, he realized that a policy decision had been made at the highest levels not to stop the Pakistanis. Sifting through old files and examining new reports from field agents and diplomats in Europe and Pakistan, Barlow found that the CIA had penetrated the Pakistani nuclear establishment so thoroughly that it possessed the floor plans for A. Q. Khan's giant enrichment complex at Kahuta. A former senior CIA officer who served in Pakistan during that period said the agency had cultivated a nuclear scientist with access to Kahuta and other installations that were part of the nuclear complex. On December 10, 1984, the CIA knew within hours that Khan had written a letter to President Zia boasting that he had enough weapons-grade uranium for at least one atomic device. The level of enrichment far exceeded the 5 percent "red line" established by President Reagan. In fact, a short time later the CIA estimated that Pakistan had enriched uranium to 93.5 percent, well into the weapons-grade realm.

Barlow was astounded: His senior thesis, based mostly on publicly available information and the few tidbits he'd picked up elsewhere, was dead-on. While a graduate student at Georgetown in 1981, he had written a paper exploring the ideological basis for possessing a nuclear weapon within Islam. Eager to make his name and publicize his theory, he drafted a paper that combined his earlier research with classified material and sought permission to publish internally for government policymakers. His CIA supervisors turned him down, telling Barlow, "Your paper would be too insulting to our friends."

It was no time to insult the Pakistanis. The Reagan administration was pouring enormous resources into Afghanistan through Pakistan, a total that was to reach three billion dollars before the end of the covert war against the Soviets. While every CIA station chief in Islamabad since the middle 1970s had made it a priority to gather intelligence on Pakistan's nuclear program, the main priority now was managing the war next door. Of the dozen or so CIA agents in the Pakistani capital in those days, only two were assigned to the nuclear portfolio. One was an attractive woman whose specialty was extracting critical information from male scientists.

Still, the CIA penetration was so complete and its information was so good that in late 1984 the agency showed a scale model of the Pakistani bomb to the country's foreign minister, Sahabzada Yaqub Khan, during a visit of his to Washington. The model had been built for the CIA's office of scientific and weapons research, with help from scientists at the Livermore lab. "We knew more about that bomb than any other bomb in the world except the Brits', which we helped build," said a former senior CIA officer. "Our intelligence was absolutely solid. The point of showing them the model was to let them know that we were on top of it. There was never any doubt that they were going nuclear."

The two sides were playing a cat-and-mouse game: The Pakistanis knew their nuclear program had been compromised, but they recognized that they could proceed as long as Washington needed their help in Afghanistan. Yet the CIA remained determined to gather as much solid intelligence as possible, even though official policy was to deny the existence of a nuclear-weapons project in Pakistan.

No one understood the gamesmanship better than Milt Bearden, a CIA veteran who replaced Howard Hart as Islamabad station chief. Bearden had joined the CIA in 1964 after serving in the U.S. Air Force, and he was part of a generation of spies who came of age in the shadow of the Cuban missile crisis. For those who rose through the ranks of the CIA in the last years of the Cold War, the war in Afghanistan was the supreme battle. William Casey, Reagan's CIA director, had personally dispatched Bearden to Islamabad to oversee the massive escalation of American aid to the Arabs battling the Soviets. But his father had worked on the Manhattan Project, so Bearden also understood the basics of nuclear weapons and the danger they represented in the hands of a country like Pakistan.

Not long after the demonstration with the model bomb in Washington, a delegation of senior American intelligence officials arrived in Islamabad, and Bearden took them to dinner with President Zia at the Army House in Rawalpindi, where Zia still maintained his headquarters. After the meal, as they were having tea, Zia told the Americans a story that he characterized as a fable. "There was a lonely woodsman walking through the woods one day not far from here, near a place called Kahuta. He was walking down a lonely road when he stopped by a stone and sat down. He was carrying an axe and decided that he would use the stone to sharpen the blade of his axe. But when the woodsman began to sharpen the blade, lo and behold, the stone began to crumble under the strokes of the axe. This was indeed surprising and so the woodsman took the stone to his village elders. They opened it and found that it was full of sensing equipment the likes of which had never been seen before in Pakistan. The woodsman's friends sent the stone to their Chinese friends and the Chinese said, 'This is very good stuff.' "

Bearden loved the story and was determined not to show any surprise that one of his listening devices had been discovered. "After the Chinese are finished, if you give me the stone I will send it to Washington for examination," he said, eliciting laughter.

THE STORYTELLING could last only as long as the fiction was maintained that Pakistan wasn't really working on a nuclear bomb. The truth needed to be concealed not just from the public but from Congress. So while the CIA reported the hard facts and intelligence back to successive administrations in Washington, the full story of Pakistan's bomb efforts and its violations of American export law were kept from Congress for fear of provoking a cutoff in assistance to Pakistan that would jeopardize the effort in Afghanistan.

On February 25, 1985, the truth emerged, if only for a brief moment in the sunshine. Seymour Hersh, an investigative reporter, wrote a front-page article in *The New York Times* exposing the connections between the krytron case and the Pakistani government. Hersh revealed that Vaid had possessed letters linking him to Siddique Butt and the Pakistani procurement effort and recounted how federal prosecutors had concealed the nature of the case. Justice Department officials denied the charge, and Pakistan's ambassador in Washington claimed that his country was not pursuing the bomb. A State Department official told Hersh that he realized the case looked like a "grand fix," but maintained that it was in fact mere bureaucratic bungling and miscommunication.

Hersh's revelation angered Stephen Solarz, a powerful Democratic congressman from New York and chairman of the House subcommittee with responsibility for India and Pakistan. The prospect of American goods fueling an arms race alarmed Solarz, and he set up a hearing before his subcommittee to explore the issue. Solarz appeared ready to start a fight aimed at cutting off aid to Pakistan, which was coming up for congressional renewal at the time. "A Pakistani agent had been caught illegally buying American technology and I took a dim view of Pakistan's effort to get nuclear weapons," Solarz said later. "A few people were arguing that it would be an Islamic bomb and that Pakistan would make it available to other countries. That seemed hyperbolic to me. I just thought it would be very destabilizing for the Subcontinent."

After lobbying by the CIA and some of his more moderate congressional colleagues, Solarz backed down. But he remained determined to impose tougher conditions, so he began crafting an amendment that would cut off assistance to any country caught trying to illegally import any type of American technology to enrich uranium or reprocess spent fuel into plutonium. He also proposed to cut off aid to Pakistan, should it detonate a nuclear device. At the same time, Senator Larry Pressler, a Republican from North Dakota, was drawing up a measure that would end American military and economic assistance to any country that possessed a nuclear weapon except for the five nations approved under the nonproliferation treaty. Like Solarz, Pressler was frustrated by what he saw as the failure of the administration and the intelligence community to tell the truth about Pakistan's nuclear program. As a member of the Foreign Relations Committee, he had received numerous classified briefings that downplayed Pakistan's nuclear ambitions, a sharp contradiction with information in the press. "The briefings were as political as talking to the Democratic or Republican National Committee," Pressler said. "We even mentioned Khan by name, and they said our information about his activities was all wrong. They would say, 'We don't believe reports by the BBC or *New York Times* are credible.' It's very hard for a congressman or senator to get at the truth of this. I said Pakistan was working on a nuclear bomb, and I kept getting the same answer from the CIA—'No, I was wrong.' "

Congress passed the Solarz and Pressler amendments, and they were signed into law on August 8. Shortly before final action in Congress, Solarz had agreed to tack on a provision that amounted to a giant loophole by giving the president the right to waive sanctions if he determined doing so was in the American national interest. Like earlier such legislation, the new laws had little impact. Reagan interpreted the possession of a nuclear explosive device in the most liberal and literal means, certifying each year that Pakistan had not violated American laws. "We knew they were almost completely finished with the bomb," Bearden said. "All they had to do was turn a screw and paint B-O-M-B on the side."

In his colloquial manner, Bearden distilled the convoluted legal interpretation by State Department lawyers used to justify continued aid for Pakistan. In one key memo to the department's chief legal adviser, government lawyers said the gap between possession and nonpossession was a narrow one, open to interpretation. "If a country has made a policy decision to halt development of its capabilities two days short of having everything in place to possess a nuclear explosive device, it would seem inappropriate to determine that they did not possess such a device," said the memo. "If the country had decided to stop its development one year short of completion, it would seem inappropriate to determine that it did possess such a device." The lawyers went even further, torturing legal logic enough to give Reagan an out if he certified that Pakistan did not possess a nuclear device yet was later proven wrong. Certification was not a guarantee of the truth, they said, and if the president acted in good faith, he was not breaking the law.

NEAR the end of 1985, Rich Barlow was sitting in his office going through files when he came across a State Department cable mentioning that a California couple, Arnold and Rona Mandel, had exported dozens of high-speed cameras and oscilloscopes to Hong Kong. Barlow knew that the equipment was widely used in nuclear programs to calibrate the compression of explosives at a weapon's core, so he began tracking the exports through various databases and CIA reports. Eventually, he found a CIA cable identifying the Hong Kong purchaser as a front company for Pakistan's nuclear program. The transaction seemed to fit into a pattern that Barlow had been seeing in raw intelligence reports about Pakistan's purchases and its nuclear progress, and he was eager to see how far he could follow the trail. Most CIA analysts would have filed the information internally, but Barlow sought permission to take the unusual step of sharing the information with the Justice Department and the Commerce Department. The prosecutors and export officials were surprised to be getting help from the CIA, but they grew enthusiastic as Barlow briefed them on the technology and the relationship between the purchaser and Pakistan's nuclear agency, the PAEC.

An enforcement agent at Customs had discovered that the Mandels had shipped $1.8 million in oscilloscopes and other nuclear-related technology to Pakistan via Hong Kong, but he had been unable to interest prosecutors in the case. Working with the agent, Barlow identified the implications of the shipments and linked them directly to Pakistan's nuclear program. After he briefed senior prosecutors in California and Washington, a criminal investigation was started by the FBI. The Mandels did not have the required export licenses from the Commerce Department for the fifteen shipments; they had merely written Commerce Department license application numbers on various forms, and the banks and shippers had sent the goods on their way. Eventually, the Mandels pleaded guilty to felony charges and were sentenced to prison terms. Few noticed that the shipments had been financed by the Bank of Credit and Commerce International, a little-known financial institution with its headquarters in London.

The successful investigation was a small but important step in breaking down the turf lines between agencies to develop a comprehensive, governmentwide strategy to combat proliferation. Barlow had demonstrated the potential effectiveness of interagency cooperation, and the result was the creation of a new group that brought together experts from the Justice Department, State Department, Customs Service, Energy Department, National Security Agency, and the CIA. It was called the Nuclear Export Violations Working Group, and Barlow was assigned to represent the CIA in it. It didn't take long for the group to find enough information to conclude that roughly 90 percent of the nuclear technology being purchased illegally in the United States was going to Pakistan, sometimes directly and sometimes through an elaborate maze of front companies.

The discovery led the group to undertake a coordinated effort to disrupt the Pakistani procurement network. When the State Department representative reported back to headquarters about the prospective campaign, alarm bells went off in the Near East and South Asia Affairs Bureau, which was responsible for relations with Pakistan and protective of the U.S.-Pakistan alliance. The big concern was that a barrage of criminal cases would trigger sanctions. The conflict between enforcing the law and disrupting diplomatic relations illustrated the inherent conflict that often found the State Department defending the suspect practices of foreign countries in order to maintain good ties and political influence. When it came to looking the other way on Pakistan's nuclear-weapons development, the striped suits at Foggy Bottom had plenty of company from the Pentagon, the White House, and influential authorities at the CIA, including Bill Casey.

Barlow felt like he had found his calling at the CIA, where he loved the challenge of deciphering the patterns of proliferation. He also recognized that the Reagan administration placed a higher priority on removing the Soviets from Afghanistan than on stopping Pakistan's march toward the bomb and enforcing the law. He just wanted the administration to come clean with Congress and explain its reasoning. "The White House should have gone to Congress and said that you can't have it both ways," he said. "If you want us to continue the war with the Russians, then change the law. That's how they started lying to Congress. They didn't want to risk losing. Proliferation was a big issue, and with the Democrats in control of Congress the administration could have lost the argument and been forced to cut its ties with the Zia regime."

The working group was hobbled but not stopped, so that when another attempt by Pakistan to obtain restricted American technology surfaced near the end of 1986, Barlow found himself working again with other government agencies. This time, a Pakistani-born Canadian had contacted a Pennsylvania company about purchasing maraging steel. The telephone call set in play a series of moves that led Barlow into the heart of a major undercover operation.

In December 1986, a man named Arshad Pervez had telephoned the international marketing manager for Carpenter Technology Corporation in Reading, Pennsylvania, saying he wanted to purchase twenty-five tons of specially strengthened maraging steel, which was used almost exclusively in nuclear facilities and was tightly controlled by U.S. export laws. The Carpenter sales manager, Albert Tomley, contacted the Department of Energy in Washington, which passed the tip on to Barlow, who informed the nuclear-export working group. The decision was made to set up another sting operation. With the steel company's help, a customs agent would pose as a salesman; Barlow was tapped to provide the undercover agent, John New, with enough technical information to play his role convincingly.

New spoke on the telephone with Pervez several times and met with him at restaurants and hotels in Toronto, where the Pakistani ran an import-export business. Pervez was surprisingly forthcoming, explaining that his client for the steel was a retired Pakistani army general, Inam ul-Haq. Pervez offered several explanations for why ul-Haq wanted the extremely strong steel, saying at various times that they planned to use it in Pakistan's space program or in the manufacture of high-speed turbines and compressors for commercial purposes. The explanations rang hollow with Barlow and his colleagues. The strength of the steel would allow Pakistan to produce rotors for the centrifuges with extremely thin walls, enabling them to spin with a speed and balance equivalent to flying a 747 ten feet off the ground. The quantity of steel signaled a major expansion of Pakistan's enrichment plant. The American government had blocked an earlier attempt by Pakistani agents to buy a similar type of steel—obtaining enough to ramp up production of the more efficient centrifuges had emerged as a major choke point in Pakistan's enrichment process.

The mention of ul-Haq's name had confirmed suspicions that the Pakistani government was involved in the purchase because the CIA had a thick file on the retired officer's involvement with Khan's procurement ring in Canada and Europe. "There is no doubt this stuff is going to Khan's enrichment plant at Kahuta," Barlow told the customs agents. "This is the clincher."

The investigators needed to catch Pervez and ul-Haq in the act, and they worried that the State Department might alert the Pakistani government if it learned of the undercover operation. Barlow and the customs agents met secretly with Fred McGoldrick, director of the State Department's office for nuclear nonproliferation and chief of the working group, to express their concerns. He promised the investigation would remain confidential and that the State Department would not be informed until the last minute.

The showdown with Pervez was set for June 9, 1987, in the bar of Toronto's Harbour Castle Hotel, overlooking Lake Ontario. Pervez and

New hunkered down at a table, sipping Johnnie Walker whiskeys and discussing the transaction. As the negotiations dragged on, they moved upstairs to New's room to make the final arrangements for price and delivery dates. Pervez insisted that Carpenter inflate the price to give him a kickback of $45,180. When New pretended to balk, Pervez sweetened the deal, promising to order eleven more shipments of steel, worth about two million dollars. He said he also wanted to buy beryllium, an element strictly controlled because of its uses in increasing the explosive power of fissile material in atomic bombs.

Suddenly Pervez stopped, looked at New warily, and said, "You could be a spy."

The Pakistani had shown no hesitation before, and New was taken aback at the thought of losing his quarry so close to the finish line. "They don't hire spies who are bald-headed and have glasses," the undercover agent replied. "They're all James Bond with the broads, you know."

Pervez was mollified and, presumably trying to make amends for any offense, told New, "The Kahuta client is ready."

"It's going to the Kahuta plant?" New repeated, emphasizing the disclosure for the videotape being made secretly by another agent in the next room. Pervez acknowledged the destination.

The initial transaction for the steel was being financed by a $447,450 letter of credit drawn on the Toronto headquarters of the Bank of Credit and Commerce International. Known as BCCI, the privately owned bank was playing a major role in financing Pakistan's nuclear-procurement operation, using its branches worldwide to provide letters of credit and payments for the purchases.

BCCI's founder was Agha Hasan Abedi, a Pakistani financier who had built the bank into a network throughout the Middle East, Europe, Africa, and North America. Among his partners in it were Kamal Adham, a former head of intelligence for Saudi Arabia, and Sheik Zayed bin Sultan al-Nahayan, the ruler of Abu Dhabi. Abedi also cultivated a close friendship with President Zia and contributed ten million dollars to a private scientific center named for Pakistani finance minister Ghulam Ishaq Khan and directed by A. Q. Khan. Among BCCI's other clients were the CIA, terrorist Abu Nidal, the Colombian drug cartels, and an assortment of arms dealers and shady businessmen. Eventually, a money-laundering case in Florida toppled the entire institution, creating one of the biggest banking scandals in history.

In Toronto, the negotiations over the maraging steel concluded with an agreement that Pervez would travel to the manufacturing plant in Pennsylvania to inspect the material for the first shipment and receive his kickback in cash. He promised to bring along ul-Haq to inspect the steel. Barlow and the team were excited, anticipating the arrest of a big fish like ul-Haq and throwing a wrench into Pakistan's progress. Before the trap could be sprung, however, they had to take a risky step. Two days before the takedown, Barlow alerted McGoldrick about the pending arrests. McGoldrick promised the information would be closely held. But the fears of a leak proved well-founded when Robert Peck, the deputy assistant secretary of state for Near East Affairs, sent a notice alerting the Pakistani government to the operation.

Ul-Haq was still in Europe, scheduled to fly to the United States the next day, when he was alerted to the sting. The less fortunate Pervez never got the word and arrived on schedule in Reading, where he was arrested in front of his wife and children, who had driven with him from Toronto. Ul-Haq's failure to show was a major blow to the team, leaving its members without the main target and without the strongest link to the Pakistani government. Some of the damage was repaired when the arresting officers seized documents from Pervez that offered direct evidence that he was working for the government's nuclear program, spelling out that the steel was for a military program and a nuclear plant. There was even a letter from ul-Haq urging Pervez not to forget that the purchase was in Pakistan's "national interest." As a result, the case was still seen as a victory, and Barlow was a hero within the CIA, praised by his superiors and nominated for the agency's "exceptional accomplishment award," one of its highest honors. "I'm famous, at least in this clandestine world," Barlow told himself.

His moment in the limelight, however, was about to end badly.

THE SUMMER of 1987 was a time of trouble and change at the CIA. The previous year, a Lebanese magazine had disclosed that the Reagan administration had sold weapons to Iran in an attempt to win release of American hostages being held in Lebanon by Hezbollah, a terrorist organization aligned with Tehran. Money from the arms was earmarked for rebels trying to overthrow the elected Sandinista government in Nicaragua. The elaborate arrangement had been orchestrated by the National Security Council inside the White House, and it violated a number of laws, including a prohibition against trade with Iran. The resulting scandal, known as Iran-Contra, implicated numerous administration figures, including CIA boss William Casey, who had died prior to testifying before a congressional committee. Casey had been replaced at the agency by William Webster, a retired federal judge with an unblemished reputation, whose chief task was to restore the integrity of the CIA.

Webster's resolve faced one of its first tests after the arrest of Pervez. Congressman Solarz demanded a top-secret briefing for his House Foreign Affairs Subcommittee from the CIA and the State Department, on the implications of the case. He suspected strongly that Pakistan had violated his amendment. When Casey was in charge of the CIA, the only person authorized to brief Congress on Pakistan's nuclear program had been David Einsel, a retired Army major general who had been brought into the intelligence community as counterproliferation chief by Casey and shared the director's unwavering commitment to defeating the Soviets in Afghanistan, no matter what the cost. In a highly unusual departure from procedure, Einsel always provided the briefings unaccompanied by anyone else from the agency and was never required to clear his talking points with anyone at the agency or elsewhere in the intelligence community. Under the newly arrived Webster, Einsel no longer had free rein, so when the Solarz request got to Langley, Barlow was chosen to represent the CIA and accompany the general to the hearing. Barlow followed procedure, spending days getting approval for his testimony and talking points from his superiors at the CIA as well as from the State Department and other agencies. He sought to ensure that any comments he made reflected the latest information about Pakistan's illegal purchases while protecting the classified aspects of the cases. "I had never had anything to do with the U.S. Congress," said Barlow. "But I wasn't worried. The general counsel at the CIA said, 'Just tell the truth.' That's what I planned to do."

Barlow and Einsel were scheduled to testify in the secure briefing room on the House side of the Capitol, and as they walked down the hallway Barlow was surprised to see a mob of onlookers outside another hearing room. Someone said Marine Lieutenant Colonel Oliver North from the National Security Council was testifying before the Tower Commission, which was investigating the Iran-Contra affair.

Barlow and Einsel were accompanied by a woman from the CIA's congressional liaison office who offered only a first name, Michelle. The three of them were escorted to a long table, and they sat down as about a dozen congressmen, along with their aides, filed into the room and took seats at the dais. Barlow noticed that the atmosphere was tense, and he attributed it to the recent front-page headlines about the Pervez case, which made Congress look foolish for continuing aid to Pakistan despite its flouting of American laws. But Barlow had a deeper concern: Just before leaving for Capitol Hill that day, his boss, Dick Kerr, had voiced concern that Einsel had been working with people at the State Department to keep the full story of Pakistan's procurement activities from Congress.

Solarz didn't waste time getting to the point, asking the witnesses about the arrest of Pervez and the involvement of ul-Haq in the steel case. "Are these people agents of the government of Pakistan?" he demanded.

"Well, we don't really know that," Einsel replied.

Barlow's head swiveled abruptly. He couldn't have heard correctly, and he looked quizzically at his colleague. Long before the Pervez case, the CIA had a thick file on ul-Haq, and everyone involved in counterproliferation at the CIA, from Einsel on down, knew that ul-Haq and Pervez were working on behalf of Khan's laboratory.

"Have there been any other cases involving agents of Pakistan?" asked Solarz.

"No," said Einsel.

Barlow was shocked by the outright lie. Trying to avoid eye contact with Solarz, he stared down at his talking points, which listed many other Pakistani attempts to violate American export laws. Finally, he shook his head vigorously to display his opposition to what Einsel was saying. Eventually the questioning turned to Barlow, who was still shaken by Einsel's testimony. Referring to his notes, Barlow said emphatically that the CIA and other agencies had plenty of evidence that Pervez and many others had been trying to buy American nuclear technology on behalf of the government of Pakistan. Furthermore, he said, there was plenty of evidence that ul-Haq worked directly for the Pakistani procurement network.

Einsel interrupted, trying to contain his anger as he said, "Richard is only repeating unreliable rumors."

"How many cases have there been?" one of the congressmen asked Barlow.

"Scores," he blurted out, before Einsel cut him off.

The CIA liaison leaned over to Barlow and snapped at him in a harsh whisper: "This is Einsel's show. Let him run it."

The contradictory testimony from the CIA officials surprised everyone in the room, including Robert Peck, the State Department official, who was sitting in the back of the hearing room. He rushed out, grabbed another government official outside the room, and told him: "You've got to testify. That S.O.B. Barlow is telling them all sorts of things, and you've got to straighten it out." The official protested that he had not been cleared to attend the briefing and could not repair the damage.

The ride back to CIA headquarters passed in stony silence. By the time Einsel and Barlow arrived, word had spread about the testimony, and congressional staffers had been on the telephone to the CIA demanding an explanation for the glaring discrepancies. The episode exposed a long-standing division within the CIA. Einsel and others demanded that Barlow be fired. But the young analyst had his defenders among those who had been reluctant to conceal information from Congress, particularly given the continued investigation into Iran-Contra. Before taking any disciplinary action, Barlow's division chief said he would wait for the transcript of the hearing, which would take several days.

Barlow's honesty threatened to pull down the curtain on the charade that had enabled the administration to continue funneling aid to Pakistan and the Afghan guerrillas. He had gone from hero to goat overnight. An agency tainted by Iran-Contra had no appetite for another scandal, accidental or not. Walking the halls the day after his testimony, Barlow glanced through the open door of an office occupied by analysts involved in the Afghan war and saw his name drawn inside a "No Smoking" sign— a circle with a line through it. Later that same day, Robert Peck telephoned from the State Department and accused Barlow of being a traitor.

When the hearing transcript arrived, a review showed no justification for firing Barlow. His immediate supervisor said Barlow had followed orders and provided Congress with nothing beyond his authorized talking points. The controversy would not die, however, and others within the agency and the State Department were adamant that Barlow had gone too far. An informal memo was circulated among the agencies that were part of the nonproliferation working group outlining changes to his duties, which included removing Pakistan from his portfolio. Barlow was transferred temporarily to the Justice Department as the CIA expert for the Pervez and Mandel prosecutions.

Alarmed and confused by conflicting signals, Barlow turned to Dick Kerr, who had spotted his talents as an analyst when he first arrived and remained a mentor. Kerr told him to keep doing what he had been doing, but Barlow couldn't escape the sense that his days at the CIA were numbered. Though Webster gave him an award for the Pervez case, Barlow felt like he was being made a scapegoat because the truth had been withheld from Congress for years. The pressure took a toll on Barlow's personal life, too. He and Cindy, who had recently joined the CIA herself, began to argue. He considered leaving the agency to save his marriage. Customs had offered him a job chasing bad guys, something that seemed black-and-white compared with the troubling grays of the CIA. In the end, however, Barlow decided that he would stick it out because he had done nothing wrong.

On December 17, Pervez was convicted of conspiracy to export maraging steel and beryllium to Pakistan. The conviction got headlines in most major newspapers, including *The Washington Post* and *The New York Times*. Members of Congress could not have missed the verdict or misunderstood its significance. Yet the day after the jury's decision, a congressional conference committee took a contradictory step and approved legislation providing another $480 million in foreign aid to Pakistan. But the conviction could not be ignored, and the next month President Reagan invoked the Solarz amendment for the first time, acknowledging that he had been forced to do so because of the Pervez conviction. Still, Reagan immediately waived the sanctions, declaring that it was in the national interest for military and financial assistance to continue flowing to Pakistan.

CHAPTER 14

MAN OF THE YEAR

K HAN RESEARCH LABORATORIES had evolved into a nuclear city-state, with thousands of employees who could take advantage of private schools, hospitals, and a world-class cricket field. A promotional video for KRL boasted that the lab's cricket team was "on the verge of improvement." Khan presided like a benevolent dictator, micromanaging details one minute and passing out thousands of dollars in cash bonus payments the next. The blank check he had negotiated years earlier with Bhutto was still good, and he had become wealthy not from his meager government salary but from kickbacks that he skimmed routinely from purchases for Kahuta. His take was never excessive enough to draw attention; it was just an accepted part of doing business in a country that was corrupt to its core.

The scientific accomplishments at Kahuta were little short of a miracle. While advanced countries had struggled for decades to master uranium enrichment, Pakistan accomplished the task in a relatively brief period, using stolen designs and black-market technology. The dramatic results were not so much due to Khan's brilliance as a scientist as they were testament to his skill in assembling the technology and attracting the teams of technicians and engineers to make it work. By the mid-1980s, Kahuta had expanded to cover more than a dozen buildings. Huge halls housed thousands of centrifuges linked by elaborate piping and vacuum systems courtesy of loose regulations in Germany, Switzerland, and other industrialized countries. Gleaming four-story research laboratories contained the latest sophisticated machinery sold by Swiss and Dutch companies. Radioactive "hot zones" were built four stories underground to guard against enemy attack. No one thought Kahuta's massive footprint in the isolated area had escaped the spy satellites, and the location was so well-known that local bus drivers referred to the stop as the bomb factory.

Near the end of 1986, India initiated the largest military exercise of its modern history in the desert area of Rajasthan, mobilizing four hundred thousand troops and more than one thousand armored vehicles just one hundred miles from the Pakistani border. General Krishnaswami Sundarji, the aggressive new Indian army leader, called it Operation Brass Tacks, but for those on the Pakistani side of the border, it seemed more like Armageddon. Zia sent almost the entire Pakistani Army racing to the border, and by the middle of January two armies faced each other within firing range, and the threat of the world's first all-out nuclear war loomed large.

In Washington, the standoff created a sense of panic, fueled by intelligence reports that Sundarji was preparing to send his forces sweeping across the border, an invasion that Pakistan's smaller forces stood no chance of stopping and would destabilize the region. Backed into a corner, Zia's only chance seemed to be the threat of a counterattack using nuclear weapons. For the threat to be credible in Delhi, however, Zia had to let the Indians know that he had a nuclear capability, so once again the intelligence agency turned to Khan.

On January 28, a Pakistani journalist named Mushahid Hussain arrived at Khan's house, accompanied by an Indian journalist, Kuldip Nayar. Khan greeted them with a white Australian parrot on his shoulder and a cat at his feet. As the houseman served tea to his guests, Khan began speaking about Pakistan's nuclear program, boasting that Kahuta had produced highly enriched uranium and that other Pakistani scientists had mastered plutonium reprocessing. Pakistan, Khan asserted, had the bomb, and he wanted the world to know. "What the CIA has been saying about our possessing the bomb is correct and so is the speculation of some foreign newspapers," Khan told the Indian journalist. Khan added a blunt warning: "Nobody can undo Pakistan or take us for granted. We are here to stay, and let it be clear that we shall use the bomb if our existence is threatened."

Nayar left Khan's house with a scoop of international significance. Surprisingly, he had difficulty finding an outlet for his blockbuster. He wanted to publish the story in the West for maximum impact, fearing it would be dismissed as propaganda if it appeared first in the Indian press. After he was turned down at several publications, the respected London *Observer* accepted Nayar's story. On March 1, *The Observer* published a lengthy article on its front page recounting the interview and quoting Khan. Diplomatic maneuvers ended Operation Brass Tacks without incident a few weeks earlier, but the article caused a sensation. The Reagan administration was deeply embarrassed and angry. Ignoring intelligence about the extent of Pakistan's nuclear program was one thing, but it was another matter when a Pakistani scientist boasted about it in the international press. Indian prime minister Rajiv Gandhi criticized the United States for allowing Pakistan to develop nuclear weapons while continuing to provide military and financial assistance to the Zia regime.

The interview had served its purpose, so when the controversy erupted, the Pakistani government persuaded Khan to issue a statement claiming he had been misquoted. He asserted that Hussain had taken advantage of their friendship and brought the Indian journalist to Khan's house, but he said his remarks had been strictly personal and that he never intended for them to be published. The Pakistani press claimed that the episode was orchestrated by Indian intelligence to embarrass Pakistan and cause trouble with the Americans. Security was increased at Kahuta in case the Indians used the incident to justify an attack on the plant. There were calls for Mushahid Hussain to be tried for treason. As part of the effort to discredit the story, the Pakistani press said the meeting between Nayar and Khan had lasted only a few minutes, not enough time for the sort of interview described in *The Observer*. To prove the point, the articles said Khan had entertained other guests that night, including two Pakistani generals and Heinz Mebus, described as a famous German engineer. What the press ignored was the fact that Mebus was one of the principal players in the illicit network of suppliers. In the end, Khan's denial provided enough cover for the Americans, and the fuss subsided. Khan later admitted to Husain Haqqani, a Pakistani diplomat and journalist, that his disclosure had been orchestrated by the intelligence service to serve as a "verbal deterrent" to the Indians.

Questions about whether Pakistan had "turned the final screw" and assembled a working nuclear device were strictly rhetorical, a convenient cover for an inconvenient truth. American intelligence knew Kahuta was producing enough highly enriched uranium for several nuclear devices and that Pakistan had tested a warhead, capable of carrying the fissile material to an Indian target. By any reasonable assessment, Pakistan possessed the bomb. "When I was in the State Department in 1985 to 1987, we had very good information about the stage of the Pakistani nuclear program, then we looked the other way," said Stephen Philip Cohen, a South Asia specialist. "In a sense, that was official American policy. Pakistan was so vital to us in terms of fighting the Soviets in Afghanistan that we held our ears, we held our nose, we kept our mouth shut. We scolded Pakistan, but we knew what they were doing and didn't do anything about that."

KHAN'S success threatened to put him out of a job. Kahuta was churning out enough highly enriched uranium to fuel an arsenal of atomic bombs, leaving him looking for a way to expand his role. In the 1970s, President Bhutto had assigned responsibility for building the actual nuclear weapon and developing the missiles to carry it to the PAEC under Munir Khan. After besting his old rival in developing fissile material, A. Q. Khan was determined to take control of the entire nuclear program by developing his own nuclear device and missiles, too, so he assigned a team of engineers to use the Chinese warhead plans as the basis for his own version, and he began searching for a source for missile technology. "You may have a Rolls-Royce, but if you don't have the gas to put in it, it isn't going to run," he told one of his colleagues. "We can enrich uranium, but without a bomb and a delivery system, it isn't going anywhere."

Articles and television reports on Khan's nuclear activities had made him infamous abroad and famous at home, where he was fast becoming the public face of a secret program. Pakistani newspapers were writing glowingly about Khan's scientific accomplishments, coverage that he helped to shape by putting some of the journalists on his payroll. By the late 1980s, Khan couldn't walk into a restaurant anywhere in Pakistan and hope to pay for his meal. His smiling face was painted on the bejeweled trucks that jammed the dusty roads and crowded streets. One newspaper named him "man of the year" in 1986. An accompanying article praised his brilliance and compared him to Muhammed Ali Jinnah, the founder of Pakistan. Journalist Zahid Malik was so taken that he asked permission to write Khan's biography, a proposal the scientist accepted readily.

Khan's life had settled into a comfortable pattern as he moved easily through Pakistan's military and business circles, attending meetings with senior government officials and receptions for visiting dignitaries. Henny remained in the background, raising the two girls and traveling often to see her aging parents in the Netherlands. Since his days as a graduate student, Khan had tried to keep up with the latest scientific research, and he began to publish articles in various journals about the intricacies of metallurgy and centrifuge development.

Khan was the senior scientist in the country's most important military effort, so the ISI kept close watch on him and found him useful. Occasionally, the ISI went to unusual lengths to protect Khan's image. In 1981, a New York publisher issued a book called *The Islamic Bomb,* a sweeping account by journalists Steven Weissman and Herbert Krosney of how nuclear technology spread to Israel, India, and Pakistan. Three chapters focused on Pakistan's nuclear program and were particularly critical of Khan's actions. The book was banned in Pakistan, and few people were brave enough to try to smuggle a copy into the country, but as Khan's influence rose the ISI decided the book had become an irritating reminder of days best forgotten. The ISI set out to change the record.

One day in 1988, motorcycle couriers were dispatched simultaneously across Pakistan to deliver new copies of *The Islamic Bomb* to influential scientists, politicians, diplomats, and government officials. Pervez Hoodbhoy, a nuclear physicist with a doctorate from the Massachusetts Institute of Technology, was in his office at Islamabad's Quaid-i-Azam University when his copy was delivered. Hoodbhoy was an outspoken critic of his country's nuclear program and one of the few people willing to criticize Khan. At one point his public attacks led Khan to persuade authorities to put Hoodbhoy on the exit control list, which prohibited him from leaving the country. It took months for Hoodbhoy to clear himself of charges leveled by Khan that he was "antinational."

Hoodbhoy had read accounts in the foreign press of *The Islamic Bomb*, but he'd never seen a copy until that day. Curious about why someone had sent him a banned book, he sat down and began to read. The work was impressive and thorough, but in the chapters about Pakistan, Hoodbhoy kept bumping into passages that seemed at odds with the overall tone of the book. Invariably, the sections praised A. Q. Khan and harshly criticized his rival, Munir Khan. Hoodbhoy found the suspect passages fishy, but he eventually set the matter aside, and the mystery remained until a visitor noticed the book on his shelf years later. When the visitor asked his opinion of the work, Hoodbhoy said he had found it very good except for some suspicious sections. The visitor photocopied the chapters on Pakistan and sent the material out of the country by Federal Express to avoid the risk of a confrontation with customs upon leaving the country. A later comparison of Hoodbhoy's copy with the original text uncovered nearly one hundred changes, some big and some seemingly inconsequential, all apparently made to protect and enhance Khan's reputation. For instance, accusations that nuclear technology had been smuggled into Pakistan had been removed, and a footnote had been added saying that Zia had renamed Kahuta in honor of Khan's "Miracle." A sample of other changes ranged from cosmetic to substantive: Munir Khan's portrayal in the original book was changed from that of "a patriot who would do anything and everything to bring atomic power and atomic weapons to his homeland" to that of an incompetent scientist who "would do everything to keep atomic power and weapons away from Pakistan." In another instance, the original said: "Only a few of the major industrialized nations had ever built their own enrichment plants, and both the technology and construction had proceeded under the strictest secrecy. How could poor, backward Pakistan ever hope to do it?" The new version appended the sentence, "Dr. Khan was the answer."

When asked about the changes, a senior Pakistani government official who had been close to the ISI explained what had happened. Pakistan had a thriving publishing industry that reproduced Western books without regard to copyright. The ISI had gone to one of those publishers and ordered the printings, with dozens of changes that rendered Khan in a favorable light and cast aspersions on his rival. "It became a well-known trick within certain circles of the ISI," said the official. "It was considered an enormous success."

CHAPTER 15

ONE-STOP SHOPPING

K HAN'S CONTACTS WITH WILLING and unwitting accomplices alike
had expanded over the years, creating a vast clandestine enterprise
capable of providing every piece of material and technology necessary to
make nuclear bombs. American intelligence agencies had watched the
ring operate for years, but they failed to understand the full extent or the
nature of the black market that Khan had created.

But by the late 1980s, Khan needed less help from outside suppliers for
Kahuta, which left his shady middlemen and manufacturers restless and
on the prowl for new customers. A handful were already selling technical
know-how to the apartheid regime in South Africa, which was well along
on its own secret program to build nuclear weapons. When it came to
new customers, Libya and Saudi Arabia were possibilities—both were rich
with oil money—but outsiders would face a hard time penetrating their
closed societies. Iraq and Iran, on the other hand, were locked in the final
stages of a long-running war that had claimed tens of thousands of lives
on both sides, and they seemed like potential clients.

Saddam Hussein was already buying technology for conventional and
nuclear weapons through a small army of clandestine procurement officers who were working out of Iraqi embassies across Europe, in a way
that mirrored Pakistan's early efforts. For its part, Iran was contemplating

restarting the nuclear program initiated by the shah and shuttered by the revolution in 1979, but its leaders were constrained because they were spending large sums on conventional weapons for the fight against Iraq.

One of Khan's suppliers who was eager for more business was Gotthard Lerch, a quiet German who was living in the picturesque Swiss village of Grabs. Lerch, a big man with the fleshy face of a brawler, had started out as a mechanical engineer in the 1960s for an aircraft manufacturer in Germany. Eventually, he moved to another German company, Leybold-Heraeus, a major player in the European market for vacuum valves that were used in the manufacture of centrifuges. Leybold was among a handful of companies that had mastered the complicated vacuum technology used in the conversion of uranium hexafluoride gas into enriched uranium. By the early 1970s, Lerch had risen to department head, a position that put him in contact with Leybold customers at Urenco, including A. Q. Khan. After Khan returned to Pakistan, Lerch continued their relationship and sold Khan the particular vacuum valves he needed.

By 1979, the size of the business with Pakistan had raised suspicions among German authorities. When they questioned Lerch, he readily acknowledged selling Pakistan valves, vacuum pumps, and a gas-purification plant worth one million dollars. The export officials noted that some of the equipment "might be adapted to be used in an enrichment plant," though no formal charges were brought against the company or Lerch. Still, Leybold executives did not like the extra government attention, and Lerch was forced to resign. Undaunted, he packed up his bags and know-how and headed for Switzerland in 1983, determined to find a better climate in which to ply his nuclear trade. Not long after he left, Leybold discovered that top-secret plans for important parts of the enrichment process were missing.

After starting his own business in the heart of Vacuum Valley, Lerch renewed his ties with Khan and once again began selling large amounts of equipment to the Pakistani. Suspicions that Lerch had stolen Leybold's plans seemed to be confirmed in 1985 when Swiss authorities stopped a Pakistan-bound shipment of equipment that seemed quite similar to that in Leybold's designs. Unfortunately, they also discovered that they had missed several tons shipped earlier. Again, no charges were brought against Lerch, because his actions were not covered by Swiss export laws. He viewed the run-in as just the cost of doing business.

Lerch developed a reputation as the man to see about all types of high-technology needs, so it was not unusual when a physicist from Iran's Atomic Energy Organization showed up at his office in 1987, looking for technology for the manufacture of conventional weapons. Lerch agreed to fill the order, but he insisted that the Iranian also watch a promotional film for his nuclear inventory. The physicist watched the short movie but repeated that he was buying for conventional weapons. For Lerch, however, the seed was planted, and a short time later he contacted Iranian nuclear officials in Tehran to see if anyone else might be interested in acquiring nuclear goods. Several weeks passed before Lerch heard back. The Iranians were indeed interested, and they suggested a meeting in Zurich.

Lerch took the train to Zurich in July and met two scientists from Iran's Atomic Energy Organization, Masud Naraghi and Mohammed Allahdad, at a hotel there. At the time, the organization was engaged in limited research using a small reactor provided by the Americans during the shah's era as part of the Atoms for Peace program. But Iran seemed to have a growing appetite for nuclear weapons because in the final months of the war, when the larger Iranian forces appeared on the verge of winning, Saddam Hussein had launched a series of attacks with chemical weapons, killing thousands of Iranians. The attacks turned the tide in favor of Iraq. Iran protested at the United Nations, arguing correctly that the weapons violated international law. But the world's superpowers had no sympathy for the Islamic republic, and their failure to take any action reinforced Iran's isolation and reminded Ayatollah Khomeini and other clerics that Iran had to protect itself. The religious and military leaders determined that Iran had to develop its own deterrence, so they started stockpiling a chemical arsenal and shopping in earnest for a nuclear weapon. In other words, Lerch's timing could not have been better.

Rather than glossy brochures and sample products, the German engineer arrived in Zurich with a rudimentary proposal scratched out in English on a single page of stationery from Siemens, a technology company that did business worldwide. He had divided the offer into four sections:

1. Drawings, descriptions, and specifications for manufacturing centrifuges.
2. One or two disassembled centrifuges to serve as prototypes.
3. Enough components to build two thousand centrifuges.
4. Blueprints and specs for a complete enrichment plant, including the full range of operating systems, and designs for fabricating nuclear-weapons components.

No one was on hand to record the moment for posterity, though the single piece of paper did survive. Lerch's offer marked the birth of a new phase of the proliferation threat. The network that had been established to supply Pakistan had reached out to a new customer and was about to evolve into an international bazaar for nuclear technology, open to any country or anyone with the money to spend.

Lerch was in full sales mode, promising the Iranians that he and his unnamed colleagues could deliver everything required to build a bomb despite export controls and restrictions on what could be sent to Iran. Many of the goods, he said, were available immediately—full sets of plans and sample centrifuges could be in Iran within weeks—and the rest of the equipment could be delivered as needed, as work progressed. When the Iranians pressed him for details, he declined to say anything about the origins of the designs and equipment, though he vouched for the quality of the products. He said he and his associates would need twenty million dollars as a down payment and untold sums later. The Iranians were definitely interested, but they said that they needed to return to Tehran to consult with their superiors before agreeing to such an expensive and treacherous undertaking. Naraghi, the head of Iran's secret program, and Allahdad promised they would get in touch with Lerch as soon as they got the go-ahead.

Iran was not new to nuclear technology. Its program dated back to the days under the shah, initiated with help from the United States and Germany. A large-scale nuclear reactor near the coastal town of Bushehr begun by the Germans had been mothballed after the Islamic revolution, which had made the country an outcast and led to international sanctions blocking the sale of nuclear technology. Back in Tehran, Lerch's proposal was passed from the Atomic Energy Organization to the Revolutionary Guards, the military organization responsible for the nation's security, and from them to the Ministry of Intelligence and Security. Eventually the one-page list made its way to the senior clerics who wielded the ultimate power—and there, someone gave it the green light.

The Iranians had run into some trouble in their efforts to buy conventional technology in Europe, and they feared being set up in a sting operation, so Naraghi tried to insist that the second meeting take place in Tehran. Lerch balked at going to Iran, however, in part because he was still under investigation by German authorities in connection with earlier shipments to Pakistan. So the two sides settled on meeting in the Persian Gulf city of Dubai, a neutral location outside the reach of European law enforcement. Even before the meeting, there had been some hard bargaining. The Iranians had spent heavily on the war, and Naraghi was under orders to bring down the initial price. Eventually, Lerch agreed to take ten million dollars as the first installment, payable upon delivery at the meeting.

Dubai is one of the seven principalities that form the United Arab Emirates. A sleepy port until a construction boom started in the 1960s, by the 1980s Dubai was a bustling free-trade zone without tariffs or taxes and little in the way of government regulation. Foreign businessmen had been drawn by the freewheeling, explosive economy. Among them was Mohammed Farooq, a stocky Indian who had set up a small import-export business in the Jebel Ali Free Zone. Like Lerch, Farooq was a veteran of the nuclear black market—he had met the engineer in South Africa years before, and they had also crossed paths over the years in their dealings with Khan. Lerch now contacted Farooq and found a willing local partner. Lerch also recruited another alumnus of the Pakistani network, Heinz Mebus. Mebus had worked at Siemens and spoke better English than Lerch, prompting later speculation that he had been the one to write the four-point proposal for Iran on some of his old stationery.

At some point, Lerch or Mebus ran the Iranian deal past Khan, who had access to the centrifuges and components that were a key part of the transaction. As a fellow Muslim who was well-known for his role in building the Islamic bomb, Khan's involvement also served to quell any worries the Iranians still had about a sting operation. Although the Pakistani scientist was willing to participate, he did not want to travel to Dubai for the meeting. Instead, he agreed to provide two centrifuges and some components. At the time, Kahuta was developing a more advanced centrifuge, known as the P-2, so all Khan had to do was to dip into his stockpile of used P-1s waiting to be melted down and ship them to Dubai. He still operated with complete immunity, without any real oversight, so the goods could be sent out of the country merely on his signature.

Later Khan would rationalize his participation in the transfer of nuclear technology to Iran in a variety of ways. Chiefly, he would argue that providing an atomic weapon to another Muslim country was a way to shift some of the West's scrutiny away from Pakistan. In private, he told friends that he had been encouraged to assist Iran by Pakistani military leaders who were interested in expanding ties with Tehran against the West and Israel. At the time of the first deal, President Zia did not trust the Americans despite the hundreds of millions of dollars in annual aid, any more than he trusted the Soviets occupying the country next door. The secure future that Zia envisioned for Pakistan rested on a new alliance stretching west to unite the region's non-Arab Muslims in Afghanistan, Iran, and Turkey. This was, in Zia's mind, a formation capable of resisting outsiders and posing a formidable counterweight to India. He had ordered his plan put down in writing and called it the Strategic Regional Consensus.

Milt Bearden learned about the plan from the ISI boss, Hamid Gul, who boasted about the alliance as something that would make the Americans expendable. "This is the dream," Gul told Bearden one day, handing him a copy of the plan to underscore his seriousness. "It's a strategic-depth concept that links Pakistan, Iran, Turkey, and Afghanistan in an alliance. It would be a jeweled Mughal dagger pointed at the Hindu heart." The CIA station chief recognized the potential danger and immediately sent a copy of the plan to CIA headquarters.

Pakistan and Iran were already working on joint defense projects involving conventional weapons, and Pakistan had signed a formal agreement in 1986 to help Iran's civilian nuclear industry. The evidence that Khan made the initial shipment to Iran with government approval is circumstantial, though in later years the volume of material sent out of

Pakistan to network customers was so large that it had to have required the complicity of the military at the highest levels.

A few days before the Iranians were due to arrive in Dubai, Khan shipped two used P-1 centrifuges and components for several others to Farooq. The equipment was accompanied by a small library of drawings and technical plans for setting up an enrichment plant and a list of potential suppliers in Europe. Farooq was afraid to store the nuclear items at his business, so he kept them in his eighth-floor apartment in central Dubai.

On the day of the meeting, Farooq was waiting at the apartment with Lerch and Mebus when the Iranians arrived. Naraghi and Allahdad were accompanied by a third official, Hormoz Azodi, from the Iranian nuclear agency. When they entered the apartment, they saw the centrifuge components standing in a corner of the living room and the engineering schematics and drawings arranged on the dining-room table. Farooq's young nephew, Buhari Sayed abu Tahir, served tea to the guests and listened to the conversation, which was conducted in English. Lerch and Mebus did the dog-and-pony show, explaining that the plans were for a huge centrifuge plant that could produce enough enriched uranium to equip up to thirty nuclear weapons per year. They sweetened the deal by showing the Iranians a fifteen-page document portraying an elaborate process for the manufacture of uranium metal, which could be cast into the precise hemispheres used to form the core of a nuclear device. The plans were unmistakably for a weapons project because uranium metal plays no role in a civilian program.

The Iranians seemed pleased. Tahir took the stacks of plans to another room to begin copying them and listened as the negotiations came to a close. Unfortunately for the network, the Iranians said they would be unable to buy more material and technology for a while because almost every penny of government money was going to the war with Iraq. They said they needed to proceed slowly, buying what they needed on their own and in small increments until the war was over. While Tahir finished, his uncle accompanied the Europeans and Iranians to the Dubai branch of the BCCI. There, the Iranians arranged to transfer ten million dollars to Farooq's account.

When the group returned to the apartment, Tahir had packed the components into two large suitcases and the papers into two briefcases. The Iranians hefted the suitcases and headed for the airport, leaving the conspirators behind to celebrate and divvy up the millions. Three million went to Lerch because he had originated the deal. Farooq and Khan received two million dollars each, and Mebus was paid one million. Friedrich Tinner, the Swiss engineer—who like Khan, had not attended the meeting—was paid $500,000, and another million went into the BCCI account of an Islamabad dentist. The involvement of the dentist remains a mystery, but some intelligence officials have speculated that he passed on the money to Pakistani government and military officials. The distribution of the final $500,000 remains unclear, though it may have gone to Tahir, whose role would eventually expand from tea boy to financial manager. Despite the Iranian desire to proceed on their own, the network participants did not think the Iranians could succeed without them, and they looked forward to tens of millions more in the future.

Within months of the Dubai deal, the Iran-Iraq war ended in a cease-fire, and customs officials in Europe and American intelligence agencies began picking up signs that Iran was on a covert shopping spree for nuclear-related technology. Front companies traced to the government were working quietly to acquire large quantities of high-strength aluminum and a range of other items that could be used in a uranium-enrichment program. At the time, there was no sign that Lerch, Mebus, or other members of the Khan network were helping Iran, but Khan had taken on an advisory role and made several trips to Tehran on his own.

CHAPTER 16

WISHFUL THINKING

THE TELEPHONE IN MILT BEARDEN'S HOME in Islamabad rang early on the morning of August 17, 1988. The caller was from the American embassy, informing the CIA station chief that there were reports that the ambassador, Arnold Raphel, President Zia, and at least ten American and Pakistani military officers had been killed in the crash of Zia's aircraft in eastern Pakistan. The deaths were confirmed the following day: Zia and Raphel had been returning from a demonstration of a new American tank, and Zia's plane lost power and crashed soon after takeoff. Beyond the immediate tragedy of the deaths, the incident threatened to have repercussions beyond Pakistan because Zia had remained a strong ally against the Soviets, who were on the verge of withdrawing from Afghanistan. His death presented the Americans with the challenge of enlisting the assistance of his successor in the fight against the Soviets and the opportunity to persuade a new leader to put the brakes on the nuclear program, which was approaching the point of no return, if it had not passed it already.

Within hours of the plane crash, Secretary of State George Shultz telephoned Robert Oakley, a career foreign-service officer assigned to the National Security Council. "I'm leading the funeral delegation tomorrow," Shultz said. "The plane is leaving at twelve. Bring two suitcases because you're not coming back. You're the new ambassador." As he packed for the trip, Oakley was well aware of the challenges.

Zia had been both Pakistan's president and chief of the armed forces. No contingency plans had been made for his sudden death. Although the constitution specified that the head of the senate would be a temporary successor, the army ignored that provision and stepped in. General Mirza Aslam Beg, the vice chief of the army, took over command of the military and invited the leader of the senate, Ghulam Ishaq Khan, to his headquarters. Both men were veterans of the musical chairs that marked Pakistani politics and knew how to play the game. Ishaq Khan, who was seventy-three years old, agreed to be acting president, but Beg, as the new commander of the armed forces, would hold the real power.

The faces changed, but the policies remained the same. For a decade, Zia had increased the role of Islam in government and tried to reduce Pakistan's dependence on the Americans through both alliances with other Islamic countries and his own nuclear-weapons program. Beg was more secular and lacked an Islamic agenda, giving the Americans some hope that he could be persuaded to freeze the nuclear program. From the outset, however, Beg rebuffed the American overtures, making it clear that a nuclear arsenal was Pakistan's greatest strategic asset and that he had no intention of backing away from it. On the contrary, he defied the Americans by ordering an acceleration of the program. Beg was a political realist and knew that the Americans would have less use for Pakistan once the Afghan war ended, so he rushed to finish the bomb because he thought Washington might be less likely to abandon a nuclear-armed Pakistan.

Eleven years of Zia's iron-fisted rule had eroded the popularity of the military, so Beg decided it was in the army's interest to conduct national elections in the fall of 1988. The task of rigging the election to install a compliant civilian government was assigned to General Hamid Gul, the chief of the ISI. Under Gul's direction, the intelligence agency created and financed a coalition of Islamic and promilitary parties to field a slate of candidates who would serve as the military's stalking horse. Not long into the campaign, however, it was obvious that the plan was in jeopardy. Benazir Bhutto, the Harvard-educated daughter of the prime minister executed by Zia in 1979, had taken over her father's Pakistan Peoples Party and was proving enormously popular. When Bhutto and her party swept the elections, Beg and the other generals were forced to strike a deal with her. They agreed not to interfere with the results so long as Bhutto retained Ishaq Khan as president and Beg as chief of the armed forces. She knew it was a necessary compromise in a country where the military held the real power.

Bhutto was sworn in on December 1, 1988. She was thirty-five years old and the first woman to head a Muslim nation in modern times. In a tacit acknowledgment of the backroom deals that allowed her elevation, Bhutto gave credit in her inaugural speech to Ishaq Khan and the generals for accepting her as prime minister. From the outset, there were limits to Bhutto's power, and she was barred from interfering with the sacrosanct nuclear program started by her father, though she was allowed to visit Kahuta and received an overview of the status of the weapons development. "They were keeping Benazir Bhutto at arm's length," said retired Brigadier General Feroz Khan, who was involved in Pakistan's nuclear security. "She was in the picture of what was going on with the bomb, but only to an extent. The fact is that Aslam Beg and Ishaq Khan never trusted her."

Bhutto said as much, years later, recalling that soon after taking office she tried to involve herself in discussions over the future of the nuclear program and was rebuffed. "I asked the army chief and he said, 'It's got nothing to do with me. It's the president.' I asked Ishaq Khan, and he said, 'There's no need for you to know.'" At various points, she said she argued that Pakistan should go slow on its nuclear development to avoid angering the Americans and possibly prompting an attack on its nuclear installations. But each time, her advice was rejected and in fact only deepened the military's distrust of her.

From the third floor of the American embassy, Bearden kept watch over the new prime minister and worked to cultivate a good relationship with her. Her father's execution never far from her mind, Bhutto worried about her security and welcomed Bearden's support. Her understanding of the precariousness of her position was underscored when she asked him if he could find body armor that could be concealed beneath her clothing. Bearden queried Langley and, in the best of bureaucratic responses, was asked to get her measurements. This seemed a bit untoward, so Bearden guessed. When the vest arrived, it must have fit because the CIA man never heard a complaint from Bhutto.

With the Afghan war winding down, Bearden's attention was beginning to shift toward Pakistan's nuclear program. He and the other CIA officers monitoring the program were not certain of Bhutto's attitudes toward the weapons effort, and there were early hopes that she might put the brakes on it. In public, Bhutto made the right sounds, suggesting that she did not favor developing nuclear weapons and parroting the long-standing lie that Pakistan was not making an atomic bomb. In private discussions with members of her administration, the prime minister took a different line, talking about extending her late father's nuclear legacy. Eventually the talk got back to Bearden, raising doubts that she would cut back the weapons program. Those doubts were reflected in a classified analysis prepared in May to set the stage for Bhutto's visit to Washington the next month. The CIA analysis said Bhutto had agreed not to interfere in Pakistan's nuclear policies as one of several conditions imposed by the army before she was allowed to take office and predicted the situation would not change. "Although Bhutto's access and leverage on nuclear issues have increased since she assumed office last December, she is unlikely to gain control over nuclear decision-making anytime soon," the CIA concluded. "Even if she were to gain the upper hand, we do not believe she would try to stop Pakistan's nuclear weapons effort or significantly reduce existing capabilities." The CIA concluded that the neophyte prime minister faced a difficult and potentially fatal dilemma: She wanted to avoid a cutoff of American aid without risking her own future.

The CIA was not the only part of the American government preparing for Bhutto's visit to Washington. Bhutto represented an important opportunity for democracy in a Muslim country, as she was someone who understood Western values. While the United States no longer required Pakistan's assistance against the Soviets, who had left Afghanistan, it wanted to retain influence in Islamabad. One way to do that was to resume large-scale military and economic assistance, including more F-16 fighter jets. Pentagon and State Department officials also argued that building up Pakistan's conventional forces was the most effective way to avoid a nuclear-arms race on the subcontinent. On the other side were counterproliferation experts within the government who argued that assistance should be withheld until there was proof that Pakistan had abandoned its goal of developing a nuclear weapon. They underscored their position by saying that U.S. law should forbid renewing or expanding assistance to Pakistan until it complied with congressional amendments that prohibited aid to countries pursuing nuclear weapons. With Bhutto's arrival less than a month away, the Bush administration remained undecided about whether to greet her with a carrot or a stick.

RICH BARLOW was struggling to rebuild his career and personal life when the debate over how to deal with Pakistan landed on his desk. By this time, his desk was not at CIA headquarters but fewer than ten miles away, at the Pentagon. In the aftermath of his testimony before Congress over the concealment of Pakistan's procurement attempts, Barlow finally left the CIA, angered by what he viewed as harassment by some of the cold warriors within the agency. Barlow's faith in government had been shaken by the lies told to Congress and by what he viewed as his own gross mistreatment. He was angry and depressed, but he still wanted to work for the government. Through contacts developed during the Pervez case and other criminal investigations, Barlow landed a job with the criminal-investigations division of the Customs Service. Criminal investigations seemed to offer a respite from the shadowy, gray world of the CIA, but it wasn't long before Barlow grew restless and started looking for something more intellectually challenging. In January 1989, he was hired as a proliferation analyst in the office of Defense Secretary Dick Cheney.

But Barlow's past followed him to the new job. When the Pentagon submitted Barlow's name for clearance to see highly classified nuclear-proliferation intelligence held by the CIA, someone at the agency blocked the request and insinuated that Barlow was a security risk. The access was critical for Barlow to be able to perform his new job, and he and his superiors at the Pentagon spent weeks fighting the denial.

The depth of the CIA's antipathy toward Barlow surfaced that spring when he tried to attend intelligence and policy meetings on Pakistan's nuclear progress with British officials in London. The CIA officer who was refusing to renew Barlow's top-secret security clearance happened to be there, and he stopped Barlow from attending the intelligence briefing because his clearance had not been renewed. Barlow's colleagues from the Pentagon protested, so he was allowed to attend the second session, which dealt with nuclear policy. When Barlow asked a British intelligence officer whether Benazir Bhutto was truly in control of Pakistan's nuclear program and the Brit said Bhutto did not appear to be, Barlow's nemesis jumped to his feet. He yelled at the British contingent not to say anything further, claiming that Barlow was a security risk who was not cleared for such sensitive information. A CIA agent escorted Barlow from the room and took him by taxi to the CIA station at the American embassy on Grosvenor Square, where he was locked in a room and forced to sign an agreement not to disclose anything he had heard at the meeting.

Barlow was angered by his treatment, but he decided to stay on in London. He had several meetings scheduled for the following two days with British officials to discuss Iraq's nuclear program, and then Cindy, his wife, was arriving for a vacation. The next morning, however, Barlow got a call at his hotel informing him that his meetings had been canceled. "I was in a wonderful mood," Barlow said sarcastically later. "I had the CIA running operations against me like a foreign government."

When he got back to Washington, Barlow persuaded his bosses at the Pentagon to find out what was going on. The message back from the CIA was ominous: If Barlow continued to poke his nose into Pakistani nuclear affairs, there would be consequences. Rather than abandon him, Barlow's boss at the Pentagon pushed to get Barlow the clearances he needed and kept him focused on Pakistan. Eventually Dick Kerr, Barlow's former boss at the CIA, intervened, telling the Pentagon that Barlow was not a security risk and that he should have access to the information he needed to do his job. As a result, the month before Bhutto was scheduled to arrive in Washington he found himself assigned to prepare an analysis of Pakistan's nuclear program for Dick Cheney.

After Gerald Ford's loss to Jimmy Carter in 1976, Cheney had returned to his native Wyoming, where he was elected to Congress two years later. In the House, Cheney established himself as a reliable conservative, voting against the establishment of Martin Luther King Day, the

U.S. Department of Education, and Head Start, the program to provide early education to poor children. In December 1988, House Republicans elected Cheney as minority whip, the number two leadership spot, though he didn't stay long. After the newly elected president, George H. W. Bush, tapped Texas senator John Tower for defense secretary, the nomination was rejected by the Senate because of reports of Tower's improper behavior with women and inappropriate ties to defense contractors; Bush turned to Cheney as his second choice. Cheney had been on the job for only a few weeks when the question arose over whether to sell the F-16s to Pakistan.

Barlow's report on Pakistan was to be part of an internal discussion with the White House. Having watched previous efforts to cover up Pakistan's nuclear progress, Barlow worried that this was going to be business as usual. "We knew the F-16s they already had were perfectly capable nuclear-delivery systems," Barlow said. "There were a few minor modifications necessary. It was not even a hypothetical. We knew they not only planned to do it but had taken the steps."

After reading the most recent intelligence reports, Barlow's views remained unchanged about what the Pakistanis were doing and about the role that the F-16s played in their nuclear strategy. The top-secret assessment he prepared for Cheney was an unvarnished account of the status of Pakistan's nuclear program and activities, of Bhutto's lack of influence over the nuclear program, and of Pakistan's intentions to use the F-16s purchased in previous years from the United States to deliver nuclear weapons, which were nearing completion. The assessment concluded that the proposed new sale violated congressional restrictions. Barlow knew he was staking out an unpopular and potentially dangerous position, so he asked the Pentagon's intelligence arm, the Defense Intelligence Agency, to prepare a separate assessment. The DIA reached the same conclusion, saying that Pakistan was preparing to use its F-16s as a nuclear delivery platform. The concerns did not stop at the Pentagon. Evaluations by nuclear-weapons experts from Lawrence Livermore National Laboratory in California also concluded that F-16s could carry a nuclear payload with relatively minor modifications well within the capabilities of Pakistani technicians. Even analysts at the CIA had reached the same conclusion.

Barlow's analysis, which covered the findings of all the other intelligence agencies, threatened to derail the sale of the aircraft, but first the report had to survive the vetting system within the Pentagon. The first step in that process was for Barlow to submit his conclusions to officials at the Office of the Secretary of Defense.

The report was sent first to Michael MacMurray, the desk officer responsible for military sales to Pakistan. A few days later, MacMurray summoned Barlow to his office and said that he objected to the findings. MacMurray said that he was alarmed because Barlow had used such unequivocal language in describing the sale as impossible because it would violate the Pressler and Solarz amendments. Barlow responded that he considered the intelligence behind his conclusion to be rock solid and he refused to change it. MacMurray pressed the issue, and eventually Barlow agreed to soften the passage slightly, altering the section saying that the sale was "impossible" to "extremely difficult or impossible."

Even the new version could derail the deal, so someone within the Pentagon hierarchy secretly altered Barlow's conclusions so radically that the version sent to the defense secretary supported the sale. Since the intelligence did not support selling the aircraft to Pakistan, the intelligence was changed; Cheney argued in favor of the transaction later that month at the White House.

WHEN BHUTTO arrived in Washington in June, Pakistan's nuclear program was high on the agenda. The last Soviet troops had left Afghanistan in February, and the new administration had already hinted that President Bush might refuse to certify that Pakistan did not possess a nuclear weapon. As Reagan's vice president for eight years and director of the CIA in the mid-1970s, Bush knew at least the broad outline of Pakistan's nuclear ambitions. As president, his daily intelligence briefings included regular updates on the topic. "The president of the United States knew more about Pakistan's nuclear program than the prime minister of Pakistan," said a senior official at CIA headquarters. "He probably had more accurate information available to him because our scientists were doing better analysis. All of our information was processed by all the smartest people who knew more about how bombs are made than anyone else in the world." Secretary of State James Baker had sent word to Bhutto before her departure that he felt the United States could no longer ignore the evidence of Pakistan's nuclear efforts.

Pakistan had never needed American aid more—its economy was in a shambles, with more than three million Afghan refugees who feared returning home because of civil conflict consuming scarce resources and sparking local resentment. Bhutto put on a charm offensive, telling a joint session of Congress that her election was a signal that democracy had arrived in Pakistan and that nuclear weapons were not part of its future. "I can declare that we do not possess, nor do we intend to make, a nuclear device," she said, winning extended applause from both sides of the political aisle.

The declaration was wishful thinking, at best. Bhutto might have been in the dark about the details of her country's nuclear ambitions, but she knew the military intended to develop a nuclear device. Any doubts she may have harbored were removed the next day when she visited CIA headquarters to meet with the director, William Webster. In the conference room adjacent to Webster's office, aides rolled out the model of the Pakistani bomb presented years earlier to the country's foreign minister. Webster explained that American intelligence not only knew the dimensions of the nuclear device being built but had the technology and resources to monitor the enrichment level produced by Pakistan's centrifuges. Bhutto was in a state of mild shock, but she composed herself enough to pledge to Webster that she would keep the enrichment level below the weapons level and promised that Pakistan would not transfer nuclear technology to any other country.

After leaving Langley, Bhutto confided to Mark Siegel, a former Carter administration official who was Pakistan's lobbyist in Washington at the time, that the briefing was more thorough than any information she had been provided by Pakistani authorities, leaving her more concerned than ever about what the military was doing behind her back.

In a private meeting at the White House the following day, Bush told Bhutto that her agreement to keep Pakistan from enriching uranium to weapons-grade level was enough to allow him to certify once again that Pakistan did not possess a nuclear weapon, which meant financial assistance would continue. Behind the scenes, however, many in the American government believed that Bhutto's assurances were empty and that Pakistan had done everything but turn the final screw. Bush's decision reflected the concern among American policymakers that a cutoff in aid would doom Bhutto's government and set back the course of democracy in Pakistan. The CIA believed the military would prohibit Bhutto from delivering on any pledge to restrict the nuclear program, regardless of her personal commitment. Bhutto herself later maintained that her opposition to going nuclear was one of the reasons she was later ousted from office.

In addition to continuing assistance, Bush provided Bhutto with additional political cover with the Pakistani military by authorizing the sale of more F-16 fighter jets. (Pakistan already had forty American-made F-16s.) The generals had urged Bhutto to secure them, and it was one of her top priorities during the visit to Washington. The $1.4 billion sale would be subject to congressional approval, however, and even before Bhutto left town opposition surfaced among congressmen who feared the sale would fuel the arms race between Pakistan and India.

Bush's agreement to sell Pakistan the F-16s failed to improve Bhutto's standing with the military. Her promises to Congress not to build the bomb had dominated the headlines in the Pakistani press, reinforcing fears that she was willing to sacrifice the country's nuclear program for closer ties with Washington. "Pakistan's nuclear weapons capability simply cannot be safe under the leadership of a westernized woman," said Maulana Sami ul-Haq, the head of one of the leading Islamic parties aligned with the ISI. "She cares more for American approval than for ensuring the *Umma*'s first nuclear bomb," referring to the worldwide Muslim community.

BEFORE giving its approval to sell the additional F-16s to Pakistan, Congress wanted further assurance that Pakistan was not pursuing a nuclear weapon and that the planes could not be modified to carry nuclear payloads. The Democrats controlled Congress, and many of them suspected that the Reagan administration had distorted intelligence about Pakistan's nuclear quest to keep aid flowing throughout the 1980s. By July, a resolution was introduced to block the deal. In response, the administration adopted a unified position that the transaction should be approved and that Pakistan had not violated American law. Lest anyone stray from the reservation, Undersecretary of Defense Paul Wolfowitz sent word throughout the Pentagon bureaucracy that he personally expected full backing for the F-16 sale.

On August 2, the House Foreign Affairs Committee heard testimony from administration officials. The principal witnesses were Arthur Hughes, who had recently become the deputy assistant secretary of defense, with responsibility for Pakistan and India, and Teresita Schaffer, deputy assistant secretary of state for South Asia. Both testified that the sale would strengthen U.S.-Pakistan relations and reinforce the Pakistani military's confidence in Bhutto's civilian government. Bolstering Pakistan's conventional forces with the F-16s, they said, would reduce the likelihood that Pakistan would feel compelled to cross the nuclear-weapons threshold.

When Democrat Dante Fascell asked whether the United States could rely on Bhutto's word that the country would not develop nuclear weapons, Schaffer replied, "We obviously place great value on the fact that Benazir Bhutto told the Congress and the world that Pakistan does not have, nor intends to produce, a nuclear weapon."

Even if Pakistan was developing nuclear weapons, Hughes assured Congress, the F-16s could not be modified to carry nuclear weapons. "In order to deliver a nuclear device with any reasonable degree of accuracy and safety, it first would be necessary to replace the entire wiring package in the aircraft," he said. "In addition to building a weapons carriage mount, one would also have to redo the fire control computer, the stores management system, and mission computer software to allow the weapon to be dropped accurately and to redistribute weight and balance after release. We believe this capability far exceeds the state of the art in Pakistan and could only be accomplished with a major release of data and industrial equipment from the U.S."

Steve Solarz, the New York Democrat, was still highly skeptical of administration pronouncements about Pakistan and pressed Hughes on that point. "Now, in your testimony, Mr. Hughes, I gather you've said that the F-16s which we have already sold them are not nuclear capable?"

"That's right, sir," replied Hughes.

Barlow was livid when he learned a few hours later about Hughes's sworn testimony, alerting his bosses at the Pentagon to what he regarded as its misleading nature. Barlow did not blame Hughes, who was new in the job and had relied on prepared testimony, but he maintained that the underlying material had been altered to an extent that misled Congress. Pentagon officials were alarmed—not by Barlow's accusation that Congress had been misinformed but that he might be on the verge of blowing the whistle.

Gerald Brubaker, the senior assistant for nonproliferation policy at the Pentagon, summoned Barlow to his office. Barlow had been promoted six weeks earlier. Suddenly, he was told he was being fired. Brubaker refused to disclose the reasons, saying only that they were classified. Barlow felt trapped in a Kafka novel. When he protested, demanding to know who was behind the move, Brubaker first refused to say. Then he told Barlow that his dismissal was approved at high levels of the Pentagon—Wolfowitz and Stephen Hadley, the assistant secretary in charge of nuclear weapons and arms control. Barlow was stunned, and he was to get another blow two days later. As he packed up his desk, he was informed that his security clearances were canceled. He still did not know anything about the allegations against him, and removing his clearances meant he might never penetrate the secret world in which his fate had been decided.

Barlow's sin was that he refused to go along with what he viewed as the manipulation of intelligence. He had written an accurate assessment of American intelligence concerning Pakistan's development of nuclear weapons, and he had refused to back down when the Pentagon altered the findings. The Pentagon bosses who had cooked the intelligence to support the administration's policy then decided they had to get rid of him. In fact, they decided to destroy him.

In attempting to justify the dismissal, Brubaker started a campaign to discredit Barlow. He told the Defense Intelligence Agency and Cheney's office that Barlow had intended to go to Congress to "give them the other side of the slant." As part of the smear, Brubaker said his concerns about Barlow's potential for harming the government were heightened when he learned that the intelligence analyst was under psychiatric care. Brubaker pressured security officers to dig into Barlow's personal life, his finances, and his marriage.

Even when the internal investigation was launched, Barlow was given no explanation for it. He was told only that it was based on a classified allegation by a senior-level Defense Department official, with the support of others who were concerned about Barlow's ability to protect classified information. The logic was circular: Barlow was told that he was not entitled to know the names of his accusers or the details of the investigation because they were classified, and he no longer held a security clearance.

Barlow was crushed and baffled, his faith in government shattered far beyond anything he had experienced at the CIA. He continued to beg associates at the Pentagon to describe the charges against him. He was convinced he had done nothing wrong. Without any solid understanding of why he had been fired, he feared the worst. Perhaps he had even been accused of being a Soviet spy. He also worried about the impact on his marriage, which had been in trouble since his downfall at the CIA. He and Cindy, who had also worked for the CIA, were undergoing marriage counseling at the time. Barlow later learned that it was the counseling sessions that led to a fabricated accusation that he was under psychiatric care.

With the investigation hanging over his head, Barlow had little money and no prospects. Some Pentagon security officials, who were familiar with Barlow's record and doubted the allegations against him, offered a solution: If he resigned from the department before his firing became official, they would give him a temporary job until the inquiry was completed and he was reinstated. He agreed reluctantly and soon found himself arranging lunches for Defense Department officials and locating public schools that would accept used computers.

As the months wore on, Barlow grew desperate to clear his name. But he faced more false accusations, ranging from claims that he had not paid his taxes to allegations that he was an alcoholic suffering from mental illness. The pressure drove Cindy to leave him, and Barlow feared that the chance to recover his career was diminishing with each passing day. He decided to hire a lawyer to help him navigate his way back to the Pentagon. Paul Warnke, a prominent Washington lawyer and former Defense Department official, agreed to take the case on a pro-bono basis. After months of depositions and litigation, Barlow was cleared of any wrongdoing. The Defense Department's own inquiry concluded that there was no information to support allegations that he had threatened to blow the whistle on misleading testimony or any of the other accusations. The suspension of his security clearance, the Pentagon found, was based on false charges, and his clearances were restored. But the man who spoke out about lies to Congress concerning Pakistan's nuclear arsenal never got his job back, despite appeals from senior Department of Defense security and personnel officials and prominent congressmen. He was damaged goods, someone whose determination that the record should reflect accurate intelligence assessments stained him. Although the allegations against him had been found to be false, they remained in his file and continued to haunt him.

Barlow could not understand why simply telling the truth had destroyed his career. He took his case to friends in other parts of the government and to the offices of congressmen he hoped would be sympathetic enough to reach out to the Pentagon on his behalf. At one point, he made an appointment with Len Weiss, optimistic that Senator Glenn's well-known concerns about Pakistani proliferation would translate into a helping hand. Weiss knew something of Barlow's circumstances, and he was indeed sympathetic, seeing in his downfall a Washington parable.

"You should understand that although there is a law to protect whistleblowers, they always find a way to get to you," he told Barlow as they sat in Weiss's Senate office. "The whistleblowers always suffer. We can do our best to see that they don't get to you, but they will get to you. They always do."

Weiss promised that he would get in touch with the inspector general at the Pentagon and ask for a review of the case, but he did not hold out much hope. As Barlow left the office, Weiss thought of him as a patriotic but naïve person, someone who believed telling the truth would be enough to protect him. But Weiss had been in Washington too long to believe that. Barlow, he knew, would have been better off if he had leaked the real information about Pakistan's procurement crimes to a friendly Senate staff member, who could have made sure that it got into the right hands without leaving Barlow's fingerprints and jeopardizing his career. Barlow's case was extreme, but it was not isolated, and Weiss regarded it as an indictment of the way the U.S. government—or perhaps any government—operates.

Barlow remains adamant that he was not a whistleblower. Rather than going to outsiders, he had voiced his concerns within the chain of command and tried to provide accurate information during congressional hearings. "If intelligence officers are destroyed for telling the truth, we are all in trouble," Barlow said years later. "I expressed only internal concerns and, if Congress had listened then, we might not be in Iraq right now because of cooked intelligence on weapons of mass destruction."

BHUTTO wasn't faring much better than Barlow. Before the end of her first year in office, she found herself hemmed in at every juncture by Beg and the military. Even the continuation of American assistance did little to relieve the pressure or slow Pakistan's nuclear progress, as she soon discovered.

Late that year, Bhutto went to Tehran for a conference of Islamic heads of state. The Iranians greeted her warmly, hosting a lavish state dinner at which she was given the place of honor next to Iranian president Hashemi Rafsanjani, the religious leader who had led the Iranian army in the final days of the war with Iraq. Rafsanjani had been elected president earlier in the year on a promise of restoring Iran's military dominance in the region because the lessons of the Iran-Iraq war had convinced the Iranians that the international community would not protect their country. Shortly after the end of the war in 1988, Rafsanjani had told the Iranian parliament: "We should at least think about [weapons of mass destruction] for our own defense. Even if the use of such weapons is inhuman and illegal, the war has taught us that such laws are just drops of ink on paper." As the dinner ended that night in 1989, Rafsanjani asked to speak to Bhutto in confidence, guiding her to a small room off to the side. Bhutto motioned to an aide to follow her.

"Our countries have reached an agreement on special defense matters," said Rafsanjani, an imposing figure in traditional cleric's robes and short gray beard. "This agreement was reached on a military-to-military basis, but I want us to reaffirm it as the leaders of our governments."

Bhutto knew nothing about any defense pact with Iran. "What exactly are you talking about, Mr. President?" she asked, gesturing for the aide to move closer to overhear.

"Nuclear technology, Madam Prime Minister, nuclear technology," said the Iranian, shaking his head as though it had just dawned on him that she had no idea what he was talking about.

Bhutto was surprised but contained her anger. "I'm not sure that I can approve such a relationship," she replied, with some firmness. "I'll have to discuss this when I get back to Islamabad."

Upon her return to Pakistan, the furious prime minister summoned General Beg. Confronted with Rafsanjani's claims, he said he didn't know anything about an agreement to send nuclear technology to Iran. Bhutto was certain the general was lying, but she could not risk challenging him. Instead, she ordered that no nuclear scientist be permitted to travel outside Pakistan without her approval.

Beg almost certainly knew of the pact with Iran. When Beg replaced Zia, he had initiated a number of joint defense exercises with Iran, though he told Bhutto they involved only conventional weapons and training. Other evidence indicates that the exchanges also involved nuclear technology. While the initial private deal between Iran and Khan's network had not gone beyond the first shipment of centrifuge components and drawings, the Pakistani scientist continued to provide technical advice and troubleshooting for Iran's new nuclear program.

In January 1990, American spy planes picked up signs that Kahuta was enriching uranium to a weapons-grade level, a clear violation of Bhutto's promise to Bush and fresh evidence that she did not control the nuclear program. When the news reached Washington, administration officials knew they could no longer certify to Congress that Pakistan did not possess a nuclear weapon. The president would have to inform Congress of the violation and impose sanctions, including canceling the F-16 deal. Bush dispatched Henry S. Rowen, an assistant secretary of defense, to Islamabad to warn Beg of the cutoff and possible international sanctions.

Beg was in no mood to acquiesce to Rowen's threat, so he offered one of his own in reply: "If we don't get adequate support from the United States, then we may be forced to share nuclear technology with Iran."

Rowen was taken aback. "If that were to happen, Pakistan would be in terrible trouble with the United States," he replied.

Rowen could not imagine that Beg was serious. The United States still had no diplomatic relations with Iran, and Washington had accused the Iranians of sponsoring terrorism and trying to destabilize the Middle East by exporting their brand of Islamic fundamentalism. Further, Pakistan and Iran were openly vying for influence in post-Soviet Afghanistan, and Rowen doubted that they could overcome their differences on that and other issues to cooperate on the nuclear front. Still, he passed on the threat to Bob Oakley, the ambassador, and made a note of it in the report he wrote about his trip.

Oakley took the threat seriously enough to request a follow-up meeting with Beg. Oakley had long opposed ending aid to Pakistan, which he believed would eliminate the moderate influence still wielded by Washington. When he broached the topic of nuclear sales to Iran with Beg, the general denied that he had been threatening the United States and said he only wanted the Americans to know that Pakistan would have to look for revenue elsewhere if it lost the aid. Selling nuclear technology to Iran's Revolutionary Guards was, in the general's view, a legitimate source of potential revenue. "He said he had a good conversation with the Revolutionary Guards about nuclear cooperation and conventional military assistance," Oakley said. "Iran was going to support Pakistan with conventional military aid and petroleum, and the Pakistanis would provide them with nuclear technology."

The military leaders of Pakistan had long seen the country's defense industry as a potentially valuable source of foreign exchange. Its conventional weapons, mostly small arms and ammunition, were marketed aggressively to developing countries. Even Khan had gotten into the act, using a Chinese design for shoulder-fired missiles to produce a version that his laboratories sold. Beg's ambitions for selling nuclear technology to Iran were even more outsized. He suggested to one government minister that the sales might bring in twelve billion dollars a year. And yet Oakley was one of the few Americans who seemed to take seriously the idea that Pakistan would peddle its nuclear secrets to Iran.

The series of conversations in 1989 constitute the clearest evidence that the Pakistani military was not only aware of Khan's nuclear transactions with Iran but that the scientist was operating with at least tacit approval because he was carrying out a policy of improving ties with Tehran that was endorsed by the commander of the armed forces and others within the military and intelligence leadership. In the years that followed, Beg repeatedly denied that anyone in authority had encouraged Khan's personal proliferation, claiming that the scientist and his accomplices were freelancers trying to enrich themselves. But even in his denials, Beg said that Khan's activities were not a crime. "If I was in it and had the people contacted me, I would have told them to go to such and such supplier," he said. "I would not be committing a crime in that I had not directly passed on any nuclear secrets or nuclear know-how."

CHAPTER 17

SADDAM'S GAMBIT

A. Q. KHAN PACED the waiting room outside the prime minister's office. Though impressed by the elaborate decorations—ornamental swords and gem-encrusted silver bowls, gifts from heads of state—they did not ameliorate his annoyance at being kept waiting. The meeting had been delayed several times by the prime minister already, but Khan needed a favor, so he tried to be patient. Eventually, an escort appeared, and the scientist was guided past the saluting guards and up the red-carpeted stairway to Benazir Bhutto's office.

"Qadeer Sahib, how pleasant to see you," Bhutto said, moving from behind the desk to greet him and directing him toward low sofas at one end of the spacious room. As they sat, turbaned waiters appeared with trays of tea and sweets.

"The honor is mine, Madam Prime Minister," Khan replied. "Thank you for agreeing to see me."

By January 1990, Khan exhibited all the trappings of success. Prosperity in Pakistan is measured in the acquisition of two things: gold and real estate. Khan favored the latter, and his stature and wealth gave him a say in virtually every major land deal in Islamabad, including arranging sweetheart deals for influential politicians and generals. Khan owned several homes, businesses, schools, clubs, a hotel, and a Chinese restaurant called the Hot Spot. Recently he had started construction on a weekend retreat overlooking Rawal Lake on the outskirts of Islamabad. The lake was the primary reservoir of drinking water for the more than two million residents of Islamabad and Rawalpindi, and zoning regulations strictly prohibited construction on its shores. Local villagers and government officials had opposed Khan's project, citing fears for the water supply and the destruction of pristine forestland, but they did not have the influence to counter Khan. When the local police chief dared to set foot on Khan's property in an effort to stop the construction, the scientist's employee shot him in the hand, an incident that brought no recriminations against Khan or the employee. Khan seemed to have more power than even Bhutto's husband, Asif Ali Zardari. Not far from Khan's plot on the lake, work had recently been halted on a 287-acre section of forest that Zardari was developing as a lakeside hotel and golf course.

Khan also exerted influence over Pakistan's press. He secretly owned one newspaper, the Pakistan *Observer,* though the public proprietor was Zahid Malik, who was nearing completion of Khan's authorized biography. Khan kept a handful of reporters on his payroll, and he often invited the press on junkets abroad to cover his speeches and scientific conferences, with expenses paid by Khan's laboratory. "He was their hero," said one journalist who covered him in those days.

Despite his success in enriching uranium, Khan still feared being overshadowed by the PAEC and Munir Khan, who often warned associates and government officials that his rival was a thief whose activities would one day bring the country into disrepute. When A. Q. Khan heard about the defamation, he decided to take another major gamble and try to persuade Bhutto to get rid of Munir Khan.

The prime minister had met A. Q. Khan soon after taking office in December 1988, when he and Munir Khan had given her a short briefing on the nuclear program. Since then, she had run into A. Q. Khan at official functions, but their relationship had remained formal, and she distrusted him. Now, after exchanging small talk about their families and the poor condition of Pakistan's economy, Khan got to the point, asking Bhutto to dismiss Munir Khan and give him control of the country's entire nuclear program. Munir, he argued, was delaying nuclear progress because he was not a good enough scientist or administrator to handle the job. Time was running out, Khan said. The Indians most certainly had an extensive nuclear arsenal, while Pakistan had yet to take the final steps.

Bhutto knew that her father had trusted Munir Khan enough to put him in charge of the nuclear program, and she was not going to remove him. Still, she knew that A. Q. Khan was a favorite of the military and the ISI, and she did not want to antagonize him. She stalled, promising to consider his request. Later, she told one of her aides that A. Q. Khan was too difficult to control and too closely aligned with the military and intelligence factions that opposed her.

As the weeks passed and he heard nothing, Khan realized his gambit had failed. So he telephoned General Beg and asked for a meeting. A few months earlier, Khan had responded quickly when Beg asked him to increase the lab's uranium enrichment to weapons-grade level, so the general was more than happy to see the scientist when he called. As the two men sat in Beg's office in Rawalpindi, Khan complained bitterly that Bhutto was hindering the advance of the nuclear program, explaining that she had restricted his travel and kept an incompetent, Munir Khan, at the top of the PAEC to stall the final push to a weapon. Bhutto was doing the bidding of the Americans, Khan contended, and the military should take steps to replace her before the Indians took advantage of Pakistan's lack of a nuclear arsenal. Beg agreed that Bhutto was an obstruction and confided to Khan that he, too, wanted to get rid of her, but it was difficult because she remained popular with the public. Nonetheless, a new alliance had been forged. Beg cemented it a short time later when he arranged for Khan to receive the Hilal-i-Imtiaz, one of the highest civilian awards presented by the government. The inscription read, "The name of Dr. Abdul Qadeer Khan will be inscribed in golden letters in the annals of the national history of Pakistan for his singular and monumental contribution to the field of nuclear science."

BHUTTO'S problems were not restricted to the dispute between the two Khans. She and her political party were proving inept at governing the fractious provinces, leaving reform-minded Pakistanis and allies in the

Bush administration disappointed and worried that she was damaging the long-term prospects for democracy in Pakistan. At the same time, tensions were escalating with India over the disputed territory of Kashmir. Tucked into the western Himalayas, the lush valleys and rugged mountains of Kashmir had remained a part of India after partition despite its Muslim majority. In early May 1990, India massed two hundred thousand troops in Kashmir and moved another twenty thousand within fifty miles of the Pakistani border in the south. Beg ordered his main tank units to the Indian border and put Pakistan on a secret nuclear alert. Pakistan had enough enriched uranium to assemble six to ten nuclear weapons in short order, and its existing fleet of F-16s was redeployed to bases throughout the country to protect against a preemptive strike by India.

American intelligence and NSA satellites immediately picked up the Indian and Pakistani troop movements, sparking fears once again of a nuclear showdown on the subcontinent. Few doubted that Pakistan would pull the nuclear trigger if India threatened to overrun the country. A senior CIA analyst monitoring the emergency from Langley recalled a meeting with Khan at a conference in Europe a few years earlier. "I was told by Khan in no uncertain terms 'Never again. Whatever else occurs, even if we tell you we've terminated, ceased working on the nuclear bomb, I can tell you that I will not be allowed to terminate, because we must continue to show the Indians that we have the ability to never again be defeated at their hands.'" Even the normally implacable Dick Kerr, by then the deputy director of the CIA, thought a nuclear exchange was imminent. "There's no question in my mind that we were right on the edge," he explained later. "This period was very intense. The intelligence community believed that without some intervention the two parties could miscalculate, and miscalculation could lead to a nuclear exchange."

Bush ordered a White House plane to take his deputy national-security chief, Robert Gates, to Islamabad and Delhi, sending along a private note asking for Bhutto's cooperation. When Gates left Washington, Bhutto was visiting the Persian Gulf states as part of a campaign to win Muslim support for free elections in Kashmir, and the American envoy tried to persuade Bhutto's aides to arrange a meeting in Cairo or Athens. The message he got back was that Bhutto insisted that Gates meet her in

Yemen, a detour that he did not think he had time to make. Bhutto later blamed the failure to meet with Gates on intentional mishandling of communications by Pakistani officials trying to undermine her relations with the Americans. At any rate, Gates headed on to Islamabad, where he met instead with Beg and Ishaq Khan and warned them that they were "bungling toward a war." To underscore his message, Gates gave them a precise scenario of an impending war that Pakistan could not win.

"Look, I'm not here to solve the Kashmir problem or discuss regional arms control," Gates said firmly. "I'm here because we think there is a short-term problem that we want to defuse." Looking straight at Beg, the American said, "General, our military has war-gamed every conceivable scenario between you and the Indians, and there isn't a single way you can win."

Gates detected no visible response from Beg, but Ishaq Khan appeared shaken. He had undoubtedly been assured by Beg and other military commanders either that India would back down or that Pakistan would prevail. The Pakistani president blinked, promising Gates that his government would stop supporting terrorism in Kashmir and shut down the insurgent training camps on Pakistani soil. The camps had trained hundreds of jihadis as part of a campaign to drive India out of Kashmir using the same tactics that had defeated the Soviets in Afghanistan.

Armed with that commitment, Gates flew to Delhi and managed to persuade the Indians to make several concessions in return. Among them was granting permission for American military and diplomatic personnel to go to Kashmir to see for themselves that no invasion by the Indian army was imminent. When the Americans found that the Indian troops were pulling back, the message was relayed to Islamabad. A potential nuclear war was averted, but interpretations over why events had unfolded that way differed.

Beg's version of the meeting with Gates was scarcely credible. He said the threat of a nuclear showdown never existed and that Pakistani and Indian military commanders were in constant conversation aimed at reducing the tensions and avoiding a ground battle. He said the American conclusion that Pakistan was prepared to launch a nuclear attack was based on a false threat drummed up by the Indian lobby to divert attention from the dispute over Kashmir. Instead, Beg argued, the nuclear parity between Pakistan and India was responsible for averting a war. "The fact is that if today there is stability," he wrote in an assessment of the 1990 crisis, "it is due to the possession of nuclear capability by both sides. It certainly has reduced the possibility of war."

ON AUGUST 2, 1990, Saddam Hussein invaded neighboring Kuwait and began massing his million-man army for what looked like a possible assault on Saudi Arabia, which would threaten the world's oil supplies. When Saddam rebuffed a demand from the United Nations to withdraw from Kuwait, the United States and other countries began readying troops for deployment to defend Saudi Arabia.

Four days later, with the world's attention focused on the Middle East, Pakistani president Ishaq Khan invoked his constitutional authority and removed Bhutto from office, accusing her of incompetence and corruption. Some of those charges seemed accurate, particularly suspicions about her husband's business dealings, but the real reason behind his action was her refusal to back Beg's decision to step up uranium enrichment to weapons-grade levels. Bhutto's ouster evoked little outcry from a distracted Washington, where her backers were disillusioned by her inability to stand up to the generals or slow the nuclear program.

Pakistan's strategic importance to the United States had reached a new low. In the fall of 1990, the CIA and other intelligence agencies declared finally that the country possessed a nuclear weapon. The decision caused some consternation within the administration because the official acknowledgment would force an end to assistance and would further deepen the divide with a country that the Pentagon and State Department still deemed important to U.S. regional interests. Before the new CIA finding could be announced publicly, Defense Secretary Dick Cheney tried to intervene, telephoning one of his senior counterproliferation experts at the Pentagon. Since his days as Gerald Ford's chief of staff, Cheney had been convinced that the Watergate scandal had weakened the presidency and that Congress had usurped authority over foreign policy that belonged to the executive branch. As defense secretary, he had come to regard Congress as "a bunch of annoying gnats," according to one friend at the time.

"Do we have to abide by this congressional amendment and decertify Pakistan?" asked Cheney, who opposed taking action that would damage ties with the Pakistani military and curtail defense sales.

"Yes, sir, it's the law, and we have to follow it," the expert replied, wondering how the defense secretary, himself a former congressman, could contemplate bypassing Congress.

In the end, there was nothing Cheney could do, and Bush notified Congress that he would no longer certify that Pakistan did not possess a nuclear weapon. The resulting sanctions ended arms transfers to Pakistan, including the sale of twenty-eight F-16s, which had been approved a year earlier and had already been paid for by Pakistan. The long charade was finally over, though it was easier for the American hard-liners to swallow because they no longer needed Pakistan to help fight the Soviets.

Senator John Glenn, who had long fought for transparency about Pakistan's nuclear industry, used tough language in assessing the performance of the last two administrations. "The Reagan and Bush administrations have practiced a nuclear nonproliferation policy bordering on lawlessness," he said. "In so doing, they have undermined the respect of other countries for U.S. law and have done great damage to the nuclear nonproliferation effort. Keep this in mind the next time someone in the administration extols the need for military action to deal with some power hungry dictator who is seeking to acquire nuclear weapons in the Middle East or elsewhere."

FOR KHAN and his network, the conflict in the Persian Gulf looked like a business opportunity, so in early October, two months after Iraq's invasion of Kuwait, the Pakistani sent an intermediary to meet with Iraqi intelligence agents in Baghdad. The meeting took place in the offices of Technical Consultation Corporation, a front organization that was already acquiring nuclear technology throughout Europe and North America. The intermediary, who gave his name only as Malik, said Khan and some associates were prepared to sell Iraq a package of nuclear-weapons technology. The offer was strikingly similar to the equipment and plans offered to Iran three years earlier, but the Iranians had gone their own way after the initial ten-million-dollar purchase of plans and components. Malik said Khan was prepared to help the Iraqis develop the capacity to enrich uranium to weapons-grade levels and provide the design for an atomic device. The goods would be shipped through a company Khan owned in Dubai. Malik wanted five million dollars as an upfront fee plus a 10 percent commission on equipment bought through the network. Khan would not be available to come to Baghdad because he was worried about the coalition troops massing in Saudi Arabia, but Malik suggested a meeting in Greece.

A top-secret memo written on October 6, 1990, by the lead Iraqi intelligence officer outlined the proposal and speculated about why Khan wanted to help Iraq. "The motive behind this proposal is gaining profits for him and the intermediary," he concluded. The Iraqis took the offer seriously enough to assign it a code name, "A-B," but they were skeptical and suspected that the proposal could be an elaborate sting designed by the Americans or their European allies and intended to cripple Iraq's clandestine nuclear efforts or even create an excuse for a massive bombing campaign. Still, the intelligence agents were intrigued enough to proceed cautiously. After all, Khan was well-known for his role in Pakistan's nuclear program, and Iraqi intelligence knew Saddam desperately wanted a nuclear weapon as soon as possible. They tried to obtain sample documents from Malik, but before the negotiations went farther, the realities of looming war intervened. Coalition troops and armored divisions massing in Saudi Arabia required the attention of all the resources of the intelligence service, and the Khan offer was filed away.

On January 16, 1991, allied forces began a withering bombing campaign against Iraq and its forces in Kuwait. The ground attack followed on February 23, and armored forces rolled through Kuwait and into Iraq. On March 3, Saddam Hussein accepted a cease-fire, and the fighting ended. As part of the bargain to end the war, Iraq agreed to accept an unprecedented degree of UN oversight. A key element of the oversight called for sending teams of inspectors from the IAEA into Iraq to search for evidence of a rumored nuclear-weapons program as well as chemical and biological weapons, but no one really expected to find much.

In the years leading up to the Iraqi invasion of Kuwait, the occasional press report had claimed Iraq was buying nuclear technology on the black market, but IAEA inspectors had never seen any evidence of a hidden program during routine inspections of Iraq's declared nuclear installations. Immediately after the invasion of Kuwait, Len Weiss had been talking with John Jennekens, the IAEA deputy director-general in charge of compliance with proliferation restrictions. American military commanders were worried that Iraq might use the highly enriched uranium at its declared sites to manufacture a crude nuclear device, but Jennekens was reassuring. "In a word, I can describe Iraq's cooperation as exemplary," he told Weiss. "Iraq's nuclear experts have made every effort to maintain compliance with the Nuclear Nonproliferation Treaty."

Jennekens was dead wrong. For nearly a decade, Saddam had concealed an ambitious clandestine program that had moved Iraq closer to an atomic bomb than anyone outside the country could have imagined. At Tuwaitha, site of the Osirak reactor, he had built an entire parallel weapons program in the shadows of the civilian installations inspected regularly by the IAEA. Just as the CIA had warned in 1981, the destruction of the reactor had driven the Iraqi program underground. Taking a page out of Pakistan's playbook, Saddam had been buying technology from a web of front companies that stretched from Europe to North America. Some of the goods were not covered by export regulations because they had civilian applications, but others were provided by companies and middlemen who evaded the controls by masking the ultimate uses of the equipment.

The public and secret programs were centered at the Tuwaitha Nuclear Research Center, which was Iraq's only approved nuclear facility. Four buildings, which contained two small research reactors, a laboratory, and a storage site, were the only facilities open to IAEA inspectors. Even within those buildings, inspectors were barred from some rooms because the Iraqis said they were not part of the nuclear program. The secret project was housed in a dozen small buildings scattered around Tuwaitha, which were visible but off-limits. To reinforce the message, the structures were set off behind berms, and Iraqi employees were under strict instructions not to let the outsiders near them.

Khidhir Hamza, a senior official in the Iraqi nuclear-weapons program, described how IAEA inspectors were carefully escorted along designated paths that kept them from seeing the buildings where the secret work was carried out. Before each inspection, Iraqi nuclear scientists and officials spent hours rehearsing answers to possible questions. Hamza said he and others in the nuclear establishment had thought at first that it was folly to construct the weapons facilities within the Tuwaitha complex, but the top administrators knew better. "They had come to understand how poorly the IAEA system worked," he explained years later, after escaping Iraq.

The cease-fire had given the IAEA its first unfettered access to Tuwaitha, but it still took months of wrangling with Iraqi bureaucrats before the first team of inspectors moved in. At its head was Jacques Baute, who had spent more than a decade with the French nuclear-weapons agency before joining the IAEA for this task. He and his colleagues soon discovered that Iraq had created what Baute called "a full-blown indigenous program" aimed at producing atomic weapons. As inspectors went through dozens of previously off-limits installations and sorted through millions of pages of records, they discovered the astonishing extent of Iraq's secret procurement operation. "The big shock was that during the 1980s Iraq was able to develop a totally independent, clandestine network," said Baute. "They had four locations under safeguards at Tuwaitha, but at the same site Iraq used all the other buildings for clandestine activities."

In hindsight, Baute and other experts realized there had been clues. Articles in American, German, and British publications had described elements of Iraq's operations, and intelligence agencies had gathered isolated pieces of what was happening without assembling the full puzzle. But American and British governments had failed to respond aggressively to those early reports because in those years Iraq was seen as a Western ally because it was fighting Iran. The IAEA had fared no better largely because it was bound by bureaucratic inertia and the long-standing precedent of taking countries at their word. "In the 1980s, Iraq had become so hungry that they were being incautious," Baute said. "Out of the press, the IAEA could have been alerted without the Gulf War, but we weren't looking."

Views of how close Saddam was to a bomb were all over the map, with some experts predicting he was within a year and others speculating that it would have taken three to five. There was a consensus, however, that one of the world's most ruthless leaders eventually would have joined the nuclear elite. The Israelis' attack on the Osirak reactor in 1981 now took on greater significance. Had they not taken out the reactor and set back Saddam's efforts, it might have been a nuclear-armed Iraq that invaded Kuwait. Defense Secretary Dick Cheney had acknowledged as much when he visited Israel in June 1991, three months after the end of the war and ten years after the Osirak attack. In a ceremony in Tel Aviv, Cheney gave Major General David Ivry, the commander of the Israeli Air Force at the time, a satellite photograph of the wrecked Iraqi reactor, inscribed by Cheney, "For General David Ivry, with thanks and appreciation for the outstanding job he did on the Iraqi Nuclear Program in 1981, which made our job much easier in Desert Storm."

Saddam had demonstrated a willingness to use chemical weapons during the Iran-Iraq war, and there was strong evidence that he had considered using a rudimentary nuclear device against the coalition troops. In January 1991, facing more than five hundred thousand coalition troops and airpower unseen since World War II, Saddam ordered highly enriched uranium removed from one of the reactors at Tuwaitha and taken to a secret location within the complex for building a crude bomb. The work had not gotten far, however, when the air assault by the coalition started, and the effort was halted.

The CIA's failure to uncover Saddam's nuclear ambitions or the full extent of his biological and chemical weapons before the war had a profound impact in Washington and was to frame American policy on Iraq in the years to come. Senior Pentagon officials, led by Cheney and Undersecretary Paul Wolfowitz, believed the CIA had stumbled repeatedly in the late 1980s and early 1990s, missing the collapse of the Soviet Union and nearly exposing American troops to Iraq's hidden arsenal of weapons of mass destruction. A deep and lasting distrust of the CIA developed among Cheney, Wolfowitz, and their aides—which was to resurface at a critical juncture a decade later, when they formed the war cabinet for the next President Bush.

CHAPTER 18

MISSED SIGNALS

B Y THE MIDDLE OF 1991, Hans Blix was beginning to recognize how masterfully he had been conned. A meticulous international lawyer by training and a measured diplomat by experience, Blix had been the director general of the IAEA for the past decade. As teams of inspectors were assessing the real nature of Iraq's nuclear ambitions, Blix realized that Saddam Hussein had succeeded in that time at concealing a threat of monumental proportions, highlighting the ineffectiveness of the international inspections regime. The sixty-three-year-old Blix was determined not to let it happen again. "The discoveries in Iraq were the ones that surprised and shocked us the most at the IAEA and they led us to the conclusion that the safeguard system had to be strengthened," Blix recalled later.

Born in Uppsala, Sweden, Blix had studied at Columbia University in New York and received a doctorate from Cambridge University. Later, he received his law degree in Stockholm and embarked on a political career, serving as Sweden's foreign minister in the late 1970s. In November 1981, he succeeded his fellow Swede, Sigvard Eklund, as head of the IAEA. That same month, a report circulating in Washington was sharply critical of the IAEA's performance as the world's frontline defense against nuclear proliferation, suggesting a tougher version of inspections was necessary.

In the decade that followed, the polite and mild-mannered Blix received mixed reviews at the agency. He increased the number of inspectors, raised the number of inspections annually by fourfold, and pushed for better techniques for monitoring nuclear sites, but the agency remained hobbled by the restrictions inherent in the safeguard system. Under the rules, inspectors could only visit facilities that were officially declared to be part of a country's nuclear program. In theory, the IAEA could conduct "special inspections" at undeclared plants, but only if another country supplied credible evidence of suspicious activity. From its inception in 1957, the agency had never invoked its authority for a special inspection and never discovered a single instance in which nuclear material had been diverted to a clandestine program.

Iraq blew a hole in the underlying assumptions of the inspection program. Saddam had demonstrated that the way to build a bomb was simply to do it at highly secret sites that were separate from the publicly declared locations where nuclear research and other activities were taking place. Not until the IAEA inspectors were granted extraordinary rights to inspect any facility of their choosing did they discover Saddam's hidden weapons facilities and begin to understand how close he had come to possessing an atomic weapon.

When critics blamed the IAEA for failing to discover Iraq's secret weapons program, Blix was sometimes defensive and sometimes contrite. "We did what we were entitled to do," he said repeatedly. "Nobody had come to us with concrete information." On other occasions, he said he had learned something from the experience. "It's correct to say that the IAEA was fooled by the Iraqis," he explained. Even that did not erase the affable Swedish grandfather's sense of protocol. David Kay, an American who was on the IAEA team sent into Iraq after the war, recalled challenging a senior Iraqi weapons official in front of Blix. Later, Blix scolded Kay for confronting "a representative of the state."

Blix recognized that there had to be something more than the threat of a special inspection if the agency was going to follow leads concerning suspicious locations and avoid another Iraq. In May 1991, he instructed his staff to begin work on a more intrusive inspections regime. The goal was to make it easier to visit a suspicious location on short notice, even when a country denied that it was involved in nuclear activities. At the same time, Blix told his lawyers to find the legal authority for inspectors to use a new technique developed in the IAEA laboratories known as environmental sampling. Using cotton swipes, the method could detect radioactive particles and discover whether undeclared nuclear activity had taken place.

The steps marked the beginning of a new era at the IAEA in which inspectors would be expected to be something closer to detectives than accountants. Laura Rockwood, an American lawyer at the agency, described the change this way: "In the past, we concentrated on correct inspections. If you tell me you have one stapler, and I see that you have one on your desk, I don't ask whether you have other staplers. Our job was seen as verifying what we could see. We realized that we should ask, Are there any other staplers in your office?"

Many countries were reluctant to relinquish sovereignty, and others did not want outsiders poking around in their nuclear closets. Still, as the startling discoveries in Iraq were beginning to emerge, a growing number of countries were worried about what their own neighbors might be doing. "The timing for reform was right," said Blix. "Before Iraq, reform would not have been accepted by governments. At a review conference for the nonproliferation treaty a few years earlier, I said the agency wanted to strengthen safeguards, but the majority of governments would not accept more intrusive international inspections. It took a catastrophe to bring readiness for action."

Any beliefs that Iraq was unique were erased by the discovery in May 1992 that another country was engaged in a secret program to build a nuclear weapon.

NORTH KOREA had signed the nonproliferation treaty in 1985, after starting work on a large reactor near Yongbyon, an ancient city about sixty miles north of the capital, Pyongyang. Despite the treaty's requirements, the North Koreans had stalled, refusing to grant the IAEA access to the new installation until 1992. By then, the huge nuclear complex covered fifty square miles, ringed by antiaircraft batteries and guard posts. Several hundred scientists and engineers lived in apartments within the complex, which also contained office buildings, industrial facilities, and a reprocessing plant where plutonium could be extracted from spent reactor fuel.

Under North Korea's agreement with the IAEA, the inspection was designed to establish benchmarks so the agency could ensure that the reactor was being used only for civilian purposes and that no fissile material was being diverted for military use. Not long into the inspection, it was discovered that some fissile material appeared to be missing already. The inspectors suspected any secret work would be under way close to the main reactor, so they identified three possible locations and asked for permission to inspect them. The North Koreans refused, claiming they were military installations and off-limits. The IAEA officials were highly skeptical, but they had no right to force the issue without actual evidence of a diversion. That evidence would come soon, however, and it would mark a dramatic change in the way business was conducted by the IAEA.

In June 1992, the Americans provided senior officials at the agency with the proof they required: copies of satellite photos of the area surrounding the reactor at Yongbyon. It was the first time that anyone had shared such material with the agency. Said a senior IAEA official involved in the episode, "The pictures showed efforts to plant trees that were so hurried and sloppy that the trees were already dying a couple pictures later in the series. It was so, so obvious that they were concealing something."

The IAEA told the North Koreans again that they wanted to visit the suspect sites, warning that they would not take no for an answer. After the Koreans refused again, the agency requested a closed session of its board of governors. A large screen was set up at the front of the main auditorium where the thirty-five members of the board sat in curved rows. As the room darkened, the images from the American satellites were projected onto the screen to dramatic effect, showing sequential construction and concealment at three locations over a period of months. When the lights went up, the audience murmured about what they had just seen. Hans Blix followed with a short and pointed report on the initial discrepancies discovered by inspectors at Yongbyon. Faced with dramatic new evidence, and with Iraq fresh in their minds, the board members authorized a special inspection. Even the Chinese, North Korea's closest allies, went along with the decision.

The disclosure of the American satellite images to the IAEA board reflected a change that had started at the agency after the Iraq discoveries. After Iraq, Blix had begun encouraging member countries to share intelligence about suspected diversion of nuclear materials and possible clandestine activities with the agency's staff. But he recognized that opening the door to outside intelligence agents carried dangers, too. "I insisted that this must be a one-way traffic," said Blix. "The agency could not trade and exchange information. It was the organ of all the members and not the prolonged arm of individual states." Blix hired a former intelligence official to serve as the liaison with foreign governments providing sensitive information and to make sure that intelligence was secure within the IAEA.

When the North Koreans still refused to admit inspectors, the board found the country in noncompliance with the Nuclear Non-Proliferation Treaty and referred the issue to the UN Security Council. In April 1994, after months of wrangling, the North Koreans withdrew from the IAEA and threatened to expel the agency's inspectors and pull out of the nonproliferation treaty altogether, an action that highlighted one weakness of the treaty—that a country could provide ninety days' notice and withdraw for "national security" reasons without repercussions. The United States regarded the prospect of a nuclear North Korea so seriously that President Bill Clinton's senior advisers considered military strikes against its nuclear facilities. Only eleventh-hour talks between former president Jimmy Carter and President Kim Il Sung of North Korea defused the crisis. On October 21, 1994, North Korea agreed to freeze its plutonium-production program in exchange for fuel oil, economic cooperation, and the construction of two light-water reactors, which would be far harder to use in a weapons program. As part of the deal, American inspectors would be permitted to monitor the reactor at Yongbyon. No one knew how long the freeze would last, but a military strike had been avoided for the time being.

The American monitors arrived in November. After three days of intense negotiations, the team boarded a dark-green, 1960s-era military helicopter emblazoned with the red-star emblem of North Korea for the trip to the complex. As the chopper swept across the mountainous terrain, Robert Alvarez from the U.S. Department of Energy sat next to Li Sang Gun, the director of the radiochemistry laboratory at Yongbyon. The Americans had been instructed by the State Department not to be too friendly because the countries remained technically at war. Li had maintained a stern visage during the three days of talks. But when the outgoing Alvarez struck up a conversation on the helicopter, he found that the Korean was sanguine, though willing to talk. Li's memories of the Korean War were still sharp and painful, and he described the napalm attacks by American aircraft and other privations during the war. He said it would be a long time before North Koreans abandoned their hatred of the United States.

When the helicopter landed, Alvarez saw the five-megawatt reactor and a handful of office buildings and other installations, all of which reminded him of an American nuclear-weapons site. The delegation was escorted to a darkened and icy lecture room, where the hosts explained that the lack of heat and electricity was the result of turning off the reactor. When Alvarez and his colleagues saw the reactor up close, they found that it resembled a 1950s British plant. Alvarez asked Li why his country had adopted that style of reactor, instead of the Russian model, and the Korean replied that the British version had been easier to build because "almost all of its important details had been available in the open literature of the 'Atoms for Peace' program since the late 1950s."

THE NORTH KOREA saga was still unfolding when South African president F. W. de Klerk presented the IAEA with another unpleasant surprise, announcing on March 24, 1993, that his country had dismantled six atomic weapons. There had been suspicions that South Africa was developing a nuclear arsenal for many years, but the IAEA had no authority to investigate because the country had not signed the nonproliferation treaty. In what was becoming an alarming pattern, the South Africans had acquired nuclear-research facilities under the guise of a civilian program. The nuclear cooperation between the United States and South Africa dated back to the waning days of World War II, when uranium ore was discovered in South Africa, after which it became one of the world's leading uranium producers. In 1965, the United States supplied a reactor to the Pelindaba Nuclear Research Center and shipped South Africa one hundred kilograms of weapons-grade uranium to fuel it. By the time the international community imposed sanctions on South Africa in the seventies for its apartheid policies, the country had built a solid foundation of nuclear expertise. All that remained was to turn to the black market in Europe and the United States for additional materials as the needs arose. Machine tools, furnaces, and an extensive list of equipment for its weapons program were imported, often from the same companies and middlemen who were helping Pakistan and Iraq. Mohammed Farooq, the Indian expatriate who had organized the sale of Pakistani centrifuge technology to Iran in 1987, sold specialized furnaces to South Africa, and Gotthard Lerch, the German engineer, provided it with vacuum technology.

In the end, external and internal factors made South Africa the first nuclear state to disarm voluntarily. Soviet interventions in southern Africa had slowed dramatically in the middle 1980s, reducing the threat to South Africa, and when de Klerk was elected president in 1989 he initiated reforms to end the country's isolation and allow it to return to good standing in the international community. De Klerk recognized that the nuclear arsenal was an obstacle, so he ordered its secret dismantling and simultaneously started negotiations to sign the nonproliferation treaty. But the South African leader also was motivated by the future rushing toward his apartheid government: Black South Africans, led by Nelson Mandela and his African National Congress, were on the verge of gaining control of the country, and de Klerk was determined that they not get their hands on a nuclear arsenal, too.

At the height of its program, the South Africans had six nuclear devices and a partially completed seventh. Under de Klerk's orders, the weapons were disassembled and the highly enriched uranium in their cores was melted down. Designs and other classified documents related to the weapons program were to be shredded, and weapons components were to be destroyed. Most of the work was done by 1991, when South Africa signed the nonproliferation treaty.

THE LESSONS of North Korea and South Africa, and to a lesser extent Iraq, demonstrated that preventing proliferation and avoiding the unthinkable demanded addressing the root causes of why nations sought nuclear weapons, raising challenges beyond the scope of the IAEA and the nonproliferation treaty. Stopping the spread of nuclear weapons required tough and enforceable safeguards, but it also demanded that the Americans and other global actors address the issues of security and national prestige driving the new proliferators. While a nation's motives are inevitably complex, the countries pursuing nuclear arsenals in the new age of proliferation faced enemies who might be deterred by the threat of nuclear retaliation: India feared China, Pakistan feared India, and Israel was surrounded by hostile Arab countries. The Iraqi decision was based more on its desire to dominate the Middle East, but its program drove Iran to developing a matching arsenal. North Korea's nuclear efforts were rooted in decades of fear of the United States; South Africa sought nuclear weapons after international sanctions left it isolated and vulnerable at a time when the Soviets were ramping up their influence in the neighborhood.

WHILE THE IAEA and most of the world's proliferation experts were focused on Iraq, North Korea, and South Africa, Khan was trying to help Iran work out the bugs in its centrifuge program. When reassembled at the Tehran Nuclear Research Center, some of the P-1 centrifuges he had supplied did not operate at all, and others spun briefly before flying out of balance. Despite the difficulties, the relationship did not end. Stymied by the international crackdown, Iranian nuclear experts had little choice but to consult Khan, flying him secretly to Tehran several times in that period.

Ali Akbar Omid Mehr, a young Iranian diplomat, was preparing for his posting to Pakistan when he came across Khan's name in Iranian government records in 1990. Before heading for the grimy frontier city of Peshawar with his wife and two daughters, Mehr had been in charge of the Pakistan desk at Iran's Foreign Ministry and had had access to the "green book," the official record of bilateral dealings between Iran and Pakistan. "I saw that Mr. A. Q. Khan had been given a villa near the Caspian Sea for his help to Iran," Mehr said later. "The villa was a gift to him for services rendered." The name didn't mean anything to Mehr until he arrived in Peshawar a few months later. In the Iranian consulate offices there, he often heard discussions of nuclear cooperation between Iran and Pakistan, and Khan's name was invariably at the center of the conversation.

Mehr was a secular man who regarded himself as a professional diplomat. Early during his assignment in Peshawar, he ran afoul of the strictures imposed by Iran's religious leaders, and he began to fear for his safety. Over several months, he hatched a secret and dangerous plan to seek refuge in a European country before he and his family were forced to return to Iran. He quietly accumulated cash and purchased airline tickets to Stockholm, where he planned to ask for asylum. Once the plans were in place, a Pakistani friend drove the Mehrs to the airport in Peshawar for the flight to Karachi, where they planned to catch a Scandinavian Airlines flight to the Swedish capital. The first leg went smoothly enough, but after boarding the plane for Stockholm, one of Mehr's daughters noticed a familiar face a few rows behind them. When she told her father, he turned and saw two security officers from the consulate. Mehr realized that his getaway had been discovered, and his heart sank. Certain that the Iranian security police would be waiting for the family in Stockholm, he quietly summoned a flight attendant. By some small miracle, she believed the desperate man's story and convinced the plane's captain to divert the aircraft to Copenhagen, where Mehr and his wife and daughters were the only ones allowed to deplane. The Danish government eventually granted the family asylum and provided them with new identities. The Mehrs moved several times to avoid Iranian agents but eventually settled in a small house in a village about an hour outside Copenhagen. Mehr worked from time to time with the Danish security authorities through the 1990s and wrote a book about his experiences in post-Ayatollah Iran. Discovery by Iranian authorities remained a constant fear for the family.

Mehr was not the only person who noted Khan's involvement with Iran in the 1990s. Another defector, a former officer in the elite Revolutionary Guards named Hamid Reza Zakeri, had worked on security at Iran's nuclear installations before leaving the country in 2002. During that time, he often saw Khan at these facilities. Zakeri, who was placed in a witness-protection program by the German authorities and testified in proceedings against a suspect in the September 11 attacks, provided a list of secret nuclear installations where he said he or his men had seen Khan working with Iranian counterparts.

CHAPTER 19

NUCLEAR NATIONALISM

L ATE IN 1992, CIA director Robert Gates found himself at the center of a fierce debate about the level of threat posed by Iran. Democrat Bill Clinton had defeated George Bush in November, and the incoming administration was weighing whether it could or should improve relations with Tehran, which had not resumed since the hostage crisis in 1979. American intelligence analysts and diplomats were divided over the intentions of Iran's revolutionary leaders and the significance of its two-billion-dollar military buildup. The division was particularly sharp when it came to discerning the purpose of Iran's renewed attempts to acquire nuclear technology.

A year earlier, the secret National Intelligence Estimate concluded that some of Iran's leaders were interested in developing nuclear weapons but that the program was too disorganized to be taken seriously. Gates, however, was of a different mind. A compact, tough-talking career CIA officer, Gates had a history of seeing the world through a bleak lens, and in the past he had been accused of slanting intelligence to justify a hard-line policy. Gates was first nominated as CIA director in 1987, but his name was withdrawn because of questions about his role in the Iran-Contra scandal. When his name was put forth again in the fall of 1991, he underwent an extraordinary three weeks of confirmation hearings in which he was both praised and condemned. The chief criticism was that Gates had tailored intelligence on the military strength of the Soviet Union for years to exaggerate and prolong the threat and to justify higher spending on the U.S. military and the CIA itself, an accusation that he heatedly denied.

Gates survived the bruising hearings and immediately began pushing a tougher position on Iran's military intentions, particularly on the nuclear front. In March 1992, he testified before Congress that Iran was engaged in a suspicious pattern of procurement that could lead to developing a nuclear weapon by the end of the decade unless the flow of Western technology was stopped. He repeated his concern shortly after Clinton's election, saying that Iran could pose a threat to the United States and its allies in the Persian Gulf within three to five years. Others within the intelligence community and at the State Department were less convinced that Iran was chasing a nuclear weapon. Iranian officials denounced the notion that they were interested in developing nuclear weapons. "We have no need for nuclear weapons," a deputy foreign minister said in late November, calling the suspicions "a lie and a plot."

When Clinton took office in January 1993, Gates was replaced as CIA chief by R. James Woolsey Jr., but his warnings echoed on. There were some early successes in interrupting Iran's purchases of nuclear technology. The Americans convinced Argentina not to sell equipment that would have enabled Iran to convert uranium ore to the uranium hexafluoride gas used in centrifuges, and they were pressuring the Chinese to delay the sale of a nuclear reactor. But the same loose control regime that Saddam Hussein had exploited still existed because the wider international community had not yet accepted the need for tighter regulations, and efforts at the IAEA were proceeding slowly. Plus, the Iranians had the added benefit of a blueprint for enriching uranium, courtesy of A. Q. Khan and his associates.

The CIA had picked up evidence in 1988 that Khan had sold some centrifuge parts to Iran, but the intelligence indicated that Iranian scientists felt the Pakistani scientist had provided them with shoddy equipment and had therefore broken off any dealings with him. So instead of worrying about Khan and Pakistan, the American intelligence and counterproliferation apparatus was focused on Europe and nuclear scientists fleeing the collapsing Soviet Union. "In the 1990s, we were not terribly worried

about A. Q. Khan and Iran," said Bob Einhorn, a senior counterproliferation official at the State Department who had access to the intelligence
gathered at the time. "In retrospect, we can see now what was happening.
We had our eye on the wrong ball. In truth, we really underestimated
what the Pakistanis were doing with their own nuclear program and we
underestimated Khan. He is the one who really enabled Iran to make
progress in developing a nuclear capability."

The intelligence was accurate in part. At the Tehran Nuclear Research Center, the Iranians were struggling to engineer centrifuges from
the components and drawings that Khan and his group had sold them in
1987. Inside hidden workshops within the research facility, teams of scientists were using uranium gas provided secretly by China to test centrifuges built from Khan's substandard components, but the machines kept
breaking down. The CIA had learned of the problems firsthand from
Masud Naraghi, the director of the Iranian program who had negotiated
the initial deal with Lerch in Zurich five years earlier. The delay in getting the centrifuges running had cost Naraghi his job, and he had walked
into the United States embassy in Bern, Switzerland, to ask for asylum in
late 1992. He and his family were flown to the United States. In exchange
for protection, Naraghi underwent a thorough debriefing by nuclear weapons analysts with the CIA, providing them with a complete rundown on
the Iranian effort to develop nuclear weapons, including its dealings with
A. Q. Khan and his network. He also said Iran was scouring Europe for new
sources of centrifuges or parts, with little success in the face of the increasing
international scrutiny.

The information was incorporated in a secret report issued on February 1, 1993, by the U.S. Joint Atomic Energy Intelligence Committee,
titled "Iran's Nuclear Program: Building a Weapons Capability." While
the report represented clear evidence about Iran's nuclear intentions and
Khan's role, the information was not shared with the IAEA. If the American government had provided the intelligence to the IAEA, its inspectors
could have demanded access to the hidden workshops. Cut off from the
intelligence, however, the centrifuge work was off-limits to the inspectors
because the Iranians used the common ruse that no unauthorized nuclear
work was underway there.

While the United States withheld the most critical intelligence, it and other countries warned the IAEA that Iran was buying nuclear equipment, and the agency officially asked Iran to respond to the accusations. The Iranians said they had nothing to hide and invited senior IAEA officials to tour its nuclear facilities. A contingent of IAEA officials spent several days on what amounted to nothing more than a wild-goose chase. The intelligence information from the Americans and others had been too general and did not identify any specific locations, so the agency's officials had had to rely on their Iranian guides. One of the few specific allegations was that weapons work was being conducted at a defense facility on a mountaintop northwest of Tehran; so on the final day of the visit, the IAEA party boarded an Iranian Air Force helicopter to visit the site. The pilot had trouble finding the remote location, eventually landing near some crude bunkhouses and other small buildings. The IAEA officials saw no signs of any nuclear work and returned to Vienna without knowing for sure that they had even been taken to the right place. The IAEA had no choice but to give Iran a clean bill of health.

Still, the international community continued to try to restrict sales to Iran, threatening to bring its nuclear effort to a standstill. The complexity of starting to build an atomic bomb from scratch meant that thousands of sophisticated machines, from centrifuges to the smallest specialty valve, had to be procured under increasingly difficult conditions. The Iranians realized that progress depended on asking A. Q. Khan and his network to obtain the technology and the material required. The Iranians had learned some lessons since 1987, and this time they demanded top-quality equipment, designs, and components for the more advanced and efficient version of the centrifuge, the P-2. In the summer of 1994, Iran's defense minister traveled to Islamabad to persuade Khan to sell his country's most advanced nuclear technology to Tehran. For a second time, Khan was going to become the unintended beneficiary of international efforts to thwart the spread of nuclear weapons.

IN PAKISTAN, Khan appeared to be untouchable, his freedom to operate unfettered, and his word unquestioned. At Kahuta, the enrichment work was going smoothly, and as he and his scientists continued to improve the centrifuge designs, the laboratory had expanded into the manufacture of conventional weapons, including surface-to-air missiles, antitank weapons, and rocket launchers. In addition, Khan Research Laboratories was peddling its nuclear wares through seminars dealing with the complexities of enriching uranium and perfecting centrifuge operations. The cover of one of the lab's brochures showed a photograph of Khan with a mushroom cloud in the background. Another brochure offered "consultancy and advisory services to government and private organizations" and, under the heading "NUCLEAR-RELATED PRODUCTS," a list of items for sale that constituted virtually a complete enrichment plant, ranging from ultracentrifuges and high-frequency inverters to a system for handling uranium hexafluoride. The lab's scientists published papers in scientific journals about how to make and test centrifuges. Khan boasted in print of getting around Western restrictions on the spread of nuclear technology, saying in one paper that he wanted to sweep away the "clouds of the so-called secrecy."

His long feud with Munir Khan had ended in 1991 when his rival had resigned as head of the PAEC and moved back to Vienna, where he had worked for the IAEA before joining Pakistan's nuclear program two decades earlier. Throughout his career, Munir Khan had maintained a low profile, even in the face of public attacks by A. Q. Khan. In his view, scientists should remain in the background. Years later, he said that he regretted allowing A. Q. to take the limelight because the fame allowed him greater license for his skullduggery. A. Q. Khan had reveled in his competitor's departure, but he was unable to persuade the government to grant him sole authority over the country's nuclear program—a new PAEC head was appointed, leaving Khan to sulk at his laboratory.

Strangely, Pakistan's nuclear status still remained officially ambiguous, and Khan was part of the charade. When British journalist Simon Henderson interviewed the scientist, he found him at once talkative and evasive. Asked whether Kahuta was enriching uranium for nuclear weapons, Khan offered a flat denial, saying the plant was "not meant for weapons production and we do not see the need of having nuclear weapons in this part of the world." Pushed about whether Kahuta could produce highly enriched uranium, Khan dismissed the idea as hypothetical, saying: "Everything has a double side: a knife can cut vegetables and a knife can kill human beings. So if you want to see it that way, so all nuclear plants and nuclear facilities and chemical plants and chemical facilities all over the world can be used for all purposes, either for saving the human race or hurting it." The scientist accused the West of discriminating against Pakistan by demanding that it open its nuclear facilities to inspection while permitting India to avoid the same. When asked whether his use of the black market indicated that Kahuta was flouting international regulations, Khan turned the question around and blamed the West for having double standards that necessitated a certain amount of subterfuge: "I can give you an example of them stopping O-rings that you can get from a shoemaker's shop. They were stopping O-rings, they were stopping materials, ordinary papers. It was not a question of circumventing. When you see that somebody is trying to stop everything which is destined for you, you ask the supplier to send to some other address. Now it is the responsibility of the supplier and the country that they observe the national laws and that they don't violate them."

Khan's remarks came at a time when the dynamics of Pakistan's foreign relations had changed. Relations with the Americans, whom he saw as his chief adversaries, had soured since President Bush cut off military assistance in the fall of 1990, and they had not improved following Clinton's election. Clinton had tried to repair the relationship by offering to sell Pakistan the F-16s, for which it had already paid five hundred million dollars, but when the deal was tied to inspections of Kahuta and other nuclear installations, the Pakistanis balked. Still, the absence of the jets left a gap in Pakistan's military strategy for attacking India with nuclear bombs, and Khan wanted desperately to fill that gap by developing a missile capable of reaching the most distant Indian cities. To that end in late 1993, he hatched a plan that took him back to the office of Benazir Bhutto.

In October 1993, more than three years after she had been ousted by the military, Bhutto had engineered her political comeback as prime minister under a new coalition government. This time around she was determined to avoid confrontation with the military and intelligence establishments, so when Khan visited her that December, Bhutto decided to cultivate a potential ally. But Khan was not the same man she had rejected as head of the nuclear program in 1990. Bhutto had run into him at a couple of official functions since returning to office and noticed changes in his demeanor. "Since my dismissal, he had clearly become more important," she explained. "But he also had changed in other ways. My first impression of him in the late 1980s was that he was a nationalist. By the time I returned to office in 1993, I felt that he was an Islamist."

Others had noticed the transformation, too. Perhaps he had become more devout. Perhaps, angered by accusations and criticism from the West, he had become a nuclear jihadist devoted to payback for grievances real and imagined. Khan frequently portrayed himself as a pious man, once telling his biographer: "I belong to the group of people who believe that nothing happens without Allah's will. What we have done for Pakistan is no less than a miracle. It is true that Allah honored me with the task of defending our beloved country."

Lieutenant General Talat Masood dealt with Pakistan's conventional-weapons programs, but he knew Khan well and had also noticed the changes in his outlook by the early 1990s. Masood believed the scientist's attitude had been shaped by the criticism and actions of the Western countries, particularly the accusation that he had stolen the keys to the bomb. "He believed that Muslim countries had been thwarted over the years while others, like Israel and India, were allowed freer rein," Masood explained. "From a Western perspective, he cheated in stealing designs, but from his point of view, he did what was necessary to achieve his goal for the country."

Pervez Hoodbhoy's job as a physicist at Islamabad's Quaid-i-Azam University and his ardent antinuclear stance meant that he often attended conferences and other meetings with Khan, occasionally debating the scientist about the need for nuclear weapons. Hoodbhoy had spent enough time with Khan to regard him as something of a chameleon, changing his colors depending on the powerful men around him, adopting his quasi-military fatigues when necessary and exhibiting a more pious side when it served his interests. Hoodbhoy did not regard Khan as a Muslim fundamentalist but rather as an ordinary believer whose outlook dovetailed with others in Pakistan's ruling circles—a pan-Islamic vision that saw the bomb as a strategic defiance of the West and a Muslim success story that brought admiration from hundreds of millions of coreligionists. Khan was deeply resentful of the United States and Israel, attributing apparent Muslim backwardness to a conspiracy by Christians and Jews, and he regarded the bomb as a victory for all of Islam. Khan was part jihadist, part nuclear nationalist.

When Khan showed up at Bhutto's office in December, he explained that he knew the prime minister was scheduled to make a state visit to China later that month. He asked if she would make a slight detour on his behalf. "If you are going to North Korea, it would be very nice if you could talk to Kim Il Sung about helping us with this nuclear thing," said Khan.

Instantly suspicious, Bhutto asked, "What do you mean, 'this nuclear thing'?"

Khan replied that he had been talking to the North Koreans, and they were willing to sell Pakistan the designs for a version of the No-Dong missile, which could carry a nuclear payload. Bhutto was puzzled and pointed out that Pakistan already had missiles capable of reaching India, but Khan said he and the generals wanted longer-range ones, with bigger warhead capacity. The prime minister was reluctant to exacerbate the arms race.

"We have a policy of doing what India does," she told him.

"We should get the technology while we can, even if we don't use it," he countered.

Bhutto recognized an opportunity to win favor with Khan as well as the hard-line generals and intelligence chiefs. She said she would make her decision in a matter of days. She then summoned General Abdul Waheed Kakar, who had by this time replaced Beg as chief of the armed forces, and Farooq Leghari, the longtime civil servant who had been elected president. Leghari told her that A. Q. Khan had already been to see him about the missiles, and he thought getting the designs was a good idea. Waheed concurred. Bhutto said that she would do as asked and instructed aides to arrange the detour to Pyongyang and a meeting with Kim, the autocratic and mercurial communist leader. Bhutto later described her motivation to an aide, explaining, "I thought the military would be very happy with me and would stop trying to destabilize my government."

A few days later, a Pakistani Air Force plane carrying Bhutto and her party landed in Pyongyang, where Bhutto was given a lavish welcome. Tens of thousands of people braved the bitter cold to line the streets for her motorcade from the airport, and that night the North Korean dictator was on hand to welcome Bhutto at a state dinner in the Kumsusan Assembly Hall. Like Pakistan, North Korea was suffering under economic hardships imposed by the international community after the discovery of its nuclear work a year earlier, and in her remarks Bhutto complained that her country and North Korea shared the problem of American-imposed sanctions. Pakistan was committed to nuclear nonproliferation, she said, but added that countries still had "their right to acquire and develop nuclear technology for peaceful purposes, geared to their economic and social developments."

North Korea was extremely poor; arms sales and currency counterfeiting were among its few sources of outside revenue. One of its most sought-after products was the No-Dong missile, so Bhutto found that Kim was willing to sell the missile plans. Bhutto's plane left the country carrying several computer disks containing the blueprints for the latest version of the missile, which she later delivered to Khan, with a reminder that the missile should not be developed unless India started work on its own long-range missile.

Khan ignored the prohibition and instructed his engineers to get to work immediately. His rivals at the PAEC had already produced short-range missiles that put most Indian cities within reach of Pakistani nuclear warheads, and Khan was determined to beat them with a missile that could go farther and carry a bigger payload. In honor of a twelfth-century Muslim warrior who fought the Hindus and with whom Khan claimed kinship, he named the missile the Ghauri. Based on a Soviet-era Scud design, the missile had an estimated range of about eight hundred miles and could carry a nuclear warhead that weighed up to 1,700 pounds. The Korean version was already popular with other countries, including Iran.

The plans were not enough to build a functioning missile, so in the months that followed Kahuta's technicians established close working relationships with their North Korean counterparts, who served as advisers. The North Koreans, including top officials from the military missile program, became familiar figures inside Kahuta, a phenomenon that did not go unnoticed by the CIA. At the same time, Khan began making so many trips to Pyongyang that he caught the eye of American intelligence agents there. The question was obvious—not what were the North Koreans doing in Pakistan, but why was Pakistan's top nuclear scientist traveling to North Korea?

The CIA suspected that Pakistan was trading Khan's knowledge of uranium enrichment for North Korean help in developing missiles, not paying for it. Pakistan's economy was suffering, and the Americans believed the country was too poor to pay for the missile help. Instead, CIA agents inside Pakistan uncovered evidence that Bhutto had set up a deadly barter, agreeing to trade Pakistan's uranium-enrichment technology for the missile secrets. When asked about the accusation after she left office, Bhutto acknowledged obtaining missile designs from North Korea but insisted that she had authorized the government to pay for the designs. If Pakistan later exchanged uranium-enrichment equipment and know-how for the technology, she said, she had no knowledge of it at the time.

A barter arrangement made sense, though, because after North Korea's plan to divert plutonium to its nuclear-weapons program was frozen by the dispute with the IAEA in 1992, its scientists had tried to start a centrifuge program as an alternative means of developing a nuclear arsenal. Centrifuge enrichment could be concealed more easily, particularly in a mountainous country where hundreds of military installations and critical factories were already buried in thousands of miles of tunnels, inspired by the national paranoia that the Americans or South Koreans would bomb the North, possibly with nuclear weapons. Hiding a few thousand centrifuges posed no problem. The problem was that the North Koreans were having a hard time mastering the enrichment technology.

Throughout 1994, the suspicion that Khan was helping the North Koreans gained further credence. Intelligence tracked shipments from Pakistan to North Korea, often on board regularly scheduled Pakistan International Airlines flights and sometimes aboard military transports. Proving what was taking place within the closed confines of Korea was virtually impossible, however, and Pakistani cooperation with American intelligence was at a low point.

There are conflicting viewpoints on whether the Pakistani military knew the full extent of what Khan was doing with the North Koreans.

The scientist was traveling often in those days, using his red diplomatic passport to visit the Middle East, Africa, and Europe. The fact that some of the crates were sent to North Korea aboard military transport planes makes it hard to imagine that Khan was operating without military approval at some level. One retired Pakistani general said there were suspicions that Khan had traded enrichment technology for missiles and pocketed the government's payment to the Koreans. Some senior military officers worried that the years of unchecked freedom and his extensive dealings with the nuclear black market to build Pakistan's arsenal had corrupted Khan, but the consensus remained that his importance to the atomic-weapons program was too high to ask too many questions. "For the military, the whole job was to protect and allow A. Q. Khan to build the bomb freely," said Feroz Khan, a retired Pakistani general who was involved in the nuclear program throughout the 1990s. "It was very clear to the military that we did not question what he was doing or how he was doing it. I used to say to the Americans and others, 'Look, we are not selling nuclear technology to the Middle East where we could get a lot of money.' We realized that if we were proliferating, our program would be in jeopardy. We got what we wanted, the bomb, we knew we were working on the black market, we knew Khan was using these dubious characters, but this was in our military interest, so some dirty tricks were allowed to go on."

Others believed that Khan could not have been engaged so openly with the North Koreans without the explicit approval of Pakistan's military leaders. The CIA and State Department saw the cooperation as part of a larger strategic partnership engineered by senior Pakistani military and civilian leaders. "We had information that this was a two-way street and nuclear technology was involved," said Bob Einhorn, the State Department's senior nonproliferation official at the time. "The strategic cooperation between Pakistan and North Korea was almost assuredly known and approved of by Pakistani military officials."

While the CIA had picked up Khan's work with the North Koreans, they were not as fortunate when it came to his cooperation with another troublesome regime.

In THE SUMMER of 1994, Iran's ambassador in Islamabad hosted a reception for a visiting military delegation from Tehran. Among the many diplomats and government officials attending was A. Q. Khan, who huddled in a corner with Iran's defense minister. The Iranian had come with a bold proposal: He wanted Khan to resume supplying Tehran with nuclear equipment on a far larger scale than before. The minister told Khan that he wanted to buy the P-2 centrifuge. Describing Iran's difficulties in obtaining other equipment on the black market, he asked Khan to reach out to some of his long-standing contacts in that world. The offer entailed some risk for Khan, but the scientist assumed that the generals would not object in the unlikely event he was discovered. Khan frequently told friends and associates that the notion of assisting another Islamic country, particularly one so opposed to the United States and Israel, appealed to him. So did the chance to earn millions of dollars. He agreed to help Iran, assuring the official that he could deliver the first shipment through his contacts in Dubai before the end of the year.

By promising to secretly siphon off some of Pakistan's most advanced centrifuge technology for Iran and enlisting his gang of black marketers, Khan was embarking on a course that would turn him into the most dangerous seller of atomic-weapons systems in history. The 1987 shipment to Iran was a small, one-time transaction, probably approved in advance by his own country, and the barter deal with North Korea provided direct benefit to Pakistan in the form of missile technology. This, however, was a private arrangement, which promised nothing to Pakistan and great wealth for Khan.

The scientist knew precisely where to turn for help in organizing the smuggling operation for Iran. Khan had kept in touch with B. S. A. Tahir, the young Sri Lankan in Dubai who had played a minor role the first time around. The two men frequently dined together on Khan's visits to the gulf port, and Tahir had helped him find an apartment in a luxury building on Al Makhtum Street, near the center of Dubai. The soft-spoken Tahir had evolved into a tough businessman, forcing his uncle, Mohammed Farooq, out of the family computer-sales business through an acrimonious lawsuit and expanding his clientele across the Middle East. On occasion, he had organized shipments of equipment from Europe to Khan's labs.

Khan telephoned Tahir and told him to expect some visitors. He'd made a deal, he explained, to move goods from Pakistan to another country, and he promised that he would get to Dubai as soon as possible to oversee the transaction. By the way, Khan said, the deal was a big one, worth six million to seven million dollars just as a down payment.

A few days later, two officers from Iran's Revolutionary Guards arrived at Tahir's SMB Computers in the city's Jebel Ali Free Zone, saying that they had come to see A. Q. Khan. Tahir told them that he expected Khan to arrive soon but that some of the items they sought were likely to be delayed. The two men spent a couple of days shopping in Dubai's glittering malls, waiting for their new partner. When Khan arrived, he brought with him detailed plans for building the P-2 centrifuge; by then, about half the parts had arrived separately at Tahir's warehouse. Unfortunately for the Iranians, Kahuta did not have enough P-2 components for Khan to take them without attracting attention, so he had substituted P-1 parts. He telephoned Tahir, who met him at his apartment, took the drawings, and then picked up the Iranians at their hotel and took them to his warehouse. The men examined the drawings without seeming to understand them and poked around in one of the crates containing the components. Tahir explained that the rest of the centrifuge components were expected in a matter of days; when they arrived, he would ship both sets to Tehran disguised as computer parts. Among the equipment to follow were about four hundred specialized bellows for centrifuges from Friedrich Tinner, and thousands of magnets and high-voltage inverters, both critical components for a centrifuge system, manufactured and supplied by two Turkish businessmen, Gunes Cire and Selim Alguadis, who had sold similar goods to Pakistan in previous years. In a rare moment of honesty, Tahir explained that though the drawings were for the P-2, the components were from P-1s. The Iranians had little choice but to accept what was offered, and they handed Tahir two heavy suitcases. After dropping the Iranians at the airport, Tahir drove to Al Makhtum Street and lugged the suitcases into Khan's apartment, where he opened them in front of Khan. The scientist's face lit up when he saw the stacks of bills, a total of three million dollars. The cash was about half what Tahir expected, but Khan explained that the remainder of the money would be paid to other participants in the network.

The arrival of the first batch of P-1 components and the additional equipment from the network provided an immediate boost to the Iranian nuclear effort, though the officials were angry that they had been short-changed on the P-2s. Up until that point, scientists at the Tehran Nuclear Research Center had succeeded in operating only a single centrifuge at nearly full speed. The new components meant that the testing could be expanded dramatically, but hiding a larger number of machines from IAEA inspectors increased the risk that someone would discover the program. So the research and production operations were moved to a nondescript complex in an industrial area on the outskirts of Tehran. The walled compound, which contained two large buildings and several smaller ones, had been home to a small clock manufacturer, Kalaye Electric Company. It was about to become the heart of Iran's nuclear project, and renovation work started even as technicians began to assemble the components into the first fifty centrifuges. Progress was to be surprisingly swift.

American intelligence completely missed the transfer of the centrifuge technology and other equipment to Iran. The notion that Khan, a Pakistani scientist whom the CIA had always underestimated, had gone from black-market buyer to seller did not occur to the intelligence agencies around the world that had been watching Pakistan for nearly two decades. The warnings about the potential for Pakistan sharing its nuclear prowess with Iran seemed to have been forgotten.

CHAPTER 20

MORE AND MORE PIECES

I N EARLY MAY 1995, Bill Clinton boarded Air Force One at Andrews Air Force Base outside Washington and headed to Moscow to attend ceremonies marking the fiftieth anniversary of the Allied victory over Nazi Germany. Because Russian president Boris Yeltsin had recently dispatched troops to quell rebels in the breakaway province of Chechnya, some White House officials opposed the trip, fearing Clinton would be seen as paying tribute to an army tarnished by atrocities. But the president had high hopes and a pressing agenda and could not be dissuaded.

High on Clinton's list was persuading Yeltsin to crack down on the sale of Russian nuclear technology to Iran. Russia's Ministry of Atomic Energy was on the verge of becoming a major supplier to Iran's nuclear program, under the guise of civilian development. The primary vehicle for transferring technology was an eight-hundred-million-dollar contract announced in January 1995 that called for Russia to complete the reactor at Bushehr. Administration counterproliferation experts wanted the president to persuade Yeltsin to cancel the Bushehr deal and other technology transfers. In preparation, the National Security Council had prepared a five-page, single-spaced report describing Iran's atomic-weapons ambitions and the roles that Russia, China, and Pakistan were playing in helping them achieve those goals. To buttress its claims, the report contained excerpts from electronic conversations intercepted by the National Security Agency as well as some raw intelligence.

Providing such sensitive intelligence to the Russian leader was highly unusual, and there was opposition to doing so from many administration officials. But Clinton's nonproliferation advisers carried the day, arguing that the information was vital to convince Yeltsin that Iran's program was military. "We know that Iran has an organized structure whose purpose is the production of nuclear material for nuclear weapons," said the report, which explained that Iran had tried to buy enriched uranium from the former Soviet republic of Kazakhstan and was importing nuclear components from European manufacturers through the same smuggling routes used by Iraq and Pakistan. Reading the report in Clinton's presence, Yeltsin was in a tough position. The Iranian deals, particularly the work on Bushehr, meant thousands of potential jobs for the unemployed and underemployed Russian nuclear scientists and technicians and a chance to increase Russian influence with Tehran. Yeltsin told Clinton he would consider the American objections, leaving the Americans hopeful.

The Clinton administration was still trying to persuade China not to sell nuclear reactors to Iran. During a conference at the United Nations to discuss extending the Nuclear Non-Proliferation Treaty, Secretary of State Warren Christopher had lunch at the Waldorf-Astoria Hotel with his Chinese counterpart, Foreign Minister Qian Qichen. Christopher argued to Qian that Iran was building a nuclear arsenal and that any cooperation with Tehran was dangerous because the technology and training could be diverted to the weapons program. Though the Americans did not know it, just such a diversion had already taken place. In 1991, the Chinese had sold Iran 1.8 tons of uranium ore and chemical forms of uranium, which the Iranians had used in testing the faulty centrifuges provided by Khan and recently transferred to the hidden facility at Kalaye Electric. Qian was unimpressed with Christopher's argument, agreeing only that Chinese experts would meet with American scientists to discuss the issue further. He refused to promise that China would end its nuclear cooperation with Iran, which was providing Beijing with badly needed hard currency and the potential access to Iran's reserves of natural gas and oil.

China officially opposed nuclear proliferation, but the reality was shaped by its self-perception as a nuclear outsider, never quite a member of the club led by the United States and the former Soviet Union. China developed its nuclear arsenal partly in response to the American threat to use nuclear devices on its troops in the Korean war and didn't test its first nuclear device until 1964. The Chinese refused to sign the nonproliferation treaty until 1992 because they regarded it as a mechanism for allowing the superpowers to maintain their arsenals while denying such weapons to other countries, some of which might have legitimate self-defense needs. The same argument is still made today by many nonnuclear countries facing what they see as outside threats.

The efforts to block Russia and China from supplying nuclear technology to Iran were commendable, but the Clinton administration and its intelligence apparatus were fighting the last war and missing the new front: the creation of a private black market comprising rogue scientists and suppliers operating outside of states and offering nuclear know-how to the highest bidder. Even when the CIA had picked up signs of a shipment of centrifuge parts from Pakistan to Iran in 1994, just as they had in the late 1980s, the incident was regarded as random and minor. No one connected the episode to Khan because the concept of private proliferation was not in the vernacular and because, once again, the Americans underestimated the Pakistani scientist. Two months after Clinton's trip to Moscow, American intelligence had another chance to connect the dots, and again it missed a golden opportunity.

ON THE NIGHT of August 7, 1995, a convoy of black Mercedes sedans sped west across the darkened border separating Iraq and Jordan. When the vehicles reached Amman, General Hussein Kamel emerged from the lead car. Kamel was Saddam Hussein's son-in-law and had been responsible for Iraq's nuclear, chemical, and biological weapons-procurement efforts. In a potentially major blow to Saddam, Kamel had decided to defect and share his extensive knowledge with the United Nations, which was still trying to guarantee that Iraq no longer possessed weapons of mass destruction four years after the end of the Gulf War.

UN inspectors had grown weary of the hide-and-seek game being played by the Iraqis, and the IAEA team was packing up to return to

Vienna for a hiatus when news broke on CNN of Kamel's defection. Hoping for new information, they unpacked. They didn't have long to wait. Saddam feared the unveiling of Kamel's secrets would undermine his government's strained credibility and jeopardize any hope of ending the UN sanctions. In a preemptive strike, he instructed Tariq Aziz, the deputy prime minister, to publicly denounce Kamel as a traitor and accuse him of concealing information about Iraq's nuclear-weapons program. A few days later, the IAEA team was headed for a chicken farm west of Baghdad. After about ten miles, they turned down a dusty road to the village of Haidar and pulled into a farming compound. The August heat was blistering as the inspectors were led by Iraqi military officers to a locked chicken coop, where they found more than one hundred wooden and metal boxes, stacked one on top of another. As the inspectors opened the containers, they found microfiches, computer disks, videotapes, photographs, and pieces of hardware.

Among the inspectors sweating inside the chicken coop that day was Jacques Baute, head of the team. Baute was collegial, articulate, and quick with a smile, but his patience had been tested by the obfuscations and obstacles thrown up for months by the Iraqis. Now, as he looked at the material being pulled out of the containers, it seemed like the IAEA's persistence was finally paying off. Though some documents and designs were for chemical and biological weapons, most of the contents dealt with the various stages of building an atomic bomb and showed that the Iraqis were much farther along than anyone knew. There were diagrams for centrifuges, schematics for cascades, and lists of equipment and suppliers across Europe. Inside one crate, Baute discovered five-foot rods of what appeared to be maraging steel. Any doubts about the sophistication of the Iraqi effort evaporated.

The Iraqis claimed the material had been hidden by Kamel without the knowledge of Saddam and other senior officials, a tale no one on the IAEA team believed. Their suspicions were proved right when satellite imagery soon revealed trucks delivering containers to the chicken farm the day after Kamel defected. Baute ordered the 150 containers sealed and transferred to Baghdad where, away from the heat and the Iraqis, he and the others would begin a careful analysis of what they had discovered.

Baute had left the French nuclear industry to join the IAEA out of a conviction that his skills could help stop the spread of nuclear weapons, and his analytical mind and expertise in weapon design made him an effective team leader. Carefully examining what he estimated to be about seven hundred thousand pages and the assorted hardware and components, Baute was convinced that Saddam would soon have produced a nuclear weapon. Among the disturbing discoveries was a thin sheaf of documents tucked deep in one of the boxes chronicling an offer to help Iraq build an atomic bomb, from a man who said he represented Abdul Qadeer Khan. Baute knew Khan as the father of Pakistan's bomb, but this was the first time he had encountered a hint that Khan might have played a role in Iraq. The first page in the file was an Iraqi government memo summarizing the meeting in October 1990 between the Iraqi intelligence service and the man identified as Malik. The senior Iraqi intelligence officer involved, code-named PC-3, suspected a sting but accepted Malik's offer to provide samples of Khan's wares; it appeared from the documents that the Gulf War had interfered.

Baute copied the Khan file and took it to a meeting with senior officials from the Iraqi nuclear agency. Before showing them the papers, he asked whether they knew anything about Khan helping the nuclear program. They said they had no idea what he was talking about. Pulling the copies out of his briefcase and handing them over, Baute repeated his question. The Iraqi officials acknowledged the approach but explained that the proposal had gone nowhere.

The offer fit too neatly into how the Iraqis operated for Baute to accept the denial at face value. For days, he traipsed from ministry to ministry, trying to solve the mystery. Eventually, he was given the names of the intelligence and nuclear officials who had received and evaluated the proposal. Some were still in Iraq, but when Baute and his team tracked them down, the officials repeated the government line that they had been dubious about the legitimacy of the offer and that it never went forward. Baute finally located PC-3, who had fled after the Gulf War, receiving asylum and eventually citizenship in a European country. Determined to get to the bottom of the story, Baute received permission from Vienna to go see the former intelligence officer, hoping that he might learn the truth because PC-3 was outside Saddam's lethal reach. Baute's luck did not change: PC-3 refused to discuss any aspect of the Khan overture.

The IAEA sent an official letter to the Pakistani government inquiring about the suspected offer. The PAEC replied that the entire incident must have been a hoax and flatly denied that Khan could have been involved in any attempt to transfer nuclear technology out of the country.

The trail had gone cold. Baute and the other team members had no doubt that the proposal was a legitimate attempt by Khan to sell his nuclear know-how to Iraq—they just couldn't prove it. "I absolutely believe the Khan offer to Iraq was real," he said. "All of us close to the question believe it was real. The name of Khan was not guessing by someone making up a fictitious proposal. The Khan network is clearly not a twenty-first-century operation. Clearly it was several decades old, based on dual-use technology taken from the Pakistani program and offered to other countries."

In a last-ditch effort, IAEA officials sent copies of the documents to American intelligence for additional evaluation. Baute thought that if anyone could get to the bottom of the story, it would be the Americans. The IAEA never got a response, leaving Baute to wonder whether the Americans had taken the prospect seriously.

Hussein Kamel never got the chance to say whether he had heard of the Khan offer. Six months after defecting, and before Baute could question him, the general was persuaded that he had been forgiven and would be welcome to return to Baghdad. Within days, he and every family member who had come home with him were executed.

INTELLIGENCE INFORMATION is rarely definitive. Western intelligence agencies and the IAEA were monitoring an array of individuals, groups, and twelve countries suspected of trafficking in nuclear technology. Patterns emerged over time as undercover operatives and deskbound analysts formed a picture of what was going on by connecting seemingly isolated incidents or disclosures. In Khan's case, American intelligence agencies had enough evidence to suspect that he was providing nuclear technology to Iran and North Korea, both regimes that were inimical to America. The suspected offer to the Iraqis was another clue.

Despite mounting circumstantial evidence, there was no concerted effort to act on the information and no push to understand the full extent of what Khan was doing or to try to close him down. "Certainly we had questions about A. Q. going way back about his predisposition to share information and technology," said a veteran counterproliferation official from the State Department. "Part of the problem with determining who knew what and when is that you get little pieces and then you get more and more pieces. You never get the whole thing dumped in your lap. And in this case, there are so many layers that we had difficulty seeing the whole picture."

What was happening was a repetition of the opportunity missed twenty years earlier in the Netherlands. The CIA and other intelligence agencies were content to keep watching Khan, collecting tidbits from intercepted telephone conversations and isolated information from people with peripheral involvement. Admittedly, the picture was incomplete and Khan was a difficult target, protected by the Pakistani government. Plus, the days when Milt Bearden and the CIA had free rein inside Pakistan were over, and penetrating the Khan group was difficult. Normally, a CIA case officer would try to develop an informant by exploiting a grievance or offering money for information, but even as the network began shipping equipment to Iran, it remained restricted to a relatively small number of well-paid Pakistani insiders beholden to Khan and a handful of outsiders whose livelihood depended on the black market. The goal of the Pakistani military and intelligence service was to protect Khan, not expose him and possibly jeopardize its atomic arsenal.

"Khan was the subject of intense scrutiny by the U.S. and others," said a former CIA case officer who was involved in recruiting informants in Pakistan. "He was pretty savvy in the way he set up his network. He used offices and faxes for a short amount of time and then moved on. He also did much of the negotiating himself. A flood of arcane and highly technical bits of information have to be analyzed to create a picture. One issue that U.S. intelligence struggles with is the inability to analyze technical information. After the Indian nuclear tests in 1974, the CIA realized that it had to bring in experts from the national weapons laboratories to look at the information they were getting to make sense out of it, but that wasn't always done."

Other factors played a role in the failure to stop Khan. Confronting the

Pakistani government could have meant disclosing sensitive information that jeopardized American intelligence-gathering methods. The National Security Agency, which operates clandestine listening posts worldwide to monitor telephone conversations and other communications, was reluctant to disclose anything that might expose a billion-dollar electronic collection system aimed at Pakistan. The Clinton administration made procedural attempts to encourage Pakistan to rein in the nuclear scientist, sending official letters of complaint and occasional delegations of State Department officials to raise the issue in a general fashion. But because the American protests contained no specific allegations, Khan turned the accusations to his advantage, portraying himself as the victim of Western propaganda, just as he had when confronted by the Dutch charges two decades earlier.

The Americans were not the only ones who were concerned. The Japanese government complained to Islamabad about Pakistan's relationship with North Korea, telling a senior Pakistani military official that the technological exchanges extended beyond missiles to the nuclear arena. After returning to Islamabad, the officer described his encounter to a meeting of high-level military and political leaders, which included Khan.

"These are lies, outrageous lies," Khan thundered as he jumped from his seat. "This is nothing more than Western propaganda to attack me and our country. The Americans are behind these lies."

Khan's outburst was a product of several factors. He had developed a genuine hatred of the United States, believing he had been branded a criminal. He often complained to associates that the Americans had been responsible for the deaths of Zulfikar Ali Bhutto and General Zia because of their nuclear aspirations, and he told them that he feared he was next on the hit list.

CHAPTER 21

A MYSTERIOUS MURDER

FROM THE WINDOW OF KHAN'S HOTEL, the Bosporus was as gray as the sky. It was a long time since the room-service waiter had left behind a Turkish breakfast of sliced melon and white cheese, olives, tomatoes, and flat bread that did not appeal to Khan. He had not come to Istanbul in the summer of 1997, however, for either the view or the food. Like countless people before him, intrigue had brought Khan to the teeming, anonymous city straddling Europe and Asia.

Khan was sixty-one years old, still erect and handsome but growing fleshy from the banquet circuit and too much of his own fried chicken. His old sense of his modest beginnings was long forgotten. These days, he was comfortable with the elite from the scientific, business, and political worlds. With underlings, he remained a stern taskmaster who never liked to ask twice for something to be done. Just a year earlier, he had been honored yet again by the government, this time on the twentieth anniversary of the groundbreaking at Kahuta. His acceptance speech was testimony to his high stature and rampant immodesty. "The gigantic pace with which the Kahuta plant was established has always amazed and enthralled people," he said. "I have been inquired of by countless people on this particular point, as it is really hard to believe that something that took two decades in the most modern countries of the world was accomplished in a record time of only six years. . . . Kahuta is an all-Pakistani effort and is a symbol of a poor and developing country's determination and defiance to submitting to blackmail and bullying."

By the time he arrived in Istanbul in the summer of 1997, however, Khan was tired, and the weariness showed. The internal battles with the Pakistani nuclear establishment had worn him out, and so had his travels throughout the Middle East and Africa. He kept an apartment in Dubai to oversee the Iran deal. He was building a twenty-four-room hotel in Timbuktu, the legendarily remote former trading center in the West African country of Mali. He planned to name it the Hotel Hendrina Khan, after his wife, and ordered a Pakistani Air Force cargo plane to fly in a load of furniture from Karachi. Sometimes Khan talked of retiring to a life of fishing and reading, perhaps spending some of his time in Mali, but in the end his appetite for power kept him in the game.

Khan spent most of the time he was on the road trying to persuade other Muslim countries to buy his nuclear wares. In the last year alone, he had made dozens of trips, often with an entourage that included a personal physician and security officer from Kahuta as well as friends like Tahir and Henk Slebos. To whet the appetite of potential customers, Khan liked to play a video produced at Khan Research Laboratories, which portrayed Khan in his trademark khaki suit as Pakistan's stalwart deterrent against an aggressive India. Through his efforts, the voice-over said, Pakistan had performed "no less than a miracle" in joining the world's nuclear elite. After panning through the centrifuge halls and research labs at Kahuta, the camera focused on Khan sitting in his office. He explained that the lab had enriched uranium by 1981 and produced enough HEU for a weapon by 1983. "On December 10, 1984, I wrote a letter to President Zia saying we are now in a position to detonate a nuclear device on the least notice," he said, his face serious. The message could hardly be clearer for prospective customers: Khan had done it for Pakistan, and he could do it for you.

Khan made several trips to Syria in the 1990s, meeting with government officials and lecturing on nuclear weapons at Damascus University. In one speech, he told his audience that Syria should protect itself from the United States by acquiring nuclear weapons. The pitch was the same in other Islamic cities, from Istanbul and Dubai to Khartoum and Riyadh. Sheikh Abdullah bin Zayed Al-Nahyan, the minister of information for the United Arab Emirates, visited Khan's lab, and Khan offered to train UAE technicians in nuclear technology. In Saudi Arabia, he delivered his message to members of the royal family, several of whom expressed interest in acquiring nuclear weapons. The Saudis had helped finance the start of Pakistan's nuclear efforts and had secretly purchased Chinese missiles capable of carrying nuclear warheads. But the Saudis, comfortable within the cocoon spun from their oil wealth, were cautious, and they initially rejected an invitation from Khan for Prince Sultan bin Abd al-Aziz, the Saudi defense minister, to visit Kahuta. Later the prince did take the tour, with Khan as his personal guide, but he continued to deny any interest in its nuclear work for his own country.

Libya, too, was resistant in the beginning. Khan had flown through Tripoli several times on his way to Timbuktu and other places in Africa. As early as 1995, he used his international reputation to try to get an audience with Colonel Moammar Gadhafi. Like the Saudis, Gadhafi had helped bankroll the early days of Pakistan's nuclear program, and Khan figured the Libyan might be interested in buying his own. Despite a series of meetings with officials of increasing rank, Khan never got to see the Libyan leader, who always seemed to be unreachable at some desert oasis. In early 1997, the scientist submitted a written description of his proposal to a senior Gadhafi aide. A few weeks later, Khan heard back: Gadhafi was interested. A Libyan official invited Khan to meet with representatives of Libya's nuclear program on the sidelines of a conference in Istanbul. At the time, Turkey was ruled by a coalition government with a prime minister, Necmettia Erbakan, who was promoting stronger ties with Libya and other Arab countries, so it was a natural spot for both the conference and the rendezvous.

Khan had picked up Tahir in Dubai, and they had flown to Istanbul together. Shortly before noon on the designated day, Khan and his young associate climbed into a waiting car and crossed the high bridge spanning the Bosporus, entering the more residential confines of the city's Asian side. They arrived at a small, anonymous café on a winding street. Waiting for them were two Libyans; Mohammad Matuq Mohammad, the head of the country's secret nuclear program, and a technician who gave his name only as Karim. Mohammad greeted Khan and Tahir, using American English he had learned studying physics in the United States in the early 1970s. Khan, Mohammad, and Karim sat down for their discussion, and Tahir moved to a small table nearby.

Gadhafi was regarded by the West as the leading sponsor of international terrorism; in their eyes, he was a man with blood on his hands. He had provided weapons to the Irish Republican Army and regularly ordered the assassination of Libyan dissidents in Europe. He was blamed also for a disco bombing in Berlin in 1986 that had killed two U.S. soldiers and a Turkish woman and injured 230 people. In retaliation, President Reagan had ordered air strikes against two suspected Gadhafi residences in Libya, killing at least fifteen people, including Gadhafi's fifteen-month-old adopted daughter, but missing the main target. Libya also was suspected of planning the explosion of a Pan Am jet over Lockerbie, Scotland, in December 1988, which killed 270 people, most of them Americans. A year later, Libya was blamed for the downing of a French airliner over Niger, in which 170 people died.

Gadhafi had been trying secretly for years to develop an atomic bomb. In the early 1980s, Libya had set up a pilot uranium-conversion facility with equipment purchased abroad. A German aviation expert had struggled to perfect centrifuge technology, and the program had stalled. What Khan had offered in his written proposal a few weeks earlier seemed to be a ticket to the elite nuclear club. In the café that day, Khan outlined his ambitious program for Libya, explaining to Mohammad and Karim that he and his network could supply an off-the-shelf nuclear-production facility, capable of turning out three or four nuclear weapons per year, taking Libya from a nuclear wannabe to a nuclear power in a matter of years. He described how he was assisting Iran in its secret effort and promised that his network could deliver similar goods to Gadhafi. The Libyans had studied the written proposal beforehand and had received preliminary approval from Gadhafi to proceed if the deal sounded legitimate. It did, they decided, and they arranged for a second meeting a few weeks later in Dubai to work out the logistics and talk about price.

The Libyan deal would dwarf Khan's arrangement with Iran and represented a challenge almost as great as the one he had undertaken in Pakistan. This time, however, he would not be starting from scratch. The Iranians and North Koreans were skilled scientists, but Libya lacked even a basic scientific and industrial infrastructure. Out of necessity, Khan would be supplying the entire operation, nuts to bolts, which would require expanding his network, reenlisting old members, and seeking out new accomplices. Complete factories would have to be built surreptitiously to produce the tens of thousands of centrifuges, a massive uranium-conversion plant would be set up, and explosive tests would have to be conducted to perfect the final bomb. As he discussed the idea with Tahir, Khan estimated a start-to-finish bomb factory would cost hundreds of millions of dollars, but he knew Gadhafi had the oil money to foot the bill. When Mohammad and Karim arrived for the second meeting in Dubai, they brought Gadhafi's formal blessing, a shopping list, and a down payment of several million dollars. Before the end of 1997, the first twenty assembled P-1 centrifuges, components for another two hundred centrifuges, and other equipment had arrived in Tripoli via sea shipments from Karachi. The wooden crates were accompanied by false invoices, which described the contents as agricultural machinery.

The network continued to supply nuclear technology to Iran, and Khan traveled to various locations there to solve technical problems. In the meantime, he was also making frequent visits to North Korea, where work was under way on an underground enrichment facility, which would use his centrifuge technology. But the Libyan deal was different because it represented a quantum leap in scope and complexity. Khan relished the new challenge, and the potential fortune, at least partly because things were not going well back home.

IN ISLAMABAD, Benazir Bhutto had been booted out of office for a second time in late 1996 after President Farooq Leghari, acting on orders from the military, accused her of corruption. It was the fourth consecutive government pushed out by the military, and it kicked off a new round of musical chairs. Nawaz Sharif, who had replaced Bhutto after she was dismissed the first time, was elected prime minister in February 1997. Sharif was widely regarded as a creature of the military, and his independence was to be challenged the following year.

In the spring of 1998, the right-wing Hindu nationalist Bharatiya Janata party won elections in India, elevating Atal Behari Vajpayee to the prime minister's office. Vajpayee was intent on demonstrating India's nuclear power, and on May 11 the country detonated three atomic devices underground, followed by two more two days later. A video of the first detonation released by the government showed the countdown followed by a deep boom that shook the earth and sent forth a huge cloud of dust.

Testing nuclear weapons can yield important information about how weapons work, and the five nuclear powers all tested devices at various stages of their development. Physicists have debated whether a nuclear weapon can be considered reliable without tests. But tests have a political dimension, too, serving to notify the world that a country has achieved nuclear status. The most dramatic example of a politically motivated test occurred in 1961 when the Soviet Union detonated the largest nuclear bomb ever created, the fifty-megaton Tsar Bomba. The device was impractical because of its weight and size, but the test was seen as a demonstration of Soviet military and scientific prowess. On the other side of the equation, Israel refrained from testing its nuclear weapons even as its arsenal grew to more than one hundred bombs through the 1990s. Israelis knew that a public announcement of its bomb would antagonize its Arab neighbors and jeopardize the billions of dollars' worth of assistance it received from the United States.

Vajpayee had decided that the test was worth the risk for India, despite its dependence on international lenders. The international community and American intelligence were taken by surprise. No one expected Vajpayee to take such a dramatic step so soon after taking office. Clinton announced an immediate suspension of aid to India and pledged to oppose more than one billion dollars' worth of loans from the World Bank and other international lending agencies. Clinton then turned his attention to Pakistan and tried to persuade it not to raise the risk of nuclear confrontation further by doing its own tests. Clinton telephoned Sharif four times in the days after the Indian tests to urge restraint and offer a package of incentives to stand down. Clinton promised to write off American loans, repeal the Pressler and Solarz amendments, and seek congressional approval for new military assistance.

Sharif was hesitant to test, fearing the economic impact of international sanctions like those imposed on India, so Clinton's offer must have been enticing. But he told the American president that he faced tremendous pressure from his generals, Islamist parties, and an overwhelming majority of the population. The Clinton administration was well aware of the pressure and where it was leading.

Three days after the initial Indian test, CIA director George Tenet testified before a closed session of the Senate and House intelligence committees, telling them that satellites had picked up preparations for underground nuclear testing in the Chagai Hills of southwestern Pakistan. The images showed heavy traffic along roads leading to the test site. The consensus in the intelligence community, he said, was that a Pakistani nuclear test was imminent.

On May 15, an emergency session of Pakistan's national-defense committee was convened to debate the pros and cons of testing, with Sharif and his cabinet in attendance along with the senior members of the military. Two items were on the agenda: Should Pakistan carry out nuclear tests? And if so, should the test be performed by the PAEC or Khan Research Laboratories? As part of the deliberations, Sharif described Clinton's incentives, but there was skepticism that the Americans would fulfill their promises. On the other hand, Saudi Arabia and other Muslim countries were urging Pakistan to test the Islamic bomb, and Sharif told the meeting that he had received a late-night call from a member of the Saudi royal family who promised to counter any Western sanctions with fifty thousand barrels of oil daily for an indefinite period on deferred payment terms. The debate lasted for several hours, with only Finance Minister Sartaj Aziz opposing the tests because he was certain it would lead to devastating economic sanctions.

When it came to deciding which organization would conduct the tests, Samar Mubarakmand, PAEC's technical director, presented the case for his agency while Khan argued on his lab's behalf. Mubarakmand said the PAEC had conducted all of the preparations at the test site in the Chagai Hills and performed the simulated nuclear explosions called cold tests, which substitute conventional explosives for highly enriched uranium or plutonium. He said he could be ready within ten days. Khan argued that his legacy gave him the right to be in charge. KRL could also be ready within ten days, he said, reminding the civilian and military leaders that his lab had enriched uranium for the devices and carried out its own cold tests. "KRL is fully independent in the nuclear field and should be given the honor of carrying out Pakistan's first nuclear tests," he told the generals and cabinet ministers.

The meeting adjourned without a formal decision on when or who would stage the tests, though the consensus was that India could not go unanswered. Sharif met with his military leaders over the next two days and decided the tests would be conducted as soon as possible by the PAEC. Khan was outraged, fearing that everything he had worked for over the past two decades would be stripped away. The public still adored him, but his relationship with Sharif was tenuous, and the army chief of staff, General Jehangir Karamat, distrusted Khan to the extent that he had tried to investigate the finances of his laboratory three years earlier. The biggest event in Pakistan's nuclear history was about to take place without Khan.

Forced to swallow his pride, Khan went to plead his case to Karamat at the Army House in Rawalpindi, asking the commander to give his lab a role even if it was not the lead agency. He argued that the nuclear devices would be using the highly enriched uranium produced by his lab. He also pointed out that he had recently tested a missile capable of carrying a nuclear payload to India. Karamat could not argue with Khan's success. In April, KRL's Ghauri missile had traveled about seven hundred miles, far enough to reach Delhi, Mumbai, or many other Indian cities. Karamat did not want to antagonize someone as popular with the public as Khan, so he promised that a team from KRL could travel to Chagai Hills to help with final preparations and that Khan would be among the honored guests invited to view the tests from a nearby bunker.

The next day, a small group from KRL joined two teams of 140 PAEC scientists, engineers, and technicians on two Pakistan International Airlines flights bound for Chagai. The unassembled weapons and other equipment followed on two C-130 Hercules military transport planes, escorted by four F-16 fighters that had instructions to shoot down the C-130s if they strayed outside Pakistani airspace. At Chagai, the components of five nuclear devices were taken into five separate rooms at the end of a three-thousand-foot, fishhook-shaped tunnel, where they were assembled under military guard. Diagnostic cables were strung out of the tunnel and connected to the devices that were to monitor the blasts. On the afternoon of May 26, the tunnel was sealed with six thousand bags of cement, and the next day the engineers certified that the cement was dry enough to contain the blast.

On May 28, Pakistani and foreign dignitaries gathered in a bunker about six miles from the blast site. Muhammad Arshad, a young science officer from the PAEC who had designed the triggering mechanism, was selected to push the button to ignite the devices. At 3:16 in the afternoon, calling out, "All praise be to Allah," he initiated the firing sequence. Five simultaneous explosions deep underground shook the mountain. Clouds of dust obscured the sun. The black granite instantly turned white from deoxidation. India had been matched. Two days later, a sixth device was to be detonated, topping India's total.

When photographers lined up to take the pictures of the assembled officials on that historic day, Khan pushed his way to the front and smiled broadly, determined to maintain his grasp on the public mantle of "father of the Islamic bomb." On the flight back to Islamabad, however, there was no official party to greet Khan at the airport except a handful of Kahuta employees gathered in the VIP lounge. The big welcome, the cheering crowd, and the prime minister came a short time later, with the arrival of Samar Mubarakmand.

President Clinton was furious and determined to punish Pakistan along with India. The United States was providing only limited assistance to Pakistan, and after the tests Clinton forged an ad-hoc multinational coalition to expand sanctions and block all nonhumanitarian assistance and loans to both countries. Japan, Pakistan's major trade partner, joined the sanctions regime. For an economy that depended on outside assistance, the fallout from broader sanctions was crippling. Loans from the American government and international financial institutions like the World Bank and International Monetary Fund were blocked, except for humanitarian purposes; American banks were prohibited from making loans to Pakistan; and sales of dual-use technology were prohibited. Sharif responded by freezing twelve billion dollars in foreign-currency deposits to avoid a run on Pakistani banks. The economic collapse that followed led to the first serious debate in Pakistan about the costs and benefits of nuclear weapons.

Even as the economy sputtered, the tests elevated Khan in the eyes of the Pakistani public and the larger Muslim world. He was embraced even more fervently by the masses. His face was painted on the back of the wildly decorated and bejeweled trucks that ply the roads and highways of Pakistan. A replica of Chagai Hills, complete with a plastic atomic bomb, was constructed on the outskirts of Islamabad in Khan's honor. Though others had played important roles, they remained in the background. Khan was the adored public face of the nuclear program, the person who made the bomb part of Pakistan's green-and-white flag. In a country where more than half the population of 132 million was illiterate, the Islamic bomb stood as the supreme status symbol. Even the elite, both secular and Islamic, saw the bomb as what Pervez Hoodbhoy described derisively as "a sign that Pakistan could succeed at something." And Khan was the ultimate nuclear hero. "You couldn't criticize him without being called a traitor," said a Pakistani journalist.

AMERICAN spy satellites monitoring the Pakistani tests sent back photographs showing several North Korean military officers among the foreign dignitaries at the detonations. Their presence renewed concerns about the type of cooperation between the two countries. The North Korean plutonium program remained frozen under the agreement reached in 1994, but the CIA was desperate to learn how much help Khan had given to them on uranium enrichment. The lengths to which the Pakistanis and North Koreans were willing to go to hide the answer to that question became apparent just days after the detonations.

On the night of June 7, a North Korean woman named Kim Sa Nae was shot to death a few yards from Khan's heavily guarded compound in his quiet Islamabad neighborhood. The Pakistani government moved quickly to head off the inevitable suspicions aroused by the murder of a foreigner. The official version of her death blamed a neighbor's cook who accidentally discharged a shotgun borrowed from a security guard. Kim was identified as the wife of a midlevel diplomat at North Korea's embassy. The coroner was not allowed to carry out an autopsy, and the police report was sealed. Strangely, the death of a diplomat's wife did not arouse a protest from the North Korean embassy.

Not everyone accepted the official version, and the potential for exposing a link between Pakistan and North Korea was tantalizing to Indian intelligence. When Indian agents began to probe the death, they uncovered a far more disturbing story. Kim was a North Korean scientist, and her husband, Kang Thae Yun, was a major arms dealer who was instrumental in the ongoing exchange of Korea's missile technology for Pakistan's uranium-enrichment technology. At the time of Kim's death, a delegation of North Korean scientists and technicians was staying in a guesthouse at Khan's compound while working at Kahuta. A few days earlier, Kim had been seen talking with an American diplomat in a local supermarket. The meeting, whether a chance encounter or something more calculated, raised fears that Kim was providing evidence to the CIA and planned to defect, a constant concern about North Koreans who were let outside of their poor, tyrannical country. One of the North Koreans was suspected of shooting Kim to keep her quiet. Kim could have given the Americans the first window into Khan's relationship with North Korea and perhaps evidence of North Korea's uranium-enrichment efforts. Three days after Kim's death, her body was flown out of Pakistan aboard a chartered Shaheen Air International jet, a private carrier controlled by the Pakistani Air Force. A Western intelligence official said the plane also carried P-1 and P-2 centrifuges as well as drawings, sketches, technical data, and uranium-hexafluoride gas for the Korean enrichment program.

But the Clinton administration was about to be distracted by another more urgent crisis.

SHORTLY BEFORE 10:30 a.m. on August 7, 1998, two teams of suicide bombers had entered two sprawling capitals in Africa. In Nairobi, Kenya, a truck packed with homemade explosives turned into the lane behind the American embassy and was detonated, blowing away the rear façade of the embassy and sending shards of glass and jagged concrete through the interior offices. Two hundred and thirteen people died, twelve of them Americans, and about four thousand people were injured. Less than ten minutes later, a second truck turned into the parking lot of the American embassy in Dar es Salaam, Tanzania, and exploded. A water tank standing between the truck and the building absorbed most of the blast, keeping the death toll to eleven Africans; another eighty-five people were injured.

A week before the embassy bombings, the CIA's counterterrorism center had issued an alert, warning of possible attacks using chemical, biological, or radiological weapons. But the CIA warning had not identified any particular threat in Africa, and the lack of specifics rendered the alert nearly useless. By then, the terrorist teams were already in place. Al Qaeda operatives had flown unnoticed to Nairobi and Dar es Salaam from Pakistan several months earlier to begin assembling the truck bombs in the backyards of rental houses.

Within hours of the embassy bombings, dozens of FBI agents were en route to Tanzania and Kenya to begin investigating, and eventually more than five hundred American agents participated in the inquiry. Although several suspect groups emerged, including Hamas and Hezbollah, the FBI and CIA soon focused on Al Qaeda and Osama bin Laden, who had issued numerous public statements from Afghanistan calling for his followers to kill Americans.

At the time, Afghanistan was controlled by the Taliban, religious zealots who had seized power after the departure of the Soviets and the crumbling of corrupt interim governments in Kabul. The Taliban was providing a haven for bin Laden and his organization, which operated terrorist training camps across the country. The CIA had received a report a few days after the bombings that bin Laden would be at the Zawhar Kili camp near Khost in eastern Afghanistan. On the evening of August 20, General Joseph Ralston, the vice chairman of the Joint Chiefs of Staff, sat down to dinner in Islamabad with General Karamat. He was there to alert the Pakistani commander that the missiles that were about to pop up on their radar were not aimed at them. A few minutes after the men finished dinner at 10:00 p.m., seventy-five Tomahawk cruise missiles roared across Pakistani airspace and crashed into the camp complex in Afghanistan. At least twenty-one jihadis were killed, and another fifty or so were wounded. The main quarry escaped—bin Laden had left the camp a few hours before the strike. The attack escalated the war between the United States and bin Laden's army of terrorists. In time, that war would make Washington and Islamabad uncomfortable allies once again.

CHAPTER 22

INSIDE THE NETWORK

W HEN B.S.A. TAHIR ARRIVED at Khan's apartment in Dubai in late 1998, the partners knew that they had arrived at a trouble-some obstacle to building Libya's bomb factory. The size and logistics of the project threatened to stretch Khan's network beyond capacity and de-manded nothing less than a complete rethinking of the way Khan and his accomplices did business. A few shipments of centrifuge parts and minor equipment had already made their way from Pakistan to Tripoli, but it had become obvious to Khan that he could not spirit away enough equip-ment from his stockpile at Kahuta to get the Libyans up and running without attracting unwanted attention. In the same way, the extent of the technology required for the project necessitated broadening the reach of his suppliers and recruiting new people for the network.

The first task facing Khan and Tahir that day was deciding where to locate the initial plant. Pakistan was out of the question for obvi-ous reasons, and Libya was unacceptable because Gadhafi lived under a blanket of sanctions because of his links to international terrorism. The logical choice, they decided, was right under their noses: Dubai. Khan was comfortable in the rapidly growing Persian Gulf city, where he owned his luxury apartment and had ensconced a mistress in a sec-ond apartment a few blocks away. Tahir's computer business, already serving as a front for shipments to Iran, offered access to large, anonymous warehouses in the free-trade zone, where the manufacturing operation could be set up. They thought that bringing huge lathes, vacuum pumps, centrifuge prototypes, and other advanced equipment into the busy port city and shipping it out again would amount to nothing more than business as usual in a place where the government's own website bragged that Dubai "enables traders to transit their shipments . . . without any hassles." American counter-proliferation expert Gary Milhollin described Dubai as "a perfect black hole into which to send a sensitive technology because you can always say, 'Well, we thought it was staying in Dubai.' "

Khan and Tahir could find and buy the necessary equipment, but someone would have to be in Dubai on a full-time basis to oversee the day-to-day manufacturing operation. Khan could not spend that much time there without attracting the attention of the Americans and the ISI, and Tahir did not have the technical background required for the job. As he pondered the dilemma, Khan hit upon the solution: Urs Tinner. Khan had known Friedrich Tinner since his days at Urenco, and he and his sons had transformed proliferation into a lucrative family business, selling their specialized vacuum technology to Pakistan's nuclear program for more than a decade. If their Swiss neighbors knew anything about the Tinner business, they did not hold it against them. Friedrich was a model citizen in their village of Haag, where he was president of the school board and active in the local branch of the Freethinking Democratic Party of Switzerland, which advocated a liberal business agenda.

During the years in which he did business with Tinner, Khan had traveled often to Haag and gotten to know the younger of Friedrich's two sons very well. He knew that Urs was an accomplished technician with the attention to quality and detail often found in Swiss craftsmen. As a young man, Urs Tinner had worked with his father and brother on many projects, including some work for Urenco's advanced centrifuge installation outside Amsterdam. "If you show him a picture of a fork, he will manufacture the perfect fork, no flaws, Swiss quality," said someone who knew him. "He was perfect for Dubai."

Just as important, Khan felt Urs could be trusted because he was a second-generation member of the network family, a loyal cog in a tightly knit and secretive enterprise that had rebuffed repeated attempts at penetration by the CIA and other intelligence agencies. At thirty-two, Urs Tinner had recently gone through a divorce from his Russian wife, and Khan suspected he would welcome a move to Dubai, which was growing popular with European tourists. First, Khan needed the father's permission. The elder Tinner agreed happily. Urs, too, liked the idea of starting over. He told friends in Haag that he was moving to Dubai to sell "power drinks," but by early 1998 he and Tahir were scouting for a warehouse to serve as the new home of Khan's operation.

The Dubai workshop was only part of the complicated scheme that Khan was putting in motion. Shipments to Iran were still moving through Tahir's computer business, but the volume expected for the Libyan project required a separate freight business as an added layer of security. Again, Khan turned to someone he had known from the old days.

In 1976, while searching for machine tools, Khan met British engineer Peter Griffin. Griffin said he became a supplier to Pakistan's program by chance, explaining that an acquaintance of Khan's in London had mistakenly telephoned Griffin's business. Later, Griffin and Khan sat down to dinner at a Pakistani restaurant not far from the House of Commons and hit it off. In the years that followed, Griffin traveled often to Pakistan and sold a wide range of industrial equipment there for factories, agriculture, and the nuclear facilities. Griffin, a tall, handsome former rugby player who could be pugnacious or charming, as the situation required, later said that his transactions with Khan did not violate export regulations or other laws, and he was never charged with a crime. As for Khan, Griffin saw him as an ambitious patriot.

"Do you ever want to be president?" Griffin asked Khan at one point.

"No way, I just want to help my country develop," replied Khan. "If it's good for Pakistan, I'd buy it from the devil."

When Khan contacted Griffin in 1998, the engineer and his son, Paul, were running a small shipping business in Dubai, Gulf Technical Industries. Griffin agreed to serve as the shipping agent for Khan's operation, though he later said that none of the Libya transactions in which he was involved were related to nuclear equipment and that Tahir had forged his company's name on some invoices.

Other former network members returned to the operation. Gunes Cire and Selim Alguadis, who ran two Turkish electronics companies that had sold equipment to Pakistan and Iran, were enlisted to supply a range of electronics for the project. Heinz Mebus, the German engineer, had died, but Gotthard Lerch was brought on to find someone to build the complicated system to control the centrifuge cascades, one of the most difficult aspects of the project. Like the centrifuges, the control system was to be built in a third country and later shipped to Libya. Lerch told Khan that he thought he knew just the man for the job.

Gerhard Wisser, a German engineer, had immigrated to South Africa in the 1960s and eventually set up a small business involved in his adopted country's nuclear-weapons program. At one point, Wisser was arrested for carrying a concealed weapon, and he justified the gun by telling the South African police that he often carried classified documents for the government. In the late 1970s and early 1980s, when Lerch was still with Leybold-Heraeus, Wisser had bought vacuum valves from him for South Africa's nuclear program. The two men had become friends and occasional partners in real-estate investments along South Africa's coast. When South Africa abandoned its program in the early 1990s, Wisser and a host of other suppliers and engineering firms faced bankruptcy. By the late 1990s, Wisser was still struggling to make ends meet by taking various small-scale engineering projects. His financial difficulties were compounded because he was in the middle of an expensive and ugly divorce. All of this made him just the man for the job.

When Lerch telephoned his old friend, he was cagey about the reason for inviting him to Dubai, saying only that he wanted Wisser to attend a dinner so he could meet some potential business associates. A few weeks later, Wisser found himself ushered into the luxurious home of a businessman who was hosting the affair. As he looked across the room, Wisser saw not only his old friend Lerch but someone else with whom he had worked in the past. A decade or so earlier, Tahir had come to Johannesburg with his uncle, Mohammed Farooq, when they were trying to buy a specialized furnace for Pakistan's nuclear program, and Wisser had met with them several times. Far from the slim, dark-skinned young man who had seemed little more than a coat holder that Wisser recalled, Tahir had grown into a well-fed and confident businessman. He wore a flashy Western-style suit, and his hair was fashionably trimmed. Wisser and Tahir chatted amiably as they waited for the dinner to be served. At one point, Tahir boasted that he owned a Rolls-Royce and other luxury cars, along with several businesses in Malaysia. Not until he was seated between Tahir and Lerch for dinner did Wisser realize that the Sri Lankan was the potential client.

During the meal, Tahir explained that he and some associates were looking for someone to manufacture certain sophisticated piping systems for an oil refinery in the United Arab Emirates, employing advanced vacuum technology. Wisser said that his company was much smaller than it had once been and no longer had the capacity to manufacture something that complex. When Tahir offered Wisser a finder's fee of one million dollars if he could arrange for the production of the system, the South African changed his mind: He eagerly promised to look around when he got home. Tahir said he would gather the technical drawings and have Lerch review them before sending them on to South Africa. Wisser couldn't believe that anyone in the Middle East would have to go to South Africa to find refinery equipment, and he did not believe there was any use for this type of technology, but he didn't question the claim. He needed the million and he had learned long ago not to ask too many questions. "With the best will in the world, I could not imagine what he wanted to do with vacuum pumps in Dubai," said Wisser. "There was no use for them there."

Even before he got back to Johannesburg, Wisser knew the person who could fill the order. A few days after his return, he went to the offices of Tradefin, an engineering and manufacturing company that was run by a former colleague from the nuclear program, Johan Meyer. Sitting with Meyer in the Tradefin office inside a large, hangarlike structure in Vanderbijlpark, fifty miles southeast of Johannesburg, Wisser explained that he had a line on a major project in Dubai, something that could run into the millions. Wisser said he didn't have the details yet, but he had been told the deal was for the oil industry. Like Wisser, Meyer had suffered from the demise of the South African weapons program, though Tradefin still had enough work to employ a sizable workforce and the capacity to execute the project that Wisser was describing. The two men were so eager for the business that they decided to fly to Dubai and meet the client. When the pair showed up unexpectedly at SMB Computer, Tahir was dumbfounded by the unwitting security breach. The whole reason for using someone as far away as South Africa was to provide an extra layer of protection for the Libyan project, and he was visibly shaken to see the two men on his doorstep. Recovering, Tahir explained that the drawings and a payment schedule were being prepared by his partners and that the material would soon be sent to them in South Africa. He apologized but said that he was too busy to see them now, and they should go home and wait. Wisser and Meyer were puzzled, but the prospect of a lucrative contract allayed their concerns, and they returned to Johannesburg.

A few days later, a box containing an eighteen-inch stack of documents from Tahir arrived at Wisser's office. He took it to Tradefin, where Meyer spread the documents across a large table. The diagrams and engineering schematics were poor copies, leaving Meyer scratching his head from time to time, but he had enough experience to recognize that they had nothing to do with the oil industry. The plans called for a sophisticated system of piping, vacuum pumps, specialized valves, and assorted other equipment built to precise tolerances far more suited to enriching uranium than refining oil. As he examined them more closely, Meyer realized he was almost certainly looking at a system to feed uranium gas into cascades of one thousand centrifuges and withdraw enriched uranium from the other end. He calculated that the job was worth thirty to forty million dollars, a big contract for his small operation. Several days later, Meyer telephoned Wisser to ask if he knew the identity of the end client. Wisser acknowledged that he wasn't sure, though he knew it wasn't Tahir. Meyer was worried about getting involved in a nuclear-weapons project, but he set aside his qualms when the initial payment arrived from a Zurich bank. In the coming months, the giant system would grow to be two stories high and cover much of the factory floor at Tradefin, leading Meyer to dub it "the beast."

A few days later, Wisser was talking on the telephone to Lerch about one of their real estate deals and brought up the piping system. When Wisser asked if Lerch knew the final destination of the piping, the German replied brusquely: "I don't know. And it's none of my business." The comment, whether true or not, exemplified the attitude that pervaded the corps of middlemen at the heart of the nuclear smuggling network.

In Dubai, Urs Tinner was struggling to set up the centrifuge plant. The problem wasn't getting the necessary equipment and material—it was finding even a small number of technicians skilled enough to operate the advanced machinery. Like many wealthy Arab oil states, the Emirates depended on workers from developing countries like the Philippines and Pakistan to do the manual labor that kept businesses and households running. The natives had no interest even in the sorts of highly skilled jobs that Tinner needed to fill, and any foreign worker interested would have to get a government work permit, which risked exposing the nature of what Tinner was doing. When he raised his problem with Khan, the Pakistani suggested that the manufacturing could be shifted to Turkey. At Khan's request, Gunes Cire made inquiries but reported back that it would be difficult to find enough skilled labor there, too.

Despite the setback, Tinner was developing a close relationship with Khan, supplanting Tahir as the Pakistani scientist's most trusted aide and surrogate son. Tahir was coordinating the network and handling the finances, which were washed through as many as six banks to conceal the payments, but he had none of the technical expertise that made Tinner so valuable in Khan's eyes. Tahir had looked upon Khan as a surrogate for his late father, and he resented watching Tinner come between them. In June 1998, Tahir planned to marry the daughter of a prominent former Malaysian diplomat in Kuala Lumpur, and he used the opportunity to display his affection for Khan, too, arranging for him to be met at the airport by a limousine and installed in a luxurious hotel suite for the duration of the opulent festivities. But to Tahir's annoyance, Tinner accompanied Khan.

THE LIBYAN project meant that Khan's network was buying more nuclear-related equipment in Europe and elsewhere, which did not go unnoticed by the CIA and European intelligence agencies. The flow of information had been trickling in for years, but the focus had always been on what Khan was importing into Pakistan. So when the reports of renewed purchases filtered in, the intelligence officials assumed that Khan was still buying for his own program. A far bigger concern to the United States was intelligence that Khan was increasing his cooperation with North Korea, which the Americans suspected was obtaining enrichment technology.

At the State Department, Bob Einhorn had been raising alarms about Khan's activities with the Koreans in back-channel conversations with his Pakistani counterparts for several months. In late 1998, he had confronted the two military officers in charge of maintaining control over the country's nuclear arsenal with intelligence reports that Khan was using aircraft from the military-controlled Shaheen Air International to carry shipments of suspected enrichment equipment to North Korea. "The only explanation is either you are complicit, or this is taking place without military knowledge, and both of these are pretty disturbing," Einhorn told the two officers.

In January 1999, President Clinton demonstrated even greater concern by sending Einhorn and Strobe Talbott, the deputy secretary of state, to Islamabad to persuade Prime Minister Nawaz Sharif to rein in Khan. The two Americans were invited to lunch at Sharif's official residence, a modern house perched on a hill overlooking the city. The dining room was decorated with polished brass urns and gilded platters. The business portion of the session came near the end of the meal, as butlers served tea and coffee.

"Mr. Prime Minister, we know that Pakistan is importing North Korean missiles," said Talbott. "We are very concerned about this. Our concern is that these transactions go beyond missile technology and could involve nuclear exchanges."

Sharif smiled and replied, "Ambassador Talbott, it is true that Pakistan has important defense cooperation with North Korea, but it is for conventional military equipment. Nothing involving nuclear technology is taking place."

Einhorn had seen the latest spy-satellite photos just before leaving Washington, which showed a Shaheen cargo plane loading missiles into its huge belly on a runway in North Korea. "Mr. Prime Minister," he interjected, "it's important to sever these connections with weapons specialists in North Korea. These transactions involve Khan Research Laboratories, your main nuclear installation. If the business continues, we would have to assume that there is more to it than conventional weapons and that nuclear issues are involved."

Sharif stared silently at Einhorn, leaving the American unsure whether the prime minister even knew that his country was swapping nuclear technology for missiles. Whether he was in the dark or not, Sharif expressed no inclination to make any accommodation to his guests, sending Talbott and Einhorn back to Washington empty-handed.

Pakistan's failure to halt Khan's trade with North Korea did not stop Clinton from trying to restore relations with both Islamabad and Delhi. If the two countries agreed to limit their nuclear and missile capabilities and resume bilateral talks, Clinton promised to work for removal of the sanctions imposed on them after the 1998 nuclear tests. The Pakistanis, faced with serious economic troubles, accepted the basic terms, even agreeing to sign a treaty limiting missile development. In February, Sharif and his Indian counterpart met for a two-day summit in Lahore and agreed to normalize relations and establish measures to reduce the risk of nuclear confrontation. Faced with the improving ties and pressure from Americans businesses eager to expand in India and Pakistan, Congress passed an amendment in July that authorized Clinton to waive the sanctions against both countries for one year.

Even before Congress voted, however, relations between the neighbors were back on a downhill path. In early May, Pakistani commandos disguised as Islamic extremists slipped into Kashmir and seized a fifteen-thousand-foot peak called Kargil, a strategic position that gave them control over supply routes from India into the disputed territory. The plan was hatched by General Pervez Musharraf, a former commando who had recently become chief of the armed forces, and approved by Sharif after receiving assurances that Pakistan's nuclear arsenal would shield it from an all-out counterattack by India. Few of Pakistan's military adventures had been more ill conceived. Within days, it became known widely that the supposed jihadis were actually regular soldiers, prompting the Indians to bomb the peak and threaten to wipe out the Pakistani army. The confrontation seemed about to escalate further as American intelligence picked up signs that Pakistan was moving its nuclear arsenal, possibly as a prelude to an attack on India. Clinton summoned Sharif to Washington and told him, "Pakistan is messing with nuclear war." The prime minister appeared surprised by the nuclear maneuvers, and he returned home immediately to announce a complete withdrawal of Pakistani troops from Kargil.

Sharif blamed the army for the incident, but the generals circulated a rumor that it was the prime minister who had promoted the disastrous escapade. In the weeks that followed, Sharif worried that Musharraf was preparing a coup against him, so on October 12, as the army commander and his wife were returning from a golf junket in Sri Lanka aboard a Pakistan International Airlines passenger jet, the prime minister fired Musharraf and ordered that the plane not be allowed to land at the Karachi airport. While the plane circled the Arabian Sea, running low on fuel, the army ousted Sharif and forced the air controller to permit the PIA jet to land. By the time Musharraf and his shaken wife stepped off the plane, Musharraf was in complete control of Pakistan.

Clinton was angry about the takeover, but his administration refused to call what happened a coup, which would have triggered renewed sanctions from Congress and damaged relations with the new government in Islamabad. Like it or not, the Americans had something more important on their agenda than criticizing Musharraf or pursuing Khan: Osama bin Laden could not be rooted out of his hiding place in Afghanistan without Pakistan's help. A few months later, a senior State Department official traveled to Islamabad for consultations with the government. Instead of Einhorn or another proliferation official, he took along a terrorism expert. A new stage in the American-Pakistani relationship had begun. The Americans planned to enlist Pakistan's help in preparing for a commando raid to snatch the Al Qaeda leader from his haven in Afghanistan.

MUSHARRAF didn't need the Americans to bring Khan to his attention. As a career army officer, he was well aware of the scientist's freewheeling ways and occasional escapades. Even before the coup, Musharraf had received a report that North Korean scientists were being given secret briefings on centrifuge technology at Khan Research Laboratories. He had ordered the army and the ISI to question Khan, but the scientist had denied any knowledge of the issue. In the years when Khan was essential to developing Pakistan's nuclear arsenal, such behavior might have been tolerated, but now that the nuclear weapons were in place, Musharraf was determined to bring some discipline to the country's nuclear industry, including its star scientist. In February 2000, he established the National Command Authority, a new agency that reported directly to him and had responsibility for oversight of the nuclear industry. A few weeks later, the agency received a tip from a disgruntled scientist at Khan's lab that centrifuge equipment was being loaded on a plane destined for North Korea, the latest installment in the long-running barter deal. The information was passed to the ISI, but when intelligence agents boarded the plane, all they found were crates of medical supplies. Musharraf later speculated that someone within the government had tipped off Khan, and the nuclear equipment had been removed. Musharraf's hold on power remained tenuous because he had not been elected and lacked a political base outside the military; even within the military, there were pious officers who thought the president too Westernized to lead an Islamic country. As a result, he had to tread carefully in going after A. Q. Khan, who remained a national hero, particularly among the Islamic political parties.

For his part, the scientist faced an openly hostile head of government for the first time, and he, too, had to plot his moves with caution.

Khan had always tried to maintain a high level of security for his smuggling operations, but in the past he had feared exposure by the Americans or another Western government, not his own. He knew the CIA had tried repeatedly to penetrate his operations at KRL. He boasted to a friend that his people were too loyal to be swayed by promises or threats. In conversations with Tahir, he expressed the same convictions about the network and its members, though the near miss at home and the rapid expansion of the Libyan project caused him to institute new security rules. He compartmentalized the Libyan operation so that, for instance, the Swiss weren't sure who was doing the work in South Africa, and the Libyans were never told much about the origins of the European equipment. The millions of dollars coming in from Libya and Iran were funneled through a series of banks in Dubai, Switzerland, and other secrecy havens before landing in the accounts of Khan and other network members. Other than Khan, only two men knew the full scope of the operation: Tahir and Urs Tinner.

Khan had long operated outside the law on the international scene, but he was not invincible. The CIA was about to get a big break.

In late 1999, a German intelligence agent working with the CIA informed the Americans that a handful of high-tech suppliers associated with Khan had a big new customer. The German wasn't sure who that customer was, but he gave the CIA the name of the Swiss banker who had overseen a series of large payments to and from accounts of several people with histories in the nuclear black market. The German's information was passed to the CIA station in Vienna, the agency's largest outpost outside Washington and the one specializing in nuclear-related intelligence. The tip was recognized immediately as a potentially important break. The CIA was well aware of Khan, and they had picked up evidence over the years that he was peddling his goods to other countries, but this represented a major new incarnation of the ring—if true.

The station chief was a senior operations officer with extensive experience in espionage in Europe and other regions. He wanted to make sure that this information was handled with great care, so when one of his case officers suggested approaching the banker directly, the chief vetoed the idea. Swiss law prohibited its citizens from cooperating with foreign intelligence agencies, so even approaching the unfamiliar banker risked causing problems and chasing away a potential source. Instead, he requested help from headquarters in developing a list of names of people associated with nuclear trafficking involving Pakistan in hopes of spotting a weak link that might open the door to Khan's operation. As analysts at Langley and agents in Vienna went over years of reports and intelligence, one name that kept coming up was that of the Tinners.

The Tinners had been flying close to the radar for many years. The CIA knew that in the 1970s Friedrich Tinner had been in charge of exports at a German firm identified by the Defense Department as shipping items with nuclear uses to Pakistan. After he set up his own company in Switzerland, Tinner was again linked to the sale of nuclear-related technology to Pakistan. In 1996, Swiss authorities had questioned Tinner about a shipment of specialized valves that ended up in Jordan, on its way to Iraq just before the Gulf War. IAEA inspectors reconstructing Iraq's nuclear-procurement efforts had discovered the shipment in a warehouse in Jordan and asked the Swiss for help. Tinner had told the Swiss that he had no idea how the valves got to the Middle East, claiming they had been shipped legally to Singapore and that it was not his responsibility where they had gone after that. The Swiss statute of limitations on export violations had expired, so the authorities did not press the matter.

"We talked to Friedrich Tinner at the time, but we couldn't prove that he knew," Othmar Wyss, head of the Swiss export control agency, told us years later. "What can you learn? The Tinners lied all the time, saying they knew nothing."

The station chief assigned a CIA agent nicknamed Mad Dog to find a way into Khan's operation through the Tinners. Mad Dog was a single-minded, methodical case officer with a great track record in recruiting agents. In this case, he got a break when he learned that Urs Tinner had recently moved to Dubai, providing an opportunity to approach him outside Switzerland and away from his father's influence. In assembling a dossier on the target, the CIA agent found out that Urs had run into some legal trouble in France, so he contacted a friend in French intelligence and asked a favor—could the French apply some pressure to rattle young Tinner? The French agent agreed, promising to get word to Urs that the French were looking for him.

When Mad Dog laid out the recruitment strategy for his station chief, the boss wrote a lengthy summary, signed and dated it, and routed it to the CIA's operations directorate at Langley, with copies to the agency's European and Near East division chiefs at headquarters. The distribution was limited to senior officers because of its sensitivity, and the idea of using someone involved actively in breaking the law sparked a debate at Langley. Some of the brass were concerned that, once recruited, Tinner might believe that his cooperation put him above the law. "You tell them they have to stop breaking the law because you might not be able to protect them," the CIA station chief explained later. "No matter what you tell them, no matter how many times you tell them that you can't defend them if they are doing something illegal, they don't listen."

Those worries were insignificant compared with the opportunity to penetrate the Khan network, however, so in early 2000 Mad Dog flew to Dubai, where he and other agents kept Tinner under surveillance for several days, watching for the places he frequented, where he could be approached alone. In the end, the best spot turned out to be a bar. One evening, the CIA agent spotted Tinner walking into a hotel bar. He was nondescript—about five foot seven, with a slight build, dark brown hair, and glasses. Mad Dog waited till Tinner sat down and then joined him, offering to buy a round of drinks. They talked casually until Tinner got up to leave. Mad Dog mentioned that he had heard Tinner was having some trouble with the French authorities, and he offered to help him out. Tinner abruptly sat back down. Over the next hour or so, the CIA agent said he could make the French case disappear if Tinner could help him learn about some goods moving in and out of Dubai. Tinner tried to extricate himself several times, but Mad Dog kept talking. Eventually, Tinner agreed to meet for dinner a few days later, and, after several conversations, he became a reluctant informant, opening an unprecedented window on the inner workings of the world's largest nuclear smuggling operation.

What had been treated for more than two decades in intelligence circles as a subordinate matter, confined largely to a few counterproliferation experts relying on electronic eavesdropping and secondhand sources, took on a much more significant complexion. Detailed reports on what the network was buying and where it was shipping the goods began to flow in from Dubai. "Tinner gave us the final ability to know what the network was doing," said a former senior CIA official who was involved in the recruitment effort and the processing of Tinner's information. "He wasn't an agent, but he agreed to cooperate with us. We did not have a huge amount of control over Urs, but he began providing the information we needed. Everything the Libyans got, we knew. We knew what was going into Iran, too."

By the spring of 2000, the CIA had obtained proof that two of the most repressive and dangerous regimes in the world—the militant clerics in Tehran and the terrorist sponsor in Tripoli—were trying to develop nuclear weapons. Coupled with what the agency already knew about North Korea, the threat posed by Khan was undeniable. As word of the new source filtered up through the command at Langley, George Tenet, the CIA director, sent congratulations to the station chief in Vienna and Mad Dog. The intelligence bonanza was funneled through Vienna to the CIA's small counterproliferation bureau at headquarters, where analysts processed the details of vacuum pumps and specialized lathes and evaluated the plans described by Tinner. Based on the shipments going through Dubai, they were able to estimate the progress Iran and Libya were making toward building a functional nuclear weapon. While the early judgments required a certain amount of guesswork, both countries were believed to be within five or six years of going nuclear.

Only government officials with the highest level of security clearance were allowed access to the information, and even then any details that might disclose Tinner's identity were scrubbed away. As the discovery that Khan was providing nuclear technology to Libya percolated through the government, concern increased at the State Department. "There was a very tight intelligence restriction on Khan and Libya," recalled Bob Einhorn. "Late in the Clinton administration, probably in 2000, we were getting good information on the Libya-Khan connection. A handful of us at State were getting briefings from the director of operations at the CIA. We knew some of the tentacles of the ring. We knew about the Tinners. We clearly knew they had moved to Dubai. The U.S. knew that Dubai was the illicit trafficking capital of the world."

Still, the government did not act against Khan and his accomplices. As the small circle of people who knew about the new source inside the Khan network grew, there was a debate over whether to take steps to shut down the operation or to continue watching. Tinner was providing enough information to close down key segments of the network, confront Musharraf, and demand action against Khan. But Tenet and others at the CIA, along with some officials in the White House and State Department, argued that more could be learned by delaying action. "The debate was, do you stop it now, or do you watch it and understand it," Einhorn explained. "I don't recall a specific decision, but the view prevailed that we'd watch and wait."

The decision carried risks. The CIA and Mad Dog expected Tinner to keep them informed about the material flowing through Dubai and provide tips on other shipments, but they could not be certain that he knew everything or that he would share everything. There was an even bigger danger: Khan had acted on his own before, and he could unilaterally sell highly enriched uranium or some other critical bomb component to Iran, Libya, or a customer out of view of the CIA and its informant. It was also possible that either Iran or Libya was actually closer to a nuclear weapon than the Americans knew, which meant that the equipment and know-how they were getting from the network could put them over the top.

Tinner's inventory of equipment destined for Libya and Iran offered a bonus—it gave the CIA the chance to engage in some of its fanciest cloak-and-dagger work by planting miniature electronic devices in some crates, so they could be tracked through every destination. On occasion, the CIA also sabotaged other equipment subtly to slow progress. In one case, specialized vacuum pumps manufactured at the national weapons laboratory in Los Alamos, New Mexico, that had been ordered with false invoices were identified and altered so they wouldn't work, before being shipped to Iran.

The information was so good that the Vienna station chief was promoted to chief of the CIA's European division and moved to headquarters in July 2001. Tenet later boasted about the extent of the CIA's penetration of Khan's operation. "We pieced together subsidiaries, his clients, his front companies, his finances, and manufacturing plants," he said. "We were inside his residence, inside his facilities, inside his rooms. We were everywhere these people were."

The obvious question, given the CIA's extensive knowledge of Khan's role, is, Why not shut him down? Despite the evidence, the administration of the new president, George W. Bush, did not press the Musharraf regime and did not provide it with the detailed information that might have forced the Pakistanis to act. "Their complaints about Khan were vague," explained Brigadier General Feroz Khan, the senior Pakistani arms-control official at the time. "We were told that more detail could not be provided, purportedly because of their need to protect sources." The CIA and the administration were employing the same passive response implemented in 1975—watch and wait. It would take a cataclysmic event to force them to act.

CHAPTER 23

TIGHTENING THE NOOSE

WHILE HE WAS ARMY CHIEF, Musharraf had tolerated Khan's refusal to submit to any government controls, but as president, Musharraf was determined to rein in the scientist for the simple reason that he no longer needed Khan; Pakistan had ample fissile material for its nuclear arsenal. The mechanism that Musharraf chose was a newly formed government watchdog agency with extraordinary powers to investigate corruption throughout Pakistan. In November 1999, Musharraf created the National Accountability Bureau to go after the endemic corruption plaguing the public and private sectors, and he underscored his commitment to that goal by appointing as its director Lieutenant General Syed Mohammad Amjad, a highly respected career officer known for his integrity. The bureau was assigned space in a small, highly secure building in a symbolic location—next to the Supreme Court and near the National Assembly—and given the authority to arrest anyone suspected of corruption and detain them for up to ninety days merely on Amjad's signature.

Amjad assembled a small and trusted staff with knowledge of banking, intelligence, the military, and law enforcement. Among them was a former Pakistani police investigator who had recently received a law degree in Britain and had a reputation as smart, ambitious, and incorruptible.

When Musharraf told Amjad in early April that he wanted the bureau to investigate one of the country's most powerful men, Amjad summoned the investigator to his office.

"I have something very sensitive and very important for you," the director explained as the investigator sat across from him. Amjad swiveled in his chair and unlocked a filing cabinet, withdrew a foot-high stack of documents, and placed them on his desk. Read these, he said, and give me your impression of them tomorrow. Amjad said he would be out the rest of the day, so the investigator should remain in his office with the records until he finished. "You can have a cup of coffee, you can smoke, but you can't leave this office," Amjad said as he stood to depart. "When I return, I want your objective, honest opinion on whether there is a case in these documents."

The name at the top of the first page was "Abdul Qadeer Khan." The investigator had met the scientist casually a couple of times and, like every Pakistani, was aware that Khan was perhaps the most influential and respected man in the country. He also assumed, like every Pakistani, that Khan had used his government position to make himself rich. In this practice, he was far from alone. A culture of bribery and kickbacks that pervaded the public and private sectors in Pakistan was condemned regularly by the World Bank and other international organizations. The regimes of Benazir Bhutto and Nawaz Sharif had both been mired in allegations of widespread corruption, and Musharraf had risen to power partly by promising to end graft at the highest levels of government. But what the investigator found was corruption on a scale unusual even by the extravagant standards of Pakistan.

The next eight hours were the most fascinating of the investigator's life. Some of the information in the eight-hundred-page dossier involved rumors about Khan's wealth that had been published in Pakistan's English-language press, which was freer to question important people, but most of it was startling and new. One section dissected Khan's personal finances, listing seven houses worth millions of dollars that he owned in Islamabad. Some of the properties were held in his name, others in the name of his wife or daughters. In London, he owned two in the affluent Kensington district in the name of his daughter, Dina, who lived in one of them. Another document listed four banks in Karachi, Lahore, Amsterdam, and Dubai where Khan maintained personal accounts, with a total balance of $8 million, an amount impossible to achieve on Khan's government salary of $30,000 per year. Another entry on the property inventory caught the investigator's eye—Khan owned the twenty-six-room Hotel Hendrina Khan in Timbuktu, and records showed that in late 1999 a Pakistani Air Force cargo plane had delivered a load of furniture for the hotel. Strangely, the documents showed that the plane had made an unexplained stop in Tripoli.

In addition to amassing a fortune in real estate and hidden bank accounts, Khan had used his wealth to curry favor with the press and prominent charities. One list in the file identified twenty Pakistani journalists who received stipends of about $175 per month from Khan, more than the salaries paid by their employers, and indicated that Khan had bankrolled the Pakistani *Observer*. In a display that struck the investigator as hopelessly egocentric, Khan had financed many charities with the understanding that he would be the recipient of the awards they bestowed for good works. There were also lists of cash payments to various military officers, politicians, and even the occasional academic. "Khan loved to be flattered," said Pervez Hoodbhoy, Khan's longtime bête noire. "Say a nice thing to him, and he'd dip into his deep, deep pocket."

The dossier also pieced together evidence of how Khan had grown so wealthy. That section was highly detailed, with names, dates, and amounts for hundreds of specific transactions involving Khan and Khan Research Laboratories. Clearly, the information had been compiled by an insider with extensive access to laboratory invoices, shipping documents, and records of kickbacks to Khan. Sometimes the records reflected a 10 percent commission for Khan, and other times he ordered more equipment than necessary, with the surplus disappearing into what the insider described as Khan's unregulated inventory. In a typical example, the lab needed fifteen to twenty feet of highly specialized, very expensive wire, but Khan had authorized buying one thousand feet. The insider suspected that Khan either got a kickback or took his cut by selling the unused portion to someone else.

The scale of Khan's thievery was so large and so obvious that the investigator could not imagine the scientist had operated so corruptly without the knowledge and tacit approval of a succession of generals and intelligence chiefs. As he thought about the evidence in the files, the investigator realized that unraveling the full extent of Khan's illegal activities would require a long investigation, the threads of which could expose corruption throughout the military and government hierarchy. The scale of the potential scandal was enormous, and, drained from the reading and the revelations, the investigator returned the documents to the locked file drawer and went home around midnight. The only record he carried with him were notes scratched in a small black diary. The next morning, he told Amjad that he had been stunned by the material and needed at least another day to reexamine and digest it. The general agreed, and the investigator spent another long day, reading and marking in his black book late into the night.

On the third day, he sat across from his boss again, saying that he needed yet more time, this time to verify some of the allegations before delivering his assessment. Amjad granted him the extra time and suggested that things might go faster if the investigator got in touch with the former Kahuta insider who had prepared much of the file. Amjad arranged the appointment, and later that day the investigator found himself facing a former top-ranking official with military intelligence and the ISI who had spent three years in charge of security at Kahuta.

"Sir, I need your guidance on an important issue," he told the retired general. "It is about a file I have been reading regarding the activities of A. Q. Khan."

The retired general nervously acknowledged that he had compiled most of the Khan dossier, and he said he had done so at the request of Musharraf. In fact, the former general said that he had delivered the only copy to the Pakistani president. "I spent three years at Kahuta, and I can tell you that Khan is a dishonest man," the general said to the investigator. "He made a lot of money from kickbacks. He had his own favorites. He turned the lab into a corrupt business empire."

Once he was over his initial nervousness, the general filled many of the gaps in the investigator's understanding of Khan's activities. Over the next two days, the investigator conducted confidential interviews with a number of other people inside and outside government, delving ever deeper inside Khan's world. He tried to phrase his questions as innocently as possible to avoid alerting his sources to what exactly he was doing, which made it difficult to verify every allegation. But he confirmed enough to compile a devastating portrait of greed and corruption that could shake the country to its foundations and land A. Q. Khan in jail.

The question was what he should do now. The investigator was torn. Going after Khan would immerse the bureau in an investigation that would take years, draining resources from other inquiries. The National Accountability Bureau and Amjad already had powerful enemies in the military and intelligence establishments. Exposing the scientist and his links to other powerful people could lead to a backlash that could extinguish the group and end any chance of uncovering the backroom deals and corruption that hobbled the Pakistani economy and its flickering democracy. And in the end, he thought, Khan might be too powerful to bring down, at least for now.

After a sleepless night wrestling with his conscience, the investigator met with Amjad and laid out the most compelling evidence against Khan. There was proof the scientist was living far beyond his government salary, he said, and his real-estate holdings alone would be enough to convict him of corruption. Everything pointed to his fortune coming from kickbacks and black-market deals.

"What do you think we should do next?" asked Amjad.

"My humble suggestion is not to open a case at this stage," the investigator replied. "We are a small team. We cannot take on this thing."

Amjad nodded thoughtfully and paused before replying. He agreed that the timing might not be right, saying that perhaps in a year the bureau would have the political strength to undertake an investigation of someone of Khan's stature. The investigator understood, but he felt guilty after leaving the office. Had he pressed, Amjad might have allowed him to assemble a team to conduct a full-scale investigation. History might have unfolded differently; the investigation might have discovered the full range of activities of Khan and his accomplices. But history took a different turn.

———

AMJAD gave Musharraf a full report on the investigation and the decision not to proceed, and the president must have agreed, but he stepped up the pressure on Khan, ordering audits of KRL's books and cutting funding for its missile program. Musharraf reasoned that Pakistan already had enough missiles to reach Delhi, Mumbai, and every other city of consequence in India. In a backdoor attempt to curtail Khan's activities with the North Koreans, Musharraf imposed new regulations that required all senior nuclear scientists and officials to report any trips that they planned to make overseas. Such security requirements were normal in the United States and other countries, and Bhutto had tried to impose them on Khan, too. Khan fumed about the interference, telling Pakistani journalist Hamid Mir that Musharraf was only trying to appease the Americans, with the end result that he would damage the country's nuclear arsenal.

The scientist refused to cooperate with the audits and ignored the travel-reporting requirement, but he could not escape the increased scrutiny, as he discovered when he tried to use a charter plane to get centrifuge equipment to Iran. Officially, the flight was scheduled to go from Islamabad to another country and back, but Khan had asked for approval to have the aircraft stop for refueling in Iran on both legs of its journey. Normally, approval would have been routine for Khan, but the stops raised flags in the president's office. Rather than explain the reason for the stops, Khan canceled the flight.

In the fall of 2000, Musharraf decided again to take a closer look at Khan and summoned the director of the ISI, ordering him to put a team of agents on Khan's trail. They were told they were to follow the scientist any time he left the country and report back directly to Musharraf. The intelligence agency, which had befriended and promoted Khan for two decades, was switching roles—its agents were to watch for evidence that might bring down the scientist.

While under surveillance, Khan arrived at the VIP terminal at the west end of Islamabad's chaotic airport in his usual two-car convoy in late October. A bulletproof Toyota Crown sedan carrying the scientist pulled to a halt in front of the terminal, blocking the aging taxis and dented minivans swirling around the entrance as two armed guards jumped from the second car to take positions alongside the Toyota. A military officer stepped out of the sedan and opened its rear door. Khan emerged in his familiar tailored safari suit and nodded regally as a wave of recognition swept over the onlookers. Somewhat incongruously for a man whose staff normally carried his briefcase, the scientist this time clutched two rumpled beige shopping bags from Good Looks Fabrics and Tailors, a dry cleaner and tailor that catered to Islamabad's wealthy. Khan was whisked through security and passport control to the first-class lounge to await his flight. As diplomats, businessmen, and generals stopped to pay their respects, the two bags never left Khan's side.

Two men in the far corner of the lounge glanced at Khan from time to time as they sipped the tea delivered to them by a waiter. Khan was accustomed to curious looks from strangers, but these men were careful not to stare. When Pakistan International Airlines flight 211 for Dubai was called, the pair hung back until Khan boarded and then hurried to their seats. The men were ISI agents on Khan's trail. When the jet landed at Dubai International Airport three hours later, they watched carefully as Khan disembarked, then they trailed him through the crowds of tourists and masses of workers arriving from Pakistan, Sri Lanka, and the Philippines to sweep the streets and clean the houses of the rich Arabs. Khan went directly to the customs booth for diplomats, flashed his red diplomatic passport, and was waved through. On the other side, he was met by Tahir, who ushered him to a waiting sedan. His only luggage was the two shopping bags. The sedan rolled past the clotted queues of Mercedes and BMWs, down the long, smooth highway leading out of the airport, and past towering palm trees and endless new construction. The destination was Khan's apartment on Al Maktoum Street, twenty minutes from the airport. The two ISI men did not bother to follow Khan closely because they knew about his apartment and, when they arrived there later, they saw that the lights were on. What they did not know as they settled in for a long night's wait was why Khan had come here.

The next morning, Khan, still carrying the shopping bags, emerged from the apartment building and got into the waiting sedan. The ISI agents trailed at a discreet distance as the car drove a few blocks to the Metropolitan Palace Hotel, where Khan strolled into the lobby and shook hands with two men in Western suits who could have been wealthy Arab bankers or traders. The three chatted amiably in the hotel coffee shop. About thirty minutes later, Khan stood and shook hands to leave. As he walked out, the ISI agents noticed that he no longer carried the bags. He must have left them with the men, whom the agents later described as "dubious characters."

For the next two days, Khan rarely left the apartment, except to visit Tahir's computer-sales office in the free-trade zone and a couple of small warehouses. The two men from the hotel were nowhere to be seen. On the third day, Khan caught the evening flight to Islamabad. The agents were on the same plane, still wondering who those dubious characters had been and what was in the bags.

The following day, Musharraf received the ISI report on Khan's unauthorized trip to Dubai and immediately summoned the scientist. Musharraf was a small man, but he had a military bearing and a way of puffing up his chest that made him seem more imposing. In tough language, he berated Khan for keeping secrets, ignoring the travel restrictions, and refusing to cooperate with the auditors at KRL. Khan was unapologetic, arguing that there was no reason he should follow rules meant for lesser men. Musharraf stopped short of firing Khan, but he ordered the scientist to comply. Instead, Khan returned to Dubai in December, again without seeking government approval. And again, the ISI followed him and reported back that Khan had met with the same two men.

This was an act of outright defiance, and Musharraf would not tolerate it. While he could not treat Khan like a common criminal, he would not put up with the continued flouting of the rules. Musharraf called his top advisers together to discuss how to discipline the recalcitrant scientist. They debated for hours before reaching a decision. In mid-January, Khan was summoned to army headquarters for a meeting with Musharraf and told that he was being sacked. Once his departure became official, Musharraf said, he would never again be allowed to set foot within the gates of KRL, the vast complex he had created. Musharraf knew he dare not humiliate Khan in public, so he told him that, since he was sixty-five years old, he would be allowed to retire gracefully in March and retain a ceremonial position as an adviser to the president.

Just as President George H. W. Bush had been willing to expose

Pakistan's nuclear bomb after the United States no longer needed its help in ousting the Soviets from Afghanistan in 1990, Musharraf no longer needed his preeminent nuclear scientist, who had become more trouble than he was worth. "Musharraf didn't want a domestic backlash, and he didn't want to belittle Khan," said a former general who was a close adviser to the Pakistani leader. "But Musharraf was determined to get Pakistan back into the international community, and he could not tolerate Khan's behavior. Nuclear deterrence was in place, the delivery system was in place. Now it was time to stop this dirty business."

After all the years of kowtowing by the generals and politicians, and despite all the money he had spread around to fund the legend of himself as the father of Pakistan's bomb, there was little Khan could do to resist. If he fought Musharraf, he risked coming under a more serious investigation that could expose his role in selling the country's nuclear secrets to Iran, North Korea, and Libya. Khan could wind up not just out of a job but in prison. Still, he was a proud man, and his first reaction was to reject Musharraf's olive branch of a title, telling the president he was done with the government. Before the official announcement of his retirement, however, Khan had a change of heart. Unable to bear the prospect of losing even an empty job, he asked Musharraf for the title and an office in the president's building. Musharraf agreed.

On March 10, 2001, A. Q. Khan's career in Pakistan's nuclear industry came to an official end. He was saluted at a retirement dinner by Musharraf, who praised his service to the nation and said Khan would become his special adviser on strategic affairs, a position that carried the same rank as a cabinet minister. To reinforce the charade that Khan was stepping down voluntarily, Musharraf ordered the chairman of the Pakistan Atomic Energy Commission to retire at the same time, portraying the two moves as a changing of the guard in the country's nuclear industry.

In the days that followed, Khan fumed at the unfairness of his fall from grace, complaining bitterly to friends that the Americans had finally engineered his removal and warning that a U.S. takeover of Pakistan's nuclear arsenal was the next step. Blaming Musharraf, Khan decided that he would challenge the little general by running for president against him. Part of his campaign involved staying in the public eye, so that summer he agreed to a rare interview with a foreign film crew in his Islamabad home. The crew was working on a documentary about the spread of nuclear weapons called *Stealing the Fire,* and as he had so many times before Khan swore that he had never provided nuclear technology to anyone outside Pakistan. "We have not indulged in any proliferation," he said, looking straight into the camera. "You cannot buy nuclear weapons. You cannot get a nuclear weapon on a platter."

That, however, was precisely what Khan was endeavoring to accomplish for Libya. Banned from Kahuta and cut off from the equipment he had been stealing from the lab, Khan now had to depend more heavily on the network. But that effort was running into trouble. Tinner and Tahir were still unable to find skilled workers in Dubai. Khan and Tahir turned to South Africa, hoping that Johan Meyer could also manufacture the critical rotors for the P-2 centrifuges. They planned to buy the less-sensitive components as dual-use items in Europe. In late 2000, Tahir purchased two specialized, flow-forming lathes from a Spanish company and had them shipped first to Gulf Technical Industries, the Dubai company run by Peter and Paul Griffin. One of the two-ton lathes was then shipped to Tradefin, so that Meyer could begin to produce the rotors. But South Africa's previous nuclear efforts meant that companies there and abroad maintained strict control over the maraging steel required for the rotors, so the lathe sat unused in its crate for months while Meyer worked on the piping. Eventually, he sent the machine back to Dubai.

Failure to provide the thousands of centrifuges threatened to derail the project until Tahir came up with an alternative. His wife was from a prominent Malaysian family with political and business connections. They lived with their two young children in a four-bedroom condominium in the chic Majestic Palace in Dubai, with expensive boutiques on the ground floor. Tahir also owned an expensive building in a suburb of Kuala Lumpur and operated several businesses there, including a chocolate franchise and a gourmet date shop. In the middle of 2001 Tahir told Khan that he could find a company in Malaysia capable of producing the rotors and other components. Khan was intrigued because Malaysia offered a good technical base, lax export controls, and a location far from the spies and customs authorities of Europe and the United States. He told Tahir to look into it.

BoB EinhorN remained the assistant secretary of state for prolifera-tion and arms control when George W. Bush replaced Bill Clinton in the White House, and he soon found a key ally. Richard Armitage, the new deputy secretary of state, was a barrel-chested Vietnam veteran who had worked at the Pentagon during the Reagan years and had harbored concerns about Pakistan and Khan from those days. In one of their first conversations, Einhorn told Armitage that the situation with Khan was so serious that he should upgrade his security clearances so that he could be briefed by the CIA. "Rich, you need to get into this compartment and get briefed," Einhorn told him.

Armitage got the clearances and called Stephen Hadley, the deputy national-security adviser, and asked him to convene a series of briefings on Khan and Pakistan. Within days, Armitage was at the White House for a detailed CIA briefing on Khan's ring. Hadley and Bob Joseph, the senior nonproliferation official at the National Security Council, also at-tended the top-secret session. There, Armitage learned that Urs Tinner had turned out to be a gold mine, providing enough detailed information for the agency to set up an elaborate monitoring operation that tracked the network's shipments. Alongside the CIA operation, the National Se-curity Agency was running a massive eavesdropping operation targeting the network, while British intelligence was contributing information from its own sources. The Bush administration had a clear picture that showed Khan providing nuclear technology to three of America's most dangerous enemies, Iran, North Korea, and Libya. Einhorn described Armitage as "really spun up about Khan," but Bob Joseph and CIA officials wanted to see what else could be learned about Khan's global network. So again, the policy remained the same: watch and wait.

Einhorn left the administration to join a think tank in Washington, and he was replaced by John Wolf, a career foreign-service officer who had served a tour in Pakistan. "By the time I came on board in 2001, we had a very broad fix on what Khan was doing," Wolf explained later. "I don't think we knew all the details, but we were inside the whole network. In Libya, we didn't know where the nuclear work was going on. We just knew they were doing it."

There was wide recognition that waiting entailed risks. The CIA suspected that Libya was making rapid progress, and its analysts knew that Iran was several years into a major bomb-building program. Equally dangerous, there was always the chance that the network was selling its technology and expertise to someone off the CIA radar, and it was possible that Khan, angered at his ouster, would retaliate by somehow arranging a shipment of weapons-grade uranium to one of his current customers or, worse, a new one.

In mid-August, two Pakistani nuclear scientists sat down beside a campfire in a compound on the outskirts of Kandahar, the city in southeastern Afghanistan that was headquarters for the ruling Taliban party and the unofficial home of Al Qaeda's leader, Osama bin Laden. Seated with the scientists were bin Laden and Ayman al-Zawahiri, the Egyptian surgeon who had emerged as bin Laden's equal and senior tactician. The Al Qaeda leader had been scouring the Middle East and former Soviet republics for chemical, biological, and nuclear weapons for years and had even obtained a fatwa, or legal ruling, from a Muslim religious leader that authorized the use of weapons of mass destruction in a holy war against the United States and Israel. Al Qaeda was conducting tests with crude chemical and biological weapons at several locations in Afghanistan, but mastering the technology was difficult. The search for nuclear material was even harder. An attempt to buy fissile material in Istanbul had fizzled when an Al Qaeda operative wound up paying a large sum for what turned out to be radioactive medical waste, which could have no use in a bomb. An earlier attempt in the Sudan had failed, too. But bin Laden remained committed to acquiring a nuclear weapon, and the two Pakistanis, Sultan Bashiruddin Mahmood and Chaudiri Abdul Majeed, offered the best chance yet. Mahmood was the more important figure, an expert in uranium enrichment who had held a series of senior posts in Pakistan's nuclear-weapons program. In 1974, when the Pakistani government was anticipating A. Q.

Khan's triumphal return from Amsterdam, Mahmood had been chosen to set up the pilot plant for the new uranium-enrichment program. As part of Musharraf's crackdown, however, Mahmood had been forced into early retirement because he had expressed sympathies for the Taliban and other Islamic extremists. In writings and speeches, he had advocated sharing Pakistan's nuclear-weapons technology with other Islamic nations to hasten the "end of days," which he believed would give rise to Muslim world dominance. Majeed was less well known, but he had important skills acquired during a career at a Pakistani installation where enriched uranium was shaped into the cores for nuclear devices.

A year before the campfire meeting, the two scientists had set up a nonprofit organization, Ummah Tameer-e-Nau, to conduct relief work in Afghanistan, including guiding the Taliban on scientific matters. Its board boasted several Pakistani generals and business leaders sympathetic to the Taliban cause, and it was one of the few nongovernmental groups that the Taliban leader, Mullah Omar, permitted to operate in Afghanistan. Not long after opening their office in a house in Kabul, the scientists met with Mullah Omar and bin Laden, and the conversation had shifted from relief work to weapons development. At one point during his visits to Afghanistan, Mahmood provided one of bin Laden's associates in Kabul with information about the construction of a nuclear weapon.

That August, the scientists spent two or three days at bin Laden's compound, listening as the Al Qaeda leader explained that he had obtained, or at least had access to, some type of radiological material from the Islamic Movement of Uzbekistan, a radical group affiliated with Al Qaeda. They discussed how the material could be used in a so-called dirty bomb, which could spread radioactive contamination over a wide area. The sessions ended inconclusively when bin Laden, al-Zawahiri, and their closest associates abruptly left for the mountains of northwestern Afghanistan. Before leaving, bin Laden told his followers that something great was going to happen, and Muslims around the world were going to join them in the holy war.

The events of September 11, 2001, redefined the American concept of national security. Suddenly aware of their vulnerability, America's leaders were determined to secure the borders and root out their enemies by whatever means were necessary. If terrorists were willing to hijack passenger planes and kill thousands of civilians by crashing them into buildings, what would stop them from exploding a nuclear device in an American city? The nuclear fears that gripped the United States at the height of the Cold War were revived, though this time the enemy was more elusive.

CHAPTER 24

"WITH US OR AGAINST US"

O N THE MORNING of September 12, General Musharraf was meeting with regional leaders in Karachi when one of his assistants entered and whispered that Secretary of State Colin Powell was on the telephone. Musharraf said he would call Powell after the meeting, but Powell insisted on talking to Musharraf immediately. The Pakistani leader excused himself to take the call in a private office. Without preamble, Powell told Musharraf that the attacks on the World Trade Center and Pentagon put the United States at war and left Pakistan with a stark choice: "You are either with us or against us." Like the rest of the world's leaders, Musharraf had been shocked by the terrorist attacks and expressed his sympathy. In the next breath, he assured Powell that he and Pakistan were with the United States in the fight against Al Qaeda.

Aligning himself with the Americans in what the former army commando suspected would be a hellish fight on his own border entailed high risks for Musharraf, whose Sunni-dominated government had long provided financial and political help to the Taliban in order to maintain a friendly regime as a buffer against its on-again, off-again relations with Iran's Shiites. He would face objections from the Pakistani population and from within his own officer corps, where many senior officers had deep ties to the Taliban leadership and junior officers shared their fundamentalist view of Islam. But what choice did the Pakistani leader have? Refusing to sign on with the Americans at this desperate hour, he realized, would expose him to the same kind of wrath they were about to rain down on Afghanistan.

Similar conversations were taking place with other nations' leaders as Washington laid out in the starkest terms that it expected complete and unstinting cooperation from all of its allies against the perpetrators of September 11. None of those countries, however, was as crucial as Pakistan to the American strategy. Just as it had served as a route for arms and assistance to the Afghan guerrillas fighting the Soviets, the intermittent ally would play a central role in the coming war. In case Powell's telephone call left any doubt, the point was reinforced later that same day by Bush administration officials who summoned Lieutenant General Mahmood Ahmed, the head of the ISI who was in Washington as a guest of the CIA, to a meeting at the State Department. Before going, he telephoned Musharraf for instructions. Musharraf told him to reinforce Pakistan's determination to cooperate and to report back immediately. According to Ahmed, Deputy Secretary of State Richard Armitage threatened to bomb Pakistan back to the Stone Age unless it cooperated in going after Al Qaeda and its allies. Though Armitage later denied making an overt threat to the Pakistani general, the message that Ahmed relayed to Musharraf reinforced that the American position was nonnegotiable. The next day at CIA headquarters, Ahmed was given a list of demands that included stopping Pakistani military assistance to the Taliban, closing its borders with Afghanistan, and allowing American reconnaissance planes to fly out of remote bases in Pakistan. Ahmed assured the Americans that Pakistan would accept the demands, but he also told them that Taliban leader Mullah Omar was a man of peace who would turn over bin Laden if the Americans convinced him that Al Qaeda was behind the attacks. Mahmood did not believe Al Qaeda was to blame for September 11, but he kept his thoughts to himself until he returned to Pakistan. There, he suggested to Musharraf that September 11 had been staged by the Americans as an excuse for making war on Islam, a theory that gained credence throughout the Muslim world in the weeks that followed.

As the United States prepared for war in Afghanistan, Pakistan followed through on its commitment, opening bases to U.S. aircraft and withholding assistance to the Taliban regime. In an attempt to avert a war, Mahmood led a delegation to Kandahar to persuade Mullah Omar to turn over bin Laden to the Americans. The terrorist attacks and the prospect of massive retaliation against Afghanistan had split the Taliban. Some argued that the United States had been Afghanistan's ally and that bin Laden lacked the religious authority to initiate a jihad against it. They argued for turning him over. Omar was angry that bin Laden had put the Taliban and Afghanistan in such a precarious position, but he reasoned that he could not remain in power himself if he gave in to American demands, so he decided that bin Laden could stay.

The prospect of an all-out American attack on fellow Muslims sent tens of thousands of Pakistanis pouring into the streets of the cities. Religious militants, who already saw Musharraf as too secular, threatened to topple his government if he helped the Americans, a position that had support among elements of the military and the ISI. Musharraf faced the dangerous task of satisfying the American demands without further inflaming passions on the streets and in the barracks.

Bush administration officials recognized the delicate balance that Musharraf was trying to maintain and worried that his ouster could destabilize the country at a critical time, probably leaving extremist elements of the military in charge of the government and its nuclear arsenal. But Washington would tolerate no wavering. In October, Powell visited Islamabad, and the security of Pakistan's nukes was part of his agenda. He told Musharraf that the United States was willing to supply technical assistance to improve the security of the nuclear weapons, including transferring technology called "permissive action links" that would prevent warheads from being armed unless a number of people entered codes. The Pakistanis worried that the Americans' real intention was to identify the location of their nuclear bombs so that they could be seized in the event of political instability. "There are some in the Pakistani hierarchy who fear a Trojan horse, that we are learning about their nuclear program because, in their minds, we may one day need to deal with it," a senior American official said at the time. The offer was rejected.

To underscore the danger of the nuclear weapons falling into unfriendly hands, Powell's delegation said the CIA had learned of Sultan Bashiruddin Mahmood and Chaudiri Abdul Majeed's meeting with Al Qaeda leaders in Afghanistan shortly before the September 11 attacks. The Pakistanis agreed to detain the scientists, who later that month were secretly taken into custody by the ISI; not even their families were told why, or where, they were held. After four weeks of interrogation, the ISI decided neither man had been involved in the weapons portion of Pakistan's nuclear program and could have been of little value to Al Qaeda, so they were released. The CIA wasn't convinced the scientists were harmless, and information obtained from Al Qaeda records found in an abandoned training camp in Afghanistan renewed their concerns. The records indicated that Mahmood and Majeed had met with bin Laden himself and that they had promised to help Al Qaeda build an atomic bomb. Adding to the fear, CIA agents operating alongside American troops had uncovered evidence at Al Qaeda training camps of experiments with chemical and biological weapons. The unfolding evidence about Al Qaeda's intentions was alarming enough that CIA chief George Tenet was convinced his people needed a crack at questioning the Pakistani scientists.

In the middle of the night on December 1, 2001, a Boeing 707 operated by the U.S. Air Force taxied to a stop in Islamabad. Three men emerged and got into an unmarked van. Accompanying Tenet were a CIA analyst named Kevin, who specialized in weapons of mass destruction, and Rolf Mowatt-Larssen, the head of CIA counterterrorism center's weapons of mass destruction branch. Mowatt-Larssen was white haired and formal, a graduate of West Point, who had served as an army officer before spending two decades as an intelligence officer for the CIA in Europe and the former Soviet Union. They had come with orders from President Bush to insist that Musharraf rearrest the scientists and permit the CIA and FBI to participate in a second round of interrogations. By this time, the American troops were routing the Taliban and Al Qaeda forces in Afghanistan, stoking the anti-American furor in Pakistan and making Musharraf's alliance with Washington more dangerous by the day—hence the secrecy of Tenet's visit.

"We have trouble, big trouble—trouble for you, trouble for us," the CIA boss told Musharraf, describing the August meeting and the new evidence. "Al Qaeda has said for years that they want a nuclear device. Now it is within reach. That is an unacceptable situation for the United States. Intolerable."

"That is not possible, Mr. Tenet," Musharraf responded. "It took Pakistan many years and a great deal of money to produce the devices we have. What you are talking about—Al Qaeda producing a bomb—is implausible."

"If it was implausible, the president wouldn't have sent me here," Tenet replied.

Mowatt-Larssen laid out the possible ways in which a terrorist organization could obtain a nuclear weapon, from the theft or black-market purchase of enriched uranium to the availability of small, portable nuclear devices. He and other American experts were concerned that Al Qaeda could fashion a crude device, even without all the components, if they acquired fissile material—and the mostly like source of that was Pakistan. Simply slamming together two subcritical masses of enriched uranium could detonate an explosion large enough to kills thousands. In addition, he told Musharraf that American intelligence had discovered that Al Qaeda cells were searching for radioactive material that could be wrapped around explosives to make a dirty bomb.

Musharraf agreed reluctantly to rearrest the scientists, saying that he hoped word of this would not become public. But news of Tenet's trip leaked three days later, causing American and Pakistani officials to claim the CIA chief had come to urge Musharraf to crack down on religious extremists leading anti-American demonstrations. By the end of the week, however, it was known that the two scientists and several of their prominent backers had been detained at the direction of the American government. To avoid a major furor, Pakistani and American officials downplayed the episode, telling reporters that the scientists were retired and did not have direct responsibilities for weapons production. Mahmood's son acknowledged that bin Laden had asked his father for help in building a nuclear bomb, but he said his father told the Al Qaeda leader that it would be very difficult. The son also said his father declined to help bin Laden. Behind the scenes, the scientists were more forthcoming when confronted with the CIA evidence, acknowledging that bin Laden had indicated that he had access to fissile material through Uzbek allies and that he had questioned them about how to fashion it into a weapon. They claimed to have told him that it would be impossible to create a weapon simply from the radioactive material, but they also admitted that their conversations with him had covered a wide range of weapons of mass destruction. Mahmood in particular appeared to the interrogators to represent the most dangerous and extremist elements of Pakistan's elite, a segment of society that advocated not only developing its own nuclear weapons but spreading them to other Islamic countries. In the end, however, the Pakistani authorities determined that the two scientists had not violated any laws, and they were quietly released again.

THE NAME that never came up in the conversation between the CIA chief and the Pakistani president was that of A. Q. Khan. From Musharraf's perspective, he had sidelined Khan the previous March. For Tenet, the issue was preventing Al Qaeda from getting access to nuclear weapons by keeping Musharraf in power, at least long enough to capture bin Laden and uproot the Taliban. As early as 1998, CIA intelligence had discovered that bin Laden had sent emissaries to contact Khan about help in building a nuclear weapon, but the scientist had apparently rejected the overtures. Khan might have felt he and his network were overextended: He was supplying enrichment technology to North Korea and in the midst of the massive project to build a nuclear weapon for Libya. Further, Khan might have felt that working with bin Laden in Afghanistan was too close to home for comfort. Nevertheless, Tenet was willing to turn a blind eye to Khan's activities to avoid jeopardizing Musharraf. "I didn't want the discussion to veer off toward Khan at this point," Tenet wrote in his memoirs. "There would be another day for that topic."

The Pakistani leader was mistaken in thinking that he had sidelined Khan. Being barred from his own laboratories may have complicated the task of supplying Libya and Iran, but the obstacles were not insurmountable. After Musharraf told Khan that he was being removed from the lab in late January, he had taken advantage of his last weeks at the facility by cleaning out not just his desk but the technology cupboard, too. He made electronic copies of a host of critical designs, including those for the P-1 and P-2 centrifuges, and ordered eight complete P-2 centrifuges shipped to Dubai.

In the fall of 2001, Tahir had begun to pursue Malaysia as the site for the centrifuge factory. It had emerged as a developing country with a growing manufacturing capacity, a skilled workforce, a good industrial infrastructure, and, most important, relatively loose controls on imports and exports. Equally important, it was far from the watchful eyes of the CIA and European intelligence agencies. Tahir had the connections to pull off the deal. His wife, Nazimah Syed Majid, was an investor in a Malaysian company called Scomi Group, which was involved primarily in the oil and gas industry. Among her partners was Kamaluddin Abdullah, the only son of Malaysia's prime minister, Abdullah Badawi.

When Tahir talked with Khan about this possibility, the Pakistani scientist immediately liked the idea of an opportunity to work in a technically advanced Muslim country, and he authorized Tahir to proceed. In December 2001, Tahir struck a deal with a Scomi subsidiary, Scomi Precision Engineering, to use one of its factories to produce what he described as metal tubing for the petroleum and water-treatment industries. He explained that Scomi's small factory would be reconfigured with new machinery and its workforce of thirty or so would be retrained for the project.

Urs Tinner agreed to move to Kuala Lumpur to take charge of the factory, and by the spring of 2002 he was on the scene and ordering the specialized lathes and other machinery. Some difficulties remained, however, particularly in obtaining some of the more sophisticated materials. Carbon fiber for the P-2 rotors was one example; its export was tightly controlled, so Tinner decided to substitute high-strength aluminum, which was more readily available. He placed an order for 330 tons of the aluminum with the Singapore offices of a German company. As the machinery and material arrived in Malaysia, Tinner used blueprints from Khan to set up a miniature version of the centrifuge production plant at Kahuta. The goal was to produce parts for at least ten thousand centrifuges.

Tinner's move to Malaysia presented both opportunities and obstacles for the CIA. He would be able to provide information about the status of the centrifuge manufacturing, but his knowledge of the ring's broader activities would be more limited because Dubai remained the central transfer point for the increasing flow of equipment to Libya. When Mad Dog learned that Tinner was moving, he notified his supervisor in Vienna and began planning a long stay in Kuala Lumpur.

Malaysian government authorities later claimed that both their inspectors and the legitimate employees of Scomi lacked the technical expertise to understand exactly what Tahir was producing at the plant. Despite the precision of the work and the use of imported parts and specialized high-strength aluminum, the authorities said the workers thought they were indeed making tubes for the oil and water-treatment industries.

As the centrifuge factory was coming together, work in South Africa was progressing on the elaborate piping system. Johan Meyer had persuaded Tahir to provide him with a videotape taken inside Kahuta that showed a similar installation. Combined with the original drawings, the video helped Meyer visualize the two-story array of pipes, valves, and high-pressure tanks. As he reported his progress back to Tahir, Meyer received installments on the thirty-three-million-dollar contract. Meyer didn't expect to finish until late 2002, but he was captivated by the complexity of the project and came to regard it as a work of art.

For Khan, the dream of providing another Muslim country with a nuclear arsenal was tantalizingly within reach. Despite the odds and obstacles, he appeared to be on the verge of pulling off another miracle. By early 2002, dozens of shipments were finding their way to Libya, and work was under way on a pilot enrichment plant, where Libyan technicians could learn how to operate the larger facility. The pilot plant was being built in a nondescript, abandoned warehouse on the outskirts of Tripoli at a place called Al Hashan. Twenty Libyan technicians had already been trained by Tinner during extended stays in Dubai. In April 2002, the first of three small centrifuge cascades was ready for testing at Al Hashan. Libya had made the first real step toward the bomb.

The centrifuge tests required a small supply of uranium hexafluoride, sales of which are highly regulated. In September 2000, Khan had managed to include two small cylinders in a large shipment of seventy-nine crates of centrifuge components from Kahuta to Tripoli. The shipment was carried by Shaheen Air International, the airline controlled by a retired Pakistani Air Force general. Mohammad Matuq Mohammad, the head of Libya's nuclear program, had insisted from the beginning that Khan provide a far larger amount of the gas for additional tests until Libya completed its own plant to convert processed uranium ore into the gas, but Khan no longer had access to Kahuta's stockpile of gas. Instead, Khan turned to the only other source he could think of, North Korea.

Even after he was sacked, Khan's nuclear trade with the North Korean regime had remained steady, and he continued to travel to Pyongyang to meet with nuclear scientists working on the secret enrichment program there. In February 2001, he arranged the shipment of large cylinders containing nearly two tons of uranium hexafluoride from North Korea to Dubai, where it was sent on to Libya. Instead of his usual barter arrangement, Khan paid for the shipment with money from Libya.

By this time, the network had received millions of dollars from the Libyans. The proceeds were laundered through a series of bank accounts throughout Europe and the Middle East, with electronic wire transfers bouncing from bank to bank. Some accounts were held by front companies or straw men who collected a small fee for the use of their names; others were numbered accounts in Switzerland and Liechtenstein. In Khan's case, his personal cut went to at least four separate bank accounts in four separate countries. The payment for the uranium hexafluoride was a good example of how the system worked. A Libyan bank wired $2 million to a Dubai account controlled by Khan. The payment, minus about $200,000 kept as commission by Khan, was then transferred to a North Korean bank in Dubai. The third bank sent the money to yet another financial institution in Macao, a region in the South China Sea with a reputation as a haven for drug runners, spies, and arms dealers and long used by North Korea to launder money. In this case, the money arrived in an account belonging to New Hap Hieng Investment Company, a North Korean government entity long accused by the United States of selling technology for chemical, biological, and nuclear weapons.

CHAPTER 25

DIPLOMATIC CHESS

WASHINGTON WAS IN THE GRIP of a heat wave on August 14, 2002, when an Iranian exile named Alireza Jafarzadeh stepped to the podium at the National Press Club. Few reporters in the room knew Jafarzadeh or had heard of the organization he represented, the National Council of Resistance of Iran, but they soon realized this story would make headlines—Jafarzadeh was about to blow the lid off Iran's secret nuclear program. "Today I am going to reveal to you top secret sites of the Iranian regime that they had succeeded to keep secret until today," he said as the TV cameras rolled and a dozen reporters scribbled in notebooks. "One of these two top secret projects is in the city of Natanz. . . . The other one is Arak's atomic facility."

Work at Arak and Natanz had been under way for some time, yet both projects had eluded detection by American spy satellites and other intelligence operations. Iranian authorities had selected the two locations carefully to conceal the nuclear work as long as possible. Each city was remote, and neither was associated with the country's military-industrial complex or its supposedly minor civilian nuclear research. Jafarzadeh's small exile group was exposing a well-kept secret, and its accusations were to reverberate in the months to come.

Natanz is a small mountain town about two hundred miles south of Tehran, known for its bracing climate and fruit orchards. There, he said, the Iranians were digging two huge holes in the ground to house thousands of centrifuges to enrich uranium. The halls would be buried twenty-five feet below the surface and covered with eight and a half feet of concrete as protection against air attacks like the one that had knocked out Iraq's Osirak reactor in 1981. Near Arak, a city of 500,000 people in western Iran best known for the weaving of fine Persian carpets, work was nearly complete on a heavy-water plant that could be used to support a re-actor capable of producing weapons-grade plutonium. In addition to those major facilities, Jafarzadeh identified several front companies and smaller installations he said were involved in the clandestine weapons program. Most of the sites identified as part of the network were part of established research centers or military installations, but one of them was a mysterious outlier. Jafarzadeh said that centrifuge development had been carried out at a company called Kalaye Electric, a supposed clock manufacturer on the outskirts of Tehran.

Jafarzadeh said the information had come from people inside Iran who were going public in hopes of discrediting and ultimately ousting the current regime. What he did not reveal was NCRI's association with the People's Mujahedin of Iran, an organization that had been designated as a terrorist group by the State Department since 1997. Even after that, however, NCRI was allowed to maintain a small office in Washington. Jafarzadeh built close ties with neoconservatives in the Bush administra-tion and emerged as both the spokesman for NCRI and an Iran analyst for Fox News.

Some of the details he provided that day eventually turned out to be slightly off. The enrichment halls at Natanz were going to be seventy-five feet underground, and the work at Arak had barely begun. But commercial satellite photos posted on the Internet the next day by a small but influ-ential Washington think tank, the Institute for Science and International Security—run by former UN weapons inspector David Albright—con-firmed that major work was under way at Natanz and that construction had started at Arak.

At the headquarters of the IAEA, the allegations hit like a bombshell. Since the discovery of Saddam's secret weapons program and the disclosure of North Korea's hidden bomb project, the agency had been struggling to invigorate its inspection system along the lines suggested by Hans Blix, to avoid the late discovery of yet another clandestine nuclear-weapons effort. The question raised by the new accusations about Iran was, Did the IAEA have the resources and ability to do just that?

The discovery that Saddam had gotten perilously close to a bomb without the knowledge of the outside world had spurred a movement to provide new powers for the IAEA, and on May 15, 1997, the agency's board had met in special session to approve a document known as the Additional Protocol, which embodied the proposals first made by Blix in 1991. Under its provisions, inspectors had the authority to visit any suspicious location on just twenty-four hours' notice—too little time, it was hoped, for a country to cover up illegal nuclear activities. The protocol also gave the agency the authority to ask formal questions about inconsistencies or suspicions involving a country's nuclear program, whether declared or not.

The change was a big step in giving the agency's investigative arm real enforcement authority, but in order for those powers to be effective, the culture had to be transformed, too. Blix and others had recognized that the IAEA needed to develop a new mind-set among its inspectors and other officials that relied on skepticism, not acceptance. But the agency is a large, labyrinthine bureaucracy, and change had been slow in coming. Toward the end of the 1990s, some senior officials realized that changing the mind-set of the existing inspectors was harder than simply looking for a new type of inspector. "In the past, they were just accountants," explained Pierre Goldschmidt, who took over in 1999 as head of the agency's safeguards division. "Now we require analytical minds, even a detective's mind. We stress teamwork and a comprehensive view that looks for inconsistencies and anomalies that might signal something suspicious is going on."

Implementing the Additional Protocol meant persuading individual countries to sign the amendment, which also required ratification by the appropriate government bodies. In the case of the United States, the Clinton administration signed the protocol in June 1998 but did not submit it to the Republican-controlled Senate because of doubts that it would be ratified. The new inspections regime could be used only in countries that had ratified the protocol. But by the summer of 2002, only twenty-six of the 140 countries with safeguards agreements with the IAEA had approved the protocol. Australia and Canada were among them, but other signers were small countries with little or nothing in the way of nuclear programs. China was the only nuclear-weapons state that had ratified the agreement. Some in the United States and Russia objected that the inspections were too intrusive; France and Britain were not to ratify until 2004. Among the other countries that had not adopted the protocol was Iran.

OLLI HEINONEN lived on the outskirts of Vienna. On August 15, a few hours after Jafarzadeh's press conference in Washington, he was sitting down to breakfast when he opened the newspaper and saw an article describing the disclosures. He could scarcely believe what he read. As a senior official at the IAEA, he knew that inspections had not uncovered a hint of trouble with the Iranian program. Not a word about a plant being built in Natanz. Nothing about a heavy-water facility in Arak or a clock factory called Kalaye. Because Iran had signed the NPT and reached a safeguards agreement with the IAEA, it was obligated to report any nuclear work to the agency, yet none of this had come to Heinonen's attention. Normally a self-contained man, he was fuming by the time he pulled into the garage beneath the IAEA headquarters and rushed to his office to get onto the Internet and track down a transcript of Jafarzadeh's press conference.

Heinonen had spent nearly twenty years at the IAEA. He had a doctorate in radiochemistry from the University of Helsinki and had worked as a researcher at Finland's nuclear-research center before joining the IAEA in 1983, out of a commitment to curtailing proliferation. Thanks to a keen intellect and dogged determination, he had risen through the ranks and was now head of Division B, one of three groups within the safeguards department that monitored compliance with IAEA agreements worldwide. Heinonen was in his early fifties, with a stocky build and shock of reddish hair that often fell across his broad forehead. A typical Finn, he rarely showed emotion, sitting impassively through diatribes by aggrieved ambassadors or calmly mediating endless bureaucratic disputes within the agency. Often after the complainants departed, Heinonen let loose a wry joke about their performance that bent his colleagues double with laughter. That particular morning, however, Heinonen was in no mood for jokes. Iran was on his watch list, and he had been on many inspection trips to its declared nuclear-research sites in Tehran and Esfahan. He knew the country had the money, industrial infrastructure, and technical know-how to undertake something of the magnitude of building an atomic bomb, yet he had had no hint of a secret weapons program.

The IAEA operates at a deliberate pace, even faced with what seemed to be an emergency. Mohamed ElBaradei, its sixty-year-old director general, was a respected Egyptian diplomat and law professor at New York University before succeeding Hans Blix at the helm of the agency in 1997. The son of a distinguished Cairo lawyer, ElBaradei had studied law at Cairo University before joining the country's diplomatic service, with postings in Geneva and New York. While in New York, he earned a doctorate in international law and developed an addiction to the New York Knicks and the NBA. He joined the IAEA in 1984 and held a series of ever-higher positions before he was chosen as director general.

Blix had begun transforming the IAEA into a more aggressive overseer, and ElBaradei had pursued that agenda with vigor. Still, he had to tread with caution to avoid antagonizing countries that felt the agency was moving too quickly, as well as those that feared it was going too slowly. His biggest worry was that nuclear weapons would fall into the hands of terrorists, but he saw communication and diplomacy as the most effective means of avoiding that catastrophe. "What I bring to the job is an understanding that a lot of these issues can only be resolved through dialogue," he said in describing his role. "It's like a small family. You will never solve your problem until you sit around the dining table and put your grievances on the table and find how to move forward. Some people equate that with being soft—that if you do not pound on the table and if you do not scream, then you are being soft. I think that is a total misconception."

The day after the Washington press conference about Iran, ElBaradei asked Heinonen to write a letter to the Iranian ambassador to the IAEA, Ali Akbar Salehi, seeking an official response to the accusations about a secret nuclear program. The Iranian's response condemned the exile group, but it did not address the specifics of the accusations. ElBaradei then summoned Pierre Goldschmidt, Heinonen, and a half-dozen other senior officials to his office on the twenty-seventh floor of the IAEA headquarters. Seated around an oblong conference table, the group debated how to get to the bottom of the accusations. The threshold question was whether the information was accurate—the exile group obviously had its own agenda and was probably not above twisting the facts or even making them up. On the other hand, the satellite photos made clear that something big was under way at Natanz.

ElBaradei was not a nuclear scientist, so he relied heavily on Heinonen to interpret the satellite photos and other information flowing into the agency about what Iran might be doing. ElBaradei and Heinonen had a strong friendship, dating to the early 1990s when they worked side-by-side in North Korea, and the director general trusted Heinonen's judgment and restraint. The Finn contended that the satellite photos alone were cause for the agency to take the allegations seriously. Other information buttressed the notion that Iran was concealing major nuclear work. Kenneth Brill, the American ambassador to the IAEA, had told ElBaradei that American intelligence regarded the information from the exiles as credible, though Brill provided little in the way of evidence, a long-standing pattern in the relationship between the agency and the United States.

The Americans shared intelligence with the IAEA when it suited their purpose and withheld information when they chose to do so. In this case, they were happy to point the finger at Iran, which was regarded by the Bush administration as part of the so-called axis of evil. The American government was the biggest single contributor to the IAEA budget and loaned numerous experts to the agency, but Washington had been reluctant over the years to share much intelligence because the agency employed nuclear scientists and technicians from a number of countries that the United States suspected of harboring or even pursuing secret nuclear ambitions. In fact, neither the Americans nor the British had disclosed anything they knew about Khan's network and its sales to Iran, North Korea, and Libya, leaving the agency in the dark as the CIA and MI6 tracked the network around the world.

In July, just a month before the disclosures about Iran, the knowledge about Khan's operation had been discussed by the heads of Britain's intelligence agencies and other senior policymakers in secret session in London. The group had gathered to examine a report that concluded Khan was selling nuclear technology to several countries in the Middle East and that he was central to clandestine nuclear-weapons development in Libya. The report made clear that the Americans and British knew that Khan had moved his base of operations to Dubai and that his ring had set up a production plant in Malaysia. The CIA and MI6 had identified numerous suppliers, bank accounts, and transportation routes used by the network in what the report described as "the first case of a private enterprise offering a complete range of services to enable a customer to acquire highly enriched uranium for nuclear weapons."

Such information would have been invaluable to the IAEA, but the only thing the American ambassador provided to ElBaradei that August was his belief that the exile group's charges regarding Iran were accurate. Still, ElBaradei was convinced the accusations were serious enough for a full-scale inquiry. He told Heinonen to persuade Tehran to let senior officials, including ElBaradei, visit Natanz and the other locations as soon as possible. The IAEA lacked the authority to demand access to Natanz, but a routine inspection of other Iranian facilities was scheduled for October.

The next morning, Heinonen called Alireza Esmaeli, an official with the Iranian delegation to the IAEA, to tell him that ElBaradei planned to accompany the October inspection team and wanted to visit Natanz and other suspicious sites. Esmaeli said Heinonen would have to talk to Ambassador Salehi for permission. Unfortunately, he added, the ambassador was on vacation.

Heinonen had dealt with Iranians enough over the years to understand that every encounter carried the likelihood of extended negotiations, and this was to be no different. His initial contact started a back and forth that was to last for years and went like this: The IAEA would ask for access to a site and then wait days, weeks, and months for a response. While the Iranians stalled, they concealed any suspicious work and concocted cover stories. In this instance, simply getting permission for ElBaradei to go to

Iran turned into a game of diplomatic chess, played purely according to the Iranian clock. On September 5, ElBaradei met with Salehi and a delegation of Iranian nuclear officials in Vienna. ElBaradei emphasized that the agency had to evaluate all of the evidence that came its way, regardless of the merits of the organization making the accusations, and he said he wanted to visit the sites. Salehi responded that he lacked the authority to permit access to the locations, but he promised to convey the request to Tehran.

The October inspection arrived without Iranian approval of ElBaradei's request, so Heinonen went without him. As usual, the team was limited to Iran's declared sites, leaving Natanz, Arak, and Kalaye off-limits. Heinonen had visited the research reactors and other declared installations in the past, but now he saw those facilities in a different light. He didn't see proof of illegal activities, but he picked up subtle signs that something was amiss—more equipment than he expected in some locations, more sections of research centers marked "off-limits."

Back in Vienna, Heinonen went back to his old files and documents, accumulated over the years from earlier inspections, to reconstruct Iran's nuclear program, keeping an eye out for imports of equipment or material that might have contributed to a hidden atomic program. He also reached out for more information from sources outside the IAEA, including contacts at foreign intelligence agencies. His persistence and thoroughness were rewarded with the discovery that Iran had secretly imported uranium hexafluoride from China in the early 1990s, without declaring it to the IAEA. The discovery was significant for two reasons: First, Iran's failure to declare receipt of nuclear material constituted a breach under its safeguards agreement with the IAEA; second, the concealment was a powerful indication that the Iranians were indeed hiding nuclear activities. Before contacting the Iranians, Heinonen asked Goldschmidt to write an official letter to the Chinese delegation to the IAEA, asking about the transfer. Surprisingly, the Chinese acknowledged that they had sold nearly two tons of uranium hexafluoride and other nuclear chemicals to the Iranians in 1991. The agency didn't want to confront the Iranians quite yet, so Heinonen filed the letter from China and put a copy in his briefcase for his next trip to Iran.

———

IT WAS not until February 20, 2003, six months after the disclosure in Washington, that the Iranian government permitted ElBaradei to visit the country. Even then, the trip was restricted to two days, and Iran insisted that it be described as a visit, not an official inspection. Not wanting to waste time, ElBaradei and his delegation went straight from the Tehran airport to the construction site at Natanz, where they found the work divided into two parts: A warehouselike structure was nearly complete in one area, and nearby earthmoving equipment was digging a vast hole in the ground. The Iranians acknowledged that the structure was for a pilot facility where they planned to begin testing centrifuges; the hole in the ground, they said, would eventually be home to a massive uranium-enrichment plant capable of holding fifty thousand or more centrifuges and producing enriched uranium to fuel a series of reactors around the country to generate electricity. The scale was enormous, and the IAEA officials were stunned that the Iranians had made such dramatic progress without the IAEA suspecting anything. The question remained whether the work violated any of Iran's obligations under the nonproliferation treaty or under the safeguards agreement with the IAEA.

Ushering ElBaradei and the rest of the delegation through the pilot plant, Gholamreza Aghazadeh, the president of the Atomic Energy Organization of Iran, was visibly proud of the technical accomplishments. Nearly one hundred centrifuges in various states of assembly were lined up in the pilot plant. Lifting a component for one of them, the Iranian official boasted that the machines were built from indigenous designs and components. The work was far enough along, he said, that the first one thousand centrifuges were to be installed by May. Aghazadeh emphasized that no nuclear material had been introduced into the pilot plant, the first step that would trigger Iran's obligation to report the facility to the IAEA. Despite the alarm bells set off by the secrecy, if Aghazadeh was telling the truth, the work at Natanz was not an obvious violation of Iran's obligations to the agency.

Heinonen dropped a few steps behind the larger group to get a closer look at the centrifuges. Impressed by the apparent quality of the machines, he thought the design looked familiar. Heinonen was not a centrifuge expert, but he had seen thousands of them on inspections around the world.

He thought to himself, "Either someone is helping these guys or they are miracle workers."

Back in Tehran, ElBaradei met with a host of Iranian political and religious leaders, from reformers like President Mohammad Khatami to hard-liners like Hashemi Rafsanjani, the former president and military commander who had restarted Iran's nuclear program in the 1980s. Even the reformers stressed that Iran's nuclear program was intended only to generate electricity in order to conserve its vast oil and gas reserves, insisting that Iran had the right under the Nuclear Non-Proliferation Treaty to enrich uranium for civilian purposes. The Iranians continued to claim they had made no effort to enrich uranium at Natanz or any of the other undisclosed sites and had not tested any of their centrifuges with nuclear material, which meant they had not breached their obligation. But why had they carried out the construction at Natanz and research elsewhere in secret? The Iranian answer was that they had been forced to work below the international radar because of sanctions imposed by the United States and other Western countries after the revolution in 1979.

No one among the IAEA experts believed Iran's program was totally indigenous. The technology and equipment that had brought them this far were available only from accomplished manufacturers and designers outside the country. The Iranians acknowledged purchasing some material in Europe and elsewhere, but they remained evasive, saying the paperwork had been lost and the people who had been involved had died.

At one point in the discussions, ElBaradei told Aghazadeh that the agency suspected the Chinese had helped Iran. When the Iranian said he knew nothing of any such transaction, Heinonen played his trump card, pulling out the letter from the Chinese. Merely possessing undeclared nuclear material was a breach of the country's IAEA agreement, and Aghazadeh was forced to acknowledge the purchase. He claimed none of the material had been used, however, and promised Iran intended to declare the material formally to the IAEA as part of its effort to come clean about its past nuclear activities. The pattern was to become familiar: Iranian officials would deny an accusation until confronted with proof, and then they would try to explain away the lies and evasions, and pledge not to do it again.

ElBaradei and his team were dubious of new Iranian claims. What they saw at Natanz and other places convinced them that Iran was farther along than Iraq had been when the Gulf War ended Saddam Hussein's dream of joining the nuclear club. It seemed unlikely that Iran could have gone so far without testing centrifuges. When ElBaradei left at the end of his allotted two days, Heinonen and several inspectors stayed behind, determined to get a look inside the other facilities so that they could get a clearer understanding of just what Iran was doing in time to report to the full IAEA board in March.

ON FEBRUARY 26, five days after ElBaradei's departure, Goldschmidt and Heinonen met with senior officials from the Atomic Energy Organization of Iran and requested for the first time that their inspectors be permitted to visit Kalaye Electric. Aghazadeh acknowledged that a workshop at Kalaye had been used to machine components for centrifuges and assemble some machines for the pilot plant at Natanz, but he denied that any testing had been carried out there with fissile material. Arranging a visit on such short notice, he said, was not possible. When Goldschmidt pressed him, Aghazadeh said he would see what he could do.

Heinonen had to return to Vienna to write the report for the board, but other team members stayed on to continue their sleuthing. On the afternoon of March 12, several inspectors were driven by their Iranian minders to Kalaye Electric. The company was housed in a three-building compound, surrounded by a high fence in a desolate industrial district on the eastern edge of Tehran. One small building contained the offices and a café for workers, but the two larger buildings were apparently where the centrifuge work had taken place. As the inspectors approached the first of the large buildings, one of the Iranian officials said, "I'm sorry. We do not have the keys for these buildings." The inspectors suspected that the Iranians never intended to let them in, but they were determined not to leave Kalaye empty-handed and asked to return to the smaller building to take photographs and conduct tests—called environmental sampling—for nuclear residue.

IAEA scientists had developed the sampling technique to detect the presence of nuclear material after the Iraq debacle. The procedure was straightforward. Cotton swabs the size of tennis balls came six to a package; an inspector would swipe them across the surfaces of a room. The cotton could pick up minute particles of nuclear residue, even if the material had been removed months earlier and the room had been cleaned thoroughly. An IAEA official compared the precision of the sampling to finding a single four-leaf clover in a field that was six miles long, nine miles wide, and 150 feet deep. The swabs were then resealed, and each was sent to a separate destination—one to be archived, one given to the country where the testing took place, one to the IAEA lab outside Vienna, and three to independent labs for testing. If particles are detected, it is conclusive proof that nuclear material was present at the location. Each nuclear particle has individual characteristics, much like fingerprints. Additional tests were capable of determining the level of enrichment and whether the particles matched samples on file at the IAEA. In the best of circumstances, the particles identified the origin of the nuclear material.

Faced with the inspectors, their swabs out and ready to begin work, the Iranians refused to permit the inspectors to conduct any sampling or take photographs, even in the smaller buildings that were unlocked, saying they had no authority to allow such activities. They promised to find the keys and return with permission before the inspectors were scheduled to go back to Vienna three days later, but on March 15 the Iranians said that religious holidays had left them unable to find the keys or get permission for the tests, and the inspectors left without photos or samples.

Another inspection team arrived in Tehran in May. One of the key members of the team was Trevor Edwards, a British centrifuge specialist. The visit to Natanz went smoothly, and this time samples were collected. There, the Iranians had nothing to hide because no nuclear material had yet been introduced. At Kalaye, the inspectors were permitted for the first time to enter the two large buildings. One of the buildings was old and smelly, and clearly no work had been done in it for years. The second building was another matter. It had undergone a recent top-to-bottom renovation, with bright lights on motion detectors, freshly painted walls, and floors tiled so recently that the grout was still wet. In a room on the second floor, the inspectors found boxes of clocks manufactured by a Japanese company, presumably part of the abandoned cover story that Kalaye was a clock company. Clearly a thorough effort had been made to erase any evidence of what had occurred there. When the inspectors began to pull out their cotton swabs for the environmental tests, they were stopped and told that sampling and photography were still forbidden. The consensus among the inspectors was that the Iranians were hiding something. "This clearly had been extensively renovated," explained one of the inspectors who had been present at Kalaye. "But if we asked questions about why, they got upset. They told us they had repainted it seven years earlier."

By the time the inspection team left Iran, suspicions were running even higher. The refusal to permit a thorough inspection of Kalaye had been repeated at other locations. But what inspectors were permitted to see raised questions, too. When Trevor Edwards visited the pilot plant at Natanz and examined the components there, he recognized that the design had most likely originated at Urenco. Edwards was in a position to know because he had worked on the Urenco project for the British government in the 1970s and 1980s. The question was, How had Iran acquired the plans?

CHAPTER 26

SPY GAMES

THE IAEA INSPECTION DRAMA unfolding in Iran in the summer of 2003 was being watched closely by American policymakers and intelligence agencies. President Bush had labeled Iran part of the "axis of evil" in his State of the Union address in 2002, and the administration had repeatedly denounced Iranian claims that its nuclear intentions were strictly peaceful. Bush himself had warned that a nuclear Iran was unacceptable and that "all options were on the table" to stop Tehran from acquiring atomic weapons. The Pentagon began making secret contingency plans for aircraft and missile attacks on key Iranian nuclear installations, consulting their Israeli counterparts in the process.

Israeli intelligence was at least as worried as Washington about Iran's progress toward a functional nuclear weapon and warned the CIA that Iran must not be allowed to master the technology to enrich uranium. "Once they learn to enrich uranium at Natanz, they will be able to take the technology anyplace inside the country, outside our view," explained an Israeli agent at the time. "The trouble with enrichment is that it can be done inside a small factory or even a mosque, and we'd never be able to find it." Still, the Israelis and Americans thought they had time before a decision had to be made on whether to take out the plant at Natanz and other nuclear installations, an attack certain to inflame the Middle East and provoke retaliation. There were plenty of targets for Iran. Thousands of American troops remained in Afghanistan, struggling to keep a fragile peace, and more than 150,000 U.S. soldiers were stationed in Iraq following the American invasion in March 2003.

For their part, Iranian leaders were nervous about being wedged between two pro-American regimes in neighboring countries and, after seeing Saddam ousted, influential factions in Tehran were more determined than ever to protect their country with a nuclear weapon. Beneath the protection of its own nuclear umbrella, Tehran could also take a more interventionist approach to helping its fellow Shiites in Iraq and protecting its own interests in Afghanistan. Iran's constant threats to destroy Israel would carry far more weight if it were armed with nuclear weapons.

The American government had good reason to voice anxiety about Iran's nuclear intentions, but Washington's credibility was in tatters when it came to warnings about clandestine nuclear-weapons programs because its primary justification for invading Iraq had turned out to be wholly unfounded. Iran could count on countries remembering the certainty with which the United States had made the case that Saddam maintained stockpiles of chemical and biological weapons and resumed his quest for a nuclear arsenal, and how wrong they had been.

The most distinct moment in that campaign occurred on February 5, 2003, when Bush sent Secretary of State Colin Powell to present the case for invading Iraq to the UN Security Council. Powell relied on slides and satellite photos to identify numerous locations inside Iraq that he asserted unequivocally were part of Saddam's weapons-of-mass-destruction programs. "The gravity of this moment is matched by the gravity of the threat that Iraq's weapons of mass destruction pose to the world," explained Powell, who probably commanded more respect from world leaders than did any other administration figure. American intelligence had ample evidence that Saddam remained determined to build an atomic bomb, he said, adding, "He is so determined that he has made repeated covert attempts to acquire high-specification aluminum tubes from eleven different countries even after the inspections resumed."

Like much of the evidence presented by Powell, the tubes had been the subject of debate within the administration. The first shipment of tubes had been intercepted in 2001, and George Tenet later told a closed session of the Senate Intelligence Committee that CIA scientists had determined that they were intended to be used as rotors for centrifuges in a hidden uranium-enrichment program. Tenet's opinion was not shared by everyone within the government, however, and experts at Oak Ridge National Laboratory had found that the tubes were not suitable for a nuclear program. Instead, they said the dimensions perfectly matched conventional artillery that Iraq was permitted to manufacture. Opinions that countered the push to justify the invasion of Iraq were ignored, and administration officials had leaked the existence of the tubes to *The New York Times*, claiming that they were hard evidence that Iraq was pursuing nuclear weapons.

"I thought when I read that there must be some other tubes that people were talking about," said Houston Wood, a consultant who had worked on the analysis at Oak Ridge. "I was just flabbergasted that people were still pushing that those might be centrifuges. Science was not pushing this forward. Scientists had made their determination, their evaluation, and now we didn't know what was happening."

Powell's use of the tubes as part of his case against Iraq also stunned experts at the IAEA. They, too, had read *The New York Times* story the previous fall and dispatched a team to Iraq to examine the tubes. The unanimous conclusion was that the cylinders were not suitable for a nuclear program. More significantly, the dozens of IAEA inspections inside Iraq over the past decade had turned up no evidence that Saddam had resumed work on a nuclear weapon. Among the skeptics about the American claims was Jacques Baute, the head of the agency's inspection team for Iraq. Baute's inspectors had found no sign of a nuclear program in Iraq, and he was confident that they had visited every potential site, since Iraq's agreement at the end of the Gulf War had given the IAEA unfettered access.

The tubes were not the only alleged evidence bothering Baute. On January 28, 2003, President Bush had used his State of the Union address to bolster the American case for going to war against Iraq, citing both the aluminum tubes and intelligence claims that the Iraqis had been shopping for uranium in Africa. "The British government has learned that Saddam

Hussein recently sought significant quantities of uranium from Africa," he said, uttering the words that became infamous. "Saddam Hussein has not credibly explained these activities. He clearly has much to hide."

Baute had first heard of the Iraqi uranium shopping in the fall of 2002 when a British dossier on Iraq mentioned that agents for Saddam had tried to buy five tons of yellowcake uranium ore in Niger. Baute had tried in vain since then to get copies of the records cited by the British so he and his inspectors could follow up. On the day of Powell's speech to the Security Council, an American official finally handed over copies to an IAEA official in New York, and a few days later they wound up on Baute's desk in Vienna—a half-dozen letters and other communications between officials in Iraq and Niger, with many of the letters written on Niger government letterhead. As Baute examined the documents, he found blatant inconsistencies that told him they were forgeries, and poor ones at that. Using just the Internet, he discovered that a letter dated October 10, 2000, had been ostensibly signed by a Niger minister of foreign affairs who had been out of office since 1989. Another letter, attributed to Niger president Tandja Mamadou, had a signature that was clearly faked and a text filled with inaccuracies. "The forgeries were so obvious that a junior case officer should have spotted them," said a senior IAEA official involved in evaluating the letters and other communications.

On March 7, with the United States on the verge of invading Iraq a month after Powell's speech, Mohamed ElBaradei appeared before the Security Council to plead for more time to complete further inspections. In precise, controlled language, he contradicted key aspects of Powell's presentation. Three months' worth of inspections at 141 sites in Iraq, he said, had turned up "no evidence or plausible indication of the revival of a nuclear weapon program in Iraq." Some of the same sites listed in ElBaradei's report as free of any evidence of nuclear activity were locations described by Powell as proof that Saddam had resumed his pursuit of nuclear weapons. Further contradicting the American claims, ElBaradei said inspectors had uncovered blueprints, invoices, and meeting notes that backed up Iraq's explanation that the aluminum tubes were part of an effort to develop a conventional artillery rocket that would resist corrosion. As for the Niger documents, the IAEA director general said his agency, in consultation with outside experts, had concluded that the material was not authentic.

Later that day, Powell responded angrily to the IAEA findings, saying: "I also listened to Dr. ElBaradei's report with great interest. As we all know, in 1991 the International Atomic Energy Agency was just days away from determining that Iraq did not have a nuclear program. We soon found out otherwise."

ElBaradei had taught international law at New York University and held the United States in high regard. So he was stung by the personal nature of Powell's attack, and by the fact that the Bush administration, in a rush to war, was ignoring facts that contradicted its view of Iraq's nuclear status. ElBaradei had watched Powell's presentation to the UN on television with key members of his staff, and the room had been filled with shouts of anger over what the IAEA officials viewed as the American official's misstatements. "ElBaradei was completely shocked and it changed him," said one of his close aides. "He found his voice, in anger maybe." ElBaradei realized that it was not enough just to issue a report, so he authorized people at the agency to reach out to the media in an attempt to get the truth out, not just about Iraq but about Iran, too. In the weeks that followed, ElBaradei began to speak out more often in the press and at conferences about disarmament and the atomic bargain that allowed countries like the United States and Russia to retain weapons.

UNDERSECRETARY of State John Bolton, the Bush administration's point man on arms control, was ElBaradei's chief nemesis in Washington even before the IAEA chief had criticized the American case against Iraq. Bolton had a reputation as a pugnacious, blunt-spoken conservative opposed in principle to multilateral organizations like the IAEA and willing to interpret facts to suit his own purposes. Critics accused him of inflating evidence against Iraq and North Korea to support tough stances against both countries. "Very often, the points he makes have some truth to them, but he simply goes beyond where the facts tell intelligent people they should go," said Carl Ford Jr., a former head of the State Department's Bureau of Intelligence and Research.

A protégé of former senator Jesse Helms, the conservative Republican from North Carolina, Bolton once said that "if the UN secretariat building in New York lost ten stories, it wouldn't make a bit of difference" and "there's no such thing as the United Nations." Soon after joining the Bush administration in 2001, he had attempted to cut American funding for the IAEA, and his anger at what he viewed as ElBaradei's coddling of Iraq grew in the aftermath of the American invasion, when military and intelligence teams were unable to find any evidence of existing programs to develop chemical, biological, or nuclear weapons.

When it came to Iran, however, Bolton found himself in the uncomfortable position of needing ElBaradei and the IAEA to point the finger at Tehran's secret nuclear program, since the international community would not believe the United States if it blew the whistle again. Like it or not, the Americans and Bolton had to play ball with the IAEA and ElBaradei.

Beginning that summer, the administration started sharing sensitive intelligence information about Iran with the IAEA. The initial exchanges went through back channels and took place in the secure room at the American mission, on the thirty-seventh floor of a modern skyscraper overlooking the IAEA complex. There, American diplomats and nuclear experts provided selected officials with the latest intelligence on Iran's nuclear efforts. Some of the most sensitive information took the form of classified satellite photos showing that trucks and bulldozers had been at work at Kalaye in April and May, weeks before the IAEA inspectors were permitted into the main building. Tons of dirt were dug up around the building and removed. At the same time, truckloads of concrete rubble, presumably from the destruction of old walls and floors, were hauled off. Without its own intelligence arm and with limited access to commercial satellite photography, the IAEA depended on the American information as part of its larger inspection strategy in Iran.

In the case of Kalaye, the photos confirmed the IAEA's suspicions that Iran had tried to remove evidence of enrichment activities from the site. Still, the inspectors were confident that, if the building had ever contained nuclear material, they would find its traces—provided they could get inside to take samples. The IAEA could not persuade Iran to allow the testing until August, a year after the site had first been identified as part of the nuclear program. Even then, the permission was granted only after Heinonen made a special trip to Tehran to tell the Iranian authorities point-blank that it was in their interest to permit the sampling and put the questions to rest. The Iranians acquiesced, apparently confident in the cleanup. Heinonen, on the other hand, fully expected the results to show traces of fissile material, despite those efforts.

On August 9, a team of inspectors with environmental-sampling kits was allowed into the building where they suspected the enrichment work had taken place. The day was sweltering, and the Iranians had shut down the air-conditioning to make the chore as unpleasant as possible. Dripping with sweat, the inspectors unwrapped the cotton swabs and began going over every available surface, pushing the swipes deep into the corners and along the windowsills. After nearly two hours, the job was done, and the team packed up its equipment, leaving the building with what its members fully expected would be proof that Iran was lying.

FROM his home in Islamabad, A. Q. Khan was engaged in his own cover-up. After the accusations about Natanz broke in August 2002, Khan realized that he had a potentially dangerous situation. Of course he was already well aware of the work at Natanz and elsewhere. After all, he had provided both the plans and a handful of centrifuges, which enabled the Iranians to manufacture their own machines. Those centrifuges would be used in the pilot plant and the huge enrichment halls at Natanz, though it had been the Iranians' idea to bury the main installation because of fears of an attack by Israel or the United States. Khan had continued to do some troubleshooting for Iran, but the flow of supplies from the network had dropped to a trickle because the Iranians were producing most of their own equipment. However, if the IAEA applied enough pressure to Tehran, it might force the Iranians to implicate Khan by revealing that he was the source of the prototypes and the blueprints.

Determined to cover his tracks, Khan had made two telephone calls. First, he talked to Tahir in Dubai, telling him to destroy all records of the transactions with Iran. Second, he telephoned a high-level contact at the

Atomic Energy Organization of Iran and instructed him to destroy any documents describing Iran's deals with the network. If the IAEA asked to speak to people involved in the early days of the nuclear program, Khan said, the Iranians should say those individuals had died. Khan was anxious, but he was far from panicking. After all, the major customers for his network were countries that had no diplomatic relations with the United States, and he was confident that they would be more than willing to lie to the IAEA.

In the fall of 2002, Khan's transactions with North Korea had also slowed after the Americans accused the Koreans of operating a secret uranium-enrichment program using equipment and know-how provided by Pakistan. The North Koreans had responded by expelling the IAEA inspectors who had been monitoring the freeze on its plutonium program and withdrawing from the nonproliferation treaty. But the network was still going gangbusters with Libya, providing Gadhafi's regime with millions of dollars' worth of technology and making final preparations to set up the bomb factory outside Tripoli.

WHILE the Americans and British continued to leave the IAEA in the dark about Khan's dealings with Iran and Libya, Washington decided it was in its interest to provide more information about Iran's program. Influential elements of the Bush administration, led by Bolton, still thought that ElBaradei was too soft on the Iranians, and they circulated stories that the director general was going easy on Tehran because he was a Muslim and falsely claiming he was married to an Iranian. Publicly, Bolton and other American officials tried to get rid of ElBaradei by opposing his bid for a third term as director general. In September, Powell argued that ElBaradei should step aside when his term ended the following year, citing an informal policy adopted several years earlier by the countries that were the largest donors to international organizations like the IAEA. Bolton increased the pressure on ElBaradei by threatening again to cut American funding for the agency, but John Wolf, Bolton's deputy for counterproliferation, opposed his boss, pointing out that withdrawing American money would cripple the agency at a time when the world and the United States needed it most.

Bolton was so determined to get rid of ElBaradei that the National Security Agency was directed to begin eavesdropping on the IAEA chief's telephone conversations. While such electronic surveillance would have required court approval in the United States, there was no law prohibiting it outside the country. By the fall of 2003, the NSA was listening in on ElBaradei's office and home calls, intercepting dozens with Iranian diplomats and scouring them for evidence that he was in bed with them. The intercepted calls produced no evidence of inappropriate conduct by ElBaradei, and when the secret tapping was disclosed by *The Washington Post* it created a backlash of support for the IAEA chief, though there was little surprise among cynical diplomats and other government officials. "We've always assumed that this kind of thing goes on," IAEA spokesman Mark Gwozdecky explained. "We wish it were otherwise, but we know the reality." ElBaradei was privately outraged, but he maintained a sanguine public attitude, later telling the German magazine *Der Spiegel*: "I have nothing to hide professionally. But it becomes unpleasant when you apparently cannot even have a private conversation with your wife or your daughter. There is also a concerted smear campaign against me. For example, they say things like: An Egyptian can't be impartial toward Islamic states and will tell them all our secrets. I refuse to comment on people at this low level."

Hans Blix, ElBaradei's predecessor at the IAEA, served as the UN's chief weapons inspector for Iraq from 2000 to 2003. He repeatedly told the UN that inspections at hundreds of suspected weapons sites had turned up no evidence that Saddam had restarted his chemical, nuclear, or biological weapons programs. During that period, Blix said later, he, too, suspected that his telephone conversations had been monitored. "If I was bugged, I wish they had at least listened a bit more carefully to what I said. It is the height of humiliation to be bugged and ignored."

At the same time the Americans were passing intelligence tips to the IAEA, the Israeli government began an ambitious campaign to exert diplomatic pressure on Iran by leaking information about its nuclear efforts. Israel's senior military leaders regarded a nuclear-armed Iran as a threat to their country's very existence, and their intelligence indicated the Iranians were farther down the road than the rest of the world realized.

Israeli military and intelligence agencies kept Tehran under close observation through a large network of informants and sophisticated electronic monitoring, sharing information with Washington and creating a circular world in which Israeli intelligence was recycled through American sources and vice versa. Like the Americans, the Israelis faced a difficult time convincing the international community that it should be concerned about a nuclear Iran because it, too, had a credibility problem. Israel's own arsenal of atomic weapons had been an open secret for years, and its weapons installations were closed to the IAEA. So Israel's Foreign Ministry and the Mossad came up with a strategy of careful and anonymous leaks, aimed at fueling worries about Iran's intentions.

Beginning in the summer of 2003, a special unit of Mossad was tasked with quietly passing on the latest information about Iran to the international press corps. The campaign was extensive and sophisticated: Israeli nuclear-weapons specialists provided secret briefings on the details of the Iranian nuclear efforts, often supported by documents from inside Iran and elsewhere. At one point, the Israelis passed on a confidential report prepared in May 2003 by the French government for the Nuclear Suppliers Group, an ad-hoc organization that tried to restrict sales of nuclear-related technology worldwide. The report summarized developments regarding Iran's nuclear program and warned that the supposedly civilian program likely concealed military aims: "France's assessment is now that this country may obtain a sufficient quantity of fissionable materials to manufacture a nuclear weapon within a few years." Mossad agents also shared information about locations where intelligence suggested that the Iranians were concealing nuclear-weapons work, accusations corroborated by satellite photos. Most of the intelligence was generated from Israel's espionage efforts, but the Israeli pipeline to the press also provided a way for the Americans to publicize their intelligence without leaving fingerprints.

This is not to suggest that the Americans did not leak, too. Bolton occasionally telephoned reporters covering the Iran file at the IAEA, offering bits of information or sanitized intelligence designed to keep the pot boiling. Diplomats assigned to the IAEA and senior officials who worked there were sometimes angered by what they viewed as misinformation coming from the Americans, so they occasionally responded with their own set of counterleaks in an attempt to set the record straight or reveal information that they felt should be in the public domain.

The resulting mix of articles in a variety of publications, wire-service reports, and television broadcasts called attention to fears about the Iranian program in general and focused suspicions on some specific locations. In some cases, IAEA officials used the articles to question Iranian authorities about activities and sites; in rare cases, the information was deemed so credible that the agency sought permission to make official visits to locations identified in the press. In that way, the leaks also protected the flow of intelligence from the United States and Israel to the IAEA. The CIA could tell the IAEA about a suspicious location, and the agency could wait to seek access to the site until the same information was published or broadcast.

The increasing press attention also renewed the focus on Khan and Pakistan. A couple of articles in the American press in the middle 1990s had suggested that Pakistan was assisting Iran with a nuclear program, but the allegations had been dismissed. But as 2003 wore on, more specific information linking Khan to the Iranian effort came out in the press, and it mirrored the suspicions of Olli Heinonen and Trevor Edwards.

CHAPTER 27

THE DROWNING MAN

THE STRAIT OF MALACCA is a narrow, perilous five-hundred-mile-long waterway that forms the main passage between the Pacific and the Indian oceans. It borders Malaysia, Indonesia, and Singapore. The thousands of oil tankers, freighters, and tugs that ply its waters carry more than one quarter of the world's trade, and they are constantly on the lookout for pirates who hide among the thousands of tiny islands and inlets. At first light one day in late August 2003, five forty-foot-long wooden crates were loaded onto one of the anonymous ships that work off the coast of Malaysia. The crates had come from Scomi Precision Engineering and were marked "agriculture machinery," with a shipping invoice that said the cargo was bound for Aryash Trading Company in Dubai. Two men discreetly watching the loading process from across the dock knew what the real contents were and where they were headed—roughly twenty-five thousand casings, pumps, tubes, flanges, and other parts, all manufactured to precise tolerances from high-strength aluminum, bound for warehouses in Libya.

The Scomi plant run by the Khan network had produced the components, the fourth and largest shipment to Libya since the plant had started operating in December 2002. The two watchers had monitored the earlier shipments, too, thanks to a steady stream of information from

Urs Tinner, who had been supervising production at the plant for nearly a year. Throughout that time, Tinner had continued to provide regular reports on the progress to the CIA through his handler, the agent nicknamed Mad Dog.

As the Malaysian ship left port and pounded through the swells of the Indian Ocean on its nearly four-thousand-mile voyage to the Persian Gulf, the CIA monitored its progress with spy satellites. The agency wasn't worried about losing the vessel because they knew that it would arrive in the Port of Dubai around mid-September, depending on the seas, where the crates would be loaded onto another ship for the last leg of the voyage. The CIA would be there to watch, too.

On the other side of the Indian Ocean from Malaysia, Johan Meyer had finished testing his masterpiece of stainless-steel tubes, valves, and tanks at his Tradefin factory outside Johannesburg. Instead of using uranium hexafluoride, he and his technicians used helium to make sure the gas feed and withdrawal systems functioned and that the vacuum valves held. The entire system had worked perfectly. After the test, Meyer took detailed photographs of each section and numbered each of the thousands of individual parts sequentially. The two-story apparatus was dismantled and packed into eleven forty-foot shipping containers. The photos of the numbered parts were then turned into flow charts so technicians could reassemble everything properly. "The plans went into great detail, including how much time it would take, to the minute, for each step in the process and the numbers of skilled or unskilled workers required for each step," said an expert who later examined the documentation. By August, the shipment was ready for delivery, but Meyer still wasn't sure where it was headed.

Meyer had his suspicions, however. In late May, two Arabs had arrived at Tradefin to watch the test, staying at a nearby Holiday Inn and arriving at the factory early each morning for a week. They said little and watched intently, talking quietly to each other in Arabic. When Meyer tried to question them about the destination for the finished product, they refused to answer. At the end of the successful test, the men nodded and disappeared. A few days after the visit, Meyer received another installment in his bank account. Previous transfers had come from banks in Dubai, but this time the money had come from Libya, a fact that alarmed Meyer. He knew from the start that he was building a system to operate an enrichment plant, but he hadn't guessed that he was doing it for the government of an outcast nation regarded as an international sponsor of terrorism.

Meyer's contraption was one of the last pieces of the nuclear puzzle being assembled for Libya. By this time, the Khan network had sent dozens of shipments of nuclear technology to Tripoli. There were electronic regulators and power supplies from Turkey, sophisticated machine tools from Switzerland and South Korea, P-2 centrifuge prototypes from Pakistan, large quantities of high-strength aluminum and maraging steel from Singapore and Malaysia, uranium hexafluoride from China. Two form-flowing lathes from Spain had found their way to Libya after an odyssey from Dubai to South Africa; once in Tripoli, the machines were equipped with computerized controls that allowed them to operate at the precision levels required to produce centrifuge rotors. Dozens of Libyan technicians were completing training in Dubai, Spain, and other countries. Several elements for the eventual bomb factory were still missing, but the basics were coming together—Libya was not far away from setting up production facilities to enrich uranium.

Some of the equipment had civilian applications and had been shipped openly to Libya by reputable companies without knowing that it was for a nuclear-weapons program. Much of it, however, arrived with false bills of lading and invoices, purposely mislabeled as industrial goods or agricultural products. From long years of illicit trafficking in goods for Pakistan and Iran, the network had established procedures designed to conceal the nature of its shipments from prying customs authorities and intelligence agents. But such subterfuge in a business where trust was in short supply had led to basic bookkeeping problems. Legitimate shipments were accompanied by detailed invoices to identify the precise contents and their costs. Buyers could check the delivery against the invoice to make sure they got what they had paid for. But when shipments were misidentified deliberately and invoices were fiction, there was no way for the recipients to make sure they were receiving everything. So the network's members had resorted to taking digital photographs of the contents of each shipment to avoid later disputes.

Secrecy had become something of an obsession among those who knew the full scope of the work being done for Libya. When engineers at the Malaysian plant finished manufacturing a particular component, Urs Tinner retrieved the drawings on which it was based, telling the employees he was protecting trade secrets. What he was really doing was erasing as much of his presence as possible in preparation for the day the CIA would stop watching and take action against the network. He expected that the Americans would protect him, but he still wanted to cover his tracks.

Tahir was the general manager and chief finance officer for Khan, Inc., and most of the machinery and equipment was first shipped to his SMB Computers in Dubai, where it was repackaged and shipped to Libya. When paying suppliers in Europe and elsewhere, Tahir used a series of international banks and front companies, bouncing millions of dollars from account to account. Like Meyer, the suppliers may have had their suspicions about the true nature of the business, but they were well paid and unlikely to ask too many questions. The subterfuge was expensive, both in terms of the premiums paid for equipment and the commissions siphoned off along the way by various middlemen, front companies, and the network's members. No one bothered with exact calculations, but rough estimates were that the Libyans were routinely charged double the going rate for much of what they bought, a fact that drew occasional complaints from Tripoli. By the summer of 2003, Libya's payments to the network totaled roughly eighty million dollars, with no bomb in sight.

And now the CIA and Britain's MI6 were closing in on two fronts: In addition to the spies who had watched the ship leave Malaysia, diplomats thousands of miles away were trying to persuade Libya to give up its weapons program through secret negotiations.

THE NEGOTIATIONS were not Libya's first attempt to make amends with the international community. Four years earlier, during the Clinton administration, a senior Libyan intelligence official had approached a CIA agent with an offer: Libya would give up its chemical weapons in exchange for easing sanctions imposed in the 1980s because of its support of international terrorism. The administration refused outright, explaining that the only way out of isolation for Libya was to take responsibility for the downing of Pan Am flight 103 over Lockerbie, Scotland, in 1988, something Gadhafi was not ready to do. The British, however, were more receptive to the Libyan approach, opening the door for quiet talks that led to reestablishing diplomatic ties and opening an embassy in Tripoli in July 1999. Over the next two years, the British led negotiations involving the United States and Libya that tried to resolve responsibility for the Pan Am bombing as a first step in Libya's rehabilitation. Progress was slow, even after a Libyan agent was convicted in Scotland in January 2001 of participating in the plot to set off the bomb. Gadhafi refused to accept responsibility for the disaster or agree to restitution for the families of the 259 passengers and crew, mostly Americans, and the eleven people on the ground who had died.

Gadhafi had come to power in 1969 and imposed his own brand of revolutionary theory on the desert country, which is three times the size of France. He presented a dashing figure, often parading through Tripoli or foreign capitals in flowing robes and surrounded by female bodyguards, and his imposing photograph appeared on billboards blanketing the country. For Western governments and his own neighbors, he was an often troublesome, frequently contradictory figure, using Libya's oil revenues to finance arms for the Irish Republican Army, ordering the assassination of dissidents living abroad, and harboring terrorist Abu Nidal for years, at the same time as he promoted women's rights and rejected Islamic fundamentalism. In the 1970s and 1980s, oil money translated into cheap housing and free utilities for every Libyan, though international sanctions after Lockerbie and other incidents had eaten into the largesse by the 1990s.

After September 11, Gadhafi recognized that international terrorism had taken a brutal turn, and he risked being crushed by the American response unless he quickly altered his ways. The Libyan leader knew from painful personal experience that the Americans could lash out when harmed or threatened. Though the Libyan leader did not receive a warning telephone call from Colin Powell on September 12, as Musharraf and other world leaders had, he was nearly frantic with fear that the Americans would bomb his country. Emerging from his desert hideaway, he delivered a series of speeches denouncing bin Laden and the terrorism against the United States. According to a confidential cable from the American embassy in Cairo, he called "every Arab leader on his Rolodex" to persuade them to condemn the attacks, too. When the Americans did not reassure Gadhafi that he would be spared in this new war, he turned to America's biggest ally in the region, Crown Prince Abdullah of Saudi Arabia, and begged him to intercede on his behalf.

Gadhafi had survived on his wits for nearly four decades, and in the end his fear of American retaliation forced him to dispatch a new team of negotiators to London to reach a deal on Lockerbie. The team that arrived in October 2001 was led by Musa Kousa, Gadhafi's intelligence chief, in some ways an odd choice for a sensitive diplomatic mission. He had studied for a master's degree in sociology at Michigan State University in the 1970s, but he was better known for the trail of terror he had left around Europe. In 1980, Kousa had been expelled as head of Libya's mission in London after two dissidents he had singled out for criticism were murdered. A 1995 report by MI5, Britain's domestic intelligence agency, described Kousa as the head of Libyan intelligence, which was responsible for terrorist acts throughout Europe and Africa. Kousa personally had been implicated in the planning of the 1986 Berlin bombing and the downing of a French passenger plane over Niger in 1989 that had killed 170 people.

But that was all in the past for both sides in the aftermath of September 11. Kousa had orders to settle the Pan Am dispute, restore Gadhafi to the good graces of the United States and Britain, and avoid an American attack. The United States had its own motives for sitting down with a regime still regarded as an enemy: The American negotiators, led by William Burns, the assistant secretary of state for Near East affairs, wanted to enlist the Libyan leader in George Bush's "war on terror."

The negotiations took several months, but in May 2002, Libya accepted responsibility for the airliner's fate and later agreed to pay $2.7 billion to the families of the victims. The decision marked a seismic shift in Libya's relations with the outside world, but the Americans and British were not done. Both countries knew that Libya maintained stockpiles of chemical weapons, but its nuclear program was a more closely guarded secret. The trick for the negotiators was to persuade Libya to relinquish its nuclear ambitions without revealing the extent to which they had penetrated the network supplying the equipment to Tripoli. Without tipping their hand, the Americans and the British envoys made clear that lifting sanctions meant that Libya would have to abandon all of its weapons of mass destruction.

Making the Lockerbie settlement was a far easier step for Gadhafi than giving up his plans for a nuclear arsenal, which would fulfill his dream of being the most powerful leader in the Arab world. The communications channel remained open on the WMD issue, but little progress was made until March 2003, when Seif Islam Gadhafi, the Libyan leader's eldest son and designated heir, contacted British intelligence and asked for a meeting to talk about reforms in the Middle East.

Seif was seen as a credible representative of his father, whose willingness to negotiate over weapons of mass destruction would be an important breakthrough. British intelligence and the CIA had been sharing information about Libya's nuclear program for nearly three years, and they had what they thought was a pretty complete picture of the progress, though senior agents recognized that they could not be certain about every aspect of a clandestine operation. The offer of negotiations provided an opportunity to get a better sense of how far along the Libyans were and, perhaps, persuade Gadhafi to give up his quest.

News about the upcoming meeting between the British agents and Seif Gadhafi was relayed to Washington, where George Tenet added the topic to his daily intelligence briefing for Bush in the Oval Office. British prime minister Tony Blair arrived at Camp David for meetings with Bush just days before the start of the Iraq war. Tenet and his British counterpart, Sir Richard Dearlove, participated in the conversation. While much of the briefing was devoted to Iraq, the Libyan overture was on the agenda, too. The group debated Gadhafi's possible motives, deciding that he had finally realized that his attempt to develop nuclear weapons was more trouble than it was worth. Tenet left the meeting with instructions from the president to find the right person to negotiate with Gadhafi.

On March 19, the day before the start of the war in Iraq, Seif Gadhafi met with two British agents at a London hotel. He was nervous, as he acknowledged in a later interview with *60 Minutes*, explaining: "It was quite unique at the time for me because I was face to face with the British secret service for the first time in my life and with the people who I regarded for a long time as devils, as enemies for me, and I was quite nervous that something goes wrong. And then one of them said one day history would recognize that a huge and historic initiative started in a small room in a small hotel."

Gadhafi wanted to talk about his father's vision for a joint initiative to reform the political process in the Middle East. The senior agent replied, "We are happy to be allies and work together in the Middle East, but first we have critical issues we have to sort out." Gadhafi suspected that the British agent was talking about Libya's weapons of mass destruction, and he agreed that it was a topic worth discussing. "I know my father very well, and I know his way of thinking," Gadhafi said. "I know for a long time that he is ready to tackle this issue, the WMD issue, with the West if there is the right deal and the right terms."

Back in Washington, the person Tenet chose to deal with Libya was Stephen Kappes, a former Marine officer who had been stationed in the Middle East and Europe since joining the CIA in 1981. John McLaughlin, deputy director of the CIA at the time, later described Kappes as the ideal choice. "You don't send just anyone to do this," he explained. "It was an enormously difficult, complicated, and high-stakes mission." Kappes was currently in Washington, where he was chief of the team that had penetrated the Khan network, so he knew well the extent of Gadhafi's nuclear-procurement operation. He also had maintained back-channel communications with Kousa over the years. In the days that followed, Tenet and Kappes met several times with Bush and Vice President Dick Cheney to discuss how to handle the negotiations with Libya. It would be tricky—at a time when Bush had declared war on terror, he could hardly be seen cozying up to a man identified with international terrorism—and Cheney cautioned that the United States had to avoid the appearance of rewarding Gadhafi's bad behavior. Still, if Gadhafi could be persuaded to give up his weapons programs, it would appear that the war in Iraq had created the kind of deterrence that Bush and Cheney desired fervently. The prize was big—no regime had given up a nuclear weapons program, with the exception of South Africa.

In the weeks that followed, Kappes and his British counterparts met several times with Musa Kousa and other Libyans in London and other European capitals. Progress remained slow. The Libyans were cagey and didn't want to admit too much in case the deal fell through, refusing to acknowledge that they had chemical weapons, let alone a secret nuclear program. The British took the lead in the negotiations because the initial contact had come through them, and they had an embassy in Tripoli and an ambassador who spoke fluent Arabic. But it was clear that Gadhafi's goal of reintegration into the international community could not be achieved without the blessing of the Americans.

"The Libya case was cut-and-dried logical," said a British government official involved in the negotiations. "Why continue with weapons of mass destruction if it was not in your interest? Plenty of sensible Libyans told me that they understood this. They told us, this is all a consequence of the end of the Cold War. It's a different game now. Libya's interests are different. Our sense of vulnerability is different."

Libya was one of the few countries whose leader had the degree of authority to decide to give up such weapons and make it stick. Gadhafi appeared to have made a sensible calculation that he had little to gain and much to lose from his nuclear program. Still, Libya had spent tens of millions of dollars, and Gadhafi was reluctant to abandon his long-sought goal just as Khan had put it within his grasp. He needed a push to take the final step.

When the negotiations bogged down in the summer of 2003, Kappes and his British counterpart, a senior intelligence agent and expert on Libya named Mark Allen, boarded an unmarked CIA Gulfstream jet outside London and flew to Tunisia for a secret meeting with Gadhafi, who was in the neighboring country on a state visit. They found the leader charming and confident and not ready to relinquish his plan for weapons. Despite long hours of conversation, they left without an agreement. In September, Kappes and Allen flew to Tripoli for their first meeting with the Libyan on his home turf. The second meeting seemed to build trust between the men, but still there was no admission by the Libyan leader that he possessed nuclear weapons, let alone an agreement to give them up. Something more was necessary to persuade the Libyan strongman to take the final, irrevocable step, and that something was bobbing across the Indian Ocean on its way to Dubai.

At the CIA, there was a strong sense that the endgame was coming for Khan. Seizing the cargo from Scomi would provide irrefutable proof that the Pakistani scientist was selling nuclear technology on the black market. While the CIA tracked the shipment from Malaysia to Dubai with the help of satellites, the White House arranged for a face-to-face meeting between Bush and Musharraf on the sidelines of the United Nations annual meeting. The Pakistani leader was regarded as such a vital U.S. ally against Al Qaeda and its offshoots that he needed to be warned of what was coming. Late on the morning of September 24, Bush and Musharraf met in Bush's suite on the thirty-fifth floor of the Waldorf-Astoria Hotel in New York for a session that was described to the press as an opportunity to discuss cooperation on the war on terror. Near the end of the one-hour meeting, the American president informed Musharraf that he would be getting a visit the next morning from George Tenet. "It is extremely serious and very important from your point of view," Bush explained.

Tenet arrived at Musharraf's suite early the next morning, and after routine pleasantries the CIA director said he had some bad news. "A. Q. Khan is betraying your country," Tenet said. "He has stolen some of your nation's most sensitive secrets and sold them to the highest bidders. Khan has stolen your nuclear-weapons secrets. We know this, because we stole them from him."

With a flourish, Tenet reached into his briefcase and placed a stack of papers and diagrams on the table in front of Musharraf—copies of the papers stolen years earlier from Khan's hotel room by British intelligence. Leafing through the material, the Pakistani leader recognized detailed drawings of the P-1 centrifuges used at Kahuta. As he looked more closely, Musharraf saw that the papers carried part numbers, dates, and signatures that linked them to his own government's nuclear program. Khan's name did not appear in the documents, but the records left no doubt that the scientist had been selling Pakistan's nuclear technology. Tenet drove home the point, extracting a blueprint for a P-1 centrifuge and saying, "He sold this to Iran." Picking up a design for the P-2, he said, "He has sold this to several countries." Finally, Tenet picked up another sheaf of papers and said, "These are the drawings of a uranium-processing plant that he sold to Libya."

The CIA chief went on: "Mr. President, if a country like Libya or Iran or, God forbid, an organization like Al Qaeda, gets a working nuclear device and the world learns that it came from your country, I'm afraid the consequences would be devastating." Tenet suggested that the United States and Pakistan join together to shut down Khan's operation.

Musharraf betrayed no emotion, though he later acknowledged that it was one of the most embarrassing moments of his life. After asking a few questions and being permitted to take the documents, he said: "Thank you, George. I will take care of this."

After Tenet's departure, Musharraf was left with the revelation that it had all taken place beneath his nose: The foreign trips, the chartered airplane flights, the enormous wealth, and the secret meetings with suspicious characters uncovered months earlier in the investigations that Musharraf had ordered, all fit into a pattern. The Pakistani leader hoped that he could deal with Khan firmly but quietly, without embarrassing the country and without devastating consequences.

A few days later, the Malaysian ship arrived in Dubai. The five crates from Scomi were offloaded and taken to a warehouse that belonged to Aryash Trading. Two days later, the crates were loaded onto the *BBC China,* a German-owned freighter bound for Libya. The ship left Dubai, sailing out the southern end of the Persian Gulf, through the Red Sea, and into the Suez Canal. Midway through the canal, the captain was hailed on the radio by the ship's owners in Hamburg, who ordered him to change course when he emerged into the Mediterranean Sea. He was told that the new destination was the southern Italian port of Taranto. The order was highly unusual, and the Hamburg office offered no explanation, but the captain immediately changed course, a switch monitored by two small U.S. Navy frigates shadowing the ship in the Mediterranean.

The next step was tricky. The Americans and their British counterparts

wanted to get the ship into a safe port and offload the cargo in secret.
They designed a cover story that was rooted in a partial truth—the German shipowners and the Italian authorities were informed that the ship
was the unwitting carrier of a load of nuclear technology that involved
A. Q. Khan, the Pakistani scientist. The ship arrived at the port on October 4, where it was met by Italian and American authorities. They handed
the captain the numbers of the crates they wanted. Crew members opened
the hatches and began the cumbersome process of locating and removing the
forty-foot crates from the ship's hold. They were loaded onto U.S. military
trucks and hauled away to an unmarked guarded warehouse. The ship's
captain never saw what was in the containers and resumed his journey
to Tripoli. The next morning, the crates were opened, and CIA experts
confirmed that they contained thousands of components for centrifuges.
Word was sent immediately to headquarters at Langley and to MI6 in
London.

Finally, the CIA had the ammunition to force Gadhafi's hand. The
cargo on the *BBC China* would allow the Americans and British to confront Gadhafi with hard evidence without exposing the inner workings
of the intelligence operation that had led to the ship's seizure. The very
day the crates were opened, Mark Allen telephoned Musa Kousa in Libya
and asked for an urgent meeting. Two days later, Allen and Kappes flew
to Tripoli with Kousa's permission. There, they boarded one of Gadhafi's
personal jets and flew to an airport two hours away, in the vast Libyan
desert. Not far from the airstrip, they found Gadhafi waiting for them
inside a well-appointed tent. As they sat in the cooling night air, a servant
lit a brazier near the entrance and fanned the hot air inside. As far as
Kappes was concerned, the time for negotiating was over. The Americans
had proof that Libya was trying to develop a nuclear weapon; if he refused
to give up the program, the months of negotiations would end, and there
would be consequences for Gadhafi and his country.

"You are the drowning man, and I am the lifeguard," Kappes told the
Libyan leader.

Gadhafi agreed to be saved.

With a deal at hand, secrecy was more vital than ever. If word leaked
that Gadhafi had agreed to give up his weapons of mass destruction, the

Arab press and his own people might embarrass the Libyan into backing out. President Bush and Prime Minister Tony Blair were informed, but only a handful of senior officials in either government knew of the deal in the desert. Technical details now needed to be resolved. First, arrangements had to be made to take an inventory of Libya's stocks of chemical weapons and nuclear equipment. Second, an agreement had to be reached to remove the most sensitive nuclear equipment from Libya and dispose of its chemical weapons. All of this was contingent upon the mercurial strongman not changing his mind and walking away from the deal.

Two weeks after the agreement, a joint team of CIA and MI6 experts in chemical, biological, and nuclear weapons boarded a CIA plane operated by a British front company and headed for Libya to get their first look at the sites where work was under way. Somehow, word of the secret flight reached a member of the European Council, the advisory body of the European Union, which threatened to expose and possibly torpedo the grand bargain. Fortunately, the legislator made the wrong assumption, leaking to the press that the aircraft had been involved in one of the CIA's "extraordinary renditions" to return a terrorism suspect to Libya. The trip lasted only a couple of days, so in early December the team returned to take a more exhaustive inventory of the nuclear sites and the warehouse where the Libyans stored barrels of chemical weapons. This time, they spent ten days compiling a catalog of advanced nuclear technology so extensive that it stunned them. The Libyans had received far more equipment than Urs Tinner had reported to the CIA, though there was no way to determine whether the Swiss technician had withheld information or simply not known about the extent of the shipments. There was still a chance that Gadhafi might change his mind, but after the second inspection the Americans and British had enough information to bomb the programs out of existence if need be.

Meanwhile, efforts were under way to resolve the political side of the equation. The diplomatic wrangling centered on how much Libya would acknowledge in public, the precise language of its admission, whether all the nuclear equipment would be removed, and whether Gadhafi would suffer the humiliation of making the announcement himself.

Late on the morning of December 16, an unlikely group arrived at the Traveller's Club, a Victorian-era gentlemen's club, which had already witnessed its share of history from its perch among the grand buildings of Pall Mall, just off Piccadilly in the center of London. They were ushered to one of the private rooms off the pillared main lobby, where they took seats around a massive mahogany table, which was set for a formal luncheon. In the middle on one side sat Musa Kousa, flanked by Libya's ambassadors to London and Rome. Across from him were William Ehrman and David Landsman, senior officials from the British Foreign and Commonwealth Office, Mark Allen, and another MI6 agent. Representing the United States were Robert Joseph, the head of counterproliferation at the National Security Council, and Steve Kappes.

The meal was over soon, but the negotiations dragged on for ten hours as the Americans and British pushed relentlessly toward a single goal: forcing Gadhafi to make an unambiguous public statement relinquishing his chemical weapons and abandoning his nuclear-weapons program. They insisted that Libya give up all of the nuclear material and equipment it had bought on the black market and destroy its stockpiles of chemical weapons. In addition, Libya would have to turn over its long-range Scud missiles, which were capable of reaching Europe, sign the Additional Protocol, and permit full inspections by the IAEA.

"It was a really tough meeting," said one participant. "They were giving up things that cost a lot of money, and a lot of people had their careers tied up in these programs. It was not an easy thing to do to shut them down and have them removed, too. There was also the political issue, how was this going to look to their Arab neighbors. And there were other impediments. There was no obligation for them to give up the Scuds. They also could have tried to keep the centrifuges and other nuclear equipment. They could simply have said this was intended for peaceful purposes, and I think the IAEA would have agreed with them and let them keep the equipment." But for the Americans and British, it was an all-or-nothing deal.

The Libyans won on a critical face-saving point. Gadhafi would not have to be embarrassed by making the actual announcement, a task given to the foreign minister. Still, Gadhafi would have to issue a brief public statement endorsing the decision as a way of signaling to the world that he had signed off on it. Eventually, the negotiations came down to the language of Libya's announcement and the responses by the British and American leaders. Each sentence was parsed over and over until the two sides found language that was acceptable to everyone. "Nothing was agreed until everything was agreed," said another participant.

As the ultimate goal loomed larger, the fears of a leak grew, causing the British and Americans to push the Libyans to announce the agreement as soon as possible. After much back and forth, the historic announcement was finally set for December 19, the earliest date by which the Libyans thought they could make the necessary preparations. In Washington, only a handful of senior people knew of the pending news. John Bolton, America's top counterproliferation official, was among those who were kept in the dark, out of fears that he would expose the negotiations. In London, one of the few British officials who knew what was coming was pacing his office and glancing at the television throughout the day on the nineteenth, waiting for word from Libya. As evening turned to night, and Tripoli was still silent, he called Anthony Layden, the British ambassador there.

"Have they broadcast it yet?" he asked Layden.

"There's a football match on television," replied Layden.

As it got later and later, the British official began to worry that Gadhafi had suffered a last-minute change of heart and would call off the whole thing.

Finally, when the soccer game ended, Libyan foreign minister Mohammed Abderrahmane Chalgam appeared on national television to announce that the country would disclose and dismantle its nuclear- and chemical-weapons programs. Gadhafi then appeared briefly to deliver his public blessing, calling it a "wise decision and a courageous step."

Shortly after 5:00 p.m. in Washington and 10:00 p.m. in London, Bush and Blair went before the TV cameras on separate sides of the Atlantic to praise Libya's decision. Nearly nine months into the Iraq war, the American teams there had failed to find any evidence that Saddam had resumed efforts to develop WMDs, stripping Bush of his principal justification for the war. As America's primary ally, Blair faced rising criticism at home. So both leaders found themselves grasping at a life preserver, this one offered by Moammar Gadhafi. Bush in particular argued that the Libyan action restored the luster of American intelligence agencies, tarnished by their failures in Iraq. Gadhafi's decision, the president said, was a direct benefit of getting tough with Saddam Hussein and other rogue regimes. American pressure on North Korea and Iran and the war in Iraq, he said in a televised address, "have sent an unmistakable message to regimes that seek or possess weapons of mass destruction: Those weapons do not bring influence or prestige. They bring isolation and otherwise unwelcome consequences."

The next day, Gadhafi sent a messenger to London with a box of dates and oranges for the prime minister, along with a note of thanks. The Khan network was about to get a different message.

CHAPTER 28

CHECKBOOK PROLIFERATION

OLLI HEINONEN WAS SHOPPING with his family at Vienna's famous Christmas Market outside City Hall on the morning of December 20, a Saturday, when his cellphone rang. ElBaradei's secretary was calling with an urgent message: Heinonen was needed at an emergency meeting in the director general's office. He left his family on the sidewalk and drove to the IAEA, promising to return home in a couple of hours. He was to be gone far longer.

Heinonen's boss, Pierre Goldschmidt, had left town the previous afternoon to spend the holidays in his native Belgium. He was pleased about the prospect of two weeks off because he had spent the previous Christmas in North Korea, negotiating in vain to prevent the expulsion of IAEA inspectors after the collapse of the agreement that had frozen the Korean plutonium program. When he opened his cellphone on the morning of the twentieth, he found a message from Vienna: "You have to come back immediately. There is a crisis with Libya." He raced to the airport in Brussels.

ElBaradei had received word of the Libyan decision the night before, within minutes of Gadhafi's announcement, when an American official telephoned his home, but he had waited until morning to contact the others. The IAEA officials were not the only ones in the dark. The

American ambassador to the IAEA, Kenneth Brill, was out of Vienna on a ski trip and knew nothing of the pending announcement, so he missed the detailed, classified communication, which arrived at the offices of his delegation at midnight. Only the duty officer was there to read the memo, which provided an extensive rundown of what had been discovered about the Libyan nuclear program and talking points for what could be shared with the IAEA the following morning.

Though Washington had continued to feed information about Iran to the IAEA, there had been a squabble over whether to involve the agency in dismantling the Libyan program. John Bolton, who himself had not learned of the negotiations with Libya until moments before Gadhafi's public announcement, argued that the United States and Britain deserved all the glory for forcing Libya out of the nuclear business, and he pressed to keep the IAEA completely out of the loop. He contended that the Libyan episode showed once again that the IAEA was incapable of uncovering a hidden nuclear program. Colin Powell overrode Bolton, persuading the White House that the IAEA had a legal role to play in dismantling the Libyan installations and that it would be good politics to involve the respected agency.

Late on that Saturday morning, two British intelligence agents arrived in Vienna and were escorted directly to ElBaradei's office. Gathered to meet them with the director were Heinonen, Jacques Baute, and a handful of other senior agency officials. Goldschmidt was still in the air. Two diplomats had come over from the American mission, but Brill had not made it back for the briefing. There were a couple of British diplomats. The intelligence agents presented an hourlong description of the types and amounts of nuclear technology discovered in Libya and the number of installations that had been inspected by the joint British-American team earlier in the month. Though the inquiry was still preliminary, the agents said that much, if not all, of the technology appeared to have come through suppliers associated with A. Q. Khan. Though the agents did not say so, the Libyans had admitted to Stephen Kappes that Khan had been their chief supplier, which was confirmed by the fact that some crates discovered at various places around Tripoli bore markings from Khan Research Laboratories.

The agents explained that Libya had agreed to give up virtually everything nuclear, down to the small amount of enriched uranium in a research reactor under IAEA safeguards. They said the Libyan government planned to invite ElBaradei to come see for himself what they had been up to. Finally, the agents said the British and American governments wanted the IAEA to play a role in overseeing the dismantling of the Libyan nuclear program and the crating and shipping of the equipment to the United States for safekeeping and inspection.

News of the decision was a complete surprise to the IAEA officials. Dismayed as ElBaradei was by the Libyan disclosures and the IAEA's failure to uncover the program on its own, he was relieved about the offer of a role for the agency in the next phase. His relations with the administration in Washington had remained testy since he had correctly challenged their claims about nuclear weapons in Iraq. The situation had deteriorated further because he continued to resist American efforts to refer Iran to the UN Security Council for possible sanctions because of its undisclosed nuclear activities. ElBaradei wouldn't have been shocked to find the agency excluded, so he was happy to assure the British agents that the IAEA would devote the resources necessary to securing the Libyan program. He also promised a thorough investigation into how the technology had gotten there in the first place.

While he had had no inkling of the talks with Gadhafi, Heinonen was not completely surprised that Libya had a secret nuclear program. During a routine inspection visit to Libya in May, he had heard a rumor that the Libyans had been buying nuclear technology on the black market, but there had not been enough information or time for him to follow up. The likelihood of Khan's involvement was even less of a surprise. Since the discovery that Iran's centrifuges matched Pakistan's designs, the agency had been investigating whether the plans had been provided to the Iranians by Khan or someone close to him. The more the inspectors stripped away the layers of secrecy in Iran, the more the finger had pointed to Pakistan and Khan. Just a month earlier, the agency had sent an official letter to Islamabad asking if their scientist could have been involved. A delegation from the Pakistani Atomic Energy Commission had arrived before the end of November to deliver the reply in person. Just as they had whenever suspicions about proliferation by their country arose, the Pakistani officials said it was impossible that Khan or anyone connected with the country's nuclear program had helped Iran.

Sitting in the director general's office listening to the briefing on Libya that Saturday morning, the significance of what the intelligence agents were describing hit Heinonen hard. The disclosure confirmed his fear that the world confronted a more complicated and potentially dangerous version of proliferation than ever before, one that would require a new paradigm. The old model had been transfers of technology from one country to another. Khan represented a new model, which operated without state control or even knowledge. A single rogue scientist had apparently provided the world's most advanced weapons technology to Iran and Libya. On top of that, the agreement with North Korea had fallen apart the previous year over allegations that the Koreans were using Khan-supplied technology. Who knew where else Khan had sown seeds of destruction?

MINUTES after the British briefers departed, a delegation from Libya arrived at the IAEA. They had flown to Vienna that morning to extend the formal invitation to ElBaradei. A week later, on December 27, for the second time in less than a year, Mohamed ElBaradei found himself on a plane to a country with a freshly disclosed clandestine nuclear program. He could take some solace from the differences: Unlike the Iranians, who were continuing to work at Natanz and other sites, the Libyans were giving up their efforts. It was a small comfort as the Austrian Airlines jet touched down at Tripoli's airport.

Stepping off the plane, the IAEA team was escorted around customs to a line of black BMWs, which whisked them past billboards carrying photographs of the great leader to the Corinthia Bab Africa Hotel. The visit was a chance for the IAEA to see first hand what Libya had bought on the black market. It proved to be a sober revelation. Libya had not bothered to conceal its secret program in well-guarded bunkers or complexes buried beneath the sands of the Sahara. Instead, the delegation toured a series of nondescript warehouses and innocuous-looking school buildings scattered around the city. They saw components for five thousand centrifuges.

Twenty of the machines had been set up and tested at one site. Other crates had not been unpacked. When they pried them open, the IAEA officials saw gleaming, well-oiled machine tools that would have enabled Libya to mass-produce tens of thousands of centrifuges. Standing in the corner of one warehouse were two cylinders containing a ton of uranium hexafluoride. It was obvious that Libya had been engaged in a complicated, long-term shopping spree, and invoices showed that equipment had arrived from around the world—advanced centrifuge parts from Khan's stocks in Pakistan, some bearing KRL labels; other centrifuge components manufactured to order in Malaysia; vacuum pumps from South Africa; specialized steel and aluminum from Singapore; balancing machines from Switzerland; power regulators from Turkey.

As Heinonen wandered among the stacks of machinery at the main warehouse, a Libyan named Karim pointed to dozens of four-foot-high metal cabinets containing regulators to govern the flow of electricity to the centrifuges. They were marked with the label of a Turkish company, Elektronik Kontrol Aletleri.

"That firm is owned by Jews," said Karim, who had attended the first meeting with Khan in Istanbul. "Nothing is holy in this world."

Once exposed, the Libyans appeared to hold back nothing. They told the IAEA officials, as they had the Americans and British, that Khan had promised to provide a complete, off-the-shelf bomb factory. The Libyans calculated that they had already paid around $80 million to the network. They said they had no idea what the final price tag would have been—$500 million? $1 billion? Iran had purchased prototypes and designs but used its own skilled workers and technical resources to develop its enrichment plant at Natanz. Libya, on the other hand, had few trained workers and little manufacturing ability, so it was forced to buy the entire infrastructure to build the bomb.

ElBaradei had asked to meet with Gadhafi, but the Libyans had been unable to confirm a time for an appointment. On the third day, as the delegation was about to head out to another site, Gadhafi sent for the IAEA chief without warning. ElBaradei and one of his aides, Canadian diplomat Mark Gwozdecky, were bundled into a government car and driven to an old army barracks in the middle of Tripoli, which had been converted into one of Gadhafi's many hideaways. The exchange was boilerplate. Gadhafi said Libya had opened a new chapter in its history and wanted to join the mainstream international community. He explained that he was committed to setting up a nuclear-free zone in the Middle East, a proposal Egypt had been pushing for years. Part of the proposal, he stressed, was for Israel to give up its nuclear arsenal. ElBaradei welcomed Gadhafi's commitment and pledged that the IAEA would work with the Libyans.

That evening, Gwozdecky and Pierre Goldschmidt went for a walk outside the hotel to get a look at street life in Tripoli, a place few Western diplomats had visited in decades. Two men in dark glasses and plain clothes followed at a discreet distance. A few minutes into the walk, Gwozdecky turned and walked back to the pair, more amused than miffed about the intrusion. When the Canadian asked what they were doing, the men smiled and said they had been told to take care of the guests. The ice was broken, and the minders turned out to be friendly and hospitable tour guides who showed the visitors the intricacies of the local market. Later, back inside the hotel, another market was on Gwozdecky's mind: the black market in nuclear technology. "It's the most dangerous phenomenon we've seen in many years," he told Goldschmidt. "It's a sophisticated global network, spanning three continents and maybe a dozen countries."

As frightening as the black market was, there was some relief in what the IAEA team had seen. The Libyans had indulged in checkbook proliferation, paying large amounts of money for a vast amount of technology. The Americans had warned that the program was well along toward developing a bomb, but to the expert eyes of the IAEA officials it did not appear that it was anywhere close. Some members of the team questioned whether the Libyans would ever have achieved the technical capabilities to build a bomb, even with Gadhafi's open checkbook and Khan's tutelage.

Any sense of relief disappeared on the last day of the visit. Mohammad Matuq Mohammad, the head of Libya's nuclear program and the point man for contacts with Khan since 1997, met with ElBaradei and the others in his office at the National Board for Scientific Research. As he had done previously with Kappes, he described his repeated meetings with Khan in Dubai, Istanbul, Casablanca, and other places. Rifling through stacks of invoices for equipment purchased through Khan and his associates, Mohammad provided the beginnings of a map of the world of nuclear trafficking that ElBaradei and the others could barely fathom. But the most startling revelation was yet to come.

At one point, Mohammad rose from the conference table, walked to one corner of his office, and picked up two innocuous-looking beige shopping bags. Setting them on the table, he explained that he wanted to demonstrate that he and his country were now cooperating fully with the IAEA. The two bags bore the markings of a tailor shop in Islamabad. Though no one in the room knew it, they were the same ones that Khan's two tails from the ISI had seen him carry to Dubai three years before and deliver to the unknown men. Mohammad reached into one of the bags and started to pull out a stack of papers, explaining that they were plans for a nuclear warhead that Khan had given to him years earlier, as a way of saying thank you for buying tens of millions of dollars' worth of technology—and as an inducement to buy more. In Middle Eastern culture, a purchase is often followed by a small gift from the seller to the buyer. In this case, the gift was the key to the world's most powerful weapon. Before Mohammad could withdraw anything, ElBaradei insisted that he stop. If the bags held what Mohammad said they did, the material was so sensitive that ElBaradei and Heinonen were forbidden to lay eyes on it. One of the cardinal rules at the IAEA was that only a handful of the 2,400 employees were permitted to look at anything that had to do with weapons designs. The few people allowed to see them were citizens from the five countries authorized by the nonproliferation treaty to possess nuclear weapons—Britain, China, France, Russia, and the United States. And even they had to have the highest levels of security clearances from their governments. The restriction was deemed necessary to prevent secrets from being stolen by employees who come from dozens of countries. Only one member of the IAEA team in Tripoli that day, Jacques Baute, had the required clearance, but even he did not want to open the bags. Instead, Baute took the two bags from Mohammad and put them in a hard plastic case normally used to carry scientific equipment and affixed an IAEA seal to it. The Libyans were told to keep the case under lock and key until Baute and another colleague with proper clearances could return to examine the modern equivalent of Pandora's box.

The Libyan was surprised by the response, explaining that he had already showed the plans to the CIA and MI6 and allowed them to make copies.

BRITISH AIRWAYS flight 898 from London arrived in Tripoli on January 18. Aboard was a fourteen-member team of American and British experts under the command of Donald Mahley, a deputy assistant secretary of state for arms control and retired U.S. Army nuclear-weapons officer. They were the first American diplomats to visit Libya officially since 1980; their passports carried special stamps from the State Department permitting them to enter a country still under sanctions. Just getting there had been difficult. There were no flights from the United States, and restrictions on travel to Libya were so tight that computers at the State Department did not list the British Airways flight. In the end, Mahley and his colleagues flew to London and paid cash for their tickets to Libya because British Airways was not even allowed to accept American credit cards for trade with Libya. Fearing Gadhafi might still change his mind, the joint team had been assembled and briefed for the trip quickly. Two weeks earlier, the last details of the protocol for dismantling and packing up the hundreds of tons of Libyan equipment had been negotiated in London. The resulting agreement specified, point by point, what was expected from the Libyans and how the removal mission would be conducted. Top priority was to remove the nuclear-warhead designs, the P-2 rotors, and other key components for the uranium-enrichment plant as soon as possible. The remaining material was to go on a later flight.

While the IAEA delegation had stayed in Tripoli's best hotel three weeks earlier, the Brits and Americans were to have a decidedly lower profile. Though Libya was a police state, Gadhafi didn't want to risk stirring up his subjects by flaunting his new alliance with old enemies. Mahley and the team were taken to a compound of low, white buildings outside Tripoli that normally was home to young men studying the Koran. About thirty staffers from a Tripoli hotel were drafted to provide food and other services. The quarters were spartan, but the team members would be spending their days and most of their nights dismantling and repacking the equipment. Mahley wanted the first load flown out within a week.

Two days later, an Austrian Airlines jetliner from Vienna touched down in Tripoli, carrying ElBaradei, Heinonen, Baute, and other experts. The Libyans saw no need to hide their presence and the delegation returned to the Corinthia Bab Africa Hotel. ElBaradei had come to review the agreement with the Libyans for removing the equipment and to reassure them that the decision to give up the illicit technology voluntarily meant the IAEA would not recommend any sanctions by the United Nations. The rest of the team was responsible for creating an inventory and attaching IAEA seals to the equipment that would be removed from Libya by the Americans. The experts also wanted to return to Vienna with samples of some of the equipment and with the uranium hexafluoride so the agency's lab could try to confirm its origins. Heinonen was most worried about the centrifuge components and related enrichment equipment, the part of the bomb equation with which he was most familiar and the part generally regarded as the biggest proliferation concern. He thought Mohammad must have been wrong about the contents of the shopping bags. The idea that Khan had been reckless enough to hand over a cookbook for a nuclear weapon was so massively stupid that it was beyond imagination. Heinonen's colleague, Baute, feared otherwise.

Early the next morning, not long after the first call to prayer from the mosques of the nearby medina, Heinonen and the others from the IAEA gathered in the hotel restaurant to go over their strategy. Heinonen would lead inspections at nine separate, previously secret locations to compile a detailed inventory of the hundreds of tons of material. Because of the volume and the need to move fast, Heinonen decided to place seals on only selected components, a sample from every category of equipment. Baute and Bob Kelley, an American nuclear-weapons specialist who also had top-level security clearance and worked at the IAEA, were assigned the sensitive job of examining the contents of the shopping bags. Just receiving permission to look inside the bags had required a high-level debate with the Americans, who were extremely possessive of the entire Libyan trove. The day before the IAEA delegation left for Tripoli, John Bolton had flown over to argue forcefully that the weapons designs were too sensitive for anyone at the IAEA to view, even a fellow American such as Kelley. ElBaradei had responded that Baute and Kelley needed to inspect the bomb plans so the agency could get a sense of how much the Khan network had given to Libya. Certainly Bolton wanted to protect against the spread of such dangerous plans, but he had other reasons for wanting to keep a lid on the existence of the warhead designs in Libya. It was possible that once the behind-the-scenes story emerged in the press, someone would discover that Khan had delivered the designs to Gadhafi well after his network had been penetrated by the CIA, a fact that could tarnish the victory. Finally, Bolton had relented, specifying that, while Baute and Kelley could examine the documents, the Americans would take ultimate custody of them.

During his years as the chief of the inspection team in Iraq, Baute had never seen anything as dangerous as actual designs for a nuclear warhead. He was alarmed simply by the presence of such material in Libya, outside any sort of control. Kelley, on the other hand, had spent the last eighteen months focusing on Iran and wondered whether the network had provided Iran with the same warhead plans he was about to inspect.

Shortly after nine o'clock that morning, Baute and Kelley were driven to the National Board for Scientific Research, where Baute had met with Mohammad on the earlier trip. Accompanying them was a Libyan minder, a silent, unsmiling man who sat next to the driver. At the so-called research center, Baute and Kelley were escorted to a small office with three desks. A few minutes after they sat down, a guard entered, carrying the hard case with the IAEA seal Baute had attached the previous month, still intact. The minder remained, reading a newspaper in a corner and only occasionally glancing at his charges, as Baute broke the seal and removed the shopping bags. He lifted out the contents, making two piles, each about a foot high, and for the next eight hours he and Kelley read through the two stacks. No sound was heard except the shuffle of papers and the drone from a window air conditioner. Occasionally, one of them would point to a particular diagram or let out a low sigh at the extent of the designs. Baute's worst fears were confirmed each time he flipped a page or opened a new document.

One of the bags contained hundreds of pages of engineering schematics, detailed drawings, and handwritten reports—at least one hundred production drawings and reports that comprised precise instructions for building an implosion-type nuclear bomb. The device would weigh around one thousand pounds, possibly small enough to fit atop the ballistic missiles in Libya's arsenal and more powerful than the bombs dropped on Hiroshima and Nagasaki. Though the reports and plans were in English, Baute's experience told him that he was looking at the designs for a device tested on a missile by the Chinese in 1966. Despite its age, the warhead design was relatively sophisticated and lighter than the first-generation nuclear warheads designed by the United States and Soviet Union.

The other bag yielded a more haphazard collection. Some documents were unclassified reports from the U.S. Department of Energy and the national weapons laboratories, which could have been downloaded from the Internet. Others were notes from seminars and visits to China that covered a variety of techniques for fabricating a nuclear warhead. These notes were numbered sequentially and appeared to cover more than a year of intensive how-to sessions. From the handwriting, it appeared that at least four scientists had attended the seminars. The notes were written in English, the international language of science, but Baute saw various clues scribbled in the margins that indicated to him that the note takers were Pakistani. "Munir's bomb would be bigger," read one note.

The plans offered an almost complete road map to a nuclear warhead, but Baute and Kelley believed that Khan had not given the Libyans everything they needed. Like a cook who leaves out an important ingredient when sharing a favorite recipe, Khan seemed to have omitted designs for at least one crucial part. Perhaps, they thought, he had planned to sell the final piece for more money. Despite the gap, the material provided an invaluable starting point for constructing a working nuclear device. Baute and Kelley decided that the information was so sensitive that they would take only limited notes in case their own papers fell into the wrong hands.

Nuclear-weapons technology was sixty years old: Inevitably, significant amounts of information had been distributed widely, and certainly the Internet had increased its availability. But the existence of actual plans for a proven nuclear warhead constituted a new level of threat in Baute's mind. His worries were deepened by his fears that the plans in front of him probably had been copied by the Libyans and that there was no way to discover who else might have received the same information from Khan's network, which no doubt had maintained its own copies.

After eight hours of wading through columns of figures and scientific ratios and diagrams on page after page, their eyes blurred and minds numbed, Baute and Kelley returned the documents to the plastic case and attached a new seal. Despite Bolton's objections two days earlier, Baute wanted to get the plans back to Vienna for further study. IAEA headquarters did not have the security required to guard nuclear-weapons plans, so Baute hoped to persuade the Americans to store them at their embassy in Vienna, where he and Kelley could have regular access to them. After repacking the material, the Frenchman carried the case down the hall to Mohammad's office, where he found Mahley waiting. "We need to take these plans back to Vienna," Baute told the American.

Mahley was in his early sixties, with the same lean, fit physique and close-cropped, iron-gray hair that he had had when he mustered out of the army as a colonel a decade earlier. He had spent twenty-eight years specializing in nuclear and biological weapons before joining the State Department as a counterproliferation expert, with the rank of ambassador. Like Bolton, Mahley thought the IAEA and ElBaradei were too soft, but he had been ordered to cooperate with the agency, so he listened to Baute's request.

"Sure," Mahley said with a wry smile. "You can have 'em, but only if you bring in a battalion big enough to take 'em."

Baute could only shrug. The plans would go back to the United States with the rest of the nuclear material.

Later that evening, with IAEA officials gathered at the hotel, Baute and Kelley offered a sanitized description of the plans they had seen and a full description of the encounter with Mahley. "These designs were made in a laboratory, and they are real," Baute explained gravely. "They are not well organized perhaps, but this is the real thing. It would provide a great starting point for any scientist trying to build a nuclear weapon. There is no question about that."

Baute told them that when he questioned Mohammad after looking at the plans, the Libyan had sworn that no one had done anything with the weapons designs and that the bags had sat untouched in a corner of his office for more than two years. There was no evidence Mohammad was lying, but he had allowed the Americans and British to make copies, raising the question of whether he made his own copy at some point. It would have been understandable insurance in case Gadhafi changed his mind. Even if they had not done so officially, what would have stopped someone from making his own copy for resale? A tested nuclear weapons design could fetch a huge sum on the black market. Listening to Baute and Kelley, Heinonen assumed securing the plans now would be too little, too late.

A COUPLE of days later, near the end of the trip, the Libyan nuclear team hosted a dinner for the IAEA delegation at a fish restaurant a short walk from the hotel. Melissa Fleming, the American who was the agency's media chief, sat next to one of the Libyans who had played a central role in buying equipment from the Khan network. He declined to give her his name, but he spoke at length about his distaste for the nuclear-weapons program and the methods used by his country to acquire the technology.

"I have a wife and children, and I want very much for them to respect me," the Libyan explained. "What we were doing was against my religious beliefs, and it was illegal. I was always uncomfortable with the way we had to conduct this business, and I am certain these black-market people cheated us."

The Libyan said he had never met Khan, but he participated in many negotiating and planning sessions with others in Dubai. He said Tahir and others in the network were always trying to get more money from the Libyans. For instance, he said, they offered to set up a training course in Dubai for Libyan technicians if Libya bought certain advanced equipment. Fleming went away from the dinner believing that the Libyan was sincere in his regrets.

After the IAEA team inspected and sealed most of the nuclear-related equipment, the Americans and British loaded it onto pallets for shipment to the States. The Defense Department planned to send a Hercules C-130 cargo plane to transport the freight to the United States, but Mahley objected. A C-130 could not be refueled in midair, which meant it would have to land somewhere along the route for refueling. Though any risk to the cargo was remote, the idea of stopping was unacceptable to a career military officer. After arguing with the Pentagon, Mahley telephoned Bob Joseph at the National Security Council and explained the problem. Joseph promised to clear it up, and within hours Air Force personnel at McChord Air Base in Washington State were preparing a special C-17 Globemaster certified to carry nuclear material and capable of midair refueling. Part of the preparations involved repainting the huge aircraft. The Libyans refused to have an aircraft with American military markings land on its soil, so the C-17 was repainted gray to cover its insignia. Even then, Musa Kousa told Mahley that the plane would have to land after dark at a former military air base outside Tripoli and depart before dawn to avoid attracting attention.

About 9:30 on the night of January 28, the C-17 lumbered to a halt on the runway outside Tripoli. The nuclear equipment was waiting inside the hangars, and the loading began at a furious pace. First aboard were the cylinders of uranium hexafluoride from Pakistan and North Korea. Next up were the P-2 rotors, the complete P-1 centrifuges, and the two Spanish lathes. The guidance sets for the long-range Scud missiles were also wheeled up the loading ramp; the missiles themselves would be part of one thousand tons of heavy stuff that would leave two months later on an American-registered ship, the *Industrial Challenger*. Mahley personally handed the case containing the nuclear-warhead plans to the pilot. At 2:17 a.m. on January 29, the plane took off for Oak Ridge, Tennessee, where the material would be taken to the Department of Energy's top-secret Y-12 National Security Complex for a detailed postmortem.

After the departure, the American and British experts had time to assess the full extent of Libya's nuclear equipment, which was still being inventoried and consolidated in a few warehouses. The Americans were finding that Libya had amassed far more nuclear technology than they had imagined previously, illustrating that even under the best of circumstances espionage rarely provides a complete picture. Activities inevitably occur outside the net cast by surveillance and informants. In Khan's case, the information from Tinner and other sources, both human and electronic, had vastly understated the extent of the technology shipped to Libya by the network, missing tons of sensitive equipment and, worst of all, the warhead plans. "We thought we knew it all about the A. Q. Khan network, and our intelligence was the best we ever had," said a senior State Department adviser. "I can tell you we were shocked by what we learned in Libya. It was amazing. They had ten times more stuff or five times more stuff than anyone had ever thought."

Mahley and the others left the country for a few weeks after the first load was sent on its way. By the time they returned in March, the *Industrial Challenger* was moored at the farthest end of Tripoli harbor, waiting to haul away the additional thousand tons of equipment. The Libyan authorities insisted that the goods be moved to the port and loaded at night, but the plan ran into trouble. "The first night we only got three truckloads," said Mahley. "The second night, four truckloads arrived. It was too slow coming through city traffic. I told the Libyan in charge that we had to do better, but the third night it was just three truckloads. I complained again."

Both sides were nervous. The Americans and Brits worried that the Libyans would stop the operation before they got everything onto the ship, and the Libyans were concerned that moving the heavy loads through Tripoli might cause a backlash if the public learned what was going on. The solution was something that could occur only in an authoritarian country: The fourth night, the authorities shut down Tripoli at 9:00 p.m., closing every street, road, and alleyway; by the next morning, everything was in the warehouse at the port. Even then, with the material one hundred yards from the ship, the last step was to prove difficult. A storm blew across Tripoli, with winds up to fifty knots sweeping across the port and making it impossible to use the ship's huge cranes to load cargo into the bay. "We had to use fifty-five-ton deck plates for stacking between the crates of equipment, and they were flying around like Frisbees," said Mahley. The storm blew itself out after thirty-six hours, and the loading was completed, allowing the *Industrial Challenger* to sail away with the remainder of the would-be bomb factory.

Estimates varied about how close Libya was to possessing a nuclear weapon. Some experts, after examining the equipment and plans, believed that an enrichment facility could have been up and running within four or five years. A warhead built according to the Chinese plans might have fit atop Libya's Scud missiles, though other means of delivery could have been developed—and there was always the opportunity to conceal a device inside a freight container. The enormity of the Libyan program, and the potential for actually building a bomb, was a dramatic demonstration of the dangers of permitting Khan to operate, even under CIA surveillance. During the months and years that his activities had been monitored, Khan had still managed to provide the plans for an atomic bomb to a rogue dictator, and it was possible that he and his accomplices had sold the same information to Iran, North Korea, or others. No one at the IAEA thought defusing Libya's nuclear ambitions had ended the greater threat.

CHAPTER 29

NUCLEAR WAL-MART

AFTER RETURNING FROM TRIPOLI near the end of January, Olli Heinonen and a handful of IAEA experts began reviewing the invoices, designs, and other papers turned over by the Libyans. They went through the lists of centrifuges, components, tool-and-die machinery, specialized electronics, and other equipment. They also went over notes from the interviews with the senior Libyan officials who had been involved in the nuclear program. For the most part, the Libyans had seemed eager to talk about what they viewed as a scientific project, though some expressed reservations about their country's quest for the bomb. The Libyans forthrightly described the initial contacts with Khan and the meetings that had followed in Dubai, Casablanca, and other capitals—information corroborated by invoices from Pakistan and equipment that still bore the labels of Khan's laboratory at Kahuta. The magnitude of the network began to emerge, with Khan as the ringmaster negotiating the deals, providing the technical advice, reassuring the scientists that the journey would end with a nuclear arsenal. Still, there were hurdles; Khan and his associates had managed to cover many of their footprints with false documents and by simply withholding information from the Libyans, leaving Heinonen the difficult task of completing the portrait of what was clearly the most dangerous proliferation operation in history.

IAEA inspectors were already suspicious that Khan and Pakistan had helped Tehran, but as Heinonen and others compared what they learned in Libya with what they had seen in Iran, it became clear that the links were much stronger than imagined. Much of the technology at Natanz and other nuclear facilities in Iran matched what was found in Libya. Most tellingly, the Urenco-based P-1 centrifuges found in Tripoli were identical to the machines being manufactured for the pilot plant at Natanz, which was nearly finished. There were still questions about the intent of the Iranians, and crucial to answering them, was finding out whether Khan had provided Iran with the same bomb plans that he had sold to Libya. Answering that would require an investigation into uncharted territory. The first step was comparing the equipment and know-how provided to Libya with what inspectors were finding in Iran. In addition to matches, omissions could be telling, too.

Before the end of January, Heinonen dispatched Trevor Edwards to Tehran to confront the Iranians over one apparent omission. Libya had turned over two P-2 centrifuges, but the Iranians had made no mention of the P-2 in earlier disclosures to the IAEA. Faced with the Libyan evidence, the Iranians admitted that they had purchased P-2 centrifuge drawings in 1994 from what they called foreign sources. Unfortunately, they said, the records of the transaction could not be found, and the government official who had arranged the deal was dead.

The reason for the lies had less to do with the actual centrifuge technology than with Iran's determination to avoid any direct connection with A. Q. Khan, fearing that admitting dealings with the father of the Islamic bomb would raise more doubts about the claim that their program was strictly civilian. Even after the Libyans pointed the finger directly at Khan, officials with the Iranian nuclear agency denied doing business with him. But that story, too, began to unravel.

About the same time Edwards was in Tehran, the laboratory results from the environmental sampling done nearly a year earlier at the secret workshop at Kalaye had come back positive—traces of highly enriched uranium had been picked up at the site. The results appeared to contradict Iran's claims that it had not enriched uranium and showed why IAEA inspectors had been barred from Kalaye while workers tried to obliterate the evidence. Confronted with the results, the Iranians adopted a new strategy, asserting that the HEU traces were only contamination from used components and centrifuges that they had purchased from Pakistan. They continued to deny that Khan had been involved.

On February 24, 2004, the IAEA staff produced a thirteen-page analysis of Iran's nuclear program in preparation for a board of governors' meeting the next month. The language of the report was scrubbed for several days, with various versions passed among senior officials for review. At one point, some of the language was shared with the Iranian delegation in Vienna, and they argued that some passages should be toned down and that they should get credit for cooperating with the inspections. The result was a compromise report that praised the Iranians for limited cooperation while still accusing them of withholding critical information and pointing out the common elements between Libya's clearly military nuclear program and Iran's, which the Iranians continued to assert was only civilian. "The basic technology is very similar and was largely obtained from the same foreign sources," the report said.

John Bolton was angered by the draft and pushed for tougher language. Kenneth Brill, the American ambassador to the IAEA, carried the complaints to ElBaradei and others, arguing that the agency had an obligation to declare that Iran's lies about its nuclear program warranted a referral to the UN Security Council for possible economic sanctions. The consummate diplomat, ElBaradei was reluctant to pursue the path of confrontation laid out by the Americans, fearing that it would lead to a war like the one under way in Iraq, without hard evidence that Iran was engaged in a weapons program.

The IAEA director general found support among the nonaligned countries represented on the agency's board of governors, such as South Africa, Venezuela, Egypt, and Malaysia. These countries accepted ElBaradei's conclusion. They were motivated partly by solidarity with Iran, which was also a member of the nonaligned movement, but more significantly by fears that their own civilian nuclear programs might be jeopardized in the future if they ran afoul of the United States. Their anger was increased because the Bush administration had recently disclosed that it was conducting research on a new generation of precision atomic weapons even as it was arguing that Iran should be denied a nuclear program because of suspicions about its intentions.

"The United States follows a double standard that allows it to develop and threaten to use nuclear weapons while denying them to smaller countries," Hussein Haniff, Malaysia's ambassador to the IAEA, said one day in his ornate office near the center of Vienna. "The Americans must reduce their nuclear arsenal, not expand it, and they must deal fairly and objectively with other countries."

While ElBaradei seemed prepared to give Iran the benefit of the doubt, he did speak out strongly to condemn Khan for helping both Libya and Iran, calling him the "chairman of the board" of a black-market network that sold nuclear equipment. When asked by a reporter whether Khan's customers extended beyond North Korea, Iran, and Libya, he replied: "This is the million-dollar question, and it's a very important question because we worry. . . . It is still an open question. We know that A. Q. Khan has not just been working for money. There is an ideology involved. We need to understand the motivations—we need to understand and try again to put some pieces of the puzzle together."

ElBaradei preferred keeping the lines of communication open with Iran as the means of getting to the bottom of its nuclear efforts. But he recognized that the IAEA could not tread as softly when it came to uncovering the increasingly alarming trail laid down by Khan. At his request, the IAEA board of governors authorized him and his staff to initiate a formal investigation. ElBaradei had already assigned Heinonen and his small group of inspectors to compare the Libyan and Iranian programs, but the authorization prompted a more wide-ranging investigation. ElBaradei told Heinonen to unravel the inner workings of what the director general had begun referring to in public as a "nuclear Wal-Mart."

The challenge exceeded anything the IAEA had undertaken in the past. Heinonen's investigation would range across the globe as he tried to reconstruct the network's activities step by step. Instead of subpoena power and the resources of the CIA or MI6, this band of trackers would depend only on its own resourcefulness and analytic skills. They would have to persuade network participants to point fingers at one another, and entice governments and companies to cooperate in the name of counterproliferation. Among his team members were Edwards, Bob Kelley, and Miharu Yonemura, a young Japanese woman who had joined the inspections division recently after working in her country's nuclear program as a chemical engineer.

"Nobody has to talk to us," Heinonen told the group in one of its early meetings. "We aren't cops, and we don't have the power to arrest anyone or make them talk. I don't really care about putting people in jail. I just want to drive a stake through the heart of this network and make sure it doesn't rise up again."

Making matters harder, Khan had had months to cover his tracks. When the work at Natanz was disclosed publicly in August 2002, he had sensed that it could mean trouble and ordered Tahir to shred documents that linked their operation with Iran. The Pakistani scientist also urged the Iranian government not to cooperate with the IAEA. "Regrettably, they were destroying evidence well before the Libya disclosure," said an American diplomat working in Vienna at the time. "They found out about the surveillance well before then."

Prior to the news of the seizure of the *BBC China* becoming public, Tahir had learned from his Libyan contacts that his five crates from Kuala Lumpur had been removed before the ship arrived in Tripoli. Suspecting the worst, he had shredded more records and erased computer files at SMB Computers before going to Kuala Lumpur, where he expected his wife's political connections would protect him. When word reached Urs Tinner that the shipment had been intercepted, he immediately packed his belongings and left Malaysia. Before departing for Switzerland, he removed the hard drive from his computer at Scomi and destroyed his personal files and other records.

It took longer for the alarm bells to ring in Johannesburg. But Gadhafi's public announcement in December confirmed Johan Meyer's suspicions that Libya was the customer for his apparatus. He telephoned Gerhard Wisser, the middleman, and Wisser rushed over to Tradefin. He ordered Meyer to destroy the system built for Libya. Send it to the smelter and melt it down, Wisser said. The stack of design drawings and the video from Pakistan, he demanded, should be committed to "an Easter bonfire." Meyer was reluctant to destroy what he had come to regard as a masterpiece; he was able to disassociate the end use of the system from its beauty as an engineering accomplishment. Besides, he was still owed the final $150,000 payment, which was due on delivery of the eleven freight containers sitting in his factory. Determined to see the evidence destroyed, Wisser paid the remaining money to Meyer out of his own pocket. Still, Meyer refused. In his growing frustration, Wisser sent a text message to Meyer saying, "The bird must be destroyed, feathers and all." In another, he wrote, "They have fed us to the dogs."

THE BRITISH had pushed to close down Khan's operation at the beginning of 2003, arguing that its activities had reached the point where it was too hard to control and too dangerous. George Tenet and Stephen Kappes had pushed back, demanding more time to gather more intelligence to eradicate every element of the network and stop Khan for good. The seizure of the cargo aboard the *BBC China* had forced Pervez Musharraf to act, but the question was how far the Pakistani leader could go in reining in his rogue scientist, who still maintained the title of presidential adviser. Since taking power, Musharraf had won financial concessions from the United States and international lenders by helping oust the Taliban in Afghanistan and playing a central role in Bush's war on terror. But faced with political instability at home, Musharraf had resisted American calls to crack down on Islamic extremists, who numbered only a few thousand but had the potential to rally the masses against his government. The same reasoning had kept him from doing more than pushing Khan to the sidelines. But Libya changed the equation, and even before Gadhafi went public Colin Powell had warned Musharraf privately: "We know so much about this that we're going to go public with it. You need to deal with this before you have to deal with it publicly."

Musharraf was left with no choice except to take steps against Khan, but the question remained, how far could the Pakistani leader go? Musharraf had narrowly survived two recent attempts on his life by Islamic extremists. Appearing to do the bidding of the United States by imprisoning a Pakistani hero, even in the face of the Libyan disclosures, would stir greater resentment. At the same time, Musharraf did not want to jeopardize the three billion dollars in financial assistance earmarked for Pakistan by Washington. But another reason demanded even more caution: When Khan's arrangement with Iran had started in 1987, some of Pakistan's military leaders had blessed the deal and others had turned blind eyes. Pushing Khan too far might provoke public disclosures by the scientist that could damage the army and possibly Musharraf himself. "We stood before the world as the illicit source of nuclear technology for some of the world's most dangerous regimes," he later explained. "I had to move quickly and decisively to stop any further activity and to find out exactly what had happened."

Musharraf polled a number of key advisers, all military officers like himself, and the consensus was that Khan had to be disciplined, though there was disagreement on how to go about it. Some generals wanted to imprison the scientist to send a clear message that Pakistan would not tolerate nuclear proliferation and reassure the international community that its arsenal was in safe hands. In the immediate aftermath of September 11, Pakistani military leaders had gone on high alert in response to rumors that the American military was about to launch raids to take control of Pakistan's nuclear arsenal. Others argued for leniency for Khan, fearing that the backlash from extremists might provoke a coup. Musharraf had to find a solution that would be accepted by Pakistani nationalists and the Americans.

In late December, Pakistani intelligence began quietly picking up scientists from Khan's lab. As word of the detentions slipped out, there were rumors that the CIA and FBI were participating in the interrogations. Khan heard the whispers, but if he thought of running, he made no attempt to do so. As before, he expected to weather the storm. As many as thirty scientists were detained and held in so-called hot rooms, where temperatures topped one hundred degrees and questioning went on for days. In late January, the government announced that six senior officials from KRL were being detained on charges of being "responsible for directly and indirectly passing secret codes, nuclear material, substances, machinery, equipment, components, information, documents, sketches, plans, models, articles and notes to foreign countries and individuals." Khan was not among them, but three were directors and the others were retired military officers. Faced with criminal charges, they began to talk, implicating Khan and ultimately winning their own freedom.

Khan had been questioned initially in December by two Pakistani generals, who described the evidence against him from the Americans and his own associates. Khan had reacted angrily, shouting at them to leave his office. When Khan learned of the formal charges against his colleagues, he was still using his office in the presidential building and decided it was time to fight back. As he had many times before, he tried to use the press to tell his story and rally public support. He telephoned Hamid Mir, a journalist and longtime acquaintance, inviting him to the office. Mir found the scientist haggard and slightly disheveled but defiant as ever. Mir asked about the arrests and recounted an article in the *Los Angeles Times* that accused Khan of helping Iran and Libya. Khan replied with a bitter denunciation of the Western press, the United States, and his own government. "It's all propaganda," he ranted. "The ISI and the CIA, they want to kill me, get rid of me anyway they can. Musharraf will arrest me and turn me over to the Americans if he can, but I can stop him."

Before Khan could say more, an ISI officer who had been eavesdropping from an adjoining office walked in and sat down without a word. Mir, experienced in the invisible lines drawn by the ISI over what could and could not be published, decided the interview had been off-the-record, finished his coffee, and left. Later, Mir offered an assessment: "He thought nobody could touch him because he is a hero. It was beyond his expectations that Musharraf could arrest him."

But the curtain was about to fall on Khan's traveling show. Early the next morning, plainclothes security agents arrived at his home, rousting him from breakfast and escorting him to a waiting car. Khan was driven to a secret location, where he was questioned by a team of senior officials from the ISI, who confronted him with evidence obtained from his former colleagues at the lab and from the Americans. There would be no hot room for the esteemed scientist, but neither would he be treated with kid gloves. Even faced with undeniable evidence, Khan resisted at first, clinging to his imperial manner and arguing forcefully that he was a national hero whose actions had all been undertaken for the benefit of Pakistan. "Who made the atom bomb?" he demanded. "I made it. Who made the missiles? I made them for you." He railed against the Americans, claiming they had set him up because he had defied their nuclear monopoly and tried to spread the lethal secrets to other Muslim countries. But after three days of insistent questioning, the sixty-six-year-old Khan, exhausted and defeated, had had enough. He agreed to confess. A meeting was arranged with Musharraf in the president's office at which Khan admitted that he had passed on Pakistan's nuclear secrets to Iran, Libya, and North Korea. A bit of bravado remained in the defeated scientist, however, and he asked for a presidential pardon, citing all he had done for the country. Musharraf knew that the public would protest any prosecution, no matter what the facts were, and he agreed to consider the request. But he stipulated that Khan would have to sign a written confession, make a public apology, and accept an indefinite term of strict house arrest. In addition, Khan would be required to apologize on national television. But his written confession would remain secret.

The apology was scheduled for February 4. That morning, Musharraf gathered the country's military and political leaders to brief them on Khan's impending confession and get them to rubber-stamp his decision to pardon the scientist. A short time later, Khan was brought to Musharraf's office, and the president informed him that he had agreed to pardon him. A photograph later distributed by the Pakistani government showed the two men seated uncomfortably in the president's office, Musharraf in his military khakis looking sternly at Khan in a western suit. Khan left to take the short ride to the studios of the national television network, where he was given the text of the statement he was to read. Before the broadcast, Musharraf appeared before a room of Pakistani journalists to explain the historic event. He laid all the blame at Khan's feet, telling the journalists: "Unfortunately, the entire proliferation took place under the orders and patronage of Dr. A. Q. Khan. I can say with certainty that no government official or military personnel were involved." Rumors had swept Islamabad throughout the day, and a reporter told Musharraf he understood that Pakistan had been asked to take three steps beyond arresting Khan: hand over all of its nuclear records to the IAEA; submit to an impartial inquiry to determine whether the military assisted Khan; and allow the United Nations to intervene in Pakistan's nuclear program.

"Negative to all three of them," Musharraf said sharply. "We will do no such thing."

A short time later, Khan appeared on television. He was somber and contrite, befitting the stage-managed event. Expressing "the deepest sense of sorrow, anguish, and regret," he said, speaking in English and occasionally glancing nervously at his statement, "I want to atone for some of the anguish and pain that has been suffered by the people of Pakistan on account of the extremely unfortunate events of the last two months. I take full responsibility for my actions and seek your pardon." Khan said that he and unnamed accomplices had passed on the weapons secrets without government authorization. "I wish to place on record that those of my subordinates who have accepted their role in the affair were acting in good faith like me, on my instructions," he said, suddenly veering from the prepared text. Khan was supposed to acknowledge an "error of judgment," and he had added the phrase "in good faith" in a last-ditch attempt to wrap himself in the cloak of patriotism.

The speech was short on specifics. He did not identify the recipients of the nuclear secrets, and he did not explain why he had sold them. His remarks raised as many questions as they answered, but Khan was hustled out of the building and was unlikely to be seen again in public. The fact that he delivered his confession in English, rather than Urdu, spoke volumes about the intended audience—the words were intended to reassure the international community that the Khan matter was over without riling the Pakistani masses. The next day, Musharraf called Khan a national hero, saying, "I revere him for his contribution to making the defense of the country impregnable." Because of his contributions to Pakistan, Musharraf said, he and the government had decided to pardon Khan. The scientist would be confined to his house, kept in isolation with his wife, allowed no newspapers, television, or Internet, and held beyond the reach of the IAEA and American intelligence agents. The few people permitted to visit the once peripatetic merchant of death said they found him depressed and in deteriorating health, passing his time feeding the monkeys in the backyard and complaining that he was the victim of an American conspiracy.

Public reaction was muted, but those three words, "in good faith," had struck a sympathetic chord. Islamic parties organized a handful of demonstrations in cities across the country, with protests carrying banners that read, "We want Qadeer Khan as President not Prisoner." A leader of the Islamic opposition, Qazi Hussain Ahmad, demanded that Musharraf step down. General Hamid Gul, chief of the ISI when Khan first started sending nuclear technology to Iran, claimed that the Americans would use Khan's confession to demand joint control over Pakistan's nuclear arsenal. The protests soon fizzled, but Pakistanis from all sides of the political spectrum believed that Khan was taking the fall for activities sanctioned by a succession of leaders, military and civilian alike. Zahid Malik, Khan's biographer, put it this way: "As he said in his statement, he behaved in good faith. To me, those words mean a lot. Dr. Khan is a responsible person and he knew Pakistan was in a difficult position and it was good of him to step aside and not prolong this difficult issue."

Khan's quarantine benefited many. Feroz Khan, a former Pakistani general, explained that Musharraf and others were afraid of what Khan might say if he were allowed to speak to the IAEA or the CIA. Whether his accusations would be true or not was immaterial, the former officer said. Lies would be enough to stir up more international condemnation for Pakistan and possibly endanger the country's nuclear arsenal. Another former military officer who had worked with Khan said there was no question in his mind that Khan had acted with the knowledge of the generals. "If Khan sent a centrifuge out of the country, he didn't carry it on his back," said the retired general. "Of course the military knew. They helped him."

There was another reason: Turning Khan over for a full debriefing by the United States or the IAEA would have risked exposing the remnants of the network at a time when Pakistan was still using them to buy technology and equipment to maintain and upgrade its nuclear arsenal. European intelligence agencies concluded that Pakistan's shopping list was extensive, involving both spare parts for its existing program and new technology for expansion.

Unlike the initial interrogation, which was intended to force a confession, the postapology questioning by the Pakistani authorities was focused on extracting as much information as possible from Khan about his operation and determining who else had been involved. The two lead in-terrogators, a general and a senior ISI official, started out gently, but a few days into the questioning the atmosphere changed dramatically. The ISI learned that in December, as rumors of his possible arrest had circulated, Khan had given a thick stack of handwritten documents to his daughter Dina, who was visiting from London. He instructed her to take them back with her and keep them as an insurance policy. If the government went after her father, she was to turn them over to Simon Henderson, a British journalist who had interviewed Khan years earlier. The Pakistani government was unsure what was in the documents, but the big fear was that he had provided details—real or imagined—of who had approved his proliferation activities.

"Now you have got your daughter involved," one of the interrogators told Khan angrily. "So far we have left your family alone, but don't expect any leniency now."

Khan had remained composed and unrepentant until that point, but the threat caused him to collapse in sobs. After being pushed harder, he agreed to telephone Dina and order her to destroy the documents. As the intelligence officers sat beside him, Khan dialed London. When Dina answered, he told her to destroy the records—three times in three languages: Urdu, English, and Dutch. The ISI official grabbed the tele-phone from him and demanded to know what Khan had said in Dutch, which no one else in the room understood. Khan explained that it was a code—if he spoke to Dina in Dutch, he said, she would know to obey his instructions.

Dina said her father had given her only a letter addressed to Henny. "At that time he was worried that he was going to be made to take the fall for the erupting nuclear scandal (a fear which later proved correct)," she wrote in a statement made public two years later. "The letter gave his version of what actually transpired and requested my mother to release those details in the event of my father being killed or made to disappear. The letter mentioned people and places, but had absolutely NO nuclear blueprints or information."

But a close friend of Khan's maintained that the scientist had given his daughter a far more extensive document, nearly one hundred pages that constituted an autobiographical account of Khan's proliferation activities over the years. Its fate remains unknown.

THE NET was closing elsewhere, too. Like Pakistan, Malaysia had been contacted before the Libyan announcement because of the importance of B.S.A. Tahir to the investigation. A month after the *BBC China* was diverted, on the evening of November 10, 2003, a CIA agent and an MI6 agent met with the director of Malaysia's Special Branch, the national-security force. They said Tahir, a forty-four-year-old Sri Lankan married to a Malaysian, was the target of an ongoing investigation of the transfer of nuclear technology from Malaysia to other countries. While Malaysia has no nuclear industry, the agents explained that Tahir had used a local company owned in part by the only son of Prime Minister Abdullah Badawi. The security chief instantly understood the implications if he refused to cooperate, and the next day he informed the prime minister, who told him to help the United States and Britain in every way possible. Tahir was placed under surveillance for the next month, and he was taken into custody following the Libyan announcement. The charge was violating the National Security Act, a vague accusation that allowed the authorities to detain him indefinitely without the unpleasantries of a public trial that might implicate the prime minister's son and other Malaysians. Tahir was held in isolation, with even his wife refused permission to visit him. Tahir had never been a hard man or a principled one, so within days, he drafted a detailed statement for the Malaysian police outlining the entire operation within the country and describing much of the network's operations elsewhere. The confession didn't win Tahir his freedom, but the sanitized, twelve-page version posted on the Internet by the government named enough names to justify arrests by authorities in other countries.

Gotthard Lerch, the German engineer, was arrested in Switzerland on charges of shipping controlled goods to Libya in exchange for thirty-one million dollars. Wisser, Meyer, and a third, South African engineer Daniel Geiges, were arrested in Johannesburg. When police raided Meyer's factory, they found the eleven containers with the superstructure for Libya's enrichment plant along with five trunks filled with photographs, designs, manuals, and other documents from Khan. Gunes Cire, one of the Turks identified by Tahir as a supplier to the Libyan program, died of a heart attack after reading about the accusations against him in an Istanbul newspaper.

The Tinners remained free, but they were frightened of being swept up. The Germans were preparing a case against Friedrich and Urs Tinner, who feared extradition. Mad Dog urged Urs to stay put, explaining that it was unlikely the Swiss would extradite him, even if he was charged. The Swiss government sent a message to Washington seeking information on the Tinners but received no response. They repeated the request three times over the next few months, always with the same result. The CIA had no interest in providing information that would expose one of its sources and the fact that it had been gathering inside information on the Khan network for years. The idea of a public trial of one of their key informants was out of the question. While the CIA did not want to help the Swiss, it was in the American interest to keep the pressure on Iran, so the agency decided to use the Tinners to get information to the IAEA. The former Vienna station chief, by now a senior official at Langley, assigned an agent in Vienna to contact Olli Heinonen with an offer of help on the investigation into the Khan network. "Keep us out of the conversation," he told her.

CHAPTER 30

WHO'S NEXT?

THE INVESTIGATION OF THE KHAN NETWORK was even larger and more complex than Olli Heinonen envisioned. From the outset, many of the companies, governments, and people involved refused to cooperate. The Pakistanis informed the IAEA that Khan was off-limits. Tahir's statement to Malaysian police offered clues that could unravel much of the operation—he had implicated a dozen and outlined their roles—but attempts to interview him were rebuffed by Malaysian authorities, who did not want to embarrass their country or highlight Tahir's political connections. Investigators in Germany, Switzerland, and South Africa were gathering their own evidence for criminal cases, so their cooperation was restricted. The Americans remained tightfisted with information, passing on occasional tidbits that focused attention on Iran's program while withholding the full scope of what they had learned about Khan's operation.

Despite the difficulties, the IAEA team was building a growing list of suspected participants. The best information came from the Libyan documents, which enabled Miharu Yonemura to construct a giant matrix of suppliers and front men. More names were added by sifting through files at the IAEA and articles in the international press. Sometimes help came from unexpected places. The Iranians provided the names of three Germans they claimed were involved in the earliest deal to buy centrifuges. Even the Pakistanis offered grudging assistance, though they continued to deny any official involvement in Khan's activities. Pakistan sent some centrifuge components from Kahuta to Vienna, where IAEA scientists matched them to the traces of HEU discovered at Kalaye. On another occasion, a visiting Pakistani nuclear specialist quietly handed Heinonen a piece of paper with the names of fifteen Europeans suspected of helping Khan on the Libyan project. Heinonen assumed the Pakistanis wanted to divert attention from Khan's role by drawing attention to others.

Still, Heinonen was far from developing a complete picture of how Khan operated, and some of the gaps were alarming. Comparing invoices discovered in Dubai with the inventory of equipment found in Libya, Heinonen found a disturbing discrepancy: A shipment destined for Libya had traveled from Malaysia to Dubai before disappearing into the ether in mid-2003. The manifest for the shipment listed centrifuge components and precision tools to manufacture them. The missing shipment fed the growing suspicion that there was a mystery customer or a secret, parallel program inside Iran run by the military.

Frustrated by the slow pace and lack of full cooperation, Heinonen had begun to fear that the chances of finding the elusive other customer were slipping away, when a woman telephoned his office in May. She refused to give her name, but she clearly knew a lot about him and his investigation. After a bit of sparring, she said she was calling because she had information that could open new doors in the inquiry. She asked if Heinonen would meet her. Six months earlier, Heinonen would never have considered agreeing to meet a strange woman at a coffee shop, but the investigation had changed the way he saw the world. The scientist's caution had been replaced by an investigator's determination to get to the bottom of the case, regardless of the means.

CIA, Heinonen thought as he hung up. He had dealt with enough Americans to recognize the accent, and he assumed the intelligence agency was monitoring his progress through moles inside the IAEA and taps on his telephone and e-mail. At one point, he had given ElBaradei some sensitive information in a telephone call, and a few days later American diplomats let slip that they knew the same information. After a series of similar minor but troubling episodes, Heinonen instructed IAEA computer technicians to install encryption software on the computers and cell phones in the hopes of keeping out the electronic snoops.

Face-to-face at Starbucks, the woman provided no more information about herself, but Heinonen didn't care. He was willing to play her game to get the information he needed. Twenty minutes or so into the conversation, with the coffee gone cold, the woman said she could set up a meeting between Heinonen and the Tinners. Heinonen recognized the name immediately from the Malaysian police report on Tahir's confession, and from his own research Heinonen knew that the Tinners had a long connection with Pakistan's nuclear program. The pleasant-looking woman was offering perhaps the biggest break yet. Heinonen said he would be happy to talk with them, and she promised to call as soon as she could arrange the meeting.

A few days later, the woman telephoned and instructed Heinonen to go to the InterContinental Hotel, across a boulevard from the grassy knolls and formal gardens of Vienna's Stadtpark. Following instructions, he arrived alone and went to the designated room on an upper floor and knocked. The door was opened by a man in his late sixties or early seventies who introduced himself in German as Friedrich Tinner and invited Heinonen in. Seated on a couch were two men in their late thirties or early forties; Tinner introduced them as his two sons, Marco and Urs. The Tinners fidgeted and tried to avoid eye contact, clearly uncomfortable sitting in the same room as a senior IAEA official. Heinonen didn't know how the woman had persuaded them to talk, but he assumed the CIA held some threat over their heads. The conversation was formal and guarded, neither side giving up much. Heinonen wanted to persuade the Tinners that they could trust him with their nuclear secrets, without giving up any leverage by disclosing how little he really knew about the network. The Tinners had grown rich and avoided trouble with the authorities by never trusting anyone. Friedrich and Marco had been surprised when Urs confessed that he had helped the CIA, but with the German authorities breathing down their necks, they hoped cooperating with the IAEA might offer some protection. The talk concentrated on the centrifuge technology sold to Libya, where the role of the network was clearest. Heinonen was careful not to press for too much detail, particularly about any other possible customers. After an hour or so, Friedrich agreed that they would meet again for a lengthier and more detailed conversation. He said the woman would call Heinonen with the time and place.

The second session was set up a few days later at the InterContinental, and Heinonen received the okay from the woman to bring Trevor Edwards, his centrifuge expert. Heinonen and Edwards listened intently as the Tinners described the arrangements with Libya and the technical aspects of the P-1 and P-2 centrifuges. Marco acknowledged building five thousand centrifuge parts in Switzerland and shipping them to his brother in Dubai. Asked about Iran, they denied that they had anything to do with sending equipment there. But under polite but persistent questioning, the architecture of the network emerged. The Tinners listed the names and companies of other participants and talked about the South African portion of the project, something that was still a mystery to Heinonen. They had brought along papers, including a list of the warehouses and offices in Dubai that the network had used to store equipment en route to Libya. When the missing shipment from mid-2003 came up, the Tinners said they had no idea where it had gone. Friedrich speculated that Tahir or Khan had cheated Libya by rerouting the equipment to another customer, but he said he had no idea who that might have been. The Tinners laughed about Khan's mistress in Dubai, saying she was a plain woman whose charms eluded them.

The conversation grew more relaxed after a room-service lunch, which was when Urs dropped a bombshell. After he fled Malaysia in October 2003, he said, Khan telephoned and told him to go to Dubai. Once there, he was instructed to make electronic copies of a particular set of drawings in a special locked filing cabinet inside Khan's apartment. When he got to Dubai, Urs said, he expected to find centrifuge drawings or something like that. Instead, he found what appeared to be complicated schematics and plans for what looked like a warhead. Still, he followed instructions, scanning the papers onto computer discs and mailing them in separate packages to Khan and Tahir. None of the Tinners had direct experience with nuclear weapons, but Urs had a good technical mind, and from his description of the plans Heinonen was certain he had copied the design for the same Chinese atomic warhead that Khan had delivered to Libya. Therefore, the detailed plans for a proven nuclear weapon were almost certainly still out there, available to anyone with a computer and enough money.

Heinonen bowed out of the session a few minutes later, anxious to report to Goldschmidt and ElBaradei. Edwards stayed behind into the night and throughout the next day to talk about technical data. In the meantime, Heinonen and Yonemura arranged to fly to Dubai to inspect the warehouses and offices identified by the Tinners. Tahir had packed up months earlier, and new tenants had moved into the spaces, but the two IAEA officials managed to talk their way into most of the locations. Though everything of obvious interest had been cleared out, that didn't mean all the evidence was gone. Yonemura had brought along an environmental-sampling kit to test for the presence of enriched uranium. She wiped down surfaces in every building. This wasn't a formal inspection, so they took the swabs to the IAEA lab for testing, with instructions that it was a rush order. The results were back within days, registering traces of weapons-grade uranium. The tests did not indicate how much HEU might have been stored in Dubai, where it was from, or where it was going. It could have been merely particles from contaminated centrifuge parts on the way from Pakistan to Iran or Libya. Or it could have been enough material for a nuclear weapon on its way to an unknown customer.

Where to search? Khan had made forty-one trips to Dubai and traveled to eighteen other countries in the ten years before he was placed under house arrest. Among them were a handful of Islamic countries regarded as likely customers, including Saudi Arabia, Syria, Egypt, Sudan, and Turkey. Saudi Arabia was the name most often mentioned, though the evidence was scant. The Saudis had helped finance the early stages of Pakistan's nuclear program and bought nuclear-capable missiles from the Chinese. The Saudi defense minister had been one of the few foreigners permitted to tour the inner sanctums of Khan Research Laboratories. On a visit to Riyadh in September 2000, Khan told an audience at the Hyatt Regency Hotel marking the joint celebration of Pakistani and Saudi national days, "Thanks to the kingdom's assistance for various development projects, we were able to divert our own resources to the nuclear program."

There were other reasons for suspicion. In 1994, Mohammed Khilewi, a senior member of the Saudi delegation to the United Nations, had defected and claimed that he had more than ten thousand documents detailing Saudi financial aid to Pakistan and its ambition to acquire nuclear weapons. Awash in oil money but technologically backward, Saudia Arabia, Khilewi said, had set aside huge sums to acquire nuclear technology and possibly weapons. Recent political developments in the Middle East contributed to a circumstantial case. Relations between Saudi Arabia and the United States had deteriorated since September 11 because fifteen of the nineteen hijackers that day were Saudis. While the Americans professed to remain strong allies, some Saudis held doubts about the reliability of the kingdom's protector. The fears of the Saudi royal family were also fueled by rising attacks from Islamic extremists inside the country.

"These fears contribute to Saudi Arabia's desire to acquire nuclear capability and to supply the entire Arab Gulf with a defense umbrella," said Richard Russell, a former CIA analyst. "The Saudis are worried that they might get left behind, particularly since Iran seems destined to possess nuclear weapons." Russell conceded, however, that he was only speculating, and there was no evidence that the Saudis had sampled Khan's wares or were pursuing an atomic bomb through other avenues.

As long as the Tinners kept talking, Heinonen held out hope of picking up enough pieces of the puzzle to determine whether there was another customer and who it was. Following the two sessions in Vienna, Heinonen and Edwards drove to Innsbruck to meet the Swiss technicians for a couple of days in July. Progress was slow, and Heinonen and Edwards were still trying to build trust with the Tinners, listening to Friedrich describe his world-class orchid collection and feigning interest in the details of Urs's divorce from his Russian wife. "The father is a tough guy," Heinonen said. "He is nice at the lunch table, but what he has done to his sons and family shows you that he is tough. They are an old Swiss-German family, and the father is the boss."

The conversations covered both the technical and financial workings of the network and gave Heinonen and Edwards a window on the dynamics within the closed circle of men who were simultaneously partners and rivals, dependent on one another without ever trusting anyone. The recollections of payments to specific middlemen for specific equipment allowed Yonemura to match the money with bank records obtained from Libya and a handful of financial institutions that were cooperating quietly with the IAEA. Yonemura carried an electronic organizer in which she kept a record of the transactions, which by now involved tens of millions of dollars bouncing from one secrecy haven to another, from Switzerland to Liechtenstein, from Dubai to Macao, from Hong Kong to Singapore. In one instance, she tracked a payment of three million euros through a bank account in Dubai in Tahir's name to a second bank in Switzerland, where it was divvied up and transferred to three separate accounts. But the well was about to run dry.

A fourth meeting in September on the Austrian-Liechtenstein border, not far from the Tinners' home, was testy, with Friedrich Tinner growing angry and trying to justify his decades-long business dealings with A. Q. Khan and with Libya. In a telling rationalization that demonstrated the psychological distance Tinner had erected between his conscience and his business, he shouted at Heinonen and Yonemura: "Just because someone makes a pistol, it doesn't mean he is a murderer. Just because we help build centrifuges, it doesn't mean we are making a bomb." Yonemura, who had left Japan's civilian nuclear industry to join the IAEA out of a conviction that nuclear weapons should never again be used, was horrified by the comment.

The Tinners were frustrated. Neither the Americans nor the IAEA had provided assurances that they could be protected from law enforcement. The Germans were investigating Urs as an accomplice in the network, and the Swiss were looking into the transfers to Libya, too. A few weeks later, in early October, Urs Tinner crossed into Germany, for unknown reasons and in violation of Mad Dog's warnings. His passport was flagged at the border, and he was arrested on charges of sending nuclear technology to Libya. Friedrich telephoned Heinonen, angrily accusing him of providing confidential information to the German authorities. Heinonen protested that he had kept everything within the confines of the IAEA, but Friedrich was unappeased. It proved to be their last conversation.

The setback meant that the most likely sources for identifying a missing customer and filling in the blanks were Khan and Tahir. Efforts to question the Pakistani scientist had remained at a standstill, the mastermind incommunicado in Islamabad. Near the end of 2004, the Pakistanis hinted at a compromise, telling Heinonen that he might be allowed to send written questions to the scientist. Heinonen and his team began preparing their questions, coming up with fifty-two detailed queries—and a prayer.

The Bush administration refused to pressure Pakistan to give the CIA or IAEA access to Khan, as it was more concerned about maintaining its alliance with Musharraf than getting to the bottom of the network. The lack of insistence was surprising because Bush seemed to believe that the threat of nuclear terrorism was real. In a presidential-campaign debate on September 30, 2004, the two candidates, Senator John Kerry and President Bush, were asked what they regarded as the top national-security danger facing the United States. The answers produced a rare moment of agreement: Kerry responded "nuclear proliferation" and repeated the words for emphasis; Bush said, "I agree with my opponent that the biggest threat facing this country is weapons of mass destruction in the hands of a terrorist network."

Bush's reelection did not bring access to Khan. But in February 2005 the Malaysian government notified the IAEA that a delegation from the agency would be allowed to interview Tahir. The following day, the team flew to Kuala Lumpur. The plan was to use this first meeting to get to know Tahir and convince him that it was in his interest to cooperate, so when the Malaysian secret police insisted that the interview take place at police headquarters, Heinonen was concerned. His worries deepened when the police who brought Tahir to the station from the remote prison where he was being held insisted on sitting in.

"Does it disturb you that the police are here?" Heinonen asked Tahir.

"Don't worry about it," he said. "It's okay."

Heinonen assumed the room was bugged anyway, so he didn't make an issue of it. He and others questioned Tahir gently about his background and how he came to be involved with Khan. Tahir did not appear to be evasive, though he was not particularly forthcoming either. He said he had tried unsuccessfully to get out of the ring on several occasions but that Khan had always brought him back in. Over several hours, Tahir began to open up, providing intriguing glimpses inside the ring, describing his friendship with Khan and the jealousies and rivalries within the network. Tahir said that Khan had grown increasingly religious during the years they had worked together; twice, he said, he had accompanied Khan to Mecca, the religious journey required by the Koran as the ultimate act of worship for Muslims. The tidbits were tantalizing, many corroborating information from the Tinners and others. Yet it was clear that there was far more to learn from Tahir. At the end of the session, Yonemura handed her digital camera to one of the policemen and asked him to take a picture of the group, promising to deliver a print to Tahir when they returned. But there was to be no next time. Twice, the IAEA officials made arrangements to see Tahir again, and each time the Malaysians canceled at the last minute, saying only that the timing wasn't right.

Come the summer of 2005, the investigation continued, but the headlines were gone and so was the pressure from the international community to get to the bottom of the Khan network. The war in Iraq was dragging on, all hope of an early American victory dashed by the growing insurgency. The way was cleared for ElBaradei to receive a third term as director general. Khan remained in protective custody in his home, suffering from high blood pressure, a hernia, and heart problems. The clamor for his release and rehabilitation had long ago subsided, though outside agencies were still prohibited from interviewing him. Urs Tinner had been extradited to Switzerland in the spring, and not long after Swiss authorities arrested his father and brother, too. In response to requests from the IAEA and published reports, the Swiss had determined that it was time to get tougher. Months later, Swiss investigators examining the role of the Tinners in the smuggling network complained that they were being hampered by a lack of cooperation from the United States. Wisser continued to await trial in South Africa.

In June, Pierre Goldschmidt retired as deputy director general in charge of the safeguards department, the agency's second-ranking position, and he was replaced by Olli Heinonen. The investigation of the network was incomplete, and Heinonen vowed to see it to the end despite the heavy new workload. His biggest headache was no longer the network, however, but the looming standoff with Iran. The United States argued that Iran continued to stonewall the IAEA and hide key elements of its nuclear program. Joined by Britain, France, and Germany in varying degrees, Washington was pushing the IAEA to send the Iranian file to the UN Security Council for possible sanctions. ElBaradei remained reluctant, fearing it could put the world on the road to war with Iran as it had with Iraq. So he argued for more time to complete inspections. To impartial observers, ElBaradei had more credibility on the subject than the Bush administration, which had finally given up on finding any evidence of a nuclear program in Iraq. "You need to be patient," ElBaradei told one interviewer.

On October 7, the IAEA director general's strategy got an enormous vote of confidence. The Norwegian Nobel Committee announced that the 2005 Nobel Peace Prize was being shared by the International Atomic Energy Agency and its director general "for their efforts to prevent nuclear energy from being used for military purposes and to ensure that nuclear energy for peaceful purposes is used in the safest possible way." The champagne corks popped in the offices of the IAEA in Vienna. An emotional ElBaradei told journalists gathered outside his office that he regarded the honor as a mandate for himself and the agency. "The award sends a very strong message: 'Keep doing what you are doing,'" he said. "We continue to believe that in all of our activities, we have to be impartial, objective, and work with integrity. Overall, my colleagues and I will go to sleep tonight with a good feeling of satisfaction that finally our effort has been fully recognized."

Heinonen celebrated with the others, but he wasn't so sure that he would sleep any better. Even with its enhanced investigative capacity and the authority that came with the world's most prestigious prize, he was far from certain that the IAEA could find the next hidden weapons program. The investigation of Khan's network had slowed, leaving Heinonen and the others doubtful that they would ever identify its other customer, if there was one. He estimated that the investigation had uncovered 75 to 80 percent of Khan's network, but frightening gaps remained. No trace had been found of the electronic warhead plans or the missing equipment.

One day in the spring of 2006, Heinonen gazed out the window at the Danube and the cityscape of Vienna. He refused to admit the obvious—that his investigation of the network was finished, overtaken by new chapters in the story of the new age of proliferation. He recognized that the IAEA still didn't have all the powers necessary to stop the spread of nuclear weapons, particularly at a time when the technology was so widely available. He was proud of the agency's performance in unraveling much of Khan's operation and focusing attention on the dangers of proliferation, but he recognized that dangers still existed.

"Even though A. Q. Khan doesn't operate, the information is still out there," he explained with a shrug. "Until we find out who got this information and technology, we cannot rest. In the past, these sorts of people have responded to difficult times by shifting the way they operate. They go where it's easy. As long as there are clients, they will have work. But we don't want to go down in history as the guys who didn't ring the bell."

IN LATE 2006, word came from Pakistan that Khan had undergone surgery for prostate cancer at the Aga Khan Hospital in Karachi. His wife and two daughters were at his side, and the room was filled with flowers and cards from well-wishers across Pakistan, who still considered him a national hero although the legacy Khan had left the rest of world was far from heroic. He had changed the global nuclear landscape in ways that would live on long after his death, ushering in a new age of proliferation by demonstrating how the old restraints had frayed.

In late October, Mohamed ElBaradei disclosed that Iran had started testing new uranium-enrichment equipment that could double the capacity of its pilot plant at Natanz, putting the country a step farther down the road toward developing fissile material. Tehran had ignored an August 31 deadline imposed by the UN Security Council to stop enriching uranium, but the group's fractious members still could not agree on whether economic sanctions were warranted as punishment.

The Iranian defiance led to new threats from the Bush administration. The Americans had determined for themselves that Iran was pursuing a nuclear weapon, though they estimated Tehran was four to ten years away. Nonetheless, articles in the American press described renewed contingency planning by the American military for attacks to knock out Iran's nuclear installations and warned that some within the administration considered war inevitable. "We'll turn Iran into a glass-covered parking lot," warned a retired army colonel. The war drums worried ElBaradei, who said there was no hard evidence that Iran was pursuing a bomb. "People confuse knowledge, industrial capacity, and intention," he said. "A lot of what you see about Iran right now is assessment of intentions."

Iran was not the only problem. At 10:36 on the morning of October 9, the North Koreans announced that they had successfully tested a nuclear device. American intelligence agencies quickly determined that the small device was based on plutonium extracted from its reactor at Yongbyon, but they cautioned that the North Koreans appeared to be preparing for a second test based on a uranium-fueled bomb developed from enrichment equipment and expertise from Khan. Reaction from Washington was swift and furious, with Bush calling the test provocative and threatening to hold North Korea "fully accountable" if its leader, Kim Jong Il, tried to sell bombs as freely as he had sold missiles. The United Nations responded by slapping sanctions on North Korea, though China and Russia watered down their scope. The Bush administration interpreted the sanctions as a warning to Iranians that they should stop their enrichment activities, but Iran's hard-liners had a far different reaction to what was essentially a weak response by the international community to a momentous event. "They must be laughing," Susan Rice, a member of the National Security Council in the Clinton administration, said of the Iranians. "You can explode a nuclear weapon and only get slapped on the wrist."

North Korea's nuclear test and Iran's continuing defiance reverberated beyond their own borders and increased the likelihood that other countries might seek parity through their own nuclear weapons. Among the likely suspects were at least three countries in Asia—Japan, South Korea, and Taiwan—and four in the greater Middle East: Saudi Arabia, Egypt, Syria, and Turkey. A week after the North Korean test, ElBaradei took up the threat in an address to a conference on proliferation controls at IAEA headquarters. The mood was somber, and many experts from the IAEA and other countries feared a new worldwide arms race. ElBaradei offered little comfort, warning that as many as thirty additional countries could soon have the technology to produce nuclear weapons in a very short time. Some countries, he said, were already far enough along that they should be regarded as "virtual nuclear weapons states." The IAEA boss did not single out any countries, preferring to issue a general warning. "The knowledge is out," he told the audience, "both for peaceful purpose and unfortunately for not peaceful purposes."

EPILOGUE

O N JANUARY 17, 2007, in an elegant nineteenth-century ballroom overlooking St. James's Park in London and in a hushed auditorium a few blocks from the White House in Washington, the world inched closer to Armageddon. In simultaneous events at the Royal Society and the American Association for the Advancement of Science, the minute hand on the Doomsday Clock, created sixty years earlier by *The Bulletin of the Atomic Scientists,* was pushed two minutes closer to midnight, the symbolic end of civilization.

At the Royal Society's headquarters on the Mall, cosmologist and mathematician Stephen Hawking spoke of the danger through a computer attached to his wheelchair. "Since Hiroshima and Nagasaki, no nuclear weapons have been used in war, though the world has come uncomfortably close to disaster on more than one occasion," he said. "But for good luck, we would all be dead."

The clock was created in 1947 as a means of reflecting the continuous danger of living in a nuclear age; at the start of the Cold War, the minute hand was set at seven minutes to midnight, and over the years it has moved backward and forward as world threats ebbed and flowed. The decision to move the clock to five minutes to midnight on January 17 was made by the board of directors of *The Bulletin of the Atomic Scientists* after consulting eighteen Nobel Laureates and a host of other luminaries. The board said the judgment reflected growing dangers from the spread of nuclear weapons and the potential for catastrophic harm from global warming. The danger of apocalypse is closer now than at any time since Hiroshima and Nagasaki.

A. Q. Khan was not on the list of reasons for the rising threat level, but two of his customers were. The North Korean test had occurred just a few weeks earlier. Experts decided that the underground explosion was relatively small, and might have been a dud, but for all intents and purposes a ninth country had joined the new generation of nuclear states. North Korea's entry into the nuclear elite mattered most as what writer Steve Coll calls "a symbol of accumulating trouble." The test was all the more ominous because the communist dictatorship has never developed a weapon that it did not offer up for sale.

The Americans and their allies appeared equally impotent when trying to deal with the likely next member of the nuclear club, Iran. Despite the threat of economic sanctions and saber rattling by President Bush and his right hand, Dick Cheney, the Iranians defiantly pushed ahead with the completion of the huge underground centrifuge plant at Natanz, preparing to install tens of thousands of the machines based on drawings and equipment from Khan and his network. Given the savage devastation occurring next door in Iraq, which had no nuclear weapon, it was hard to fault Iran's revolutionary leaders for wanting some deterrence against an attack by the United States. Indeed, short of sustained military strikes on dozens of nuclear facilities inside Iran, there appears to be no way to stop Iran from developing its own bomb, particularly given the Bush administration's contempt for diplomacy.

Another of Khan's clients, Libya, had relinquished its nuclear ambitions in an attempt to rehabilitate its outlaw reputation and rejoin the international community. But its leader, Moammar Gadhafi, was growing restive at the slow pace of his country's reintegration into the world economic order. Some experts worried that he might rekindle his plans, possibly with equipment and designs hidden from the American and British intelligence agents.

Then, there was the threat of the mysterious fourth customer of the

Khan network, rumored to be Saudi Arabia, Syria, Egypt, or Al Qaeda. Three years after the network was shut down, the fact that critical equipment from its inventory had still not surfaced offered no solace to the officials at the IAEA. Among the missing items were electronic copies of the Chinese nuclear warhead. Iran had already demonstrated how easy it was to conceal a nuclear program, having hidden its dealings with Khan for fifteen years.

Khan played a central role in ushering in the second nuclear age, an era in which the monopoly on atomic weapons maintained by five major powers was threatened by a new type of proliferation. In this new age, history's most lethal weapon became available to less developed countries and possibly to well-funded terrorist organizations. One of the most disturbing aspects of Khan's successful operation was how clearly it demonstrated the failure of the nuclear-proliferation regime. From his days working in Amsterdam until his downfall, Khan exploited weak export controls and lax enforcement. His network relied not on state-to-state transfers of technology but on the easy availability of nuclear-related equipment and material on the gray market, as governments and industries promoted high-tech exports. Globalization and the Internet offered even easier and faster methods of distributing sensitive information and technology.

The spread of nuclear know-how and related technology has gone far beyond the traditional weapons states and outstripped their capacity to control it. In 2005, Britain's MI5 revealed that more than 360 businesses and individuals worldwide were suspected of playing a role in the development of chemical, biological, and nuclear weapons. MI5 said these entities and people were concentrated in the developing countries of the Middle East and South Asia.

Recent history offers little reason for optimism that this proliferation can be contained. President Kennedy's dire prediction in 1963 that there would be twenty countries with nuclear weapons by 1975 did not come true. But the Nuclear Non-Proliferation Treaty of 1968, which helped hold down the number, is in danger of falling apart because of defiance by North Korea and Iran and the threat of new entrants in the atomic sweepstakes. The biggest danger lies in the domino effect: North Korea and Iran are likely to be followed by Japan, South Korea, Saudi Arabia, and Egypt. Unlike some of those countries, Japan is a highly industrialized country with the nuclear and military infrastructure in place to flip the switch and go from zero to nuclear in almost an instant, which could trigger a wider arms race. What will Washington do if an ally like Japan or oil-rich Saudi Arabia decides to go nuclear? Probably nothing.

The challenge of proliferation control lies not in the lack of proven techniques but in the absence of moral suasion and sustained diplomacy by the world's leaders. The American government subsidized the spread of nuclear knowledge through the Atoms for Peace program to counter Soviet influence, and at virtually every critical juncture since then successive administrations have set aside long-term proliferation goals in favor of short-term strategic priorities. Jimmy Carter did it in 1979 when he abandoned sanctions on Pakistan in exchange for help fighting the Soviets in Afghanistan; Ronald Reagan continued the policy throughout the eighties; George W. Bush sacrificed the opportunity to uproot Khan's network to maintain the support of the Musharraf regime in the fight against Al Qaeda. As a result, independent nodes of Khan's network went to ground and have since reinvented themselves to proliferate another day. In each case, the more immediate U.S. goals seem worthy—until the day comes that a nuclear weapon is detonated in a major city and incinerates tens of thousands of people.

The logical question is, What steps are required to restrain the ambitions of the nuclear aspirants? Several are readily identifiable, though not so easily adopted:

The first order of business is restricting the supply of highly enriched uranium. A moratorium should be imposed on new enrichment plants, coupled with additional layers of international inspection on existing plants to lessen the chances of diversion. Countries that agree to forgo enriching uranium for their civilian reactors should be guaranteed access to internationally regulated supplies of the fuel. Mohamed ElBaradei has proposed this approach, but developing countries object to curtailing rights to enrichment created under the nonproliferation treaty. To further restrict access to bomb material, the dozens of research reactors worldwide that use highly enriched uranium should be replaced with versions relying on the less dangerous low-enriched uranium.

The nonproliferation treaty, which remains the world's primary arms-control regime, is battered and in desperate need of reform. A critical change is closing a gaping loophole that allows a country to acquire nuclear-weapons capabilities and then withdraw from the treaty without penalty, as North Korea did and as many expect Iran to do. A group of twenty-three nuclear experts at Stanford University's Center for International Security and Cooperation proposed that the UN Security Council establish sanctions to impose on any country that withdraws from the treaty and tries to build weapons using fissile material and facilities obtained for supposedly peaceful purposes.

Reforms must go beyond taking from the have-nots. When the treaty was drawn up, the vast majority of the countries agreed to forgo nuclear weapons on condition that the five existing nuclear powers eventually reduce their arsenals. While the Russians and Americans made substantial progress in the years after the end of the Cold War, they have not gone far enough—and they still possess twenty-six thousand nuclear weapons between them. More troubling, the Americans are threatening to reverse the trend. The Bush administration initiated research into a new type of tactical nuclear weapons, called "bunker busters," and began designing the nation's first new nuclear weapon in two decades. In 2002, the administration released its "Nuclear Posture Review," which recommended a continued reliance on nuclear weapons to "achieve strategic and political objectives" and advocated using them to "dissuade adversaries from undertaking military programs or operations that could threaten U.S. interests or those of allies and friends."

The Bush nuclear doctrine undermines its arguments that others should give up or not acquire nuclear weapons. The next American president needs to make a commitment to further reductions in the arsenal and abandon the development of new weapons and the strategy of using them for tactical warfare. Other nuclear powers must restrain themselves, too, pulling back from what author Jonathan Schell calls a "nuclear renaissance" in which China, India, Pakistan, North Korea, and Britain are increasing their arsenals or improving their delivery systems—or both.

If the United States is to reduce the threat of a nuclear attack in the coming years, the next president must do a far better job of balancing long-range proliferation concerns with short-term strategic goals. This will require enforcing restrictions on sales of nuclear technology to allies as well as adversaries, and recognizing that the dangers of nuclear annihilation far outweigh the benefits of coddling nuclear aspirants even if they appear to be friends. Containment is more challenging today than it was during the Cold War or before September 11; it is also more important to the security of Americans and the rest of the world. Along with taking challenging unilateral steps, the United States must recognize the gravity of the nuclear threat by assuming a leadership role in strengthening existing international treaties and developing new methods and eschewing the inflammatory rhetoric of unilateralism.

The IAEA is the best hope for enforcing new treaties, but the agency requires more cooperation from its member states and the ratification of new power in order to carry out its mission of safeguarding nuclear facilities and uncovering hidden sites. An important step in expanding its reach is embodied in the Additional Protocol, but since its passage in 1995 only 112 countries have signed the agreement, and eighty-one of them have ratified it. Among the countries that have not yet signed are several with substantial nuclear activities, including Argentina, Brazil, and Egypt.

As the Khan network proved, nuclear proliferation is the result of dedicated clandestine programs that are not always related to existing civilian nuclear programs and diversion from power plants. Enforcing a tougher nonproliferation treaty will not go far enough. Stopping the spread of atomic weapons in the new nuclear age also depends on close monitoring of the nuclear industry and strengthened international cooperation through full transparency with regard to sales of nuclear-related technology and improved intelligence sharing.

These are steps that offer the promise of slowing global proliferation, though few believe that it can be stopped without more radical action, such as the abolition of all nuclear weapons. The idea is not as far-fetched as it sounds: The vast majority of countries in the UN General Assembly have voted regularly to get rid of all nuclear weapons, and two thirds of Americans responding to a public-opinion poll in 2006 agreed with the statement "no country should be allowed to have nuclear weapons"; the favorable response was even higher in other countries.

LEONARD WEISS, who has spent thirty years working on counterproliferation, advocates going a dramatic step farther, arguing that abolishing nuclear power is the only certain way to avoid Armageddon. As long as nuclear power plants exist, he reasons, so will the opportunity to divert fissile material to weapons. Since retiring from Senator Glenn's staff in 1999, Weiss has worked as a consultant to Lawrence Livermore National Laboratory and written extensively about nonproliferation policy. After Khan was exposed, Weiss wrote passionately about the United States turning a blind eye to Pakistan's nuclear development and bemoaned the absence of a consistent proliferation policy, just as he had during his days as a Senate staffer.

"Instead of following a single standard for everyone, we made distinctions between countries, between our friends and our enemies," he said one day in the spring of 2007 as he sat in a small apartment at the edge of the Stanford University campus, where he is a fellow at the Center for International Security and Cooperation. "When you get down to fundamentals—things like nuclear weapons—you must treat your friends and enemies the same. Only then can you have a nonproliferation policy."

Richard Barlow has had little time to relish Khan's downfall and finds no satisfaction in being proved right. Instead, he remains obsessed with winning the pension he was denied after his dismissal from the Pentagon. His efforts have been hampered because there are few protections against retaliation for intelligence officers and other national security staffers who reveal wrongdoing. He lives with two dogs in a motor home and works sporadically as a fishing and hunting guide in New Mexico and Montana. "The government viciously tried to destroy my life, personally and professionally," he said forcefully one night over dinner in Los Angeles. "Not just my career, but they went after my marriage, my livelihood, and smeared my name in truly extraordinary ways that no one has ever seen before or since, at least until Joe and Valerie Wilson were victims of the same people." Valerie Wilson was a covert CIA agent whose cover was exposed after her husband criticized claims by the Bush administration that Saddam Hussein had sought uranium in Niger, one of the justifications for the war in Iraq. I. Lewis "Scooter" Libby, Vice President Cheney's former chief of staff, was sentenced to thirty months in prison for lying to federal investigators looking into the leak of Wilson's identity as a CIA agent.

In Islamabad, Abdul Qadeer Khan remains a figure of adulation in some circles, despite his confession to peddling his country's dearest secrets. Officially, he remains under tight house arrest, with visitors restricted and his compound under constant military guard. But when he was hospitalized in the summer of 2006 with heart problems and high blood pressure, Prime Minister Shaukat Aziz sent flowers, and prayers for his recovery were recited across the country. About the same time, the Pakistani Senate passed a resolution opposing American requests to interrogate Khan as interference in the country's internal affairs. By the middle of 2007, Pakistani authorities were easing the restrictions on Khan, allowing the scientist to have visitors at home and make brief excursions outside. Despite the American aid flowing into Pakistan at the rate of $1 billion a year, Khan remained outside the reach of interrogators from the United States or the IAEA.

Others sought to rewrite Pakistan's nuclear history, downplaying the disgraced scientist's role. In May 2006, *Defence Journal*, a publication controlled by the Pakistani military, devoted thirty-six pages to relegating Khan to the dustbins of the country's golden nuclear era, replacing him on the pedestal with his old rival, Munir Khan. That fall, Musharraf published his memoir, *In the Line of Fire*, in which he described the discovery of Khan's proliferation network as one of "the most serious and sad crises" he had ever faced. As for the scientist, Musharraf wrote: "The truth is that he was just a metallurgist, responsible for only one link in the complex chain of nuclear development. But he had managed to build himself up into Albert Einstein and J. Robert Oppenheimer rolled into one."

For a simple metallurgist, Khan wreaked enormous damage and played a critical role in ushering in the second age of proliferation. His ego and his nationalism, his skill at subterfuge, and his religious fervor all combined to push the Doomsday Clock a little closer to midnight.

ACKNOWLEDGMENTS

THE CREDIT for this book belongs to our sources, the scores of people who provided us with insights into the complexities and nuances of nuclear proliferation, espionage, and geopolitics. Many of them sat for multiple interviews over the course of many months, sharing their knowledge and trusting us to convey it as accurately and fairly as possible. Some of them are named in the endnotes, but others must necessarily remain anonymous. We are sincerely grateful to all of them for their help, and we accept all responsibility for any errors or omissions in compiling this book.

More than any others, the staff at the International Atomic Energy Agency in Vienna was instrumental in bringing this book to life. They guided us through their arcane world with unflagging commitment to the truth and with patience and good humor. We cannot name all of those who assisted us, but special thanks go to members of the communications staff—Mark Gwozdecky, Melissa Fleming, Peter Rickwood, and Elizabeth Dobie-Sarsam—and members of the safeguards division—Olli Heinonen, Pierre Goldschmidt, and Miharu Yonemura—as well as Jacques Baute, Terry Dunn, and Tariq Rauf.

Many excellent journalists came to this subject before us, and many competed with us over the last five years. We could not have written this without relying on their contributions to the body of knowledge about nuclear proliferation and A. Q. Khan. Seymour Hersh of *The New Yorker* broke major stories about this topic, from the early 1990s until the present. David Sanger and William Broad of *The New York Times* and Dafna Linzer of *The Washington Post* were dogged in their coverage of the Khan network and the IAEA. Louis Charbonneau from Reuters was the best beat reporter at the IAEA, perhaps ever, and a good friend, too. Steve Coll wrote extensively and thoughtfully about this topic at *The Washington Post* and most recently at *The New Yorker;* his marvelous book *Ghost Wars* provided innumerable insights into the CIA and its relationship with Pakistan during the Soviet occupation of Afghanistan. At the *Los Angeles Times,* we were assisted by Josh Meyer, a persistent and knowledgeable reporter, Bill Rempel, a trusted colleague, and former Johannesburg researcher Salma Patel. In 2003, then managing editor Dean Baquet and Marjorie Miller, the foreign editor, helped launch the reporting that led to this book. In Switzerland, Bruno Vanoni of Tages Anzeiger proved an able guide to the complexities of the export bureaucracy.

Len Weiss devoted hours to explaining the history of U.S. proliferation policy and correcting our misunderstandings about all things nuclear. We are grateful for the friendship of Len and his wife, Sandy. Richard Barlow was always available to answer any question, and he illuminated the mistakes of the Pentagon and CIA for us.

Among the many denizens of the world's think tanks and policy institutes, a handful was particularly instructive and always helpful. George Perkovich at the Carnegie Endowment for International Peace in Washington, D.C., offered excellent insights on American policy in South Asia. David Albright, president of the Institute for Science and International Security in Washington, has written extensively and provocatively about this subject for many years. Jeffrey T. Richelson, author and senior fellow at the National Security Archive in Washington, shared his knowledge and some key documents. Avner Cohen of the Center for International Security Studies at the University of Maryland knows more about Israel's nuclear-weapons program than any person willing to talk about it, and we benefited from his generosity. Frank Slijper and his colleagues at the

Dutch Campaign Against the Arms Trade prepared an extensive history of Khan's activities in the Netherlands for Greenpeace International.

Our understanding of Pakistan, however flawed it may be, was enhanced enormously by the help of our friend Stuart Hughes and his diplomatic colleague, Aized Ali. Husain Haqqani, a journalist and professor at Boston University, graciously shared his extensive knowledge of his homeland. Hassan Abbas of Harvard University's Belfer Center for Science and International Affairs proved a formidable guide to the intricacies of Pakistani bureaucracy and law enforcement. Pervez Hoodbhoy, professor of nuclear physics at Quaid-i-Azam University, is simply one of the most honest and brave people we know, and we are honored to have spent time with him. Numerous Pakistani journalists and former government officials, who for their own safety cannot be named, spent hours schooling us.

The concept of Twelve Books is brilliant, and so was our editor there, Jonathan Karp. Sometimes we thought he understood the subject better than we did, which was always comforting. We are also indebted to Nate Gray, the editorial assistant at Twelve, and Cary Goldstein, publicist extraordinaire. Our agent, Kathy Robbins, fought for our book at every step, and we cannot thank her enough. Thanks, too, to her tireless assistant, Coralie Hunter.

And finally, a special thanks to friends and family who listened over and over again to the refrain, "This week we are going to finish the book." With their help and understanding, we finally did.

NOTES

The following is a guide to the main sources of information in the book. For complete end notes, with detailed references to source material and links to original documents, please refer to our Web site, www.thenuclearjihadist .com.

The primary source of factual material was hundreds of hours of interviews with people who had firsthand knowledge of the subject matter. In many cases, more than one participant in an event was interviewed; some people were interviewed multiple times over the course of many months. The interviews were augmented with thousands of pages of public and confidential documents from government agencies and courts around the world, personal notes taken by participants, and reports by the International Atomic Energy Agency.

Many people spoke to us only after being promised confidentiality. The reasons for requesting anonymity varied: Some were not authorized to provide the depth of detail that they shared with us; others feared reprisals by their governments or employers. We have respected these requests and endeavored to corroborate as much information as possible from other sources to provide the fullest and most complete picture possible.

The book was written in a narrative style that places readers as close as possible to major events. As a result, occasionally it was necessary to reconstruct conversations in order not to interrupt the narrative flow for attribution. Many of these reconstructions are from official transcripts and post-conversation summaries prepared by participants; in other instances, the information was provided later by one or more participants. In some cases, the authors' notes examine discrepancies between versions of events.

PROLOGUE

The encounter between Olli Heinonen and the CIA agent in Vienna came from multiple interviews with senior officials at the International Atomic Energy Agency and the Central Intelligence Agency. Information about the "Dragonfire" incident in October 2001 came chiefly from Graham Allison's excellent book *Nuclear Terrorism: The Ultimate Preventable Catastrophe* (New York: Times Books/Henry Holt and Company, 2004), and Massimo Calabresi and Romesh Ratnesar, "Can We Stop the Next Attack?" *Time*, March 11, 2002. The impact of a nuclear detonation on an American city was compiled from interviews with Allison and his Harvard colleague Matthew Bunn, and Gary Milhollin, director of the Wisconsin Project on Nuclear Arms Control, as well as various Web sites.

The Dutch decision not to arrest A. Q. Khan in 1975, with the knowledge of the CIA, was described in detail in an interview by Ruud Lubbers, the former Dutch prime minister, who was involved in the incident. It was first mentioned in an article by William J. Broad and David E. Sanger, "Unraveling Pakistan's Nuclear Web," *New York Times*, December 27, 2004.

CHAPTER 1. THE SMILING MAN

Details of Khan's arrival at the Physics Dynamic Research Laboratory in 1972 and many other events during his time there came from several interviews with Frits Veerman and from a privately published manuscript by Veerman and Jacques Ros, "Atomic Espionage" (Amsterdam: Centerboek Weesp, 1988). Additional details about Khan's early years in India and Pakistan came from the authorized biography of Khan by Zahid Malik, *Dr. A. Q. Khan and the Islamic Bomb* (Islamabad: Hurmat Publications, 1992), and from various speeches and articles by Khan over the years.

General information about the birth and history of Pakistan came from a trio of fine books: Stephen Philip Cohen, *The Idea of Pakistan* (Washington: Brookings Institution Press, 2004); Husain Haqqani, *Pakistan: Between Mosque and Military* (Washington: Carnegie Endowment for International

Peace, 2005); and Hassan Abbas, *Pakistan's Drift into Extremism: Allah, the Army, and America's War on Terror* (New York: M.E. Sharpe, 2005).

CHAPTER 2. AN ACCIDENTAL OPPORTUNITY

President Dwight D. Eisenhower's "Atoms for Peace" program was described by Leonard Weiss, "Atoms for Peace," *The Bulletin of the Atomic Scientists*, November–December 2003; and Allan M. Winkler, *Life Under a Cloud: American Anxiety About the Atom* (Urbana and Chicago: University of Illinois Press, 1999). Ronald I. Spiers recounted the proposal that led to the creation of the IAEA in an interview.

Reports by the CIA and other American intelligence agencies about early proliferation threats were recounted by Steve Weissman and Herbert Krosney in *The Islamic Bomb: The Nuclear Threat to Israel and the Middle East* (New York: Times Books, 1981). Both authoritative and prophetic, the book describes the origins of Pakistan's nuclear ambitions and the roles played by the French and other nations in supplying equipment to the fledgling program.

Khan's wife has spoken little in public about her husband's work and their life. Much of the information here comes from the transcript of an interview she gave May 17, 1986, to *Hurmat*, a weekly newspaper in Islamabad. In addition, several friends and associates of the Khan family provided insights into their domestic life. Henk Slebos was interviewed outside a Dutch courtroom where he was awaiting trial on charges related to nuclear exports to Pakistan.

Martin Brabers's recollections of Khan's student days and many details about conditions at Urenco are contained in a report commissioned by Greenpeace International and written by Joop Boer, Henk van der Keur, Karel Koster and Frank Slijper "A. Q. Khan, Urenco and the proliferation of nuclear weapons technology: The symbiotic relation between nuclear energy and nuclear weapons," (May 2004). Security regulations at Urenco were described in two reports by the Dutch government, one a study made public in 1979 and the other a classified version completed in 1982.

CHAPTER 3. THE MUSLIM ALLIANCE

Zulfikar Ali Bhutto's rallying speech at Multan was described by Weissman and Krosney in *The Islamic Bomb*. Additional details were provided in an interview with Khaled Hasan, who attended the meeting as Bhutto's press secretary and now lives outside Washington. Hasan also provided information about Bhutto's campaign to raise money for the nuclear program from Colonel Moammar Gadhafi of Libya and other Muslim leaders; in addition, Weissman and Krosney described the arrival in Pakistan of couriers with suitcases of cash in *The Islamic Bomb*, as well as in a BBC-TV Panorama program broadcast June 16, 1980.

The Indian nuclear detonations in May 1974 and the history of the country's nuclear program were described in penetrating detail by George Perkovich in his book *India's Nuclear Bomb: The Impact on Global Proliferation* (Berkeley: University of California Press, 1999) and in *The Islamic Bomb*. Henry Kissinger's response to the Indian nuclear explosion was portrayed by Dennis Kux in his book *The United States and Pakistan, 1947–2000: Disenchanted Allies* (Washington: Woodrow Wilson Center Press, 2001).

Robert Gallucci provided a rundown on what the United States knew about Pakistan in the wake of the Indian tests in interviews. His recollections were augmented by declassified reports from the State Department and the Arms Control and Disarmament Agency, many of which are available through the National Security Archive at George Washington University (www.gwu.edu/~nsarchiv/).

CHAPTER 4. GOING HOME

FDO officials refused to discuss anything related to Khan's employment there, but details of his work at FDO and in the "brain box" at Almelo came from the later Dutch government reports, the Veerman interviews, and the Malik biography. Malik described Khan's encounter with the two Pakistani scientists at FDO and his later attempts to join the Pakistani nuclear program. Khaled Hasan fleshed out details of Khan's courtship of Bhutto in his interview. Ria Hollabrands talked about Khan's domestic life in Zwanenburg in an interview outside her home there. Bhutto's skepticism was relayed by Hasan and by another former aide to the Pakistani leader who asked not to be identified. The same sources described the arrangements that turned Khan into a spy.

CHAPTER 5. THE PAKISTANI PIPELINE

Siddique Butt's role in the Pakistani pipeline was described in numerous sources, most extensively in *The Islamic Bomb* by Weissman and Krosney, the

Greenpeace International report, and interviews with former American intelligence officials. The episode involving the ultra-thin foil, which led to the initial suspicions about Khan, is contained in confidential IAEA documents provided to us and amplified in interviews with IAEA officials. The failure of the Americans to grasp the threat posed by Pakistan's acquisition of nuclear-related technology originated in interviews with numerous former American diplomats and intelligence officials, most of whom were granted anonymity. The British technician's discovery of the extra-specialized lathe at Rochling, the German company, is contained in confidential IAEA documents.

Ruud Lubbers discussed the surveillance of Khan by Dutch security officials in an interview, which was augmented by an interview with a former BVD officer involved in the investigation, who spoke on condition of anonymity; and by a former senior CIA official, who also was granted anonymity. The outlines of the surveillance were also recounted by Broad and Sanger in "Unraveling Pakistan's Nuclear Web." Robert Einhorn called the decision to let Khan proceed a monumental error in an interview with us.

CHAPTER 6. DOUBLE STANDARDS

Information about Leonard Weiss came primarily from several interviews with him over the course of three years. Principle sources of information about Cheney, including his codename "Backseat," were James Mann, *Rise of the Vulcans* (New York: Penguin Books, 2004), and Joan Didion, "Cheney: The Fatal Touch," *New York Review of Books*, October 5, 2006. Information about the Ford administration's plans to sell nuclear technology to Iran was described in a series of declassified memos from administration archives; Dafna Linzer, "Past Arguments Don't Square With Current Iran Policy," *Washington Post*, March 27, 2005; "Iran's upheaval derails a dynamic economy," *Business Week*, November 27, 1978; and Henry Sokolski, "The Washington Post Bombs Nuclear History: Did Dick Cheney, Donald Rumsfeld, and Paul Wolfowitz Try to Stoke Iran's Nuclear Ambition in the '70s?" *Weekly Standard*, March 30, 2005. Kissinger's quote about proliferation not coming up in discussions about Iran is from Linzer's article. Tony Benn's complaints about the American attitude toward Iran were from an article he wrote, "Atomic Hypocrisy: Neither Bush nor Blair is in a position to take a high moral line on Iran's nuclear programme," *Guardian*, November 30, 2005.

The description of Israel's nuclear weapons program was based on Avner

Cohen, *Israel and the Bomb* (New York: Columbia University Press, 1998), files from the National Security Archives, and author interviews with former Israeli nuclear officials. The exchange involving Kissinger and Reginald Bartholomew on the Symington amendment and Pakistan's nuclear program, along with the warning from the shah about Bhutto's nuclear intentions, came from a declassified Memorandum of Conversation, State Department, May 12, 1976.

CHAPTER 7. THE ROAD TO KAHUTA

Khan's early days in Pakistan after his flight from Amsterdam and his rivalry with Munir Khan were described by Malik in his authorized biography and by Khan himself in an article he wrote in volume 21 of *Defence Journal*, a publication of the Pakistani military, titled "The Kahuta Story—Twenty Years of Excellence and National Services." Additional information came from a lecture by Khan on September 9, 1990, to the Pakistani Institute of National Affairs in Lahore. Khan's criticism of Munir Khan to Bhutto came from a former senior Pakistani government official and from Khan's personal recollection of the conversation for his biographer, Malik. Khan's description of beginning the enrichment program as a gigantic task was from his *Defence Journal* article. (After Khan's confession in 2004, the *Defence Journal* article was removed from the publication's Web site. In 2006 *Defence Journal* published a new history of Pakistan's nuclear program, which diminished Khan's role and promoted his late rival, Munir Khan.) Henny's attitude toward life in Pakistan was from the *Humrat* interview.

CHAPTER 8. OPERATION BUTTER FACTORY

Veerman described his correspondence with Khan and provided copies of the letters quoted here. The Dutchman also recounted his dealings with the security police. The Brabers quotes came from the Greenpeace International report, but they are also contained in newspaper and magazine articles.

Information about the contract with CORA came from Weissman and Krosney in *The Islamic Bomb* and Leonard Downie Jr., "US Prepared to Resume Nuclear Cooperation; Swiss, US Set to Resume Nuclear Energy Cooperation," *Washington Post*, December 31, 1980. Slebos described his dealings with Khan in an interview, details also recounted in various newspaper articles, the Greenpeace report, and court files in the Netherlands.

Sonja Haas described her father's relationship with Khan in an interview. Officials with the Swiss government, the IAEA, and the CIA provided additional information about the Tinner-Khan ties. Friedrich Tinner's quotation came from a senior IAEA official to whom it was addressed.

Zia's recollections of his journey from India to the newly formed country of Pakistan were from Steve Coll's Pulitzer-Prize winning book, *Ghost Wars: The Secret History of the CIA, Afghanistan, and bin Laden, from the Soviet Invasion to September 10, 2001* (New York: The Penguin Press, 2004). Coll's mastery of those years is unparalleled, and his book provided essential background material for us.

Khan's advertisements for workers at Kahuta and other recruitment efforts were from the Canadian Broadcasting Corporation's program, *The Fifth Estate,* "Secret Cargo," December 9, 1980, and from private correspondence provided to us between Khan and Abdul Aziz Khan and other Pakistanis living abroad.

CHAPTER 9. ACTIONABLE INTELLIGENCE

The description of the CIA station in Islamabad was provided by Milt Bearden in an interview with us. Information about CIA tactics came from Coll's *Ghost Wars* and other publications. A former senior CIA official told us about the detention of an agency asset by the ISI and described the CIA's knowledge of Khan dating to the middle 1970s. Other former American officials and Lubbers confirmed that Khan was "on the radar" at that time. In addition, declassified United States government memos and reports from the 1960s and 1970s demonstrate early concern about Pakistan's nuclear aspirations; they are available from the National Security Archives.

Weiss told us about his trip to Paris to meet with Bertrand Goldschmidt and his other involvement. Bob Gallucci's quotations came from an interview with us and were corroborated by declassified documents, chiefly a January 22, 1975, memo, "Pakistan and the Non-Proliferation Issue," and a formal complaint sent to Pakistan by the State Department on January 30, 1976. Cyrus Vance's working group and its concerns are embodied in a detailed, 32-page white paper on Pakistan prepared by the State Department on April 25, 1978, later declassified and available through the National Security Archives. Gallucci's comment about the option of assassinating Khan came from an interview. The former government official who said Khan should have been killed made the initial comment on the record, but he later requested anonymity because of his continuing dealings with the Pakistani government.

CHAPTER 10. A NUCLEAR COWSHED

The technical problems experienced by Kahuta were described by Khan in personal correspondence and in various declassified reports by the United States government. The CIA and other intelligence agencies ultimately discounted the chance of Khan's success based on these initial reports of difficulties, which is one of the reasons the agency did not pay enough attention to him.

The transaction involving the inverters from the British subsidiary of Emerson Electric and the comments of Frann Allaun, the British MP, were from Don Oberdorfer, Michael Gatier, and Maralee Schwarts, "Pakistan: The Quest for Atomic Bomb; Problem Discussed by West, Moscow, Peking," *Washington Post*, August 27, 1979; David K. Willis, "On the Trial of the A-Bomb Makers: Antinuclear Battle Nears Climax," *Christian Science Monitor*, December 1, 1981; Weissman and Krosney, *The Islamic Bomb*; and a BBC-TV Panorama program, June 16, 1980. Khan's concerns were expressed in a letter to Abdul Aziz Khan that we obtained.

Khan's outburst about his alleged persecution by Americans and Jews is contained in a letter that he wrote to Aziz Khan on June 4, 1979. The quotation "Those of us who knew what was going on . . ." came from a former Pakistani diplomat who was interviewed multiple times and refused to allow his name to be used.

The meeting with the IAEA director general was described in detail in a three-page, declassified telegram from the United States Embassy in Vienna to the State Department, dated July 9, 1979. Additional information came from the interview with Gallucci. The September 13 meeting was memorialized in a secret transcript prepared by the Arms Control and Disarmament Agency and declassified in 2004. Gallucci described his covert trip to see Kahuta. The trip and Zia's reaction were from an article by Simon Henderson, "We can do it ourselves: The father of Pakistan's nuclear program speaks out," *Bulletin of the Atomic Scientists*, September 1993.

CHAPTER 11. SEE NO EVIL

Zia's fateful bicycle trip through the streets of Rawalpindi was described by Abbas in *Pakistan's Drift into Extremism* and Coll in *Ghost Wars*; the latter also provided extensive details on the reaction of the people inside the United States Embassy to the rioters, material that was augmented with newspaper and magazine accounts of the episode.

The assessment of Pakistan's tilt toward religious extremism and the justification in the Koran for using nuclear weapons came from a declassified report by the Bureau of Intelligence and Research, Department of State, "Islam and the Pakistani Officer Corps," February 5, 1981, which was provided to us by Jeffrey T. Richelson, author of *Spying on the Bomb: American Nuclear Intelligence from Nazi Germany to Iran and North Korea* (New York: W. W. Norton & Company, 2006).

Zbigniew Brzezinski described his reaction to the Soviet invasion of Afghanistan in a memo written for President Carter, "Reflections on Soviet Intervention in Afghanistan," December 26, 1979, released by the Cold War International History Project. Ronald Spiers's recollections about the Carter administration's policy toward Pakistan came from an interview. The inability of Weiss to persuade Glenn to oppose lifting the sanctions came from an interview with Weiss.

President Reagan's remarks about Pakistan's nuclear program came from a packet of briefing papers and talking points prepared by the State Department on December 5, 1982, as well as notes from the actual meeting, all of which came from the archives of the Ronald W. Reagan Presidential Library, Simi Valley, California.

Khan's courtship of Pakistani journalists was described in interviews with several journalists, who spoke on condition of anonymity because of fear for their jobs and safety.

The progress at Kahuta and the incident in which MI6 agents broke into Khan's hotel room came from two confidential British documents from 1981 and 1983 and from interviews with a senior British counter-proliferation official and a former CIA official, both of whom declined to be identified because of the sensitive nature of the information. Zia's reaction to Vernon Walters was from Simon Henderson, "Anxious U.S. Could Probe Zia over N-Plans," *Financial Times*, December 8, 1982; and Kim Rogal, William J. Cook, and Jane Whitmore, "Worries about the Bomb," *Newsweek*, December 20, 1982.

The events leading up to the Israeli attack on Iraq's Osirak reactor and its aftermath came from an interview with a senior Israeli intelligence official and from a book by former Mossad agent Victor Ostrovsky and Claire Hoy, *By Way of Deception: The Making and Unmaking of a Mossad Officer* (New York: St. Martin's Press, 1990); Major General David Ivry, "The Attack on the Osiraq Nuclear Reactor—Looking Back 21 Years Later," *Israel's Strike Against the Iraqi Nuclear Reactor 7 June, 1981* (Jerusalem: Menachem Begin Heritage Center: 2003); Federation of American Scientists, "Israel's Strike Against the Iraqi Nuclear Reactor," June 7, 1981; and CIA Directorate of Intelligence, "The Iraqi Nuclear Program: Progress Despite Setbacks," June 1983.

CHAPTER 12. CRIMES AND COVER-UPS

The best account of Pakistan's procurement in Canada is by John J. Fialka, "How Pakistan Secured U.S. Devices in Canada to Make Atomic Arms," *Wall Street Journal*, November 26, 1984. Additional material came from CBC-TV's *Fifth Estate* broadcast on December 9, 1980. Additional details were derived from Khan's personal correspondence with Aziz Khan and others, and from interviews with Richard Barlow, the former CIA and Pentagon analyst.

The Vaid case was documented extensively in a fine article by Seymour Hersh, "Pakistani in U.S. Sought to Ship A-Bomb Trigger," *New York Times*, February 25, 1985. Hersh reprised some of the details in "The Deal," *The New Yorker*, March 8, 2004. The Vaid case was also discussed by Fialka in his *Wall Street Journal* article. On July 22, 1987, the House of Representatives Committee on Foreign Affairs Subcommittee on Asian and Pacific Affairs delved into the Vaid case and other examples of Pakistani proliferation in a public hearing, which provided authoritative testimony concerning the procurement operation.

Deane Hinton's classified evaluation was from Coll's *Ghost Wars*.

Descriptions of the lack of security at FDO and Almelo, and Khan's activities there, were drawn primarily from the interviews with Veerman and two reports by the Dutch government, a draft issued in 1979 and the final version a year later, February 29, 1980; quotations about the assumptions regarding Khan's work were from the final declassified version. The best account of Khan's reaction to the Dutch charges against him in 1983 is contained in the Malik biography. Henny Khan also described her husband's anger over the accusations in her *Humrat* interview.

Gallucci recalled the top-secret memo in an interview; the later memo prepared by his staff in 1983, "The Pakistani Nuclear Program," June 6, 1983, was obtained from the National Security Archives. Khan's interview and Zia's response were from "Zia Chastises Western Media for Accounts of Khan's Remarks on Weapons Capability," *Nuclear Fuel*, February 27, 1984; "Zia Denies Pakistan Building Atom Bomb," *Japan Economic Newswire*, February 14, 1984; "Pakistani Nuclear Program," *Washington Post*, February 14, 1984.

Weiss described his reaction to the Cranston speech and legislation in an interview, augmented by a memo that he wrote to Glenn on August 7, 1984. The quotation from Barlow's senior honors thesis came from a copy of the thesis provided by Barlow.

CHAPTER 13. NUCLEAR AMBIGUITY

Richard Barlow's story has been recounted several times over the years. The first lengthy account was provided by Seymour Hersh, "On the Nuclear Edge," *The New Yorker*, March 29, 1993. We interviewed Barlow more than a dozen times, often over several days. He also provided us with hundreds of pages of court records and other documents that corroborated his version of events. The Kerr quote about Barlow was from the Hersh article, "On the Nuclear Edge."

The quotation "We knew more about that bomb than any other bomb in the world except the Brits'" came from an interview with a former CIA officer who monitored Pakistan's nuclear program for many years and asked not to be identified because some of the information remains classified. Milt Bearden told us the story about the lonely woodsman who found the strange stone and provided the quotation about Pakistan being almost finished with the bomb.

Former congressman Stephen Solarz and former senator Larry Pressler were both interviewed, and their recollections were augmented by transcripts of numerous congressional hearings and newspaper accounts.

Barlow talked about the discovery of the information that led to the Mandel case in an interview. Additional information about the case and its outcome came from Michael R. Gordon, "U.S. Indicts 3 in the Export of Equipment to Pakistan," *New York Times*, July 18, 1987.

Similarly, Barlow described previously undisclosed details of the Arshad Pervez case in interviews, which were augmented by published accounts; the most extensive was Hedrick Smith, "A Bomb Ticks in Pakistan," *New York Times Magazine*, March 6, 1988. Additional material came from "Pakistani Seized by U.S. in a Plot on A-Arms Alloy," *New York Times*, July 15, 1987; and "An Arrest Spurs New Debate over Pakistan and the Bomb," *Insight Magazine*, August 17, 1987.

The connection between BCCI and Khan was mentioned in a report to the United States Senate Committee on Foreign Relations, "The BCCI Affair," compiled by Senators John Kerry and Hank Brown in 1992. The tie to the Pervez smuggling case was provided by Barlow in an interview and confirmed by a former BCCI officer in an interview. Background on the bank was from James Ring Adams and Douglas Frantz, *A Full-Service Bank: How BCCI Stole Billions Around the World* (New York: Pocket Books, 1992).

Barlow's testimony before Congress and his confrontation with his supervisors at the CIA afterward came from interviews with Barlow and Solarz and published accounts, reports, and documents. Among the most helpful documents was a memo prepared by Louis Fisher, for the Congressional Research Service, "National Security Whistleblowers," December 30, 2005. Additional background information came from the transcript of the hearing conducted in July 1987 by the House of Representatives Committee on Foreign Affairs Subcommittee on Asian and Pacific Affairs.

Most of the conversations quoted in this section of the book relied on Barlow's recollections. In every case possible, we tried to obtain corroborating documents or to talk with others involved in the incidents. In the end, after reviewing hundreds of pages of hearing transcripts, court records, and other material, and talking with his supporters and critics, we concluded that Richard Barlow is a credible person whose account stands up.

CHAPTER 14. MAN OF THE YEAR

The promotional videotape of KRL was played for us by a senior official at the IAEA. Additional descriptions of KRL and its workings came from interviews with two former workers there and various published accounts.

The account of the Khan interview intended as a warning to India during Operation Brass Tacks was based on interviews with two former ISI officers, both of whom demanded anonymity; an interview with Husain Haqqani, a former Pakistani diplomat and journalist; and the article published in the *London Observer* based on the interview by Indian journalist Kuldip Nayar.

The quotation by Khan about the need for a delivery system for Pakistan's nuclear weapons came from an interview with the former colleague to whom Khan made the remark. The episode involving the distribution of *The Islamic Bomb* and the subsequent discovery of the changes made by ISI came from an interview with Pervez Hoodbhoy and our review of the two versions of the book. The former government official who said the ISI considered the changes a significant success requested anonymity to avoid antagonizing the intelligence service.

CHAPTER 15. ONE-STOP SHOPPING

Lerch's early involvement with Khan was chronicled in testimony at his criminal trial in 2006 in Mannheim, Germany, and numerous articles; among the most informative and authoritative of this is a two-part piece by Juergen Dahlkamp, Georg Mascolo, and Holger Stark, "Network of Death on Trial," *Der Spiegel*, March 13, 2006; and a series of articles by Mark Hibbs in *Nuclear Fuel*, an industry newsletter, on February 28, 2005, August 28, 2006, and September 25, 2006.

Lerch's initial meeting in Zurich with the two Iranians was described in interviews with two senior diplomats who saw the notes taken by the Iranians listing the four sections of the offer. The same diplomats provided information from their conversations with Iranian nuclear officials about the specifics of the first transaction between the Khan network and Iran. Among the new elements they disclosed was that Iran paid the network $10 million for the first components and plans, twice the amount used in most publications. They also provided the first breakdown in the allocation of the money, based on bank records.

Khan's justifications for his involvement in the transfers to Iran came from interviews with friends and former associates of the scientist. Although Pakistan's Strategic Regional Consensus plan by Zia has been written about previously, Bearden described to us how Gul boasted about it and provided him with a copy, which he sent back to CIA headquarters.

Tahir provided a description of the 1987 deal in an interview with Olli Heinonen and other IAEA officials, and the results of that interrogation were provided to us. The network's first transaction with Iran was mentioned briefly in a twelve-page statement released on February 4, 2004, by the Malaysian police after the arrest of B.S.A. Tahir in Kuala Lumpur. The statement, available at www.iranwatch.org/goverment;Malaysia/malaysia-police-libyareport-02204.htm, is devoted primarily to describing the ring's later dealings with

Iran and Libya, but it provides a primer on how things worked and names many of Khan's associates.

CHAPTER 16. WISHFUL THINKING

The telephone call regarding Zia's aircraft crash was recounted by Bearden in an interview in which he also described other aspects of his time as Islamabad station chief. George Shultz's comments were from an interview with Robert Oakley; the scene was also described by Coll in *Ghost Wars*. Benazir Bhutto's rise to power and political and economic conditions in Pakistan at the time were drawn from Cohen, *The Idea of Pakistan*; Haqqani, *Pakistan*; and Abbas, *Pakistan's Drift into Extremism*. Benazir Bhutto was interviewed several times between December 2001 and July 2005.

Barlow's tenure at the Pentagon was described by him in a series of interviews; we also relied on numerous documents from the various investigations that concluded he had done nothing wrong, including Report of Investigation, Inspector General, Department of Defense, December 24, 1991; Hersh, "On the Nuclear Edge"; Ken Silverstein and David Isenberg, "What happens when U.S. spies get the goods – and the government won't listen?" *Mother Jones*, January/February 2002; and Lyndsey Layton, "Whistle-Blower's Fight for Pension Drags On," *Washington Post*, July 7, 2007.

The quotation about President Bush's knowledge of Pakistan's bomb came from a former senior CIA official who insisted on anonymity because details of briefings to the president remain classified. Bhutto described her briefing from William Webster, and details of the encounter were also drawn from William Burrows, *Critical Mass: The Dangerous Race for Superweapons in a Fragmenting World* (Los Angeles: Reed Business Information, 1994).

The hearing before the House Foreign Affairs Committee came from a transcript of the session; Barlow's reaction was described in an interview. Gerald Brubaker's involvement was described by Barlow and in testimony by Victor Rostow, a former Pentagon official, in a civil case brought by Barlow. The conversation between Leonard Weiss and Barlow was described by Weiss; Barlow's recollection of the meeting differed slightly because he does not regard himself as a whistleblower since he never took his complaints outside the government.

The exchange between Bhutto and Hashemi Rafsanjani was recounted by Bhutto in an interview and later confirmed by the aide who attended the meeting with her. Henry Rowen was interviewed by us. General Aslam Beg was interviewed twice, once in person in Islamabad and a second time by telephone; he acknowledged engaging in exchanges of conventional weapons and training with Iran, but he disputed advocating transferring nuclear technology or weapons to Tehran or threatening to do so. Oakley discussed his exchange with Beg in his interview. A good rundown on the exchanges between Beg and Rowen was published by the Associated Press, "Pakistan threatened to give nukes to Iran, ex-officials say," on February 28, 2004.

CHAPTER 17. SADDAM'S GAMBIT

Bhutto remembered her encounter with Khan in interviews. The background about Khan's construction project on Rawal Lake and general information about his rising influence came from interviews with current and former Pakistani officials and journalists, most of whom declined to be named because of the risk of retaliation by Khan's supporters or by the government. Information from Malik's biography of Khan was augmented by an interview with Malik in Islamabad in 2005. The switch of Khan's allegiance to Beg was described by a former senior Pakistani government official and by a former colleague of Khan's at KRL.

The quotation from Khan to the senior CIA official and the quotations from Dick Kerr and Robert Gates, as well as general background on Operation Brass Tacks, came from Hersh, "On the Nuclear Edge." The broad outlines were confirmed in interviews with former CIA and Pakistani officials. The confrontation was also described by Lawrence Lifschultz, "Doom Thy Neighbor: After Hiroshima and Nagasaki . . . Lahore and Bombay?" Alicia Patterson Foundation, volume 19, no. 1.

The exchange between Cheney and the counterproliferation expert was described by the latter, who spoke on condition of anonymity.

Khan's offer to Iraq was described in Iranian documents and secret memos provided to us by Western diplomats. Weiss told us about his conversation with John Jennekens. A similar comment by Jennekens is contained in "The Bomb in Iran's Future," by Henry Sokolski, published in *Middle East Quarterly*, June 1994.

Khidhir Hamza's account of Iraq's nuclear program came from various news articles about him and his book, *Saddam's Bombmaker* (New York: Scribner, 2000), coauthored with Jeff Stein. Hamza's accounts have been disputed over the years, but the information here was in line with information from other sources, including IAEA officials.

Jacques Baute was interviewed many times about the discoveries in Iraq by international weapons inspectors. His recollections were corroborated by inspection reports and other files at the IAEA and United Nations.

Cheney's presentation of the Osirak photograph to General David Ivry was described by an American diplomat who was present during the ceremony and spoke on condition of anonymity.

CHAPTER 18. MISSED SIGNALS

We interviewed both Hans Blix and Laura Rockwood. David Kay's recollection was from Michael Dobbs and Walter Pincus, "Persistent or Pushover: Views of Blix's Record Vary," *Washington Post*, December 5, 2002.

The sharing of American spy satellite photos with the IAEA was described by an IAEA official and a former United States official, both of whom requested anonymity because of the sensitive nature of the information. Blix also described the episode.

Robert Alvarez described the inspection visit to North Korea in an interview, in which he also described his interaction with Li Sang Gun.

The involvement of Mohammed Farooq and Gotthard Lerch in South Africa's nuclear program is contained in documents that we obtained from the court case in Pretoria, South Africa, against Gerhard Wisser and Daniel Geiges.

Khan's visits to Iran to help the nuclear program were described in interviews with Ali Akbar Omid Mehr and Hamid Reza Zakeri. The visits were also described in newspaper articles, including Douglas Frantz, "Iran Closes In on Ability to Build a Nuclear Bomb," *Los Angeles Times*, August 4, 2003. After Khan confessed to helping Iran and other countries, the Pakistani government continued to deny that he had traveled to Iran. Mehr also described his flight from Pakistan in interviews conducted at the safe house in Denmark where he lives under an assumed name.

CHAPTER 19. NUCLEAR NATIONALISM

Robert Gates's testimony before Congress about Iran's nuclear program was from Steve Coll, "U.S. Halted Nuclear Bid By Iran; China, Argentina, Agreed to Cancel Technology Transfers," *Washington Post*, November 17, 1992. Additional background information came from John Prados, *Safe for Democracy: The Secret Wars of the CIA* (Chicago: Ivan R. Dee, 2006). Einhorn acknowledged that the American intelligence and counterproliferation agencies had underestimated Khan in an interview.

The description of the clandestine work at Tehran Nuclear Research Center came from interviews with current and former IAEA inspectors and officials and from IAEA reports based on later disclosures by the Iranian government. The visit to Khan by Iran's defense minister in 1994 was described by an IAEA official who based his knowledge on debriefings of senior Iranian officials. Khan's role in setting up the second round of sales to Iran was corroborated by Tahir under questioning by Western diplomats and government officials, the results of which were shared with us by the officials and diplomats.

Khan's brochures were obtained by us from an IAEA official. His long feud with Munir Khan was described in the Malik biography, various writings by A. Q. Khan, and former colleagues of both men. George Perkovich of the Carnegie Endowment for International Peace described the late Munir Khan's reaction to Khan in an interview with us.

Simon Henderson's interview with Khan appeared in the September 1993 issue of the *Bulletin of the Atomic Scientists*, under the title "We Can Do It Ourselves."

Bhutto recounted the changes in Khan's personality and her agreement to obtain the missile plans from North Korea in one of our interviews. Her recollections of the trip to North Korea were corroborated by an aide who accompanied her; the episode is also contained in newspaper and magazine articles. What remains in dispute is whether Bhutto paid cash for the plans or was aware of a barter arrangement in which North Korea received nuclear technology and assistance from Khan in return for the missile know-how. Bhutto is adamant that her government paid for the plans, something that several former American intelligence officials doubted in interviews.

Lt. General Talat Masood spoke of Khan's motives in an interview with us in Islamabad. Pervez Hoodbhoy also discussed Khan's personality in an interview.

The progress at KRL on building the missile was monitored by CIA assets and described in interviews with former CIA officials and in some published accounts.

Feroz Khan spoke of the relationship between the military and Khan in interviews, and Einhorn described American knowledge of the cooperation between Pakistan and North Korea in an interview.

Khan's relationship with Tahir was described in interviews with IAEA officials and others who interrogated Tahir after his detention by the Malaysian police; they provided the most detailed rundown of how the two men operated. It was also the subject of numerous newspaper articles, including William J. Broad, David E. Sanger and Raymond Bonner, "A Tale of Nuclear Proliferation," *New York Times*, February 2, 2004; David E. Sanger, "In Face of Report, Iran Acknowledges Buying Nuclear Components," *New York Times*, February 23, 2004; Alan Sipress and Ellen Nakashima, "Sri Lankan Accused of Helping Pakistani Sell Arms Components to Libya, Iran," *Washington Post*, May 29, 2004; and Douglas Frantz and William C. Rempel, "New Find in a Nuclear Network: Pakistani Scientist Used South African Affiliates in an Effort to Outfit Libya with a Uranium Enrichment Plant," *Los Angeles Times*, November 28, 2004.

The absence of Masud Naraghi, the Iranian nuclear official, from the second round of negotiations in Dubai was first reported in a German documentary film, *The Mullahs' Physicist*, by Egmont R. Koch, which was broadcast on German public television on February 22, 2007.

CHAPTER 20. MORE AND MORE PIECES

The report that President Clinton shared with Boris Yeltsin was first disclosed by Jim Hoagland, "Briefing Yeltsin on Iran," *Washington Post*, May 17, 1995. Warren Christopher's lobbying of Qian Qichen was from Elaine Sciolino, "Beijing Rebuffs U.S. on Halting Iran Atom Deal," *New York Times*, April 18, 1995.

Hussein Kamel's flight from Iraq was detailed in a report by the UN Secretary-General, "Note by the Secretary-General," S/1996/848, October 11, 1996; and a transcript of the UN interview with Kamel, "General Hussein Kamal [sic] UNSCOM/IAEA Briefing," provided to us by a UN official. Jacques Baute provided a detailed description of the inspection team's efforts in Iraq, its visit to the "chicken farm," and his dealings with Iraqi officials in a series of interviews.

The quotation about the mounting questions concerning Khan's nuclear activities was from an interview with a former State Department official who asked for anonymity because of the sensitivity of the information. The quotation about Khan being the subject of intense scrutiny was from a former CIA officer who now works undercover for another agency and did not want his identity disclosed.

The same former officer helped us understand other reasons why the American intelligence community was reluctant to blow the whistle on Khan. The incident in which Khan jumped from his seat to defend himself was dawn from interviews with Feroz Khan, who was present at the meeting.

CHAPTER 21. A MYSTERIOUS MURDER

Khan's visit to Istanbul was described by Tahir under questioning by Western diplomats and by one of the Libyan officials who attended the session in conversation with IAEA officials in Tripoli; the diplomats and IAEA officials shared the information with us on a confidential basis. The Libyan also described Khan's earlier trips to Tripoli. Some information about Khan's dealings with Libya is also contained in IAEA reports.

Information about the hotel Khan built in Timbuktu is available in numerous published articles. The Khan video was played for us by a Western diplomat who had obtained a copy from the Pakistani government. Information about Khan's travels to various countries trying to sell nuclear technology was described in many published articles, including Edward Harris and Ellen Knickmeyer, "Head of Pakistan's nuclear ring made repeated visits to uranium-rich Africa," Associated Press, April 20, 2004.

The Indian test, and the events leading up to it, is best described by Perkovich, *India's Nuclear Bomb*. The Pakistani response, including the debate and Khan's role, was detailed in *Defence Journal*, an official publication of the Pakistani military; the article, "When Mountains Move—the Story of Chagai," was written by Rai Muhammad Saleh Azam. In April 1999, Jang, one of the most respected newspaper groups in Pakistan, published a special edition about the country's nuclear test and the background for its nuclear program. The elevation of Khan to hero status was described in interviews by Hoodbhoy and a Pakistani journalist who spoke on condition of anonymity because he is not authorized to speak by his newspaper.

The murder of Kim Sa Nae was drawn from Paul Watson and Mubashir Zaidi, "Death of N. Korean Woman Offers Clues to Pakistani Nuclear Deals," *Los Angeles Times*, March 1, 2004

CHAPTER 22. INSIDE THE NETWORK

The obstacles to mass production of centrifuges for Libya were outlined in debriefings of Tahir and Urs Tinner by Western diplomats and CIA officials, who relayed the information to us. Some of the material also was referred to in various reports published by the IAEA. Gary Milhollin described Dubai as a black hole in an interview. Urs's claim to friends that he was going to Dubai to sell beverages was from an interview with Bruno Vanoni, a Swiss journalist.

Peter Griffin and his son Paul were identified as Khan associates by Tahir, according to the statement released by the Malaysian police. The history of the relationship between the two men was described in testimony by Matthew S. Borman, a deputy assistant secretary of commerce, before the Subcommittee on National Security, Emerging Threats, and International Relations of the House Committee on Government Reform, March 9, 2004; and in an article by Owen Bowcott, John Aglionby and Ian Traynor, "Businessman under scrutiny 25 years ago after ordering unusual supplies," *Guardian*, March 5, 2004. Griffin described his dinner with Khan in Steve Coll, "The Atomic Emporium: Abdul Qadeer Khan and Iran's race to build the bomb," *The New Yorker*, August 7, 2006.

Peter Griffin declined requests for interviews through his lawyer, but the lawyer and Griffin have both denied repeatedly that he had any knowing involvement in the shipment of nuclear technology to Libya or Iran. Griffin has blamed Tahir for forging his signature on documents. Neither Griffin nor his son have been charged with any criminal violation.

Gunes Cire and Selim Alguadis were implicated in the network by Tahir's statement to the Malaysian police, and equipment from Alguadis was later found in warehouses in Libya. Cire died soon after his involvement was disclosed. In an interview in Istanbul in 2005, Alguadis acknowledged that he knew Khan and said that he once gave him a tour of the city. But he denied knowingly providing nuclear-related technology to Libya or Iran.

Wisser's involvement with South Africa's nuclear program and his dealings with the Khan network were described in great detail in hundreds of pages of affidavits, sales records, and other documents from the case file in Pretoria, South Africa, on the criminal case against Wisser and Geiges. Among those documents are two lengthy statements given by Wisser to law enforcement officials in Germany and South Africa, as well as photographs of the centrifuge piping system manufactured for Libya by Johan Meyer. The records are the primary source of information on Wisser and his colleagues, though interviews were also conducted in Johannesburg with lawyers for him and Meyer. In addition, IAEA officials evaluated the contents of the court records and shared their findings with us.

Lerch acknowledged in an interview with Swiss authorities that he knew Khan, Wisser, and Tahir, but he denied that he had any role in setting up a uranium enrichment facility for Libya, according to a transcript of the interview provided to us.

Urs Tinner's difficulties establishing a centrifuge plant came from CIA and IAEA officials who spoke with Tinner and from the debriefing of Tahir by Western diplomats.

The Clinton administration's efforts to stop Pakistan's nuclear program and the lunch with Nawaz Sharif and Strobe Talbott were described by Einhorn in an interview. Talbott also referred to the lunch in *Engaging India: Diplomacy, Democracy, and the Bomb* (Washington: The Brookings Institution, May 2004).

Clinton's comment that Pakistan was "messing with nuclear war" during the Kargil confrontation was from "Pakistan 'prepared nuclear strike,' " BBC-TV, May 16, 2002, based on an interview with Bruce Riedel, who was on the White House National Security Council during the incident and later wrote a paper about the episode for the Center for Advanced Study of India at the University of Pennsylvania.

The tip to General Pervez Musharraf was recounted in an interview with a former senior Pakistani law enforcement official, who provided extensive details from his written notes and memory about Musharraf's determination to assert control over Khan. The former official spoke on condition of anonymity out of fear of reprisal. Khan's boast that he knew the CIA had tried to penetrate his network came from an interview with a former colleague.

In 2006 a handful of articles suggested that Urs Tinner had been recruited by the CIA. The articles were not conclusive and they did not speculate on when Tinner might have started supplying information to the Americans. Tinner's recruitment was, we believe, a turning point in the CIA's knowledge of the Khan network, so we want to explain our methodology in unraveling the mystery, though the names of some of the sources must remain anonymous.

We first learned that Tinner, his father, and his brother had begun cooperating with the IAEA from two Western diplomats in Vienna. The diplomats were uncertain how the arrangements were made, but eventually one of them conceded that a mysterious woman had telephoned Olli Heinonen, the

IAEA official heading the investigation of the Khan network, and set up the first meeting with the Tinners. Heinonen said in an interview that he did not know the identity of the woman, though he suspected she was from the CIA. Later, a former CIA case officer who worked in Vienna suggested that the meeting had been arranged by the agency. We interviewed two former CIA officials before tracking down a former chief of the CIA station in Vienna, who had later returned to a senior post in Washington and eventually left the agency. He provided many of the details about the recruitment of Tinner by the agent identified as Mad Dog, and he acknowledged dispatching the woman agent to contact Heinonen. The quotation that Tinner "gave us the final ability to know what the network was doing" came from the former station chief. Another former CIA official provided additional details of Mad Dog's relationship with Tinner. As a result, we were able to confirm that the CIA began receiving direct and detailed reports about Khan's supplies to Iran in early 2000, earlier than previously disclosed. Some of these findings were corroborated by a British counterproliferation official who also declined to be identified.

Einhorn confirmed the improved flow of information about Khan's connection to Libya in an interview, but he knew nothing about the source.

Tenet's boast about the CIA penetration of the Khan network came in a speech he made at Georgetown University in Washington on February 5, 2004.

CHAPTER 23. TIGHTENING THE NOOSE

The investigation of Khan by Pakistan's National Accountability Bureau was described by Farah Stockman in "Pakistan Had Case Against Scientist," *Boston Globe*, February 13, 2004; and Douglas Frantz, "From Patriot to Proliferator: The myth of a Pakistani scientist as his nation's savior long protected him," *Los Angeles Times*, September 23, 2005. Our account is much fuller and relies heavily on a series of interviews with the Pakistani man who carried out the investigation. The investigator's recollections were augmented by notes he had taken during his inquiry, which were also shared with us. The investigator now lives in the United States and requested anonymity to protect family members still in Pakistan. We made every attempt to corroborate his information. For instance, the investigator read us a list of Pakistani journalists who received payments from Khan, some of which we were able to corroborate by talking with journalists. General Syed Mohammad

Amjad vouched for the reliability of the investigation in an interview, but he declined to discuss any details of the inquiry into Khan. In addition, we reviewed reports filed by Pakistani security officials.

Musharraf referred to the investigation and his suspicions about Khan in his autobiography, *In the Line of Fire* (New York: Simon & Schuster, 2006). He also discussed the difficulty in pursuing Khan in an interview with David Rohde and Amy Waldman, "Pakistani Leader Suspected Moves by Atomic Expert," *New York Times*, February 10, 2004.

Hamid Mir described Khan's reaction to the investigation in an interview. The name on the shopping bags was provided by a Western diplomat who later saw the bags in Tripoli. Details of the surveillance of Khan came from the investigator, who had access to the intelligence reports as part of his inquiry.

Events surrounding Khan's dismissal were described by Musharraf in his memoir and numerous published articles. The quotation about Musharraf fearing a backlash came from an interview with a former Pakistani general who spoke on condition of anonymity. Khan's complaints were described by several of his former associates; one of his friends told us about Khan's plan to run for president. John S. Friedman and Eric Nadler, the co-producers of the 2002 documentary *Stealing the Fire*, graciously provided us with a transcript of their full interview with Khan.

The network's purchase of the Spanish lathes came from the court files in South Africa, which include invoices for the machines, as well as from interviews with South African law enforcement officials. Tahir's conversations with Khan about moving the manufacturing to Malaysia were described by the Western diplomats who debriefed Tahir while he was in prison.

Einhorn described his conversation with Richard Armitage in an interview. A second former Bush administration official, who requested anonymity, recounted the briefings at the White House. John Wolf was interviewed after he left government.

The August 2001 meeting of the Pakistani nuclear scientists with Osama bin Laden was described in detail in numerous newspaper articles, including Douglas Frantz, James Risen and David E. Sanger, "Nuclear Experts in Pakistan May Have Links to Al Qaeda," *New York Times*, December 9, 2001; Kamran Khan and Molly Moore, "2 Nuclear Experts Briefed bin Laden, Pakistanis Say," *Washington Post*, December 12, 2001; Akhtar Jamal, "Pakistani Nuke Scientists to Face Charges for Al Qaeda Contacts," Eurasianet.

org, December 13, 2001; and David Albright and Holly Higgins, "Pakistani Nuclear Scientists: How Much Nuclear Assistance to Al Qaeda?" Institute for Science and International Security, August 30, 2002. George Tenet provided a detailed analysis of the meeting and its ramifications in his autobiography, *At the Center of the Storm* (New York: HarperCollins, 2007). It was also mentioned in Ron Suskind, *The One Percent Doctrine: Deep Inside America's Pursuit of Its Enemies Since 9/11* (New York: Simon & Schuster, 2006).

CHAPTER 24. "WITH US OR AGAINST US"

Musharraf wrote about his conversation with Secretary of State Colin Powell in his memoir, *In the Line of Fire*; the exchange was also described in various publications. General Mahmood Ahmed's confrontation with Armitage was disclosed by Musharraf in an interview with CBS-TV's *60 Minutes* on September 24, 2006; and by Hassan Abbas, "Inside story of Musharraf-Mahmood tussle," *Daily Times of Pakistan*, September 26, 2006. Armitage denied making the threat in an interview with NBC-TV on September 22, 2006, and in a PBS documentary, *Return of the Taliban*; the PBS transcript is available at www.pbs.org/wgbh/pages/frontline/taliban/interviews/armitage.html.

The information about the American efforts to secure Pakistan's nuclear arsenal and the Trojan horse quote is from Frantz, Risen and Sanger, "Nuclear Experts in Pakistan May Have Links to Al Qaeda."

Tenet's arrival in Islamabad on December 1 was described from interviews conducted by us in Pakistan; we also relied on Tenet's *At the Center of the Storm* and Suskind's *One Percent Doctrine*.

Khan's decision to make electronic copies of centrifuge designs and ship centrifuges to Dubai came from IAEA reports and interviews with IAEA officials and Western diplomats in Vienna, all of whom spoke on a confidential basis. In addition, we were given access to confidential reports prepared by the IAEA, which provided a detailed description of the network's activities based on interviews conducted by the agency with network participants and officials of various governments and intelligence agencies.

Tahir's lifestyle was described by two of his former associates in interviews and by Anwar Faruqi, "Accused Smuggler Lived Lavishly," Associated Press, February 14, 2004. The details of Tahir's deal with Scomi were drawn from the Malaysian police report. Mad Dog's move to Kuala Lumpur was described in an interview by the former senior CIA official.

The South Africa project was described in the court file against Wisser and Geiges. The training of Libyan technicians in Dubai was from an IAEA report and interviews with IAEA officials who had been given a rundown on the network's operation by Libyan authorities.

The $2 million Libyan payment was described by a Western diplomat involved in the investigation who copied bank records tracking the money.

CHAPTER 25. DIPLOMATIC CHESS

The transcript of Alireza Jafarzadeh's press conference is available at www .iranwatch.org/privateviews/NCRI/perspex-ncri-topsecretprojects-081402 .htm; we also interviewed him. The outlines of Iran's clandestine nuclear program were reported by Frantz, "Iran Closes In on Ability to Build a Nuclear Bomb." The response to the disclosure by the IAEA was described in interviews with three IAEA officials who were involved.

Changes at the IAEA after the discovery of Saddam's secret nuclear program were described in interviews by Hans Blix, Pierre Goldschmidt, Laura Rockwood, and other IAEA officials. We also had access to minutes from IAEA board meetings and other internal records.

ElBaradei's quotation about how he sees his job was from Tom Hundley, "UN nuclear chief, agency win Nobel Peace Prize," *Chicago Tribune*, October 8, 2005. The details of his meeting with senior officials and the letter to the Iranian representative were from interviews with other IAEA officials and agency records.

The fact that the United States and Britain had not provided information about Khan's network to the IAEA came from interviews with six IAEA officials and Western diplomats in Vienna, all of whom had knowledge of the agency's inner workings and its relationship with the two countries. The fact that the Americans and British were aware of Khan's network became obvious with the release of the so-called Butler report, officially *The Review of Intelligence on Weapons of Mass Destruction*, on July 14, 2004.

Contacts between IAEA officials and their Iranian counterparts were laid out in an internal chronology provided to us and through interviews with IAEA and Iranian officials who were involved. Additional analysis of the Iranian enrichment program came from a twenty-page internal assessment by a senior IAEA expert, which was provided to us.

The visits to Kalaye Electric Company were described by IAEA officials and Western diplomats who were either part of the inspection team or were later given detailed briefings about the inspections.

CHAPTER 26. SPY GAMES

Israel's views about Iran's nuclear program and its campaign to leak news about it came from interviews with several high-ranking Israeli military, intelligence, and foreign ministry officials, all of which were conducted under rules that prohibited disclosing their identities. Additional information was from "Israel Casts Wary Eye on Iran," broadcast by CBS-TV on September 29, 2004.

The story of the aluminum tubes was recounted in numerous newspaper and magazine articles. The quotation from Houston Wood was from an interview he gave to CBS-TV, which was broadcast February 4, 2004, on *60 Minutes* II. Baute described his analysis of the Niger claim in an interview.

John Bolton's attitude toward ElBaradei and international organizations in general was from Sonni Efron, "Critics say blunt-spoken weapons expert has exaggerated," *Los Angeles Times*, November 10, 2003. Bolton also was interviewed in late 2003.

The American decision to provide limited intelligence on Iran, including the satellite photos of Kalaye, to the IAEA was described in interviews with two American diplomats in Vienna and confirmed by IAEA officials.

Khan's response to the disclosure about Natanz was from a Western diplomat who was involved in the interrogation of Tahir, and the destruction of some documents was confirmed by an IAEA official.

The eavesdropping on ElBaradei was disclosed by Dafna Linzer, "IAEA Leader's Phone Tapped; U.S. Pores Over Transcript to Try to Oust Nuclear Chief," *Washington Post*, December 12, 2004. Mark Gwozdecky's comment came in an interview. El Baradei's comments to *Der Spiegel* appeared under the heading, "Al Qaeda also Wants the Bomb," February 12, 2005.

CHAPTER 27. THE DROWNING MAN

The CIA observation of the shipment to Libya was described by a former senior CIA official in an interview. Meyer's progress and the arrival of the two Arabs came from the court files in Pretoria. The existence of power supplies from Turkey and other equipment in Libya was from IAEA reports following Libya's abandonment of its nuclear program and from interviews with IAEA officials who spent time in Libya. Tahir's role as paymaster for the network was described by two international investigators.

The Butler report examined the negotiations with Libya, as did numerous newspaper and magazine articles, which detailed the talks and the seizure of the *BBC China*. Among the articles used were Barton Gellman and Dafna Linzer, "Unprecedented Peril Forces Tough Calls," *Washington Post*, 26 October 2004; David Albright and Corey Hinderstein, "Libya's Gas Centrifuge Procurement: Much Remains Undiscovered," *ISIS*, March 1, 2004; Bill Powell and Tim McGirk, "The Man Who Sold the Bomb," *Time*, February 14, 2005; Dafna Linzer and Craig Timberg, "S. African's Arrest Seen as Key to Nuclear Black Market," *Washington Post*, September 4, 2004; Stephen Fidler and Mark Huband, "Turks and South Africans Helped Libya's Secret Nuclear Arms Project," *Financial Times*, June 10, 2004; and Frederick Lamy, "Export controls violations and illicit trafficking by Swiss companies and individuals in the case of A. Q. Khan network," Geneva Centre for Security Policy, August 19, 2004.

Seif Gadhafi's quotation was from a report by Allan Urry, "Britain 'knew about nuclear network,' " BBC-TV, August 17, 2004. Additional background information on the talks and the eventual resolution came from Peter Beaumont, Kamal Ahmed and Martin Bright, "The meeting that brought Libya in from the cold," *Observer*, December 21, 2003; and Douglas Frantz and Josh Meyer, "The Deal to Disarm Kadafi," *Los Angeles Times*, March 13, 2005. Additional information about negotiations over Lockerbie, and insights into the Libyan rationale for relinquishing its nuclear program, was drawn from Flynt Leverett, "Why Libya Gave Up on the Bomb," *New York Times*, January 23, 2004.

The quotation from John McLaughlin about Stephen Kappes was from Mark Mazzetti, "A Storied Operative Returns to the CIA," *New York Times*, May 30, 2006. Additional biographical information about Kappes and his role in the Libyan negotiations came from Walter Pincus, "Kappes Is Expected to Boost CIA Morale," *Washington Post*, June 19, 2006. Information from these and other articles was augmented by interviews with British and American officials who were involved in the negotiations with Libya and who all spoke on condition of anonymity. The encounters between Musharraf and Bush and Tenet were described by Musharraf in *In the Line of Fire* and Tenet in *At the Center of the Storm*.

The progress of the *BBC China* was from an account given by a former

American intelligence official who was involved in monitoring the ship, and from an officer of the German company that owned the vessel.

The trip by Kappes and Mark Allen to Libya after the seizure of the ship was from the interview with the former American intelligence official and from an interview with a senior British counterproliferation official, both of whom were involved in the Libyan negotiations. Senator John W. Warner, Republican from Virginia and then chairman of the Armed Services Committee, cited Kappes's role in negotiating with Libyans and attributed the "drowning man" quote to him on the Senate floor on May 10, 2006.

The scene and negotiations at the Traveler's Club were described in interviews by two participants as well as in Beaumont, Ahmed and Bright, "The meeting that brought Libya in from the cold," and Frantz and Meyer, "The Deal to Disarm Kadafi." The delay in Gadhafi's announcement because of the soccer match was recounted by the British official in an interview.

CHAPTER 28. CHECKBOOK PROLIFERATION

The special meeting on Libya with the British intelligence agents called by ElBaradei and the responses of various IAEA officials were described in interviews with many people at the agency, including Heinonen and Goldschmidt. Bolton's opposition to involving the IAEA was told to us by one of his former associates at the State Department, John Wolf.

The IAEA trip to Libya in December was described in detail by several officials who participated and in internal and public IAEA documents; additional details were from Louis Charbonneau, "UN Inspectors Visit Libya Nuclear Weapons Sites," Reuters, December 28, 2003. Heinonen told us about the encounter with Karim. Two of the participants in the IAEA inspection told us about Mohammad Matuq Mohammad's unveiling of the Chinese warhead plans and the reaction of the IAEA officials.

One of the leaders of the joint American and British team in Libya provided a detailed rundown of the operation, from start to finish, in a series of interviews. Much of his information was corroborated by IAEA officials and Western diplomats also involved in dismantling the Libyan nuclear program. The IAEA officials also provided information about their inspections there. The contents of the two shopping bags were described by two Western officials who were involved in the Libyan episode. The identities of our sources are protected here because of sensitivity of the information.

Melissa Fleming told us about her encounter with the Libyan scientist in an interview.

The incident with the C-17 cargo plane and other details of the final loading of the equipment were provided by one of the American officials involved, who spoke on condition of anonymity. Donald Mahley provided an extensive rundown of the dismantling of the Libyan nuclear equipment in the November 2004 issue of *The Arena*, a publication of the Chemical & Biological Arms Control Institute. He offered an interesting conclusion: "It is relatively easy, even in a country where the bulk of the territory is open desert, to conceal elements of a WMD program if there is national dedication to do so."

The quotation from the senior State Department advisor regarding how little the Americans really knew about Khan's sales to Libya was obtained by Josh Meyer of the *Los Angeles Times* as part of his joint reporting with Frantz for the newspaper. Details of the equipment shipped to Oak Ridge were from Frank Munger, "Libyan nuke materials displayed; Energy czar on hand as journalists briefed about content in Oak Ridge," *Knoxville News-Sentinel*, March 16, 2004.

The estimate of the weight of the Chinese warhead and whether it would fit atop a Scud missile was provided to us by Jeffrey Lewis, a proliferation expert who runs the excellent Web site www.armscontrolwonk.com.

CHAPTER 29. NUCLEAR WAL-MART

The reconstruction of the IAEA investigation after the Libyan disclosure was assembled from a variety of sources, which included IAEA and American officials, Western diplomats, and public and confidential documents from the IAEA. Most of the interviews were conducted on background, so the identities of the sources are concealed. Additional information came from a BBC-TV interview with ElBaradei by Mark Urban, which was broadcast on March 3, 2004; and Paul Kerr, "IAEA Says Iran Failed to Disclose Key Nuclear Activities," *Arms Control Today*, March 2004.

Bolton's anger over the IAEA draft was described by an American diplomat in Vienna. The quotation from Hussein Haniff was from an interview.

Western diplomats and international investigators familiar with the debriefings of Tahir and Tinner told us how the two men tried to cover their tracks following the seizure of the *BBC China*. Wisser's reaction was from Meyer's statement to South African authorities, which is contained in the court files there.

Musharraf's deliberations were recounted in his memoir, *In the Line of Fire*, and in interviews with two of his close aides, who were involved in the talks. Pakistani newspapers also provided accounts of the arrests of KRL scientists. Hamid Mir told us about his last encounter with Khan in an interview. Khan's comment about making the missiles and bomb was from an interview with him broadcast January 23, 2004, on GEO, a private television network in Pakistan.

Musharraf's claim that no military or government officials helped Khan and that he would not submit to an outside inquiry or allow UN intervention in Pakistan's nuclear program was from a transcript of his session with journalists provided to us by a Pakistani reporter, who requested anonymity. Zahid Malik was interviewed in Islamabad. The former Pakistani military officer who said the military knew about Khan's activities spoke in an interview after being promised anonymity.

The interrogation in which Khan telephoned his daughter, Dina, and told her in code to destroy the documents he had given her was described by a retired Pakistani military official who participated in the session, and it was confirmed by a second former Pakistani official who was briefed on the episode. Dina's version was contained in a statement that she issued in 2006 from London. The close friend of Khan's who said he saw the 100-page document spoke to us on condition of anonymity.

CHAPTER 30. WHO'S NEXT?

The matrix constructed by the IAEA investigators was provided to us. Much of the information in this chapter was drawn from that and other internal documents as well as interviews with IAEA and American officials and with other diplomats in Vienna. The missing equipment was first disclosed by Frantz, "Vital Nuclear Parts Missing," *Los Angeles Times*, April 22, 2005.

The first word of the CIA contact with Heinonen came from an IAEA official; it was later confirmed and expanded upon by the former senior CIA official who assigned the agent to call him. Details of the meeting and the subsequent talks with the Tinners were provided by Western diplomats involved in the operation. The most alarming aspect of the talks, that Urs Tinner had made electronic copies of the nuclear warhead plans, was confirmed by two senior international investigators; the copies have never surfaced.

Mohammed Khilewi's assertions were first reported by Marie Colvin, "How an Insider Lifted the Veil on Saudi Plot for 'Islamic Bomb,' " *Sunday*

Times of London, July 24, 1994. A thorough rundown of the assertions and references to other articles was prepared by the Federation of American Scientists and is available on their Web site www.fas.org/asmp/profiles/saudi_arabia.htm.

Richard Russell talked about Saudi Arabia's nuclear ambitions in an interview.

The interrogation of Tahir in Malaysia was described by a participant. Additional information was obtained from a written summary of the session.

The lack of American cooperation with Swiss authorities investigating the Tinners was highlighted in an article posted on a Swiss government Web site on May 29, 2006, "US frustrates Swiss nuclear probe." The article quoted congressional testimony about the American refusal a week earlier by David Albright; it is available at www.swissinfo.org/eng/front/detail/US_frustrates_Swiss_nuclear_probe.html. The Americans later cooperated somewhat, according to Balz Bruppacher, "U.S. assists Swiss probe of family accused of aiding Libyan nuclear program," Associated Press, November 28, 2006.

Heinonen reflected on the outcome of his investigation in an interview.

Susan Rice's comments about the weak response to the North Korean nuclear test were from Matthew B. Stannard, "Sanctions on North Korea unlikely to sway Iran, experts say," *San Francisco Chronicle*, October 19, 2006.

EPILOGUE

The Doomsday Clock can be found, along with a host of valuable articles and data, at the Web site of the *Bulletin of the Atomic Scientists,* a nonprofit publication that leads the way in covering proliferation issues: www.thebulletin.org. The movement of the clock was described by Jeremy Manier, "Doomsday Clock to start new era: Scientists update 60-year-old monitor of nuclear threats to include new worries," *Chicago Tribune*, January 17, 2007.

We obtained a copy of the classified report by Britain's MI5 about the number of businesses and individuals engaged in proliferation.

INDEX

ABOUT TWELVE

Mission Statement

TWELVE was established in August 2006 with the objective of publishing no more than one book per month. We strive to publish the singular book, by authors who have a unique perspective and compelling authority. Works that explain our culture; that illuminate, inspire, provoke, and entertain. We seek to establish communities of conversation surrounding our books. Talented authors deserve attention not only from publishers, but from readers as well. To sell the book is only the beginning of our mission. To build avid audiences or readers who are enriched by these works—that is our ultimate purpose.

For more information about forthcoming TWELVE books, please go to www.TwelveBooks.com